INTERNATIONAL ENVIRONMENTAL OBLIGATIONS AND LIABILITIES IN DEEP SEABED MINING

Should deep seabed mining (DSM) stop or proceed? The international community is now facing a difficult choice. No matter what decision is made, environmental consideration is the core of the issue. This book tackles the compelling question of how to secure the marine environmental protection in DSM from an international law perspective. It deals with two major research questions: what are the international environmental requirements of participants – the contractor, the sponsoring State and the International Seabed Authority (ISA)? And what are the legal consequences for them when environmental damage occurs? In doing so, it analyses the international DSM legal regime and general international environmental principles, observes the functioning of the ISA, and draws on law and practice of various environmental treaty mechanisms. The examination reveals the practical difficulties as well as fundamental obstacles in the application of international environmental rules and principles in the specific context of DSM.

LINLIN SUN is Assistant Professor at the Law School, Zhongnan University of Economics and Law, China. She has had internships at China Ocean Mineral Resources Research and Development Association (2012), the International Seabed Authority (2015), the International Maritime Organization (2016) and the International Tribunal for the Law of the Sea (2016, as a Nippon Fellowship recipient).

INTERNATIONAL ENVIRONMENTAL OBLIGATIONS AND LIABILITIES IN DEEP SEABED MINING

LINLIN SUN

Zhongnan University of Economics and Law

CAMBRIDGE
UNIVERSITY PRESS

CAMBRIDGE
UNIVERSITY PRESS

Shaftesbury Road, Cambridge CB2 8EA, United Kingdom

One Liberty Plaza, 20th Floor, New York, NY 10006, USA

477 Williamstown Road, Port Melbourne, VIC 3207, Australia

314–321, 3rd Floor, Plot 3, Splendor Forum, Jasola District Centre, New Delhi – 110025, India

103 Penang Road, #05–06/07, Visioncrest Commercial, Singapore 238467

Cambridge University Press is part of Cambridge University Press & Assessment,
a department of the University of Cambridge.

We share the University's mission to contribute to society through the pursuit of
education, learning and research at the highest international levels of excellence.

www.cambridge.org
Information on this title: www.cambridge.org/9781108488303

DOI: 10.1017/9781108770125

First published 2023

A catalogue record for this publication is available from the British Library.

Library of Congress Cataloging-in-Publication Data
Names: Sun, Linlin, 1983- author.
Title: International environmental obligations and liabilities in deep seabed mining / Linlin Sun,
Zhongnan University of Law and Economics, China.
Description: Cambridge, United Kingdom ; New York, NY : Cambridge university press, 2023. |
Includes bibliographical references and index.
Identifiers: LCCN 2023029290 (print) | LCCN 2023029291 (ebook) | ISBN 9781108488303
(hardback) | ISBN 9781108725811 (paperback) | ISBN 9781108770125 (ebook)
Subjects: LCSH: Ocean mining–Law and legislation | Ocean bottom–Law and legislation. |
International Seabed Authority. | Environmental law, International. | Liability for
water pollution damages. | Marine pollution–Law and legislation.
Classification: LCC KZA1390 .S87 2023 (print) | LCC KZA1390 (ebook) |
DDC 341.4/55–dc23/eng/20230802
LC record available at https://lccn.loc.gov/2023029290
LC ebook record available at https://lccn.loc.gov/2023029291

ISBN 978-1-108-48830-3 Hardback
ISBN 978-1-108-72581-1 Paperback

To my parents and brothers
with love, laughter and tears

CONTENTS

Foreword xii
NICO SCHRIJVER

Preface xvii
Acknowledgements xix
List of Abbreviations xxi

1 **Introduction** 1
1.1 Background: Development of Deep Seabed Mining and the Legal Regime 1
1.2 Research Questions and the Scope 6
1.3 Terminology 7
1.3.1 Obligation 7
1.3.2 Liability 8
1.3.3 Participants in DSM 15
1.3.4 International DSM Legal Regime 16
1.4 Validity and Limits of the Book 17
1.5 Structure and Outline of the Book 17

2 **Common Heritage of Mankind and Protection of the Marine Environment** 22
2.1 Introduction 22
2.2 Elements of the Common Heritage of Mankind in the Context of DSM 23
2.2.1 The Area and Its Resources as Global Commons Subject to International Administration 24
2.2.2 Common Interest, Benefit-Sharing and Preferential Treatment of Developing States 26
2.2.3 Peaceful Use of the Area and Its Resources 30
2.2.4 Protection of the Marine Environment 31
2.2.5 Summary 34
2.3 Common Heritage of Mankind in Comparison with Related Concepts in Other Fields 34
2.3.1 Common Interest/Common Heritage of Mankind in Outer Space 35

2.3.2 Common Interest of Mankind in Antarctica 38
2.3.3 Common Interest of the International Community as a Whole in International Law 41

2.4 Protection of the Marine Environment in Deep Seabed Mining 44
2.4.1 The Conceptual Level: Marine Environmental Protection as Obligation *Erga Omnes* 45
2.4.2 The Operational Level: The Significant Role of Marine Sciences 49

2.5 Conclusions 56

3 International Seabed Authority and Its Environmental Mandate 57

3.1 Introduction 57

3.2 Nature of the International Seabed Authority 57

3.3 Organs and Subsidiary Bodies 59
3.3.1 The Assembly 59
3.3.2 The Council 61
3.3.3 The Legal and Technical Commission 65
3.3.4 The Secretariat 70
3.3.5 The Finance Committee 73
3.3.6 The Enterprise and the Economic Planning Commission 74
3.3.7 Summary and Comments 79

3.4 Powers and Obligations Relating to Marine Environmental Protection 80
3.4.1 Power to Adopt Rules, Regulations and Procedures 81
3.4.2 Issuing Recommendations, Standards and Guidelines 84
3.4.3 Safeguarding the Marine Environment while Administering Activities 86
3.4.4 Responding to Environmental Emergencies 91
3.4.5 Obligation to Apply the Precautionary Approach 93
3.4.6 Promoting and Encouraging Marine Scientific Research 97

3.5 Ongoing Development of the Exploitation Regulations 102
3.5.1 Features of the Drafting Work and Changed Approach to Environmental Regulation 102
3.5.2 Continuing Assessment of Marine Scientific Knowledge 105

3.6 Conclusions 108

4 International Environmental Obligations of the Sponsoring State and Contractor 110

4.1 Introduction 110
4.1.1 The Role and Status of the Sponsoring State in a Dual-Track Regulatory System 110
4.1.2 Structure 113

4.2 International Environmental Obligations of the Sponsoring State 114

4.2.1 The Overarching Principle of Sustainable Development 115
4.2.2 Obligation of Prevention 118
4.2.3 Obligation to Apply the Precautionary Approach 123
4.2.4 Obligation Concerning Environmental Impact Assessment 132
4.2.5 Obligation to Cooperate 141
4.3 International Environmental Obligations of the Contractor 142
4.3.1 Obligations to Conduct EIAs and Submit EISs 143
4.3.2 Obligations to Prepare for and Respond to Environmental Emergencies 149
4.3.3 Environmental Management and Monitoring Obligations 151
4.3.4 Obligation to Apply the Highest Standards of Environmental Protection 154
4.3.5 Other Environmental Obligations 157
4.4 Conclusions 158

5 Definition and Measure of Marine Environmental Damage 161

5.1 Introduction 161
5.2 'Marine Environmental Damage': A Broad Definition with Threshold Requirement 162
5.3 Measure of Marine Environmental Damage in DSM: Drawing on Experience of the International Oil Pollution Compensation Funds 167
5.3.1 Definition of 'Pollution Damage' 168
5.3.2 Criterion for Admissibility of Claims for Marine Environmental Damage 169
5.3.3 Costs of Preventive Measures 172
5.3.4 Costs of Reinstatement Measures 173
5.3.5 Costs of Post-spill Environmental Impact Studies 175
5.3.6 Lessons for the Measure of Marine Environmental Damage in DSM 176
5.4 Measure of Marine Environmental Damage in DSM: Drawing on Experience of the 'F4' Claims before the United Nations Compensation Commission 178
5.4.1 Claims and Payment for Direct Environmental Damage 179
5.4.2 Costs of Monitoring and Assessment Activities 180
5.4.3 Costs of Preventive Measures 183
5.4.4 Costs of Restoration Measures 184
5.4.5 Pure Environmental Damage 185
5.4.6 Lessons for the Measure of Marine Environmental Damage in DSM 187

5.5 Measure of Marine Environmental Damage in DSM: Drawing on the US and EU Laws and Discussions in the Context of the Convention on Biological Diversity 189
- 5.5.1 Natural Resources Damage Assessment in US Law 189
- 5.5.2 Remediation of Environmental Damage in EU Law 191
- 5.5.3 Liability and Redress in the Context of the Convention on Biological Diversity 193
- 5.5.4 Lessons for the Measure of Marine Environmental Damage in DSM 194

5.6 A Two-Step Pattern for the Measure of Marine Environmental Damage in DSM 195
- 5.6.1 Applying a Cost-Based Method as the First Step 196
- 5.6.2 Valuation of Pure Environmental Damage or Interim Loss as the Second Step 197

5.7 Conclusions 200

6 International Environmental Liability of the Contractor 203

6.1 Introduction 203

6.2 Channelling Liability to the Contractor 203

6.3 The Polluter-Pays Principle 207

6.4 Establishment of International Environmental Liability of the Contractor 214
- 6.4.1 Environmental Damage 214
- 6.4.2 Internationally Wrongful Acts of the Contractor 214
- 6.4.3 Causal Link between Environmental Damage and Wrongful Acts 221

6.5 Forms and Contents of Liability: Remediation of Marine Environmental Damage 224

6.6 Implementation of International Environmental Liability of the Contractor 226

6.7 Special Liability Issues: The Enterprise as Contractor and States as Contractors 230
- 6.7.1 The Enterprise as Contractor 231
- 6.7.2 States as Contractors 235

6.8 Conclusions 236

7 Alternatives to International Environmental Liability of the Contractor 238

7.1 Introduction: A Paradigm Shift from Civil Liability to Other Regimes 238

7.2 Compulsory Insurance or Financial Security Schemes 239

7.3 Compensation Fund for Environmental Damage 246
- 7.3.1 Conceptual Clarification: Relationship between Compensation Fund and Liability Regimes 247

7.3.2 Environmental Compensation Fund in the Context of DSM 250

7.4 Administrative Approach to International Environmental Liability of the Contractor 256

7.4.1 Turning to an Administrative Approach to Environmental Liability 257

7.4.2 International Regulatory Environmental Liability of the Contractor 260

7.5 Conclusions and Potential Ways Forward 266

8 International Environmental Liabilities of the Sponsoring State and the International Seabed Authority 271

8.1 Introduction 271

8.2 International Environmental Liability of the Sponsoring State: Commentary Notes on the Seabed Disputes Chamber's 2011 Advisory Opinion 272

8.2.1 Establishment of International Environmental Liability of the Sponsoring State 272

8.2.2 Differentiation of State Liability *Ex Delicto* from State Responsibility 276

8.2.3 Connection between International Environmental Liabilities of the Sponsoring State and of the Contractor 281

8.2.4 Forms and Contents of Liability: The Full Reparation Principle for Environmental Damage 283

8.2.5 Invocation of Liability of the Sponsoring State: *Locus Standi* 287

8.2.6 Conclusions 294

8.3 International Environmental Liability of the International Seabed Authority 296

8.3.1 Establishment and Contents of International Environmental Liability of the ISA 296

8.3.2 Liability of Member States for Acts of International Organizations 297

8.3.3 Invocation of Liability of the ISA 307

8.3.4 Conclusions 308

9 Conclusions 309

9.1 The Roles of Participants in DSM 309

9.2 The Role of Marine Sciences and Response to Their Limitations 311

9.3 International Environmental Obligations 312

9.4 International Environmental Liabilities 317

9.5 Final Observations about the Future Development of the international DSM Legal Regime 322

Bibliography 326

Index 351

FOREWORD

This book addresses a highly pertinent topic: the merits and the pitfalls of engaging in deep seabed mining and what international law has to say on this. On the one hand, currently there appear to be some shining prospects for the technological and economic feasibility to mine and process at last a considerable harvest of polymetallic nodules from deep seabed areas beyond the limits of national jurisdiction (also called the Area). Such exploitation can be meaningful for a variety of purposes, including facilitating the much-warranted energy transition from fossil fuels to renewable resources by enhancing the capacity of stockpiling of energy in batteries produced partly with lithium and other rare metals extracted from the polymetallic nodules from the deep seabed. Yet, there is still significant scientific uncertainty about the actual environmental effects of deep seabed mining on the other. What will be the potential pollution, the disturbance of vital marine ecological systems and the loss of marine biological diversity caused by these deep seabed mining activities? Based upon her in-depth research and supplemented by the experience of her encounters with practitioners, the author of this book takes the audacious position that by now the international community could proceed towards actually initiating deep seabed mining, albeit under strict environmental regulations and close international management and supervision.

Dr Linlin Sun's book meticulously builds upon and rearticulates the international law principle of the common heritage of humankind as the fundamental principle for any deep seabed mining regime. Its basic tenets are well known and include: non-appropriation, an international legal regime, sharing of benefits, use for peaceful purposes only, and respect for the rights of future generations. Consequently, Dr Sun finds that this principle implies not only rights and benefits but also obligations and burdens, reflecting a delicate balance between development in the public interest of the international community and conservation of nature and protection of the environment. She demonstrates that by now the environmental dimension of the principle is an integral and inherent restrictive element of the principle of the common heritage of humankind, thus also highlighting its capacity to respond to a fundamental change of circumstances if compared with the time of its inception. Moreover, she convincingly argues that international environmental obligations in deep seabed mining are of an *erga omnes* character, which means that they can also be invoked by non-injured third States and other international actors. It also means that all activities as well as their evaluation must rely upon solid marine scientific knowledge and the best and most environmentally friendly techniques. However, the current status of marine sciences continues to signify great gaps of marine scientific knowledge, which also in the author's view constitutes a fundamental impediment to the speedy development of deep seabed mining as well as its environmental protection. In this way, her book highlights both the crucial role of marine sciences and the necessity to respond to its shortcomings. In doing so, the author delves into the precautionary approach and an administrative approach to the liability of the contractor as two specific legal responses when those from marine sciences are silent or reach their limits.

The book explains in considerable detail the role each participant plays in the marine environmental protection in deep seabed mining, be it a state, a contractor or an international organ. Dr Sun advocates a dual-track regulatory system. The International Seabed Authority (ISA), as established under Part XI of the UN Convention on the Law of the Sea, is regarded as the primary regulator which exercises international public authority *vis-à-vis* the contractor directly. The sponsoring State plays a complementary regulatory role. The latter should focus on enforcement of the regulations at the national level and as a backup to the practical capacity of the ISA. Furthermore, it is up to the contractor as the main operator of deep seabed mining activities, albeit subject to regulations of both the ISA and the sponsoring State, to follow the rules, regulations, procedures, standards and guidelines concerning deep seabed mining. The contractor should do so at both the international and the national level. However, all participants in deep seabed mining may actually contribute, independently or collectively, to marine environmental damage during deep seabed mining activities, although playing different roles and of different nature. Therefore, to prevent and minimize risks or mitigate damage, they all must observe essentially the same international environmental obligations. Most prominently, they are all required to apply the principle of prevention, the precautionary approach, conduct or review EIAs, prepare for and respond to an environmental emergency, and take seriously the obligation to cooperate. Furthermore, all participants must adhere to and endorse the overarching goal of sustainable development as encapsulated in the World Agenda for 2030.

Against this backdrop of scientific uncertainty about the impact of deep seabed mining, the obligation to apply the precautionary approach is of the utmost importance. The book highlights the fact that the ISA takes the lead in applying the precautionary approach. An international consensus about the contours and the specific meaning and implications of the precautionary approach in the field of deep seabed mining is in the making but still to be achieved. This is at the centre of concern in the ongoing negotiations on the Mining Code: Draft Exploitation Regulations. Nonetheless, in recent years, the ISA has been able to employ already various environmental management tools as they emerged in practice. This distinctive way of applying the precautionary approach reflects a new result-oriented thinking of the ISA with respect to the discharge of its environmental mandate. The sponsoring State is squarely expected to follow the ISA's example in applying the precautionary approach. It should also endorse the EIA guidelines issued by the Legal and Technical Commission of ISA and cooperate with the ISA in adopting and implementing regulations. Moreover, it is widely considered that also general or customary international environmental law is incumbent upon States, by analogy to the application to the ISA and the contractor. New regulatory rules and practices in the context of deep seabed mining DSM in their turn also contribute to the emergence of new developments in international environmental law. As for the contractor, it is now well established that they are required to conduct continuously EIAs and submit environmental impact statements (EISs) and maintain environmentally responsible management and monitoring. Notably, the contractor plays an active role in dealing with environmental emergency by making and implementing 'Emergency Response and Contingency Plan'. In sum, the contractor is under the obligation to meet the highest environmental standards.

However, this is not to say that determination of breaches of environmental obligations of participants is not a difficult task of a scientific character. Therefore, such determination leaves for the time being considerable room for wide margins of appreciation. Even if breaches of environmental obligations are identified, this is not automatically enough for triggering liabilities of participants. For the book demonstrates that international environmental liabilities are still preconditioned on the actual occurrence of environmental damage and their goal of restoring or compensating environmental damage. In practice, international environmental liabilities of the three principal participants should be taken together as they result into common environmental damage. Nevertheless, evaluation and attribution of environmental damage in deep seabed mining will be far from an easy task. Hence, the author cautions that the role of the liability regimes for marine environmental protection in deep seabed mining should not be overestimated in view of the formidable practical difficulties in the satisfaction of each of these three constituent elements for establishing liabilities. These include internationally wrongful act, environmental damage and the causal link between the act and the damage. Yet, such liability regimes are still badly needed because their very existence could probably serve the function of prevention or deterrence. Considering the difficulties in the application of liability, alternative mechanisms of allocation of loss and damage, including compulsory insurance and the establishment of an environmental compensation fund, and the further development of the administrative approach towards liability of the contractor are explored. So far, the international environmental liability is placed primarily on the contractor as the operator.

These are only some of the takeaways of this rich and well-written book, based as it is upon in-depth academic study and analysis with interesting flashes of their tests in the practice of policy and standard-setting in deep seabed mining. A major contribution of this study is that it presents not only a clear and comprehensive picture of deep seabed mining as a topical issue of the twenty first century, but also explores, analyses and even outlines the newest development of international environmental law in this frontier area of an international legal regime for deep seabed mining. However laudable this already is, in my view the highlight of the book lies in the liability part. This clarifies the concept of international environmental liability through a historical account of the work of the International Law Commission on the topic of 'international liability' and scrutinizes the landmark 2011 advisory opinion by the Seabed Disputes Chamber of the International Tribunal of the Law of the Sea. The author analyses the existing environmental liability regimes in the context of deep seabed mining and examines for this purpose in a comparative way a large number of relevant multilateral environmental treaties and related institutional arrangements. Equally important, Dr Sun also lifts the veil of the practical difficulties in implementing the environmental liability regimes. Her systematic analysis of the liability issue from the three constituent elements mentioned above deepens the understanding of international environmental liability regimes in general and in the context of deep seabed mining in particular. In doing so, the book also provides highly valuable guidance to their operations in the practical realm.

It is with deep respect and admiration for the research efforts by Dr Linlin Sun that I recommend a wide readership of academics, policy makers and practitioners to take note, and learn from, the analysis and findings of this fine book.

Nico Schrijver
Professor of International Law and former Academic Director of the Grotius Centre for International Legal Studies, Leiden University, The Netherlands.

PREFACE

The advisory opinion of 1 February 2011 delivered by the Seabed Disputes Chamber of the International Tribunal for the Law of the Sea reignited an interest in deep seabed mining (DSM) among international lawyers. Subsequently, research projects on the topic have been getting increasingly popular. What is interesting is the fact that most of the legal studies had a focus on the environmental aspect as if by prior agreement. Why was the resurgent interest in DSM among international lawyers converged on the issue of marine environmental protection in the twenty-first century? This was because, in spite of advancement in marine technologies, marine scientists (in particular, marine biologists) warned of the big unknowns of the deep sea, which generated a major concern about the risks of serious and/or irreversible environmental damage that would be caused by DSM activities. This environmental concern has become the primary constraint for the development of both DSM activities and the DSM legal regime. Questions arose: if DSM activities are not prohibited or suspended, how should participants in DSM behave to protect the marine environment in a context of scientific uncertainty about their activities' environmental impacts? What would be the legal consequences if they failed to protect this environment?

This book belongs to the research wave just described and takes up the above-mentioned questions. It is a revised version of my PhD thesis, the output of a research project (2012–2017) at the Grotius Centre for International Legal Studies of Leiden University. It adopts a conceptual analysis approach. The aim of the book is to conduct a comprehensive examination of the international environmental obligations and liabilities of all participants in DSM. It examines environmental rules and principles under both the international DSM regime (*lex specialis*) and general international (environmental) law. It attempts to pinpoint the situations where environmental rules and principles are clear and where they are still ambiguous; the difficulties of environmental liability regimes' application in practice; the development or deviation of certain rules and principles in comparison with the existing international environmental law; and the situations where the contractor would be left with ample room for self-regulation rather than adhering to regulations of either the International Seabed Authority (ISA) or the sponsoring State. In short, this book clarifies the legal meanings of international environmental rules and principles and assesses their practical applicability in the specific context of DSM. It interprets the basic legal framework for perceiving and debating the issue of environmental protection in DSM.

In the process of researching and writing this book, I wanted to check my legal interpretations against practice as much as I could. For that purpose, I conducted internships at the ISA, International Tribunal for the Law of the Sea (ITLOS) and International Maritime Organization (IMO) as well as at China Ocean Mineral Resources Research and Development Association (COMRA, a contractor with the ISA) and I interacted with marine scientists, diplomats, contractors and environmentalists. Those experiences and interactions, in particular the on-site observation of the functioning of the ISA at its twenty-first session (2015), left footprints on this book. Hence, this book should not be taken as a product made solely in quiet libraries or studies; it reflects to some extent the ethos of DSM in the twenty-first century as well.

As this book has been ten years in the making (2012–2022), the ethos of DSM has changed in the process. The initial seemingly optimistic prospect of DSM gave way to divided expectations. Such a change, coinciding with the outbreak of the COVID-19 pandemic, was exemplified by the opposing positions of those who argued for a 'speed-up towards exploitation' and those who called for a 'moratorium'. In the meantime, as the drafting work of Exploitation Regulations proceeds, discussions about DSM are getting increasingly technical. Correspondingly, academic research among international lawyers has turned to an interdisciplinary approach. In spite of those changes, the basic legal framework for environmental protection will remain unchanged and will need constant (re)interpretation, for as long as the very topic of DSM is not disregarded. The information in this book was current as of 4 October 2022.

ACKNOWLEDGEMENTS

This book would not have existed had I not met Professor Nico Schrijver at the Xiamen Academy of International Law in the summer of 2011. That initial acquaintance led me to do PhD research under his supervision in Leiden, starting in September 2012 and finishing at the end of 2017; the PhD defence was taken in June 2018. This book is based on my PhD thesis. As my PhD supervisor, Professor Schrijver set a high academic standard for me to meet but at the same time left me the space to develop on my own. During the five years of my stay in Leiden, Professor Schrijver provided me with the most generous help and strong support. I would like to express my wholehearted thanks to him for all he has done for me. I would also like to extend deep gratitude to my second PhD supervisor Professor Eric de Brabandere. I thank him for his always timely responses to my questions and requests, for the many discussions of my chapters, and above all, for his confidence in me.

I benefited from talks with many individuals who are highly knowledgeable in either international law or marine sciences. Specifically, first, I greatly benefited from the discussions with Professor Blokker in the writing of Sections 3.3.6, 6.7.1 and 8.3. Secondly, the discussion with Professor Rene Lefeber at Amsterdam University on the environmental liability issue was inspiring for the writing of the liability part of this book. Thirdly, the discussions with the senior legal officer at the International Maritime Organization Jan de Boer and the legal counsel of International Oil Pollution Compensation Funds Kensuke Kobayashi were helpful in writing Section 5.3. Fourthly, the long talks with marine geologist Dr Sven Peterson at GEOMAR were very valuable in giving me a basic understanding of marine sciences. Fifth, I also benefited from the talks with the Secretary-General of the ISA Michael Lodge on various occasions. Sixth, a part of the published article titled 'Dispute Settlement Relating to Deep Seabed Mining: A Participant's Perspective' was incorporated in Sections 1.1, 8.2.5 and 8.3.3. That article was completed under the supervision of the associate legal officer Dr Naomi Burke during my internship at the International Tribunal for the Law of the Sea (ITLOS). Judge Liesbeth Lijnzaad at the ITLOS, Professor Seline Trevisanut at Utrecht University and Professor Marcel Brus at Groningen University served as members of the reading committee for my PhD thesis; they gave me invaluable advice for improvement of the manuscript. So did the anonymous reviewers. To all of them I would like to express my sincere gratitude.

Meanwhile, credit should go to the following institutions as they furnished me with the necessary conditions for conducting research and writing a book. The China Scholarship Council funded my PhD research for a period of four years (2012–2016); Leiden University Fund financially supported me to do the field study at the ISA in the summer of 2015; and ITLOS granted me a Nippon Scholarship for the three-month internship at ITLOS in the winter of 2016. From the Peace Palace Library at The Hague, I found almost all the books I needed. The Grotius Centre for International Legal Studies of Leiden University was the best academic home I could ever imagine. It is during my Assistant Professorship at the Law School of Zhongnan University of Economics and Law since August 2018 that I managed to transform my PhD thesis into a book.

The making of this book has taken a long time. I am much indebted to many friends. I thank the former principal legal officer of the ISA Dr Kening Zhang, the current senior legal officer of the ISA Yongsheng Cai, Professor Yuwen Li at Erasmus University Rotterdam, and my former PhD fellows at Leiden, Ruben, Vid, Andrea, Hanna, Floris, Xuechan, Yudan, Hilde, Qiuyin and Xiang, for their various kinds of help, encouragement and companionship. Cecily was generous enough to share with me her experience of academic writing and publication. Nico reminded me from time to time to get this book done when the focus of my work drifted away from deep seabed mining upon my graduation from Leiden; so did Xiangxin. In this respect, I owe special thanks to my editor Joe Ng for his tolerance, patience and gentle push. Additionally, I am grateful to my colleagues and students at Zhongnan for the many hours we spent together at table tennis courts and in classrooms; these activities have been vital for me to maintain a stable psychological state, especially during the difficult time of the COVID-19 pandemic. Last but not least, the unreserved love, sacrifice and expectations of my family are the ultimate source of strength for me to overcome all kinds of difficulties in this long journey. This book is dedicated to them.

ABBREVIATIONS

ABMTs	area-based management tools
AJIL	American Journal of International Law
APEIs	areas of particular environmental interest
ARIO	Articles on the Responsibility of International Organizations
ASR	Articles on State Responsibility
ATCM	Antarctic Treaty Consultative Meeting
AustYBIL	Australian Yearbook of International Law
B.C. Envtl. Aff. L. Rev.	Boston College Environmental Affairs Law Review
B.C. Int'l & Comp.	Boston College International and Comparative Law Review
BASE	best available scientific evidence
BATs	best available technologies
BEPs	best environmental practices
BGR	Federal Institute for Geosciences and Natural Resources (of Germany)
BYIL	British Yearbook of International Law
CBD	Convention on Biological Diversity
CCAMLR	Convention on the Conservation of Antarctic Marine Living Resources
CCZ	Clarion–Clipperton (Fracture) Zone
CDR	Central Data Repository
CEE	Comprehensive Environment Evaluation
CERCLA	Comprehensive Environmental Response, Compensation, and Liability Act
Chinese JIL	Chinese Journal of International Law
CHM	common heritage of mankind
CIL	customary international law
CLC	International Convention on Civil Liability for Oil Pollution Damage
COP	Conference of Parties
Cornell Int'l L. J.	Cornell International Law Journal

CRAMRA	Convention on the Regulation of Antarctic Mineral Resource Activities
CUP	Cambridge University Press
CVM	contingent valuation methodology
DSM	deep seabed mining
ECF	environmental compensation fund
ECJ	European Court of Justice
EIA	environmental impact assessment
EIS	environmental impact statement
EJIL	European Journal of International Law
EMMP	environmental management and monitoring plan
EMP	environmental management plan
EMS	environmental management system
EPC	Economic Planning Commission
EU ELD	EU Environmental Liability Directive
EU	European Union
FinnishYBIL	Finnish Yearbook of International Law
Front. Mar. Sci.	Frontiers in Marine Science
GDV	German Insurance Association
Geo. Int'l Envtl. L. Rev.	Georgetown International Environmental Law Review
GESAMP	Joint Group of Experts on the Scientific Aspects of Marine Environmental Protection
GIP	Good Industry Practice
GRIR	Geneva Papers on Risk and Insurance Review
GSR	Global Sea Mineral Resources NV
Harv. Int. Law J.	Harvard International Law Journal
HELR	Harvard Environmental Law Review
HNS	hazardous and noxious substances
ICJ	International Court of Justice
ICLQ	International and Comparative Law Quarterly
IDI	International Law Institute (Institut de Droit International)
IEE	Initial Environment Evaluation
IEL	International Environmental Law
IJMCL	International Journal of Marine and Coastal Law
ILA	International Law Association
ILC	International Law Commission
ILM	International Legal Materials
IMMS	International Marine Minerals Society
IMO	International Maritime Organization
Ind. J. Global Legal Stud.	Indiana Journal of Global Legal Studies

INEA	International Environmental Agreements: Politics, Law and Economics
IOLR	International Organizations Law Review
IOPC	International Oil Pollution Compensation
IPCC	Intergovernmental Panel on Climate Change
IRZs	impact reference zones
ISA	International Seabed Authority
ISO	International Organization for Standardization
ITLOS	International Tribunal for the Law of the Sea
JEM	Journal of Environmental Management
JMLC	Journal of Maritime Law and Commerce
JOGA	Journal of Ocean Governance in Africa
JPI-O	Joint Programming Initiative-Oceans project
JYIL	Japanese Yearbook of International Law
La. L. Rev.	Louisiana Law Review
LJIL	Leiden Journal of International Law
LTC	Legal and Technical Commission (of the ISA)
MARPOL	International Convention for the Prevention of Pollution from Ships
MaxPlanckUNYB	Max Planck Yearbook of United Nations Law
Mich. J. Int'l L.	Michigan Journal of International Law
Mich. L. Rev.	Michigan Law Review
MIDAS	Managing Impacts of Deep-Sea Resource Exploitation project
MJECL	Maastricht Journal of European and Comparative Law
MJIL	Melbourne Journal of International Law
MPEPIL	Max Planck Encyclopedia of Public International Law
MPIL	Max Plank International Law
MSR	marine scientific research
N.Y.U. Envtl. L. J.	New York University Environmental Law Journal
NEPA	US National Environmental Policy Act
NGOs	non-governmental organizations
NIEO	New International Economic Order
NILR	Netherlands International Law Review
Nordisk Tidsskrift Int'l Ret	Nordisk Tidsskrift for International Ret (Nordic Journal of International Law)
NRDA	Natural Resources Damage Assessment
NYIL	Netherlands Yearbook of International Law
NZYIL	New Zealand Yearbook of International Law
Ocean Coast Manag.	Ocean & Coastal Management
ODIL	Ocean Development and International Law
OECD	Organisation for Economic Co-operation and Development

OPA	US Oil Pollution Act
OUP	Oxford University Press
PCA	Permanent Court of Arbitration
PCIJ	Permanent Court of International Justice
PRZs	preservation reference zones
RdC	Hague Academy (of International Law) Collected Courses (Recueil des cours de l'Académie de la Haye)
RECIEL	Review of European Community & International Environmental Law
REMPs	regional environmental management plans
RIAA	Reports of International Arbitral Awards
SDC	Seabed Disputes Chamber (of the ITLOS)
SEA	Strategic Environmental Assessment
SIMPLY	The Scandinavian Institute's Maritime and Petroleum Law Yearbook
SJILC	Syracuse Journal of International Law and Commerce
SPC	The Pacific Community
Stan. Envtl. L. J.	Stanford Environmental Law Journal
Tex. Intl. L. J.	Texas International Law Journal
Tul. L. Rev.	Tulane Law Review
UN	United Nations
UNCC	United Nations Compensation Commission
UNCLOS	United Nations Convention on the Law of the Sea
UNECE	UN Economic Commission for Europe
UNEP	United Nations Environment Programme
UNESCO-IOC	International Oceanographic Commission of the United Nations Educational, Scientific and Cultural Organization
UNFCCC	UN Framework Convention on Climate Change
UNGA Res.	UN General Assembly Resolution
US	The United States
Utrecht L. Rev.	Utrecht Law Review
Va. J. Int'l L.	Virginia Journal of International Law
Va. Law Rev.	Virginia Law Review
Vand. L. Rev.	Vanderbilt Law Review
WTAC	willingness to accept compensation
WTP	willingness to pay
WULQ	Washington University Law Quarterly
YILC	Yearbook of International Law Commission
YIntlEnvL	Yearbook of International Environmental Law

1

Introduction

1.1 Background: Development of Deep Seabed Mining and the Legal Regime

It was in 1873, during the *HMS Challenger* expedition (1872–1876), that polymetallic nodules were first discovered on the seabed.[1] Yet, it was not until the 1960s that the economic value of these nodules became an issue of international interest.[2] Soon, exploration for and exploitation of the mineral resources on the seabed area beyond national jurisdiction (the 'Area') – that is, deep seabed mining (DSM) – appeared as a topic on the agenda of the United Nations General Assembly. From 1967, under the auspices of the UN, negotiations began for an international DSM legal regime. The final outcome of the long-lasting negotiations was Part XI of the 1982 United Nations Convention on the Law of the Sea (UNCLOS).[3] However, owing to the disapproval of industrial countries of the contents of Part XI of the UNCLOS, the Convention did not enter into force until Part XI was amended by the 1994 Agreement.[4]

[1] International Seabed Authority: Exploration Contracts. International Seabed Authority (isa.org.jm).

[2] In 1962, John Mero said that 'the nodules are indicated to be forming at an annual rate of 6×10^6 metric tons in [the Pacific] ocean'. The same estimation was repeated in his influential book *The Mineral Resources of the Sea*. According to this estimation, the potential economic value of manganese nodules would be huge. Although it turned out to be far too exaggerated, this estimation stimulated great international interest in deep seabed mining. John Mero, 'Ocean Floor Manganese Nodules' (1962) 57 *Economic Geology* 747, 756–758; John Mero, *The Mineral Resources of the Sea* (Elsevier 1965) 235.

[3] Adopted on 10 December 1982; entered into force on 16 November 1994.

[4] Agreement relating to the Implementation of Part XI of the United Nations Convention on the Law of the Sea of 10 December 1982, adopted on 28 July 1994, entered into force 28 July 1996 (the '1994 Agreement'). States' divergent attitudes were exemplified in the unilateral national legislation of a group of industrialized countries, and in the mini-treaty arrangement between these states in the 1980s. See Yuwen Li, *Transfer of Technology for Deep Sea-Bed Mining: The 1982 Law of the Sea Convention and Beyond* (Martinus Nijhoff 1994) 87–90. The unilateralism movement created a crisis in the international DSM legal

The International Seabed Authority (ISA) was established upon Part XI's entry into force in 1994, and came into operation in 1996. The ISA is empowered under the UNCLOS to 'organize and control activities in the Area, particularly with a view to administering the resources of the Area'.[5] It controls activities in the Area by granting permits in the form of contracts.[6] As of the 27th session of the ISA in July 2022, the ISA has signed 31 contracts for exploration in the Area.[7] Behind these 31 contracts, there are 22 contractors that fall within three categories: States, publicly funded companies or institutions and private companies.[8] Private companies were not involved in exploration in the Area until 2011 when Nauru Ocean Resources Inc. (sponsored by Nauru) signed a contract with ISA as the first private company. Thereafter, more private companies joined, which brought the total number of private contractors to ten. All these private companies are currently conducting exploration for polymetallic nodules in the Area.

regime. As a response, the then Secretary-General of the UN initiated a serial of informal consultations (1990–1994) which resulted in the amendment of Part XI of the UNCLOS. See ISA, *Secretary-General's Informal Consultations on Outstanding Issues Relating to the Deep Seabed Mining Provisions of the United Nations Convention on the Law of the Sea: Collected Documents* (Collected Documents, ISA, 2002) 1.

5 Article 157, UNCLOS.

6 Article 153(3), UNCLOS.

7 The 2022 report of Secretary-General of the ISA, ISBA/27/A/2. The up-to-date data is available online at: https://isa.org.jm/exploration-contracts.

8 There are four contractors in the first category: the governments of India, South Korea, Russia and Poland.

Eight contractors belong to the second category: Interoceanmetal Joint Organization (IGO); JSC Yuzhmorgeologiya; China Ocean Mineral Resources Research and Development Association (COMRA); Japan Oil, Gas and Metals National Corporation (JOGMC); Deep Ocean Resources Development Co., Ltd (DORD); Federal Institute for Geosciences and Natural Resources of the Federal Republic of Germany; Institut Français de Recherche pour l'Exploitation de la Mer; and Companhia De Pesquisa de Recursos Minerais.

Ten private contractors in the third category as follows: Nauru Ocean Resources Inc. (2011, sponsored by Nauru); Tonga Offshore Mining Limited (2012, sponsored by Tonga); G TEC Sea Mineral Resources NV (2013, sponsored by Belgium); UK Seabed Resources Ltd (2013, sponsored by the UK); Marawa Research and Exploration Ltd (2015, sponsored by Kiribati); Ocean Mineral Singapore Pte Ltd (2015, sponsored by Singapore); Cook Islands Investment Corporation (2016, sponsored by Cook Islands); China Minmetals Corporation (2017, sponsored by China); Beijing Pioneer Hi-Tech Development Corporation (2019, sponsored by China); and Blue Minerals Jamaica Ltd (2021, Jamaica).

The involvement of private companies[9] resulted in diverse contractors. More importantly, private investment served as a strong impetus to bringing DSM into the exploitation stage. Unlike States or publicly funded companies or institutions that might have strategic goals and long-term plans for DSM, private companies are normally commerce-oriented. For them, the viability of making profits in a relatively short term is of significance. Along with private companies, there were also calls from some developing countries for progress in the exploitation stage.[10] The likely incentive underlying their suggestions was the potential benefits they might share in accordance with the principle of the common heritage of mankind (CHM). Additionally, the ISA itself was of the opinion that 'commercialization of marine minerals in the [Area] . . . [was] well within reach and could be attained in the foreseeable future'.[11] Thus, it seems that, in spite of the existence of obstacles such as gaps in marine scientific knowledge,[12] the nascency of technology,[13] fluctuations

[9] In Dingwall's opinion, 'the UNCLOS DSM regime is an unlikely hybrid of capitalist and communist values, embracing the role of private actors while enshrining principles of resource distribution'. Private companies' prioritizing the protection of investment and economic benefits would cause a sharp tension with the requirements of environmental protection and equitable share of benefits. See Joanna Dingwall, *International Law and Corporate Actors in Deep Seabed Mining* (OUP 2021).

[10] This position was vividly exhibited at the 22nd annual session of the ISA during a discussion of the Legal and Technical Commission's report on 'applications for extension of contracts for exploration of polymetallic nodules'. Brazil maintained that it was necessary that the draft decision pertaining to extensions be reworded to ensure that contractors proceed to the exploitation stage at the end of the five-year exploration stage. Cameroon, Chile, Kenya and South Africa supported the position of Brazil. See: ISA, 'Seabed Council Approves Plan of Work for Crusts Exploration by the Republic of Korea; Delays Approval of Five-Year Extension of Six Exploration Contracts' (Press Release, SB/22/8, 18 July 2016).

[11] ISA, 'Commercialization of Marine Minerals in Deep Seabed Well within Reach, International Seabed Authority Secretary-General States as he Introduces Annual Report' (Press Release, SB/22/11, 19 July 2016) 1.

[12] Reference to Section 2.4.2.

[13] Ecorys, 'Study to Investigate the State of Knowledge of Deep-Sea Mining' (Final Report, 28 August 2014) 55–71; Elaine Baker and Yannick Beaudoin (eds.), 'Sea-Floor Massive Sulphides — A Physical, Biological, Environmental, and Technical Review' (Review, Secretariat of the Pacific Community, 2013) 43–48. Available at: http://dsm.gsd.spc.int/public/files/meetings/TrainingWorkshop4/UNEP_vol1A.pdf; Elaine Baker and Yannick Beaudoin (eds.), 'Manganese Nodules: A Physical, Biological, Environmental, and Technical Review' (Review, Secretariat of the Pacific Community, 2013) 43–48. Available at: http://dsm.gsd.spc.int/public/files/meetings/TrainingWorkshop4/UNEP_vol1B.pdf; Elaine Baker and Yannick Beaudoin (eds.), 'Cobalt-Rich Ferromanganese Crusts: A Physical, Biological, Environmental, and Technical Review' (Review,

in the metals market[14] and the absence of Exploitation Regulations (in the process of development),[15] DSM is in a crucial transitional period moving towards the exploitation stage.

In June 2021, Nauru requested the ISA to complete the framing and adoption of Exploitation Regulations within two years, thereby paving the way for granting permit for exploitation in the Area.[16] Such a request, dubbed as the trigger for the 'two-year deadline',[17] has provoked a storm of protest from those who are concerned with and would give priority to the protection of the marine environment. The concerned individuals and groups rallied and strong reactions followed. In September 2021, IUCN World Conservation Congress voted for 'Motion 069', calling for a moratorium on deep seabed mining.[18] For the very first time there were two diametrically opposing positions towards DSM. This abrupt change seems to indicate that DSM has come to a crossroads.

It merits noting that the conflicting positions with respect to DSM are by no means a new phenomenon. Since the environment became an international concern in the 1970s, the struggle between the 'development' camp and the 'conservation' camp has almost never failed to manifest itself in the political and legal contestation concerning the utilization of natural resources. Experience shows that mostly compromise between the two camps was reached in the end, but there were exceptions too. The bridled mineral resource and whaling activities in

Secretariat of the Pacific Community, 2013) 41–45. Available at: http://dsm.gsd.spc.int/public/files/meetings/TrainingWorkshop4/UNEP_vol1C.pdf.

14 Ecorys, 'Study to Investigate the State of Knowledge of Deep-Sea Mining' (Final Report, 28 August 2014) 112–136.

15 Reference to Section 3.5.1.

16 By the letter dated 25 June 2021: https://isa.org.jm/files/files/documents/NauruLetter-Notification.pdf, 'Nauru requests the President of ISA Council to complete the adoption of rules, regulations and procedures necessary to facilitate the approval of plans of work for exploitation in the Area', ISA News: https://isa.org.jm/news/nauru-requests-president-isa-council-complete-adoption-rules-regulations-and-procedures.

17 See Pradeep A. Singh, 'The Two-Year Deadline to Complete the International Seabed Authority's Mining Code: Key Outstanding Matters that Still Need to Be Resolved' (2021) 134 *Marine Policy* 104804. The trigger of the 'two-year deadline' has also provoked a strong reaction from international lawyers who are concerned with the readiness of Exploitation Regulations in such a rush.

18 IUCN World Conservation Congress 'Motion 069': www.iucncongress2020.org/motion/069 for the voting record, see: www.savethehighseas.org/momentum-for-a-moratorium/. Later, on 14 December 2021, at the 26th session of the Assembly of the ISA, DSCC requested for a moratorium on DSM in its intervention: https://isa.org.jm/files/files/documents/DSCC_item9.pdf.

Antarctica are two examples. Here, questions arise, 'Will the polarized positions towards DSM activities, as exemplified by Nauru's request and IUCN's call, respectively, bring a dreadful "either/or" question before all participants in DSM'? 'Can compromise be achieved'? 'Which way to take for DSM in the future'? One needs to wait and see what answers turn out to these questions. This book does not attempt to conduct systematic analyses of these questions of a contingent nature, but the position taken by this book is explained in the following paragraph.

This book does not favour a moratorium on DSM for the sake of marine environmental protection, nor does it favour a rush towards the exploitation stage. It rejects an environmentalist's proposition of moratorium because such a position gives priority to marine organisms, species, communities and ecosystems but fails to take human conditions and welfare into consideration. The deep seabed appears as a new source of mineral resources that has the potential to meet, to some extent, the growing demand for metals in general, and for certain critical metals for the development of innovative technologies necessary for tackling climate change in particular. True, DSM activities may have (significant) detrimental effects on the deep-sea environment, and historically, we human beings ourselves are causes for ecologic crisis, global warming and other environmental problems we are facing now.[19] To capture the pervasive human influence on nature, Crutzen coined the well-accepted concept 'Anthropocene'.[20] We should certainly learn lessons from history and protect the marine environment in DSM as possible as we can. Nonetheless, to impose a moratorium on DSM is to swing the pendulum to an extreme. In a 'risk society',[21] (environmental) risk cannot be avoided in its entirety but must be managed or regulated. Refusing to take any (environmental) risks would mean a denial of all chances for satisfying human needs. That is a price too high to afford. What is the human reality now? There is a huge and growing world population who are aspiring for a better life and there is a need to resort to innovative

[19] Lynn White Jr., 'The Historical Roots of Our Ecologic Crisis' (1967) 155(3767) *Science* 1203. White investigated the relationship between religion, particularly Christianity, and attitudes towards nature. In particular, he considered the Christian human-centred idea as a deep root reason accounting for the ecologic crisis.

[20] Paul Crutzen, 'Geology of Mankind' (2002) 415(6867) *Nature* 23. In Crutzen's opinion, we have entered into a new geological period of 'Anthropocene' since late eighteenth century when the curtain of industrialization era opened.

[21] Ulrich Beck, *Risk Society: Towards a New Modernity*, translated by Mark Ritter (Sage 1992). The book was originally published in German in 1986.

technologies to fight climate change. If the world population is not to decrease, if people's aspiration for better life is not to be discouraged and if the transition from fossil fuels to clean energies is not to discontinue, then DSM is worth trying.[22] This book embraces the concept of 'conservation science' which recognizes 'the dynamics of coupled human-natural systems'.[23] On the other hand, it rejects the private contractors' commerce-oriented approach because such a position gives priority to investment and profits but disregards everything else of vital value to humanity and ecology. In a word, this book takes the position that DSM should proceed but with extreme care with respect to the protection of the deep-sea environment.

1.2 Research Questions and the Scope

Against this background, this book addresses two major research questions concerning all participants in DSM. First, what are the international environmental obligations of the participants in DSM? Second, what are the legal consequences for them when environmental damage occurs? (this is the international environmental liability issue). The scope of research of the book can be defined by the following three dimensions. First, it discusses the subject matter of DSM at the international level. Second, it deals only with the environmental aspects of DSM. Marine environmental protection constitutes an inherent restraint to the development of DSM. Yet, unlike other restraint elements such as mining technologies and the metals market, the environmental aspects are expected to become increasingly challenging and complex with the advancement of DSM. Third, it addresses the issue of protection of the

[22] Kim argued that 'more fundamental societal transformation should be sought after to cope with the foreseeable shortage of metals and guard them against future exhaustion'. He also argued that metal recycling and more efficient governance could be ways to tackle the problem of shortage of metals. See Rakhyun Kim, 'Should Deep Seabed Mining Be Allowed?' (2017) 82 *Marine Policy* 134–137, 135 and 136. Similar arguments were also raised by those who suggested or supported a moratorium on DSM. However, one would be reasonably dubious about the practicability of a fundamental change of the way of life of people as well as the extent to which recycling and more efficient governance would work in meeting the demand of metals. That said, it does not mean that these ways are not worth trying but that they cannot be sufficient reasons for excluding other ways, such as seeking for new sources of mineral resources in the seabed – DSM.

[23] Peter Kareiva and Michelle Marvier, 'What Is Conservation Science?' (2012) 62(11) *BioScience* 962–969, 962.

marine environment in DSM from a legal perspective. And the legal analysis revolves around the two core concepts: obligation and liability.

1.3 Terminology

1.3.1 Obligation

As it is stated,

> The notion of a legal obligation is fundamental both for the understanding of the legal regulation of conduct and for the analysis of other concepts used in the description and exposition of the law, such as rights, powers and trusts, property, possession and conveyance.[24]

Indeed, the concept of 'legal obligation' is central to law, no matter which school of law one follows. However, there are different understandings of 'obligation'. For Pufendorf, a proponent of pure natural law, the concept of obligation is the key to turning the natural state into a moral sphere: Obligation has 'an operative moral quality' and 'it places a kind of moral bridle upon our liberty of action'.[25] For Bentham and his disciple Austin, obligation exists in both legal and moral contexts, and a key feature of a legal obligation is the probabilistic sanctions in case of disobedience.[26] However, in Hart's opinion, it is of utmost importance to perceive obligation from 'an internal point of view'.[27] A legal obligation necessarily implies the existence of a rule or law. 'Law', as per Hart's narrative, is not imperative order backed with threat, but 'a combination of primary rule of obligation and the secondary rules of recognition, change and adjudication'.[28]

Then, in what sense does this book employ the word 'obligation'? First of all, 'obligation' is not discussed in a moral but a legal context. Second, in general this book takes a positivist approach in the sense that the main source of obligation is found in positive international law. Third, this

[24] H. L. A. Hart, *Essays on Bentham: Jurisprudence and Political Philosophy* (OUP 1982) 127.

[25] Samuel Pufendorf, *Two Books on the Elements of Universal Jurisprudence*, translated by William Abbott Oldfather (Oxford: Clarendon Press 1931). Pufendorf used about one-quarter of Book I to clarify 'obligation' as one out of twenty-one important definitions.

[26] H. L. A. Hart, *Essays on Bentham* (OUP 1982).

[27] H. L. A. Hart, *The Concept of Law* (OUP 1961) 79–88.

[28] Ibid., 89–97. Please note that the terms of 'primary rule' and 'secondary rule' used by Hart in *The Concept of Law* should be distinguished from the same terms used by Ago in the ILC's work on 'State responsibility'.

book aims at furthering the understanding of legal obligation seen from participants' perspective, which is an internal point of view. Namely, it elucidates the rules which the participants in DSM perceive as binding on them or the rules that constitute the reason for the participants to act in conformity with certain guidelines and other obligations. Additionally, it is noted that the terms 'duty', 'responsibility' and 'requirement' are used in some contexts which bear the same meaning as the term 'obligation'.

1.3.2 Liability

However, the very use of the concept of 'liability' invites confusion: at the national level, its legal meaning differs between States (particularly between States following common law and those following civil law traditions), and at the international level, it has an intricate relationship with the concept of 'State responsibility'. Considering the same concept of liability is used at both the national and international levels and in different contexts, the meaning of the concept is indeed very confusing.[29] For this reason, it is necessary to define the concept of 'liability'. In this book, the concept of 'liability' is employed and used in the same sense as the International Law Commission (ILC) in its work on the topic of 'international liability for injurious consequences arising out of acts not prohibited by international law' ('international liability') because DSM is a specific kind of 'activity not prohibited by international law'. The remainder of this subsection will elaborate on the conceptual evolution of 'international liability' in the work of the ILC, which automatically explains the meaning of the term used in this book.

1.3.2.1 State Liability *Sine Delicto* as Primary Obligation under International Law

The topic of international liability emerged out of State responsibility. In 1970, the then special rapporteur Roberto Ago emphasized that the issue of 'responsibility for risk' should be treated separately from State responsibility.[30] His explanation for doing this was that since the basis of responsibility for risk is totally different from that of State responsibility,

[29] Nathalie Horbach in her dissertation examines the various meanings of the concept of liability in different contexts in great detail. See Nathalie Horbach, *Liability versus Responsibility under International Law, Defending Strict State Responsibility for Transboundary Damage* (S.l.: s.n. 1996) [Proefschrift Rijksuniversiteit te Leiden].

[30] The 1970 report on State responsibility of Ago, UN. Doc. A/CN.4/233.

the nature, content and forms of the rules governing them should also be different. A joint examination of them would create confusion. In his opinion, responsibility for risk arises out of 'the exercise of an activity which is in itself lawful', while State responsibility relates to 'the breach of a legal obligation'.[31]

In 1978, the ILC approved the new topic on international liability and appointed Quentin-Baxter as the first special rapporteur. Yet, doubts about the autonomous status of the new topic existed from the very moment of its inception. Hence Quentin-Baxter was faced with the challenge of defending the autonomy of international liability. In his first three reports,[32] he addressed the conceptual basis of international liability. He found that

> [t]he regime of liability in respect of acts not prohibited does not detract from the universality of the regime of responsibility for wrongful acts, because the two regimes exist upon different planes. Obligations arising in respect of acts not prohibited are the product of particular 'primary' rules: the violation of these or any other 'primary' rules brings into play the 'secondary' rules of State responsibility for wrongful acts.[33]

Identifying international liability as primary rules provided Quentin-Baxter with 'an iron-clad' separation wall[34] to prevent international liability from 'trespassing into the Commission's topic of responsibility'[35] which dealt exclusively with the secondary rules. In this manner, Quentin-Baxter defended the autonomous status of the topic of international liability *vis-à-vis* that of State responsibility.

Despite its structural advantages, this approach had its Achilles' heel. Quentin-Baxter argued for international liability as primary rules that did not require a wrongful act, that is, State liability *sine delicto*. It meant that States were liable in the event damage occurred. However, States resisted this proposition during the negotiations within the Commission. Treaty practice as well as international judicial practice did not support this idea either.[36] The resistance of States during the negotiation and a paucity of

[31] Ibid., para. 6.

[32] The preliminary report, 1980 (UN. Doc. A/CN.4/334); the second report, 1981(UN. Doc. A/CN.4/346); and the third report, 1982 (UN. Doc. A/CN.4/360 and Corr.1).

[33] The preliminary report of Quentin-Baxter, 1980 (UN. Doc. A/CN.4/334), para. 21.

[34] The second report of Quentin-Baxter, 1981(UN. Doc. A/CN.4/346), para. 15.

[35] Julio Barboza, *The Environment, Risk, and Liability in International Law* (Martinus Nijhoff 2011) 78.

[36] See especially the two surveys of State practice relevant to international liability prepared by the Secretariat in 1985 (UN. Doc. A/CN.4/384) and in 1995 (UN. Doc. A/CN.4/471).

treaty and judicial practice eventually prompted the second special rapporteur Barboza to completely abandon the effort to codify or progressively develop a general rule on State liability *sine delicto*. Barboza further developed the concept of international liability along two different paths. On the one hand, State liability *sine delicto* gave way to State liability *ex delicto* which requires a breach of the obligation of prevention and is triggered by environmental damage. As a consequence, State liability *ex delicto* fell within the scope of State responsibility. On the other hand, State liability was substituted with what is known as the civil liability system, which imposed liability primarily on the operators; this latter path was afterwards further developed into a notion of 'allocation of loss'.

1.3.2.2 State Liability *Ex Delicto*'s Falling within the Scope of State Responsibility

The understanding of State liability changed within the Commission; the ILC moved from State liability *sine delicto* to State liability *ex delicto*.[37] That change was mainly due to the different views on the relationship between prevention and liability among the three special rapporteurs. As described by Barbazo,[38] Quentin-Baxter did not want the topic of international liability to be assimilated into State responsibility. He therefore broadened its scope to include obligations of prevention from the very beginning. As to the relationship between prevention and liability, Quentin-Baxter saw them as 'compound primary obligations'. He envisioned State liability as 'a continuum' that started with prevention and minimization and then ended with compensation. In addition, Quentin-Baxter adopted a 'soft approach' with respect to the legal effect of the obligations of prevention and international liability (the obligation of reparation).[39] In his view, failure to take preventive measures, such as providing information, 'shall not in itself give rise to any right of action'.[40] In other words, the prevention obligations were just 'soft' obligations. Consequently, no legal consequence ensued from their

[37] The phrase 'liability for wrongful acts' appeared in the tenth report of Barboza,1994 (UN. Doc. A/CN.4/459) for the first time.

[38] Julio Barboza, *The Environment, Risk, and Liability in International Law* (Martinus Nijhoff 2011) 78; see also the fourth report of Quentin-Baxter, 1983 (UN. Doc. A/CN.4/373 and Corr.1 and 2.), para. 39.

[39] The fourth report of Quentin-Baxter, 1983 (UN. Doc. A/CN.4/373 and Corr.1 and 2.), para. 43.

[40] The third report of Quentin-Baxter, 1982 (UN. Doc. A/CN.4/360 and Corr.1), para. 8 and section 2 of the schematic outline.

breach. Similarly, reparations should be negotiated between States in accordance with their 'shared expectations'.[41] Quentin-Baxter's approach attracted criticism. La Fayette stated that the rule prescribing prevention obligations is not soft but hard law.[42] Graefrath contended that the consequence of a breach of prevention obligations by States fell under the law of State responsibility. For him, 'it seems clear that with the growing precision of preventive rules, i.e. specifying international obligations of States, the whole subject comes closer and closer to international responsibility'.[43]

Like his predecessor, Barboza also envisaged a proper role for prevention within an overall scheme of liability.[44] Yet he disagreed on the effect of a failure to fulfil those obligations. He acknowledged that the consequences of a breach of the obligations of prevention fell within the field of State responsibility:

> Having established the State's obligations of prevention in the ninth report, we must now consider the potential consequences of its failure to fulfil those obligations. Normally, they would be the consequences laid down for a breach in part two of the draft articles on State responsibility [. . .].[45]

With this understanding, Barboza changed from State liability *sine delicto* governed by primary rules to the 'State liability for wrongful acts' governed by secondary rules in his tenth report in 1994.[46] In so doing, the 'iron-clad' separation wall which segregated the topic of international liability from responsibility was demolished. Immediately, doubt about the autonomy of the topic of international liability were revitalized; members of the ILC debated whether it was necessary to separate State

[41] Ibid., section 4 of the schematic outline.

[42] Louise de la Fayette, 'The ILC and International Liability: A Commentary' (1997) 6(3) *RECIEL*, 328.

[43] Bernhard Graefrath, 'Responsibility and Damages Caused: Relationship between Responsibility and Damages' (1984) 185 *RdC*.

[44] See Part II of the 1996 working group commended draft articles. UN Doc. A/CN.4/L.533 and Add. 1. The articles on prevention constitute the main contents of that draft articles. See also the first report of Rao, 1998, UN. Doc. A/CN.4/487 and Add. 1.

[45] The tenth report of Barboza, 1994 (UN. Doc. A/CN.4/459), para. 31. He also said, 'Once consideration of the issue of prevention has been completed, the two types of liability to which our articles would give rise must be considered: State liability for the failure to fulfil obligations of prevention, which constitutes liability for a wrongful act, and the liability in principle of the private operator.' It seems that Barboza used the phrases 'State liability for wrongful acts' and 'State responsibility' interchangeably.

[46] The tenth report of Barboza, 1994 (UN. Doc. A/CN.4/459), para. 5.

liability from responsibility if both deal with the legal consequence of internationally wrongful acts – the breach of primary obligations.

When the third special rapporteur Rao took on the topic in 1998, he started with the work on the subtopic of obligations of prevention and completed it with the 'Draft articles on Prevention of Transboundary Harm from Hazardous Activities' in 2001 ('the 2001 ILC Draft Articles on Prevention'). Yet the work on State liability was never resumed. Actually, both Rao and States saw State liability as a wrong path undertaken.[47] It is ironic to recall that by extending the scope to include the obligations of prevention, the first special rapporteur intended to reinforce the autonomous status of the topic of international liability, yet, eventually it was exactly due to the development of the obligations of prevention which made State liability as an autonomous concept redundant. Ultimately, the ILC reached no conclusion about the rule of State liability in general terms, be it *sine delicto* or *ex delicto* or as a whole. After more than thirty years, the work on the liability aspect of the topic seems to have gone back to its point of departure.

1.3.2.3 From State Liability to Liability of the Operator and Further to 'Allocation of Loss'

Until the sixth report of Barboza in 1990, States were the only subject of international liability in the discourse of the ILC. From then on, international liability of the private operator coexisted with State liability in the ILC's reports on the topic. The sixth report introduced a significant change, by including for the first time a new chapter titled 'Civil Liability'. It split the avenues for obtaining remedy for international environmental damage between the domestic and international levels.[48] In doing so, the ILC established a two-track international liability system, namely civil liability and state liability. The line of civil liability eventually evolved into a new concept of 'allocation of loss', as set out in the 2006 Draft Principles on the Allocation of Loss in the case of

[47] The first report (subtopic on international liability) of Rao, 2003 (UN. Doc. A/CN.4/531), paras. 16–19.

[48] To illustrate these two levels' remedy mechanism, see chapter III of the ILC's draft articles on international liability proposed by the 1996 Working Group (UN. Doc. A/CN.4/L.533 and Add. 1): Article 20 (non-discrimination) set out the minimum requirement of the State of origin to secure domestic means for remedies for transboundary harm, while Articles 21 (nature and extent of compensation or other relief) and 22 (factors for negotiations) pinned down the inter-state negotiations.

Transboundary Harm Arising Out of Hazardous Activities (the '2006 ILC Draft Principles').

Instead of setting model rules on civil liability at the international level that call for harmonization of liability rules at the national level, the 2006 ILC Draft Principles allocate loss among different actors involved in the operations. These rules represent a new way of thinking. The core of this new idea of 'allocation of loss' embraces one objective and two essential elements. The objective of ensuring prompt and adequate compensation for innocent victims serves as the justification for the ILC's turning away from liability and moving towards the concept of allocation of loss. The two essential elements are: First, 'any scheme of allocation of loss should place the duty of compensation first on the operator'.[49] Second, States still play an important role in the allocation of loss scheme, even when no internationally wrongful act is attributable to them. Principle 4 of the 2006 ILC Draft Principles reflects this idea and sets out a model of allocation of loss. This provision suggests that a State regime for ensuring prompt and adequate compensation for victims should include the imposition of liability on the operator, the requirement of financial security of the operator and the establishment of industry-wide funds. In addition, the State should ensure the availability of additional financial resources. However, neither the idea of allocation of loss nor the model depicted in Principle 4 was completely new in the 2006 ILC Draft Principles. In effect, Principle 4 of the 2006 Draft Principles is based on the models of allocation of loss in the existing civil liability treaties.[50]

In essence, the 2006 Draft Principles promulgate a regime on allocation of loss consisting of civil liability of the operator, which is reinforced by a financial security mechanism and supplemented by additional financial sources. Therefore, the concept of allocation of loss does not contradict the notion of liability of the operator. On the contrary, the latter serves as the fundamental element of the former. However, the

[49] The second report (subtopic on international liability) of Rao, 2004 (UN. Doc. A/CN.4/540), para. 36(5). It is noted that this position was first established in the Working Group on International Liability for Injurious Consequences Arising out of Acts Not Prohibited by International Law, 2002 (UN. Doc. A/CN.4/L.627), para. 10. It was stated that 'the operator, having direct control over the operations, should bear the primary liability in any regime of allocation of loss'.

[50] Rao conducted a sectoral and regional analysis of the existing civil liability treaties in his first report, and based on that analysis he discerned some common features of the models of allocation of loss.

newly added dimensions – financial security and other supplementary financial source mechanisms that enable the involvement of other actors including the State – signal a conceptual evolution from civil liability to allocation of loss. With this concept of allocation of loss adopted in the 2006 Draft Principles, the conceptual evolution of 'international liability' during a period of nearly three decades (1978–2006) finally came to an end.

However, Principle 2 of the 2006 Draft Principles, which defines environment broadly, opens possibilities for further developments of environmental liability regimes.[51] Indeed, three related provisions of the 2006 Draft Principles – Principle 2, paragraph (a)(iv) and (v), Principle 3, paragraph (b) and Principle 5 entitled 'response measures' – hint at a new approach to environmental liability. Differing from the regimes on civil liability or allocation of loss where focus is on the compensation of the victim, the promising new approach would deal specifically with the damages to the environment *per se*, where the emphasis is on the restoration or reinstatement of the damaged environment.

1.3.2.4 Conclusions

In summary, while the initial objective of the work by the ILC on the topic of international liability was to codify and progressively develop general rules on State liability *sine delicto*, most of the work focused on obligations of prevention. The development of rules concerning obligations of prevention in turn played a critical role in transforming State liability *sine delicto* into State liability *ex delicto*, which however fell within the scope of State responsibility. Simultaneously, it is considered that the operator should primarily assume liability. From there, a further conceptual evolution was made as a result of a new way of thinking. The concept of 'allocation of loss', which centred on the liability of the operator but was reinforced by financial securities and supplemented by additional financial sources, was accepted in the final result of the work on the topic of international liability, namely the 2006 ILC Draft Principles.

Through historical reflection on the work of the ILC as explained earlier, the meaning of the concept of international liability is clearer. Strictly speaking, international liability is not a specific but a generic concept that

[51] The third report (subtopic on international liability) of Rao, 2006 (UN. Doc. A/CN.4/566), para. 14.

embodies both primary and secondary rules and covers both States and private entities. When referring to international liability, it could mean either State liability *sine delicto* or State liability *ex delicto* or liability of the operator in light of specific civil liability treaties. Firstly, State liability *sine delicto* governed by primary rules does exist in international law. Yet State liability *sine delicto* in international law is more an exception than a rule. The Convention on International Liability for Damage Caused by Space Objects is the only example of this kind.[52] Secondly, owing to its entry into the field of the secondary rules, State liability *ex delicto* falls under the scope of State responsibility. However, there are subtle differences between these two concepts in the field of international environmental law. This point will be clarified in Section 8.2.2. Thirdly, civil liability under international law is imposed on operators by specific treaties, which normally is implemented within national judicial systems. Treaty practice, however, shows that liability of the operator is normally reinforced and supplemented by other compensation mechanisms such as compulsory insurance and compensation funds. This helps to transform the civil liability regime to a regime on allocation of loss.

1.3.3 Participants in DSM

Participants in DSM can be categorized differently according to different criteria. Based on the nature of the subjects, the participants in DSM can be grouped as: ISA, State and private entities. Yet, based on the roles the subjects play, participants in DSM can be grouped as: ISA as the regulator at the international level, the sponsoring State as the regulator at the national level and as an assistant to ISA at the international level and the contractor, which includes ISA as the contractor (the Enterprise), State as the contractor and the private contractor. The two methods of categorization of the participants in DSM can be combined and illustrated as follows:

I. The ISA:

  I (a) The ISA as the regulator at the international level
  I (b) The ISA as the contractor (the Enterprise)

[52] Adoption on 29 November 1971, entry into force on 1 September 1972. Controversially, the *ex gratia* payment by States in environmental accidents might also be considered as State practice of State liability *sine delicto* in this respect.

II. State:

II (a) The sponsoring State as the regulator at the national level and as an assistant to the ISA at the international level

II (b) State as the contractor

III. Private entity as the contractor

This book adopts the second method of categorization, namely, to group the participants in DSM into three subcategories on the basis of their different roles. They are: the ISA as the regulator, the sponsoring State as the regulator and the contractor. In this book, the first two categories are referred to as the ISA and the sponsoring State, respectively.

1.3.4 International DSM Legal Regime

As indicated earlier, this book takes a positivist approach. Thus, it is important to identify clearly the positive laws as the sources of obligations and the legal bases for establishing and implementing liabilities of the participants in DSM. These laws are referred to under a broad label of 'international DSM legal regime'. Thus far, the DSM legal regime at the international level is composed of:

(a) The UNCLOS, including particularly Annex III (basic conditions of prospecting, exploration and exploitation), IV (Statute of the Enterprise) and VI (Statute of the International Tribunal for the Law of the Sea);
(b) The 1994 Agreement;
(c) The rules, regulations and procedures of the ISA adopted in accordance with the UNCLOS, including: Exploration Regulations, Recommendation of Guideline issued by the LTC;[53] and
(d) The Exploration Contracts.[54]

Beyond the international DSM legal regime identified earlier, customary international law and the general principles of law compatible with the UNCLOS could also serve as legal bases for the international environmental obligations and liabilities of the sponsoring State and the ISA.[55] Moreover, considering that the contents of legal sources (c) and (d) keep

[53] Article 38, Annex VI to the UNCLOS.

[54] The terms of contracts are applicable concerning activities in the Area in matters relating to those contracts. Ibid.

[55] Article 293(1), UNCLOS.

changing, the international DSM legal regime is thus of an evolving character. In addition, the Seabed Disputes Chamber of the International Tribunal for the Law of the Sea (SDC) can provide authoritative interpretation of the international DSM legal regime through delivering advisory opinions. To date, there has been one such case: Advisory Opinion of 1 February 2011 on 'Responsibilities and Obligations of States Sponsoring Persons and Entities with respect to Activities in the Area' (the '2011 Advisory Opinion of the SDC').

1.4 Validity and Limits of the Book

This is qualitative research. It aims at identifying the applicable legal rules concerning the marine environmental protection of participants in DSM and interpreting their meanings. The book is valid on the condition that DSM is considered as lawful activities under both the DSM legal regime and general international law. Suppose that either general international law or the DSM legal regime were to impose a prohibition or moratorium on DSM in the future, this book would no longer be valid. As to the limits of this book, there are mainly three. First, considering that the subject matter of the marine environmental protection in DSM is very much a scientific issue, and that one main theme of this book is that the legal regime for the marine environmental protection in DSM should be based on sound marine scientific knowledge, the survey of scientific documents concerning marine environmental protection in DSM is very limited. Secondly, this book relies heavily on the ISA for documents, data and information. Thirdly, owing to the fact that commercial exploitation in the Area is yet to commence, practice concerning the topic of environmental protection in DSM is scarce. In spite of these limits, this book is of both theoretical and practical significance because it detects and clarifies the fundamental legal bases for the discussion about the issue of 'marine environmental protection in DSM'.

1.5 Structure and Outline of the Book

The next chapter of the book elaborates on the principle of common heritage of mankind (CHM): the fundamental theoretical basis upon which the current and future DSM legal regime is built. To begin with, it identifies eight elements of the principle of CHM in DSM. Then, the principle is compared with related concepts in other contexts. Thereafter, it zooms in the environmental aspects of the principle, deliberating over the *erga omnes* nature of international environmental obligations at the conceptual level and the critical role played by marine sciences at the operational level of environmental protection in DSM. The remaining chapters can be grouped into two parts: Chapters 3 and 4 are the obligation part while Chapters 5–8 the liability part.

Chapter 3 enquires into the nature, composition and environmental mandates of ISA. It gives an overview of the functioning of the ISA since its operation in 1996, in particular, it identifies the problems faced by its organs in practice. Thereafter, it reveals how the ISA discharges its environmental mandates by exercising powers and fulfilling obligations: it analyses its powers to adopt regulations, issue recommendations on environmental impact assessments (EIAs) and safeguard the marine environment when administering activities and its obligations to apply the precautionary approach, respond to environmental emergency and promote and encourage marine scientific research. Finally, it singles out the main features in the drafting process of Exploitation Regulations and suggests possible ways for the ISA to overcome the fundamental obstacle for the making and implementation of environmental regulations and standards – gaps in marine scientific knowledge.

Chapter 4 continues to examine international environmental obligations in DSM of other participants. At the beginning, it explains about the sponsoring State's legal status and roles in the DSM legal regime. Then, Section 4.2 elaborates on international environmental obligations of the sponsoring State: it focuses on its obligation of prevention, the obligation to apply the precautionary approach, the obligation concerning environmental impact assessment and the obligation to cooperate. Analyses in this section draw on legal bases of both the *lex specialis* of DSM regime and general international (environmental) law. The examination shows in what circumstances and how obligations under the *lex specialis* of DSM regime are consistent with or deviate from those under general international (environmental) law. Mostly, discussions over relevant general international (environmental) law in this section could apply by analogy to the ISA and also serve as a reference point for the contractor. Section 4.3 investigates international environmental obligations of the contractor. It covers the obligations to conduct EIA, prepare and respond to environmental emergency, environmental monitoring and management and apply the highest environmental standards. In contrast with Section 4.2, analysis in this section is based only on the *lex specialis* of DSM regime. Additionally, it refers frequently to draft Exploitation Regulations and Standards and Guidelines to be adopted by the ISA.

As to the liability part, it is noted that the reflection on the work of the ILC on the topic 'international liability' in this Introduction chapter provides a conceptual background against which the international environmental liability regimes in DSM are analyzed. The scope of the analysis includes the following three dimensions. First, the analysis covers only DSM activities; activities other than DSM in the Area are excluded. DSM activities by their nature are 'hazardous activities not prohibited by international law', which falls into the coverage in the ILC's work on international liability. Secondly, the analysis deals in general with situations where the environmental effects of DSM activities take place in the Area or the high seas which are regarded as global commons. The situation that DSM activities conducted in the Area (threaten to) cause damage to a coastal State is excluded.[56] Thirdly, the analysis focuses primarily on damage to the marine environment *per se*. It is noted that, initially, international environmental liability regimes provide remedies only to victims who suffer damages through the impairment of the environment; damages to the environment *per se* are included alongside the traditional forms of damage at a later stage,[57] and examples where environmental damage refers exclusively to damage to the environment *per se* are rare. A comparative reading of the definitions of damage in those environment-related liability instruments will reveal this point. In this respect, La Fayette made a keen observation:

[56] This is however an exceptional situation merits special note. Pursuant to Article 142(3) of the UNCLOS, that coastal State is entitled to take measures consistent with the relevant provisions of Part XII as may be necessary to prevent, mitigate or eliminate grave and imminent danger. However, Article 142(3) does not indicate whether that coastal State is entitled to seek remedies when damages have been incurred, and if so from whom. The contractor? the sponsoring State? or the ISA? A further question is: Should this situation fall into a transboundary context? Or a global commons context?

[57] Examples of international instruments which cover damages to the environment itself include: Article 2(7)(c) and (d) of the 1993 Convention on Civil Liability for Damage Resulting from Activities Dangerous to the Environment (Lugano); Article 2(c)(iv) and (v) of the Basel Protocol on Liability and Compensation for Damage resulting from Transboundary Movements of Hazardous Wastes and their Disposal (adopted at the Fifth Conference of Parties (COP-5) on 10 December 1999); Article 1(6) of the 1992 Protocol to the Civil Liability Convention and the IOPC Fund Convention; Article 23 of the1998 ILC Resolution 67(2) on Responsibility and Liability under International Law for Environmental Damage ('environmental regimes should separately from or in addition to the reparation of damage relating to death, personal injury or loss of property or economic value'.); Article 2(b) of the 2001 Draft Articles on Prevention ('harm' means harm caused to persons, property or the environment); Article 2(a)(iv) and (v) of the 2006 Draft Principles by the ILC.

> It appears that definition of "environmental harm" or "pollution damage" fall into two main categories: (i) those that focus on the traditional heads of damage in national tort law, such as personal injury, property damage, and economic loss; and (ii) those that focus on damage to the environment *per se*.[58]

She further indicated that most international liability regimes fall into category (i) and the regimes for Antarctica and deep seabed mining fall into category (ii). Therefore, in reality, the term environmental damage is used in two different senses: 'damages through the environment' and 'damages to the environment'. This book discusses 'environmental damage' in the latter sense.

Chapter 5 is dedicated to the definition and measure of 'environmental damage' which are related to the issues of environmental obligations and liabilities. Indeed, this book revolves around 'environmental damage' as the principal objective of environmental obligations is to prevent environmental damage, while that of environmental liabilities is to provide remedies to environmental damage. In particular, Chapter 5 is an integral part of Chapters 6 and 8 since environmental damage is a common triggering element for the establishment of international environmental liabilities of the contractor, the sponsoring State and the ISA. Following the line of the ILC's work on international liability, it is believed that primary liability should be imposed on the operator who has the direct control over the DSM activities. Thus, the international environmental liability of the contractor is dealt with first.

Chapter 6 examines the theoretical basis, establishment and invocation of international environmental liability of the contractor. It also covers remediation of environmental damage and special issues of the Enterprise as contractor and States as contractors. Furthermore, as the reflection on the ILC's work on international liability has also shown, schemes on allocation of loss function as reinforcement or supplementary mechanisms to the liability of the operator. Thus, Chapter 7 discusses compulsory insurance or financial security and trust fund for marine environmental damage as the possible schemes on allocation of loss in the context of DSM. These are two alternatives to liability of the contractor. In addition, Chapter 7 considers a third alternative – the administrative approach to the liability of the contractor.

[58] Louise de La Fayette, 'The Concept of Environmental Damage in International Liability Regimes', in Michael Bowman & Alan Boyle (eds.), *Environmental Damage in International and Comparative Law* (OUP 2002) 181.

Chapter 8 scrutinizes international environmental liabilities of the sponsoring State and ISA. With respect to the liability of the sponsoring State, as has been explained in the reflection on the ILC's work, once entering into the field of secondary rules, State liability falls within the scope of State responsibility. For this reason, the general rules on State responsibility as reflected in the 2001 ILC Articles on State Responsibility (ASR) are employed in analysing the establishment, content and invocation of the liability of the sponsoring State. Nevertheless, the subtle differences between the notions of 'State liability' and 'State responsibility' will also be displayed. With respect to international environmental liability of the ISA, the establishment of the international environmental liability of the sponsoring State can be applicable *mutatis mutandis* to the ISA by analogy. Yet, a special liability issue that is involved concerning the ISA but not the sponsoring State will be discussed in detail. This is the question of attributing liability to member States. Finally, Chapter 8 also touches on the problem of invocation of liability of the ISA.

2

Common Heritage of Mankind and Protection of the Marine Environment

2.1 Introduction

The concept of the common heritage of mankind (CHM) has dominated international discussions about the subject of deep seabed mining (DSM) within the United Nations since the very beginning. It was formally introduced by Malta's proposal to the forum of the twenty-second session of the UN General Assembly on 17 August 1967[1] and further articulated by Malta's Ambassador Arvid Pardo on 1 November 1967.[2] Pardo's speech caused a sensation within the UN General Assembly.[3] On 17 December 1970, the General Assembly adopted the Declaration of Principles Governing the Sea-Bed and Ocean Floor, and the Subsoil Thereof, Beyond the Limits of National Jurisdiction (the 1970 Declaration of Principles).[4] The contents of the 1970 Declaration of Principles were later incorporated into the 1982 UN Convention on

1 Declaration and treaty concerning the reservation exclusively for peaceful purposes of the seabed and of the ocean floor, underlying the seas beyond the limits of present national jurisdiction, and the use of their resources in the interests of mankind. UN Doc. A/6695.

2 For a historical account of the context of the speech, see Surabhi Ranganathan, 'Global Commons' (2016) 27 *EJIL* 693–717.

3 The reaction by the UN General Assembly was immediate. On 18 December 1967, the UN General Assembly adopted Resolution 2340 (XXII) to establish the Ad Hoc Sea-Bed Committee to study the peaceful uses of the seabed and the ocean floor beyond the limits of national jurisdiction. A year later, on 21 December 1968, upon adoption of Resolution 2467 A (XXIII), the General Assembly established a permanent Sea-Bed Committee on which the same mandate as its predecessor was conferred. Upon adoption of Resolution 2750 (XXV) on 17 December 1970, the Committee's mandate was expanded to include preparation for the third Law of the Sea Conference to be convened in 1973. Correspondingly, the Sea-Bed Committee was reformed. Since then, the mandate concerning the peaceful uses of the seabed and the ocean floor beyond the limits of national jurisdiction had been under the trust of Subcommittee I of the Sea-Bed Committee until the completion of the draft of the UNCLOS. See Yuwen Li, *Transfer of Technology for Deep Sea-Bed Mining: the 1982 Law of the Sea Convention and Beyond* (Martinus Nijhoff 1994).

4 UNGA Res. 2749 (XXV).

the Law of the Sea (UNCLOS). With the adoption of the UNCLOS, CHM turned into an overarching legal principle governing all aspects of the DSM legal regime, including the protection of the marine environment. Indeed, as Li puts it, 'the principle of CHM constitutes the essence of the [DSM legal] regime in the sense that it is the starting point as well as legal basis for the regime'.[5]

This book does not cover all aspects of the DSM legal regime, but focuses only on environmental aspects. Nevertheless, since marine environmental protection is both an integral element of and closely connected to other elements of the principle of CHM, this chapter starts with an examination of the full legal meaning and nature of CHM in the context of DSM (Section 2.2). In this regard, it disagrees with Pinto on that CHM is a myth[6] and concurred with Lodge that Part XI of the Convention gives precise legal meaning to this term.[7] To further the understanding of CHM in the context of DSM, the concept is then compared with that in the contexts of outer space and the Antarctic, and also compared with the notion of 'common interest of international community as a whole' ('community interest') in general international law (Section 2.3). Thereafter, the focus of the investigation zooms in on the environmental aspects of CHM (Section 2.4).

2.2 Elements of the Common Heritage of Mankind in the Context of DSM

Article 136 of the UNCLOS states that 'the Area and its resources are the common heritage of mankind'. In Section 2 of Part XI, the UNCLOS elaborates on the meaning of CHM in the context of DSM. Specifically, Article 137 prescribes the global commons status and international control of the Area and its resources. Articles 140, 143, 144 and 148 touch upon the idea of distributive justice,[8] which has four components, namely DSM for the benefit of mankind as a whole; equitable sharing of

[5] Yuwen Li, *Transfer of Technology for Deep Sea-Bed Mining: The 1982 Law of the Sea Convention and Beyond* (Martinus Nijhoff 1994) 38.

[6] M. C. W. Pinto, 'Common Heritage of Mankind: From Metaphor to Myth, and the Consequences of Constructive Ambiguity', in Jerzy Makarczyk and Krzysztof Skubiszewski (eds.), *Theory of International Law at the Threshold of the 21st Century: Essays in Honour of Krzysztof Skubiszewski* (Kluwer 1996).

[7] Michael Lodge, 'The Common Heritage of Mankind' (2012) 27 *IJMCL* 733–742, 734-736.

[8] Edwin Egede, *Africa and the Deep Seabed Regime: Politics and International Law of the Common Heritage of Mankind* (Springer 2011) 244.

economic benefits arising from DSM; preferential treatment of developing countries; and marine scientific research (MSR) for the benefit of mankind as a whole. Articles 141 and 145 depict the requirements on the peaceful use of the Area and its resources, and the protection of the marine environment, respectively.

2.2.1 The Area and Its Resources as Global Commons Subject to International Administration

Article 137 of the UNCLOS reads as follows:

> 1. No State shall claim or exercise sovereignty or sovereign rights over any part of the Area or its resources, nor shall any State or natural or juridical person appropriate any part thereof. No such claim or exercise of sovereignty or sovereign rights nor such appropriation shall be recognized.
> 2. All rights in the resources of the Area are vested in mankind as a whole, on whose behalf the Authority shall act. These resources are not subject to alienation. The minerals recovered from the Area, however, may only be alienated in accordance with this Part and the rules, regulations and procedures of the Authority.
> 3. No State or natural or juridical person shall claim, acquire or exercise rights with respect to the minerals recovered from the Area except in accordance with this Part. Otherwise, no such claim, acquisition or exercise of such rights shall be recognized.

From the first paragraph, it is clear that the Area, like the high seas, Antarctica or celestial bodies in outer space, is considered as *res communis (omnium)*, which means 'things of the (entire) community',[9] usually called 'global commons' since they are beyond the sovereignty of any State and can be subject to the no-appropriation principle. In Schrijver's view, global commons resemble in many ways the concept of common goods or common property as explained by Hugo Grotius in his seminal work *mare liberum*.[10] Grotius argued that because common goods such as the high seas by nature cannot be subject to anyone's possession and they are for the public utility, they shall be open to the free access of all.[11] This argumentation led to the pronouncement

[9] Aaron Fellmeth and Maurice Horwitz, *Guide to Latin in International Law* (OUP 2009) 250.

[10] Nico Schrijver, 'Managing the Global Commons: Common Good or Common Sink?' (2016) 37(7) *Third World Quarterly* 2.

[11] Ibid.

of one of the most fundamental principles of the law of the sea: the freedom of the seas.

However, the Area as global commons under Article 137 of the UNCLOS is different from the seas as common goods under Grotius's *mare liberum*. From the second and third paragraphs of Article 137, it is seen that 'these resources [in the Area] are not subject to alienation', that any access to and utilization of the resources in the Area must be through the International Seabed Authority (ISA), which shall act on behalf of 'mankind as a whole', and that rights to 'minerals recovered from the Area' cannot not be legally recognized unless in accordance with Part XI of the UNCLOS. Pursuant to Article 137, paragraphs 2 and 3, access to the Area and utilization of its resources are subject to international administration. This is one of the critical differences between the principles of CHM and freedom of the seas: internationally controlled access and utilization versus free access and utilization of the global commons.

Scholars attempted to provide justification or a theoretical explanation for such an evolution. Schrijver observes that '[o]ver time this [the over-exploitation of marine resources] has also brought to the fore the limitations of the Grotian concept of common goods, and with it the principle of the freedom of the seas'.[12] And since 'some original tenets of Grotius's concept of *res communis*, in particular the idea of inexhaustibility, can no longer be upheld', 'the freedom of access to the global commons has become increasingly qualified and supplemented, if not replaced by a new law of international co-operation aimed at conservation and sustainable use of natural wealth and resources beyond the limits of national jurisdiction'.[13] To some extent, the principle of CHM can be seen as the result of a long evolution from the principle of the freedom of the seas with a purpose of countering the limitations of the latter.

Hardin offered a theoretical explanation as to why freedom with respect to the commons should be restricted or abandoned in his well-known publication 'The Tragedy of the Commons'.[14] In his article, Hardin demonstrated that rational individuals are driven by self-interest

[12] Ibid., 3.

[13] Nico Schrijver and Vid Prislan, 'From *Mare Liberum* to the Global Commons: Building on the Grotian Heritage' (2009) 30 *Grotiana* 168.

[14] Garrett Hardin, 'The Tragedy of the Commons' (1968) 162(3859) *Science* 1243–1248. Ranganathan analyses the context and subcontext of Hardin's 'Tragedy of the Commons' and compares them with those of Pardo's 'CHM'. She concludes that although both concepts seemingly emerged from different world views, they revealed both parochial and cosmopolitan tendencies, they both had illiberal and imperial dimensions, and the

to maximize their own gains, while the resources of the world are limited. Thus, an unlimited freedom towards the commons will inevitably bring ruin to all. In his words, 'the inherent logic of the commons remorselessly generates tragedy'.[15] Originally an article by a biologist addressing the problem of overpopulation, 'the Tragedy of the Commons' has been transformed into a widely accepted theory that can provide justification for public control (typically through legislation or regulation) over the commons. The Area and its resources are just such a pertinent example: international control over the access and utilization of the Area and its resources can be justified by the theory of the tragedy of the commons.

To avoid the dismal scenario of the tragedy of the commons, there is a need for regulation. In the context of DSM, the primary task of Part XI of the UNCLOS is to establish an international regulatory system governing the Area and its resources. The ISA was created to exercise international public authority with the purpose of safeguarding the interests of mankind as a whole. Indeed, the ISA as the institutional arrangement is so important for the operationalization of the principle of CHM that thirty out of the fifty-nine provisions of Part XI of the UNCLOS are concerned with the ISA. To sum up, Article 137 presents two elements of the principle of CHM: first, the Area and its resources as global commons and, second, the international administration by the ISA over the Area and its resources. The element of CHM concerning international administration by the ISA makes it distinct from the principle of freedom of the seas.

2.2.2 *Common Interest, Benefit-Sharing and Preferential Treatment of Developing States*

The principle of CHM also reflects the idea of distributive justice. In the context of DSM, four elements of CHM are related to the idea of distributive justice: DSM and MSR activities in the Area for the benefit of mankind as a whole, equitable sharing of economic benefits arising out of DSM and preferential treatment of developing States.

Articles 140(1) and 143(1) of the UNCLOS adopt the same for-the-benefit-of-mankind-as-a-whole model for both DSM and MSR activities

integrative approach played a critical role in the production and impact of both concepts. See Surabhi Ranganathan, 'Global Commons' (2016) 27 *EJIL* 693–717.

15 Garrett Hardin, 'The Tragedy of the Commons' (1968) 162 *Science* 3859, 1244.

in the Area.[16] For this reason, the principle of CHM is distinguished further from the principle of the freedom of the seas since the latter works on a first-come-first-served basis, which encourages self-interest. Yet, although both DSM and MSR are required to be carried out for the benefit of mankind as a whole, the ISA plays different roles in the sharing of the benefits generated from these two activities. The ISA is empowered to distribute the economic benefits generated from DSM (Article 140(2)), but it is only entrusted to encourage and promote the dissemination of the scientific knowledge and information generated from MSR (Article 143 (2)). Furthermore, DSM and MSR activities in the Area are not equally regulated. In contrast to international administration by the ISA with respect to DSM activity, the 'freedom of scientific research' as depicted in Article 87(1)(f) is still in principle applicable to MSR in the Area.

Article 140(2) of the UNCLOS addresses the issue of the distribution of the economic benefits generated from DSM activities. It prescribes that: The Authority shall provide for the equitable sharing of financial and other economic benefits derived from activities in the Area through any appropriate mechanism, on a non-discriminatory basis, in accordance with article 160, paragraph 2(f)(1).

This provision conveys two messages. First, 'the equitable sharing' is chosen as the governing principle over the distribution of economic benefits among States. Second, the ISA is entrusted with the duty of designing and implementing concrete mechanisms for the equitable sharing of economic benefits.

Moreover, the idea of distributive justice is reflected not only in the principle of the distribution of the economic benefit but also in the exploitation system. Article 153 of the UNCLOS establishes a parallel exploitation system. On the one hand, the Enterprise is designed as an operational arm of the ISA to conduct DSM on behalf of and for the benefit of mankind directly.[17] On the other hand, States and entities

[16] Article 140(1) prescribes that: 'Activities in the Area shall, as specifically provided for in this Part, be carried out for the benefit of mankind as a whole, irrespective of the geographical location of States, whether coastal or land-locked, and taking into particular consideration the interests and needs of developing States . . .'. Article 143(1) states that: 'Marine scientific research in the Area shall be carried out exclusively for peaceful purposes and for the benefit of mankind as a whole.' [a question: when should a full stop mark within or outside the quotation mark?]

[17] Article 170, UNCLOS; Section 2, Annex to the 1994 Agreement. At the time of writing, the Enterprise is still not functioning. However, as will be shown in Chapter 3, the functioning of the Enterprise is already under discussion within the ISA.

(under the sponsorship of States) are also eligible to conduct DSM. For the latter scenario, special attention is given to ensuring the equal participation of all States, including in particular developing States.

Based on the realistic consideration of the unequal capacities between developed and developing States with regard to DSM, the UNCLOS accords preferential treatment to developing States. The latter part of Article 140(1) stipulates that 'the interests and needs of developing States' shall be taken into particular consideration. Moreover, Article 148 states that:

> The effective participation of developing States in activities in the Area shall be promoted as specifically provided in this Part, having due regard to their special interests and needs, and in particular to the special need of land-locked and geographically disadvantaged among them to overcome obstacles arising from their disadvantaged location, including remoteness from the Area and difficulty of access to and from it.

To ensure the effective participation of developing States, Article 144 (2) prescribes that training opportunities in marine science and technology shall be provided to nationals from developing States.[18] Article 15 of Annex III to the UNCLOS specifies the contractor as the party obliged to provide and fund training opportunities. This obligation of the contractor is further elaborated in the Exploration Regulations and incorporated into every contract the contractor signs with the ISA.[19]

In practice, developing States have so far benefited most from the training opportunities under Article 144(2). Since the first contract granted by the ISA in 2001, many training programmes have been implemented.[20] It is a task of the Secretariat of the ISA to negotiate with each of the contractors and their sponsoring States on the training programmes, and to supervise, review and assess the implementation of those training programmes. Developing States have also benefited significantly from Articles 8 and 9, Annex III to the UNCLOS, which

[18] The compulsory transfer of technology requirement as depicted in Article 144(1) is repealed by Section 5, Annex to the 1994 Agreement.

[19] Regulation 27 of nodules exploration regulations (ISBA/19/C/17, 2013) and Schedule 3 of exploration contracts.

[20] 'Between 2013 and 2017, a total of 69 training places were provided by 11 contractors' and 'if all existing contracts and approved plans of work were implemented according to the recommendations made by the Legal and Technical Commission with respect to training programmes, approximately 200 training places will be made available by contractors between 2017 and 2021', the 2018 Annual Report of the Secretary-General of the ISA, ISBA/24/A/2, paras. 106 and 108.

accords privileges to developing States concerning activities in the reserved area. To date, there have been six contracts under the sponsorship of developing States that cover the reserved area within the Area.[21] It should be noted, however, that the preferential treatment of developing States is not a purpose in itself; rather, it is a means to achieving the goal of equal participation in DSM. The Seabed Disputes Chamber (SDC) highlights that, except for the preferential treatment accorded by specific provisions, developing States shall engage in activities in the Area on an equal footing with developed States.[22] Particularly, there shall be no preferential treatment accorded to developing States when it comes to the liability issue of the sponsoring State.[23]

But why was the idea of distributive justice associated with the principle of CHM? To understand the underlying reasons, it is important to turn to the historical background of the formation of CHM. Pinto observed that: It [the principle of CHM] was an inspiring vision offered to a world at a time when it seemed feasible to establish a 'new international economic order' founded on distributive justice and co-operation that would replace an old order of exploitative relationships based essentially on power disparities and competition.[24]

Indeed, the provisions of Part XI of the UNCLOS identified in this subsection reflect the tenets of the international movement for a New International Economic Order (NIEO),[25] which are fully demonstrated in the 1974 Declaration on the Establishment of a New International Economic Order (the 1974 NIEO Declaration) and the Charter of Economic Rights and Duties of States.[26] The third paragraph of the preamble to the 1974 NIEO Declaration expresses the aspirations of developing States for 'the establishment of a New International

[21] These six developing sponsoring States and the dates for the conclusion of the corresponding exploration contracts are: Nauru (22 July 2011), Tonga (11 January 2012), Kiribati (19 January 2015), Singapore (22 January 2015), Cook Islands (15 July 2016) and China (12 May 2017).

[22] ITLOS, Advisory Opinion of 2011 (No. 17 case), para. 158.

[23] Ibid.

[24] M. C. W. Pinto, 'The Common Heritage of Mankind: Then and Now' (2012) 361 *RdC* 113.

[25] The NIEO also found its way into the fifth paragraph of the preamble to the UNCLOS which states that the UNCLOS intends to contribute to 'the realization of a just and equitable international economic order which takes into account the interests and needs of mankind as a whole and, in particular, the special interests and needs of developing countries, whether coastal and land-locked.'

[26] UN Doc. A/RES/S-6/3201, 1 May 1974 and GA Res. 3281 (XXIX), 12 December 1974.

Economic Order based on equity, sovereign equality, interdependence, common interest and cooperation among all States'. Article 4 of the 1974 NIEO Declaration stipulates that 'the new international economic order should be founded on full respect for the following principles: ... (c) full and effective participation on the basis of equality of all countries in the solving of world economic problems in the common interest of all countries'. Now, in spite of the disappearance of the NIEO movement, the related elements of the principle of CHM by and large stand. This is certainly in part because law, unlike the political movement, is more stable. But the more fundamental reason is that those elements are consistent with a broader trend in developments in international law – the community interest – which are examined in Section 2.3.3.

2.2.3 *Peaceful Use of the Area and Its Resources*

The principle of CHM also reflects developments in international law in areas other than the law of the sea. Two such examples are the requirements that 'the Area shall be open to use exclusively for peaceful purposes by all States' (Article 141) and that 'necessary measures shall be taken to ensure effective protection for the marine environment' (Article 145).

The origin of Article 141 of the UNCLOS can be traced back to Article 1 of the 1959 Antarctic Treaty and Article IV of the 1967 Outer Space Treaty.[27] Furthermore, the development of Article 141 was closely connected to the historical background of the arms race in the Cold War. Particularly, it has to do with the negotiation of two treaties: the 1963 Treaty Banning Nuclear Weapon Tests in the Atmosphere, in Outer Space and Under Water and the 1971 Treaty on the Prohibition of the Emplacement of Nuclear Weapons and Other Weapons of Mass Destruction on the Sea-Bed and the Ocean Floor and in the Subsoil thereof.[28] But above all, the element of peaceful use of the Area and its resources can be seen as a corollary of the principle of prohibition of the threat or use of force as enshrined in Article 2(4) of the UN Charter and

[27] Yuwen Li, *Transfer of Technology for Deep Sea-Bed Mining: the 1982 Law of the Sea Convention and Beyond* (Martinus Nijhoff 1994) 40.

[28] Commentary to Article 141, para. 141(2), Satya N. Nandan, Michael Lodge and Shabtai Rosenne (eds), *United Nations Convention on the Law of the Sea 1982: A Commentary (Vol. VI)* (Martinus Nijhoff 2002).

also incorporated in Article 301 of the UNCLOS. Nowadays, peaceful use of the Area and its resources is well accepted and observed.

2.2.4 Protection of the Marine Environment

Like the requirement of 'peaceful use' under Article 141, the requirement of environmental protection under Article 145 of the UNCLOS is by no means unprecedented. The protection of the marine environment has been an international legal issue for many years. Prior to the milestone Stockholm Conference in 1972, there were the 1954 International Convention for the Prevention of Pollution of the Sea by Oil[29] and the 1969 International Convention on Civil Liability for Oil Pollution Damage (the 1969 CLC). At about the same time as the 1972 Stockholm Declaration, the Convention on the Prevention of Marine Pollution by Dumping of Wastes and Other Matters was adopted (the 1972 London Convention).[30] Very soon after the 1972 London Convention, another convention was under negotiation – the 1973 International Convention for the Prevention of Pollution from Ships (the MARPOL).[31] The MARPOL took into consideration the 1972 UN Conference on the Human Environment, particularly Annex III on General Principles for Assessment and Control of Marine Pollution.[32] It also took into account the Third Conference for the Law of the Sea Convention, particularly the discussion on the protection of the marine environment. Part XII of the UNCLOS prescribes a comprehensive international legal framework on the protection and preservation of the marine environment. Moreover, beyond maritime law and the law

[29] Adopted on 12 May 1954, entered into force on 26 July 1958.

[30] Adopted on 13 November 1972, entered into force on 30 August 1975. The 1996 Protocol to the 1972 London Convention (entry into force on 24 March 2006) created a simplified but more stringent system with respect to dumping at sea. Now the two systems under the 1972 London Convention and the 1996 Protocol are co-existent, each with its own States Party. Yet, the 1972 London Convention and the 1996 Protocol share the same secretariat – Office of London Convention/Protocol and Ocean Affairs of the IMO. Moreover, eventually the 1996 Protocol will replace the 1972 London Convention, thereby merging the two systems.

[31] Adopted on 2 November 1973, amended by the 1978 Protocol before its entry into force. The MARPOL 73/78 entered into force on 2 October 1983. Upon its entry into force, it replaced the 1954 International Convention for the Prevention of Pollution of the Sea by Oil.

[32] Report of the UN Conference on the Human Environment, Stockholm, 5–16 June 1972, A/CONF. 48/14/Rev.1, 73–74.

of the sea, the requirement of the protection of the marine environment has developed alongside similar requirements of environmental protection in other fields. These international environmental treaties or provisions may be referred or systematically integrated as the other rules of international law when international environmental obligations in DSM are interpretated.

Yet, in comparison with most international environmental provisions, Article 145 of the UNCLOS is special in that, first, it assigns the primary responsibility concerning the protection of the marine environment to an international organization –the ISA – rather than States, and second, the ISA is entrusted with quasi-legislative power.[33] This assignment and empowerment of the ISA with respect to environmental protection in Article 145 can be correlated with Article 157 which empowers the ISA to control and manage DSM activities; they can be regarded as two sides of the element of the principle of CHM that DSM is subject to international administration. Indeed, the ISA occupies a central place in the international DSM legal regime. Discussions over international environmental obligations in DSM in this book are centred on the ISA too.[34] As will be shown in Chapter 3, the ISA has exercised new powers not explicit in the UNCLOS to discharge its environmental mandates, such as the employment of various environmental management tools. Moreover, in recent years, there has been a growing demand that the ISA should be more transparent and allow for wider public participation in its decision-making process. The expansion of environmental mandates of the ISA and the growing voice of civil society's participation in the global governance (in particular the environmental aspects) of the DSM can both find their rationale in the principle of CHM. More specific, the global commons status of the Areas and its resources and the ISA's role as the international administrator (to control and manage DSM activities and to protect the marine environment) on behalf of mankind as a whole could provide not only theoretical basis but also rhetoric to a flexible

[33] It is prescribed: '. . . To this end, the Authority shall adopt appropriate rules, regulations and procedures for *inter alia* . . ..'

[34] It is important to keep in mind that assigning the primary responsibility with regard to the protection of the marine environment to the ISA does not, however, exclude the roles played by other participants in DSM (the sponsoring State and the contractor, see Chapter 4) and even non-participants.

understanding of the ISA regarding the content of its environmental mandates as well as the way it discharges those mandates.[35]

In recent years, with a prospect of commercial mining activities in the near future, environmental protection in DSM has increasingly become a global concern. This changed situation prompts some to propose for a 'contemporary vision of the global seafloor' which brings new meanings to CHM[36] but some to reaffirm the importance of respecting the delicate balance enshrined in the principle of CHM and to fully appreciate (in particular the environmental aspects of) CHM 'as a limit to exploitation of the global commons'.[37] It is argued here that the principle of CHM is flexible enough to respond to the changed situations. Indeed, the word 'heritage' in the phrase 'CHM' should be understood as denoting not only benefits and interests/rights but also burdens and obligations. If the four elements under the rubric of 'distributive justice' focus on the positive side of DSM activities and MSR – 'benefit-sharing and common interests/rights', then the elements of marine environmental protection and peaceful use of the Area and its resources could be said to refer to the negative side – 'common burdens and obligations'. In a sense, these 'burdens and obligations' of the protection of the environment are the necessary costs for getting the 'benefits and interests/rights' through utilizing mineral resources in the Area. Thus, the former constitutes an inherent constraint to the latter. However, unlike the element of 'peaceful use of the Area and its resources' which only requires actors to refrain from resorting to armed forces, the 'protection of the marine environment' requires actors to take active measures. Marine environmental protection in DSM is a complex issue. The difficult problem is not whether but how the marine environment should be protected against detrimental effects of the lawful use (exploration and exploitation) of the Area and its resources. This is the overarching research question of this book.

[35] On how the idea of 'the common' could provide theoretical basis and rhetoric to a new mode of global governance, see Samuel Cogolati and Jan Wouters (eds.), *The Commons and a New Global Governance* (Edward Elgar 2018).

[36] Sabine Christiansen et al., 'Towards a Contemporary Vision for the Global Seafloor: Implementing the Common Heritage of Mankind' (2019) Heinrich Boll Stifung (Publication Series Ecology Vol. 45).

[37] Karin Mickelson, 'Common Heritage of Mankind as a Limit to Exploitation of the Global Commons' (2019) 30(2) *EJIL* 635–663.

2.2.5 *Summary*

To summarize, the principle of CHM in the context of DSM implies not only rights or benefits but also obligations or burdens. It embodies eight elements: (1) the status of the Area and its resources as the global commons (Article 137); (2) international administration by the ISA over DSM activities (Articles 137, 157); (3) common interest of international community in DSM in the Area (Article 140(1)); (4) common interest of the international community in MSR in the Area (Article 143); (5) equitable sharing of the economic benefits arising from DSM among States (Articles 140(2), 148, 144); (6) preferential treatment of developing States (Articles 143(3), 144(1), 144(2), 152, 160, 162 and Articles 8 and 9 of Annex III); (7) peaceful use of the Area and its resources (Article 141); and (8) protection of the marine environment in DSM (Article 145). Individually, these elements are not unique to CHM. It is the combination of all these elements that makes the principle of CHM in the context of DSM unique. To understand the principle as a whole, one should examine the total of the parts, otherwise, one would get into a situation like 'the blind men and the elephant'.

The elements of the principle of CHM carry different weights and they are interconnected. The most fundamental element is the Area and its resources as the global commons; it constitutes the prerequisite for all the other elements. Closely related is the element of international administration of the Area and its resources – the international regime centred on the ISA; this element is the key to the operationalization of the principle of CHM. The elements of peaceful use of the Area and its resources and the protection of the marine environment are integrated into the principle of CHM which constitute restraints on the use of the Area and its resources from two different angles. Particularly, DSM must be balanced against the consideration of marine environmental protection. The contrast of weights between the two sides of the balance determines principally the direction of the development of the principle of CHM and the international DSM legal regime in the future. The four elements relating to distributive justice are not as generally acknowledged as the other four elements beyond the context of DSM.

2.3 Common Heritage of Mankind in Comparison with Related Concepts in Other Fields

In this section, concepts related to CHM beyond the context of DSM will be examined. CHM is first compared with the concepts of 'common interest/common heritage of mankind' in the context of outer space (Section 2.3.1) and with the 'common interest of mankind' in Antarctica (Section 2.3.2), respectively. Then, CHM is compared with the notion of 'community interest' in general international law (Section 2.3.3).

2.3.1 Common Interest/Common Heritage of Mankind in Outer Space

'Ever since the first human-made satellite orbited the Earth in 1957, the UN has been committed to space being used for peaceful purposes'.[38] In 1958, the United Nations Office for Outer Space Affairs (UNOOSA) was created within the UN Secretariat. In 1959, the General Assembly of the UN established the permanent Committee on the Peaceful Uses of Outer Space (COPUOS). In 1961, the UN General Assembly adopted Resolution 1721 (XVI) on the International Cooperation in the Peaceful Uses of Outer Space which recognized 'the common interest of mankind in furthering the peaceful uses of outer space and the urgent need to strengthen international cooperation in this important field'[39] and declared that 'outer space and celestial bodies are free for exploration and use by all States in conformity with international law and are not subject to national appropriation'.[40] These principles have been repeatedly endorsed by all the sequential legal instruments in this field.[41]

[38] United Nations Office for Outer Space Affairs: www.unoosa.org/oosa/en/ourwork/copuos/history.html.

[39] Preamble, para. 1, UN General Assembly Resolution 1721 (XVI) on the International Cooperation in the Peaceful Uses of Outer Space (adopted on 4 December 1961).

[40] Ibid., Preamble, para. 2(1)(b).

[41] To date, there are five treaties in this field: the 1967 Treaty on Principles Governing the Activities of States in the Exploration and Use of Outer Space, including the Moon and Other Celestial Bodies (Adoption by UN GA Res. 2222(XXI) on 19 December 1966, entry into force on 10 October 1967); the 1968 Agreement on the Rescue of astronauts, the Return of Astronauts and the Return of Objects Launched into Outer Space (Adoption by UN GA Res. 2345 (XXII) on 19 December 1967, entry into force on 3 December 1968); the 1972 Convention on International Liability for Damage Caused by Space Objects (Adoption by UN GA Res. 2777(XXVI) of 29 November 1971, entry into force on 1 September 1972); the 1974 Convention on Registration of Objects Launched into Outer Space (Adoption by UN GA Res. 3235(XXIX) on 12 November 1974, entry into force on 15 September 1976); and the 1979 Agreement Governing the Activities of States on the Moon and Other Celestial Bodies ('the 1979 Moon Agreement') (Adoption by UN GA Res.34/68 on 18 December 1979, entry into force on 11 July 1984. As of 4 October 2022, it has eighteen parties).

The 1979 Moon Agreement took a considerable step further: Article 11 declares that 'the Moon and its natural resources are the common heritage of mankind'. The Article also gives meaning to the concept of CHM. Paragraphs 2 and 3 affirm the prohibition of appropriation of the Moon and its resources. Paragraph 4 asserts the equality in the exploration and use of the Moon. In addition, paragraphs 5, 6 and 7 touch upon the to-be established international regime. Paragraph 5 stresses the necessity of the establishment of an international regime. Paragraph 6 states that in order to facilitate the establishment of the international regime, States Parties are required to inform the Secretary-General of the UN of related information. Paragraph 7 describes the purposes of the international regime, which are to secure the orderly and safe development and rational management of the natural resources of the Moon, expand the opportunities in the use of these resources and enable all States Parties to equally share the benefits derived from those resources, while the interests and needs of the developing countries shall be given special consideration.

CHM as prescribed in Article 11 of the 1979 Moon Agreement is very similar to that under the DSM legal regime. Nevertheless, a distinctive difference is that: in the context of DSM, not only a full-fledged international regime has been established but it had already been in operation for more than two decades. Whereas in the context of the 1979 Moon Agreement, the international regime envisaged is still to be established. Even if the international regime were established, almost all of the handful spacefaring States are not yet States Party to the Agreement. Hence, in the absence of the international regime as well as the spacefaring States' legal status as non-States Party to the 1979 Moon Agreement, so far, the concept of CHM has not been operationalized in the field of outer space.[42] In effect, the concept of CHM is being challenged by national law, such as, the 2015 US Commercial Space Launch Competitiveness Act.[43] The Act acknowledges in Section 403 that

[42] It is acknowledged that the non-inclusion of the principle as a customary norm makes the relevance of common heritage of mankind in the present world debatable and uncertain. (Naman Khatwani, 'Common Heritage of Mankind for Outer Space' (2019) 17(2) *The International Journal of Space Politics and Policy* 89–103.) Yet, one should also note that an analysis of the principle of CHM should not be left out. And it is necessary to stress the necessity of an international regime for the exploitation of space. (Shadi A. Alshdaifat, 'Who Owns What in Outer Space? Dilemmas regarding the Common Heritage of Mankind' (2018) 21 *Pecs Journal of International and European Law*.)

[43] Public Law No: 114-90 (11/25/2015), source from US Congress: www.congress.gov/bill/114th-congress/house-bill/2262/text.

'it is the sense of Congress that by the enactment of this Act, the United States does not thereby assert sovereignty or sovereign or exclusive rights or jurisdiction over, or the ownership of, any celestial body'. However, in accordance with Section 51303 of the 2015 US Commercial Space Launch Competitiveness Act:

> A United States citizen engaged in commercial recovery of an asteroid resource or a space resource under this chapter shall be entitled to any asteroid resource or space resource obtained, including to possess, own, transport, use, and sell the asteroid resource or space resource obtained in accordance with applicable law, including the international obligations of the United States.[44]

Therefore, the United States approved the concept of common interest of mankind but rejected the concept of CHM as envisaged in the 1979 Moon Agreement. What the Act upholds is the ideas of the free access and first-come-first-served, but not the ideas of international control and equal sharing of benefits.

To conclude, 'common interest of mankind' is the basic concept of the outer space legal system. This concept embodies three elements: (1) the global commons status of the outer space (including the free access to and non-appropriation of the outer space); (2) the use of outer space for peaceful purposes; and (3) international cooperation in the use of outer space. The 1979 Moon Agreement transforms the concept of 'common interest of mankind' into 'common heritage of mankind'. In comparison with the concept of common interest of mankind, CHM also includes the elements of non-appropriation, for peaceful purposes and international cooperation. Yet, it substitutes the element of free access with international control over the access to and the use of the resources. In addition, it requires equal sharing of the economic and other benefits therefrom. Nevertheless, owing to the fact that the 1979 Moon Agreement has not been successful in attracting spacefaring States as its States Party, the idea of CHM is still more as an ideal than as a binding principle. Additionally, there are certain institutional arrangements, the UNOOSA and the COPUOS, to safeguard the global commons status and the peaceful use of outer space, and to promote international cooperation in the field. Yet, such institutional arrangements are insufficient to

44 The term 'space resources' means an abiotic resource in situ in outer space, including water and minerals (Section 51301 of the 2015 US Commercial Space Launch Competitiveness Act).

operationalize the principle of CHM as envisaged in the 1979 Moon Agreement.

2.3.2 *Common Interest of Mankind in Antarctica*

Like outer space, Antarctica is also seen as an area in which mankind has a common interest. The 1959 Antarctic Treaty declares that 'it is in the interest of all mankind that Antarctica shall continue forever to be used exclusively for peaceful purposes and shall not become the scene or object of international discord'.[45] The 1980 Convention on the Conservation of Antarctic Marine Living Resources (CCAMLR)[46] and the 1988 Convention on the Regulation of Antarctic Mineral Resource Activities (CRAMRA)[47] both have similar statements. Thus the peaceful use of Antarctica is one element of common interest of mankind in Antarctica.

Another element of the concept of common interest of mankind in Antarctica is the protection of the Antarctic environment and dependent and associated ecosystems. As the 1991 Protocol on Environmental Protection to the Antarctic Treaty (the 1991 Environmental Protocol) states, 'the development of a comprehensive regime for the protection of the Antarctic environment and dependent and associated ecosystems is in the interest of mankind as a whole'.[48] Environmental protection as a common interest of mankind has been increasingly accepted. This point will be elaborated in Section 2.5.1. Here in the context of Antarctica, it is clear that with the adoption of the 1972 Convention for the Conservation of Antarctic Seals,[49] the 1980 CCAMLR and, in particular, the 1991 Environmental Protocol, environmental protection constitutes a main pillar of the Antarctic Treaty System – all agreements made by States to coordinate activities and relations in Antarctica.

[45] Preamble, paragraph 1 of the Antarctic Treaty (adopted on 1 December 1959, entered into force on 23 June 1961).

[46] Preamble, paragraph 9, the 1980 CCAMLR (adopted on 20 May 1980, entered into force on 7 April 1982).

[47] Preamble, paragraph 2, the 1988 CRAMRA (adopted on 2 June 1988, it became obsolete before entry into force).

[48] Preamble, paragraph 8 of the 1991 Protocol (adopted on 4 October 1991, entered into force on 14 January 1998).

[49] Convention for the Conservation of Antarctic Seals (adopted on 1 June 1972, entered into force on 11 March 1978).

The environmental protection regimes within the Antarctic Treaty System provide illustrative examples of how environmental protection as the common interest of mankind is safeguarded. The environmental consideration was already included in the 1959 Antarctic Treaty: Article 5(1) prescribes that 'any nuclear explosions in Antarctica and the disposal there of radioactive waste material shall be prohibited'. Article 4 of the 1988 CRAMRA prescribes that mineral resources activities may only be undertaken if assessments show that they would not have significant detrimental impact on the Antarctic environment and dependent or associated ecosystems. However, as a consequence of the protest against mineral resources activities in Antarctica, the 1988 CRAMRA was soon revoked by the 1991 Environmental Protocol.[50] The 1991 Protocol establishes a comprehensive environmental regime: under Article 2, Antarctica is designated 'as a natural reserve, devoted to peace and science'. Article 3 states that 'the protection of the Antarctic environment and dependent and associated ecosystems and the intrinsic value of Antarctica [. . .] shall be fundamental considerations in the planning and conduct of all activities in the Antarctic Treaty area'. According to Articles 11 and 12, the Committee for Environmental Protection was established for the purpose of providing advice and formulating recommendations to the Parties on the fulfillment of their environmental obligations. Under Article 14, activities undertaken in Antarctica must be subject to the inspections arranged by the Antarctic Treaty Consultative Meeting (ATCM).[51] Last but not least, the 1991 Protocol includes six Annexes which focus on several critical aspects of the Antarctic environment.[52]

[50] It was exactly due to environmental considerations that Article 7 of the 1991 Environmental Protocol bans 'any activity relating to mineral resources, other than scientific research'.

[51] The activities are mostly scientific investigations, but there are also tourism and some other activities such as bioprospecting. It is phrased as follows: 'Any activities undertaken in the Antarctic Treaty area pursuant to scientific research programmes, tourism and all other governmental and non-governmental activities in the Antarctic Treaty area for which advance notice is required under Article VII(5) of the Antarctic Treaty, including associated logistic support activities'. See also Article 3(4) and Article 8(2) of the 1959 Antarctic Treaty, Article 15 of the 1991 Protocol and Annexes III and IV of the 1991 Protocol.

[52] Annex I: environmental impact assessment; Annex II: conservation of Antarctic fauna and flora; Annex III: waste disposal and waste management; Annex IV: prevention of marine pollution; Annex V: area protection and management; and Annex VI: liability arising from environmental emergencies. The Annexes form an integral part of the 1991 Protocol (Article 9 of the 1991 Protocol).

Still another basic tenet of the concept of common interest in Antarctica is the freedom of scientific investigation. Article 2 of the Antarctic Treaty prescribes that

> [f]reedom of scientific investigation in Antarctica and cooperation toward that end, as applied during the International Geophysical Year, shall continue, subject to the provisions of the present Treaty.

Moreover, Article 3 stipulates that scientific observations and results from Antarctica shall be exchanged and made freely available. However, it should be noted that although the Antarctic Treaty area is open to all for scientific investigation, there is no free access, like the high seas. According to Article 7, prior notification is required. In addition, as already mentioned, all activities in Antarctica, including scientific investigation, shall be subject to inspections by the designated observers.

To conclude, strictly speaking, Antarctica does not secure a status as global commons because Article 4 of the 1959 Antarctic Treaty creates an interim regime to maintain the *status quo* of Antarctica by freezing the territorial claims by States in the area. Nevertheless, since Antarctica is open to all States and since the Antarctic Treaty System is devoted exclusively to the common interest of mankind in the protection of the Antarctic environment and dependent and associated ecosystems, treating Antarctica as global commons does make sense. There are three elements of common interest of mankind in Antarctica: (1) the use of Antarctica for exclusively peaceful purposes; (2) environmental protection; and (3) the freedom of scientific investigation. An international regulating regime overseen by the Antarctic Treaty Consultative Meeting exists for the purpose of safeguarding common interests in Antarctica.

In comparison, the concepts of common interest of mankind and CHM in the contexts of outer space, Antarctica and DSM have common elements: they all imply the (quasi-) global commons status and the use of areas and resources for peaceful purposes. For this reason, many people employ the same concept of CHM in these three contexts. But there are also differences. The main difference between CHM in the context of DSM and common interest/common heritage of mankind in outer space is that a strong international organization is established to operationalize the principle of CHM in the former but not in the latter. This shows that the legal regimes in the two contexts are at different stages of development. The main difference between common interest of mankind in the context of Antarctica and CHM in DSM is that, although international arrangements exist in both contexts, in the context of

Antarctica it is for the protection of the Antarctic environment and the freedom of scientific investigation, while in the DSM context there are triple purposes, namely the utilization of mineral resources, marine environmental protection and marine scientific research for the benefit of mankind. This shows the different policy orientation of the two legal frameworks.[53] Yet, the implications of the concepts in different contexts should not be viewed statically. In the long run, outer space law could develop into a more advanced stage. For instance, an international mining regime in outer space could be established at a later stage, and such a regime could model itself on the DSM regime. Also, the DSM regime could shift in the same direction as the Antarctic regime if the contrast of weight between environmental consideration and economic benefits of DSM overwhelmingly tilts towards the environment side.

But irrespective of contexts and time, the essence of CHM cannot be reduced or changed. In the next subsection, an attempt has been made to grasp the essence of CHM by placing it against a broader intellectual background – common interest of the international community as a whole ('community interest') in general international law.

2.3.3 *Common Interest of the International Community as a Whole in International Law*

The existence of community interest is increasingly acknowledged in general international law. Advocating for community interest has become a salient feature of the scholarly identities of some established international lawyers. Jessup proposed in 1948 that 'the notion of community interest should be realized in the revised international legal order in the future'.[54] Jenks wrote in 1958 that

> [c]ontemporary international law can no longer be reasonably presented in the framework of the classical exposition of international law as the law

[53] As a consequence of Article 7 of the 1991 Protocol on Environmental Protection to the Antarctic Treaty, the Antarctic regime transformed 'from a regime essentially designed for the exploitation of mineral resources into a legal framework for the protection of the Antarctic environment' (Bruno Simma, 'From Bilateralism to Community Interests in International Law' (1994/VI) 250 *RdC* 217–384, 363); In contrast, the DSM legal regime adopts 'a primarily utilization-oriented approach' and 'addresses environmental problems only incidentally' (Ulrich Beyerlin, 'State Community Interests and Institution-Building in International Environmental Law' (1996) 56 *ZaoRV* 602–627, 610).

[54] Philip Jessup, *A Modern Law of Nations* (Macmillan 1948) 2.

> governing the relations between States, but must be regarded as the common law of mankind in an early stage of development.[55]

Community interest in international law has been a recurring theme for a series of lectures at The Hague Academy of International Law. Friedman was famous for the distinction between 'international law of coexistence' and 'international law of cooperation'.[56] He argued that the emergence of international law of co-operation brought a vertical structure of the international legal order. He further emphasized international cooperation for the realization of common interests.[57] Mosler looked at international law from the point of view of international society as a legal community. He emphasized that

> [i]nternational law cannot be defined solely in terms of bilateral or plurilateral relations between subjects who possess legal capacity. The collection of subjects participating in the international legal order constitutes a community, and all subjects of international law are its members.[58]

Based on the perspective of international society as a legal community, Mosler indicated that 'international public order' was a necessity for maintenance of the community. Like Friedman, he also identified the new phenomenon of international law of cooperation; he saw international organizations as institutionalized international cooperation. In the 1990s, a series of lectures was given at The Hague Academy of International Law on the same topic of community interests in international law, albeit on different aspects. Tomuschat discussed 'obligations arising for states without or against their will',[59] Frowein explored 'reactions by not directly affected states to breaches of public international law',[60] while Simma delved into the doctrinal expression of

[55] C. Wilfred Jenks, *The Common Law of Mankind* (Stevens 1958), para. 1 of the Preface. Although the objective of this book was to highlight the new trend of 'the progress of universality', that is, the change of international law from a characteristic of European-centred to the inclusion of all civilizations, he did touch upon the notion of international community.

[56] Wolfgang Friedmann, 'General Course at The Hague Academy' (1969) 127(2) *RdC* 41–246.

[57] Certainly not all common interests are community interests, but community interests are one kind of common interests.

[58] Hermann Mosler, 'The International Society as a Legal Community' (1973) 140(3) *RdC* 1–320, 11–12.

[59] Christian Tomuschat, 'Obligations Arising for States without or against Their Will' (1993) 241(4) *RdC* 199–374.

[60] Jochen Frowein, 'Reactions by Not Directly Affected States to Breaches of Public International Law' (1994) 248(4) *RdC* 345–438.

community interest and, particularly, community interest in treaties.[61] A tentative definition of community interest was given by Simma as:

> A consensus according to which respect for certain fundamental values is not to be left to the free disposition of States individually or inter se but is recognized and sanctioned by international law as a matter of concern to all States.[62]

Cançado Trindade argued for an international law for humankind.[63] This was an attempt to humanize as well as universalize international law. To construct such an international law for humankind, he resorted to the concepts of *jus cogens*, obligations *erga omnes*, international crime, common heritage of mankind and common concern of mankind,[64] all of which, in his opinion, are expressions of community interests.

Indeed, notions such as '*jus cogens*',[65] 'obligations *erga omnes*',[66] 'third-party invocation of State responsibility',[67] as well as 'common heritage of mankind' or 'common concern of mankind'[68] are manifestations of the community interest in international law. Such manifestations, in Villapando's observation, 'have arisen in a compartmentalized and asynchronous way'.[69] Namely, 'each of the manifestations described

[61] Bruno Simma, 'From Bilateralism to Community Interest in International Law' (1994) 250(6) *RdC* 221–384.

[62] Ibid., 233.

[63] Antônio Augusto Cançado Trindade, 'International Law for Humankind: Towards a New *jus gentium*' (2005) 316 *RdC* 9–439.

[64] Ibid., Part V.

[65] Article 53 of the 1969 Vienna Convention on the Law of Treaties defines a peremptory norm of general international law (*jus cogens*) as 'a norm accepted and recognized by the international community of States as a whole as a norm from which no derogation is permitted and which can be modified only by subsequent norm of general international law having the same character'.

[66] The famous *obiter dictum* of the ICJ in the 1970 *Barcelona Traction, Light and Power Company (Belgium v. Spain)* states as follows: An essential distinction should be drawn between the obligations of a State towards the international community as a whole, and those arising *vis-à-vis* another State in the field of diplomatic protection. By their very nature the former are the concern of all States. In view of the importance of the rights involved, all States can be held to have a legal interest in their protection; they are obligations *erga omnes*. (para. 33)

[67] Article 48(1) of the 2001 Draft Articles on State Responsibility (the second reading) stipulates that any State other than an injured State is entitled to invoke the responsibility of another State if the obligation breached is owed to 'the international community as a whole'.

[68] This notion is often used in international environmental law; it will be discussed preliminarily in Section 3.5.1.

[69] Santiago Villalpando, 'The Legal Dimension of the International Community: How Community Interests Are Protected in International Law' (2010) 21(2) *EJIL* 387–419, 408.

above has initially been tested in a limited and contained legal environment and developed independently'.[70] The concepts were consolidated and linked in legal theory and practice only at a later stage, which resulted in an emerging web of interconnected transformations of the international order being characteristic of the protection of community interests.[71]

Therefore, CHM is by no means an isolated concept; rather, it is an exemplary case of a new trend in international law, an eminent manifestation of community interest. The fundamental reason for the existence of CHM, as well as other types of community interest, is the changed nature of the international community. Specifically, it is because of the need for international cooperation and the consensus of the international community about certain fundamental values. This partly accounts for why the tenet of CHM could stand against the substantial change in the DSM regime by the 1994 Agreement: because of the need for international cooperation, the consensus of the international community in the field of DSM remained unchanged. A connection between the concepts of CHM and community interest provides a deeper understanding of where CHM stands in international law now and the direction in which it could head in the future.

Yet, the recognition of community interest in international law gives rise to a difficult question. That is, how to protect community interest? Villalpando commented that 'the protection of community interests in international law has been effected through the adaption, not abandonment, of existing legal regimes'.[72] On this point, CHM is special because a specialized international legal regime was created for the operationalization of CHM in the context of DSM.

2.4 Protection of the Marine Environment in Deep Seabed Mining

Upon an examination of the principle of CHM in general, this section focuses on the element of marine environmental protection in DSM. The issue is appraised at two levels: at the conceptual level, it argues that the requirements of marine environmental protection in DSM are obligations *erga omnes* imposed on all the participants in DSM; at the operational level, it argues that the effective protection of the marine

[70] Ibid. 409.
[71] Ibid.
[72] Ibid.

environment in DSM is preconditioned on sufficient scientific knowledge of the deep sea. Observations at these two levels set a broad intellectual background against which the two major research questions of this book – international environmental obligations and liabilities of the participants in DSM – are to be discussed in the following chapters.

2.4.1 *The Conceptual Level: Marine Environmental Protection as Obligation* Erga Omnes

International environmental protection is widely accepted as a key example of 'community interest' among the scholars mentioned in Section 2.3.3 and many others.[73] Besides 'community interest', the notion of 'common concern of humankind' or 'international concern' is also employed to refer to the global environmental issues of, such as, 'climate change' and 'conservation and sustainable use of biological diversity'.[74] As explained in the ILC's work on 'the protection of the atmosphere', the concept of common concern of humankind means issues or problems that are no longer contained in 'the reserved domain of domestic jurisdiction', since they are 'matters of international concern'.[75] The

[73] For instance, Feichtner categorizes community interests into four types: the protection and creation of common goods; the protection of common values; the internationalization of common spaces and redistributive and intergenerational justice. She considered that environmental protection is recognized as a typical example of community interests in the category of 'the protection of common values' (Isabel Feichtner, 'Community Interest'), MPEPIL (last updated February 2007). For another example, Sand considered that the 'F4' Panel functioned as a guardian of community interest by dealing with environmental damage claims (Peter Sand, 'Environmental Damage Claims from the 1991 Gulf War: State Responsibility and Community Interests', in Fastenrath, Ulrich et al., (eds.), *From Bilateralism to Community Interest: Essays in Honour of Bruno Simma* (OUP 2011)).

[74] UNEP, The Meeting of the Group of Legal Experts to Examine the Concept of the Common Concern of Mankind in Relation to Global Environmental Issues (Co-Rapporteurs: A.A. Cançado Trindade and D. J. Attard), 1991, available at: http://historico.juridicas.unam.mx/publica/librev/rev/iidh/cont/13/doc/doc29.pdf. Take climate change as an illustrative example: In 1988, the UN General Assembly declared in Resolution 43/53 that 'climate change is a common concern of mankind, since climate is an essential condition which sustains life on earth'. The 1992 UN Framework Convention on Climate Change (UNFCCC) acknowledges in paragraph 1 of the preamble that 'the change in the Earth's climate and its adverse effects are a common concern of humankind'. The 2015 Paris Agreement to the UNFCCC reaffirms in paragraph 11 of the preamble that 'climate change is a common concern of humankind'.

[75] ILC, The first report on the protection of the atmosphere (Special Rapporteur Shinya Murase), 2014, A/CN.4/667, para. 89. In 2015, however, the ILC decided to remove the

Secretary-General of the UN stated that 'the notion of common concern of humankind recognizes the legitimate interest of the international community to concern itself with certain issues and values which, by their nature, affect the community as a whole'.[76] Shelton,[77] as well as Castillo-Winckels,[78] stated that issues or problems of common concern not only transcend national boundaries but also require concerted or collective actions of all States to effectively address such issues or problems. Similarly, Bowling et al. considered the concept of common concern of humankind as particularly suitable for environmental issues because environmental problems very often transcend national boundaries and 'at the very least, a common concern of humankind designation expresses the need for international cooperation through strong global institutions to face a shared problem'.[79] The notions of 'community interest' and 'common concern' both capture the essence of international environmental issue, but they express it from different angles. Simma commented that international concern for the environment provides a particularly impressive illustration of the movement 'from bilateralism to community interest in international law'.[80] This change impacts the nature of international environmental obligation and its legal effect.

Here the notion of 'obligations *erga omnes*' should be turned to.[81] The famous *obiter dictum* of the International Court of Justice (ICJ) in

concept of common concern of humankind from its Draft Guidelines on the Protection of the Atmosphere.

76 Report of the Secretary-General of the UN, Rio Declaration on the Environment and Development: application and implementation, E/CN.17/1997/8, 1997, para. 44.

77 Dinah Shelton, 'Common Concern of Humanity' (2009) 39(2) *Environmental Law and Policy*, 83.

78 Nadia Sanchez Castillo-Winckels, 'Why "Common Concern of Humankind" Should Return to the Work of the International Law Commission on the Atmosphere' (2016) 29 *Geo. Envtl. L. Rev.* 131, 134.

79 Chelsea Bowling, Elizabeth Pierson, Stephanie Ratte, 'The Common Concern of Humankind: A potential Framework for a New Internationally Legally Binding Instrument on the Conservation and Sustainable Use of Marine Biological Diversity in the High Seas' available at the UN Division for Ocean Affairs and the Law of the Sea: http://www.un.org/depts/los/biodiversity/prepcom_files/BowlingPiersonandRatte_Common_Concern.pdf.

80 Bruno Simma, 'From Bilateralism to Community Interest in International Law' (1994) 250(5) *RdC* 221–384, 238.

81 The focus of the notion of obligations *erga omnes* is on the legal effect. Christian Tomuschat, reply to the first report of Giorgio Gaja, 'Obligations and Rights *Erga Omnes*: First Report (March 2002)' (2005) 71-I *Yearbook of the Institute of International Law*, 160–161. Weil criticized that the acknowledgement of such a notion as obligations *erga omnes* diluted the normativity system of international law (Prosper

1970 spelled out two criteria for the identification of obligations *erga omnes*: The obligations must by their very nature be 'the concern of all States' and 'in view of the importance of the rights involved, all States can be held to have a legal interest in their protection'.[82] It is seen that the *erga omnes* character of an obligation finds its basis on the concepts of community interests or international concern. Gaja observed that

> [t]he emergence in the second part of the 20th century of the category of obligations *erga omnes* under international law [...] reflects what has been termed as the emergence of public interests in the international community: the growing concern for the protection of interests that States perceive as common and the consequent building of rules and institutions that are designed to protect those interests.[83]

The 'F4' Panel of the United Nations Compensation Commission (UNCC) repeatedly emphasized that 'the common concern for the protection and conservation of the environment' 'entails obligations towards the international community and future generations'.[84] The protection of the marine environment in DSM is exactly such an obligation that has an *erga omnes* character. As the Institute of International Law (IDI) resolution states,

> Under international law, certain obligations bind all subjects of international law for the purposes of maintaining the fundamental values of the international community. A wide consensus exists to the effect that [...] obligations relating to the environment of common spaces are examples of obligations reflecting those fundamental values.[85]

Weil, 'Towards Relative Normativity in International Law' (1983) 77 *AJIL* 413–442). Yet, Fastenrath and Villapando hold different positions. Fastenrath argued that relative normativity in international law is a conceptual reflection of reality of the international community (Ulrich Fastenrath, 'Relative Normativity in International Law' (1993) 4 *EJIL* 305–340). While Villalpando explained that the shift towards the protection of community interests in international law was the result of the objective existence and needs of certain common goods or values and the subjective awareness of such existence and needs by the international community (Santiago Villalpando, 'The Legal Dimension of the International Community: How Community Interests Are Protected in International Law' (2010) 21(2) *EJIL* 387-419, 390).

82 ICJ, *Barcelona Traction, Light and Power Company (Belgium v. Spain)*, Judgment of 1970, paras. 52–53.

83 Giorgio Gaja, 'Obligations and Rights *Erga Omnes*: First Report (March 2002)' (2005) 71-I *Yearbook of the Institute of International Law*, 119–151, 119.

84 Peter Sand, 'Environmental Damage Claims from the 1991 Gulf War: State Responsibility and Community Interests', in Fastenrath, Ulrich et al. (eds.), *From Bilateralism to Community Interest: Essays in Honour of Bruno Simma* (OUP 2011).

85 Institut de Droit International (the Fifth Commission) Resolution: Obligations and Rights *Erga Omnes* in International Law (Rapporteur: Giorgio Gaja), adopted at

However, recognition of community interests, common concern and obligations *erga omnes* in theory is one thing; protection of community interest, tackling common concern and enforcement of obligations *erga omnes* in practice is another.[86] As the ILC stated,

> It may be too early at present to interpret the concept of common concern as giving 'all States a legal interest, or standing, in the enforcement of rules concerning protection of the global atmosphere', in view of the absence of appropriate procedural law to implement such an interpretation. It may also be premature to consider the concept of common concern as creating rights for individuals and future generations.[87]

Indeed, at the current stage of international law, mechanisms and procedures for enforcement of obligations *erga omnes* are by and large rare.[88] This reality impedes an adequate protection of the community interests or a sufficient solution to an international concern. Nonetheless, things are changing. A vivid example can be found in the practice of flourishing climate change litigations in recent years.[89] Likewise, changes are found in DSM practices too. Chapters 3 and 4 will demonstrate a shift to a more informative, inclusive and transparent model of global environmental governance of DSM: public consultations are included into the drafting process of Exploitation Regulations and Standards and Guidelines, the EIA review process, the preparation and implementation of various management plans, emergency plans, etc., and the obligation of cooperation among DSM participants is emphasized. Chapters 6 and 8 will demonstrate that the *erga omnes* character of marine environmental obligations in DSM has significant impact on the question of who is

Karkow Session on August 27, 2005, paras. 1 and 2, preamble. Available at: www.idi-iil.org/idiE/resolutionsE/2005_kra_01_en.pdf.

86 Christian Tams, *Enforcing Obligation Erga Omnes in International Law* (CUP 2005).

87 LTC, The first report of Special Rapporteur Shinya Murase on the protection of the atmosphere, 2014, A/CN.4/667, para. 89.

88 Article 48(1) of the 2001 ASR is normally considered as endorsing the enforcement of international obligations *erga omnes (partes)*, yet it provides no concrete mechanism. Establishing the ISA to operationalize the principle of CHM in DSM may be considered one such mechanism.

89 Although climate change cases have so far been brought before national courts, some of these national courts develop international climate change law in some cases. Furthermore, some small island States are attempting to request for advisory opinion on climate change from either the ICJ or the ITLOS or both, see Annalisa Savaresi, Kati Kulovesi and Harro van Asselt, 'Beyond COP26: Time for an Advisory Opinion on Climate Change?' EJIL: Talk! blog posted on December 17, 2021, available at: www.ejiltalk.org/beyond-cop26-time-for-an-advisory-opinion-on-climate-change/.

entitled to invoke liability of the contractor, the sponsoring State and the ISA for environmental damage. In a word, one should not take a static view over mechanisms and procedures for enforcing environmental obligations in DSM, as the CHM status of the Area and its resources and the *erga omnes* character of environmental obligations in DSM inherently make a big room for innovative practices in the future.

2.4.2 The Operational Level: The Significant Role of Marine Sciences

On the operational level, it is argued that the environmental rules and policies should be science-based as assessments of whether the marine environment faces damage or risk of damage from DSM, and if so, what particular types of damage or risk entail and how they may best be prevented or remedied must all rely on marine scientific knowledge.[90] It means that not only the making but also the implementation and compliance of the environmental rules should be based on scientific knowledge about the marine environment and the environmental impacts of DSM. As it is indicated, 'in appreciating what is involved in such issues [as the impact of mineral extraction etc.], let alone what might be done to avoid unwelcome consequences, accurate scientific knowledge of the sea is imperative'.[91]

What then is the current status of scientific knowledge about the marine environment? A brief answer is that there are great gaps owing mainly to the fact that oceanography is still at an early stage of its development. It is generally acknowledged that the *SMS Challenger* expedition (1872–1876) marked the birth of modern oceanography because the expedition standardized methods to collect data and investigated the physics, chemistry, biology and geology of the ocean. It is also because the expedition produced results which laid the foundation for

90 It is to be noted: although not discussed as much as marine sciences at this stage, deep sea mining technology and engineering also play an important role in safeguarding the deep-sea environment in DSM. The Netherlands proposed the ISA to develop an assessment methodology and subsequent approval process for equipment, operational procedures and processes used in DSM exploitation activities. See 'Development of environmentally responsible mining technologies: towards an approval process for mining equipment', submitted by the delegation of the Netherlands, ISBA/23/C/5, 2017.

91 Margaret Deacon, Tony Rice and Colin Summerhayes (eds.), *Understanding the Oceans: A Century of Ocean Exploration* (Routledge 2001) 1.

oceanography.[92] Oceanography is related to the study of all aspects of the ocean. Yet, the physical, geological, biological and chemical aspects of the oceans each constitutes the subject matter of a marine science. It was not until 1942 that the first comprehensive book on oceanography was published which attempted to integrate all marine sciences.[93] The book especially emphasized the close interrelationship and mutual dependence of the marine sciences.[94]

To assess the environmental impact of DSM requires investigation into all four aspects of the oceans.[95] Yet, since the goal of marine environmental protection in DSM focuses primarily on the health of the marine ecosystems,[96] and since an ecosystem is defined as 'a biotic assemblage and its associated physical environment in a specific space',[97] the

92 The *Challenger* expedition (1872–1876) was the most ambitious and innovative scientific project ever attempted – a global survey of the deep ocean. The assignment of *Challenger* was to determine 'the conditions of the deep-sea throughout all the great oceanic basins'. The expedition, still the longest, covered nearly 70,000 nautical miles in 4 years, carried out almost 500 deep soundings and 133 dredgings and obtained various data from 362 stations (one every 200 miles). As a result of the expedition, 715 new genera and about 4,500 new species were described. James Kennett, *Marine Geology* (Prentice-Hall 1982) 5.

93 H. U. Sverdrup, Martin W. Johnson, Richard Fleming, *The Oceans: Their Physics, Chemistry, and General Biology* (Prentice Hall, 1942). This book is called 'the Bible of Oceanography'.

94 For instance, it was said that marine geology 'is dependent upon the results of nearly every other marine science' and 'the contacts between marine biology and the chemistry of sea water are so intimate that it is difficult to indicate where the biology stops and the chemistry begins'. Ibid., 5.

95 For instance, The SPC-EU deep seabed minerals project investigated the physical, biological, environmental and technical aspects of mining on Manganese Nodules, Seafloor Massive Sulphides and Cobalt-rich Ferromanganese Crusts. The project was initiated in 2011 and ended in 2013. It was run at a budget of EUR 4.4 million. A primary objective of the project is to support informed and careful governance of any DSM activities in the Pacific Island countries. Source from: www.sopac.org/dsm/index.php.

96 For instance, it is said that 'conservation objectives should relate to the concept of ecosystem-based management and to the dynamic structure and function of the ecosystems' (ISA, 'Environmental Management of Deep-Sea Chemosynthetic Ecosystems: Justification of and Considerations for a Spatially-Based Approach', Technical Study No. 9 (2011), 29). It is also said that 'the MIDAS project aimed at helping the nascent deep-sea mining industry, regulators and civil society to understand the potential impacts of mining on deep-sea ecosystems'. (The final report of The Managing Impacts of Deep Sea Resource Exploitation project ('MIDAS') 2016, 5). In the UNCC 'F4' Panel report, it was stated that 'the aim of restoration would be to restore the overall ecological functioning [. . .] of the marine ecosystem' (UNCC, the third 'F4' report, 2003, para. 48).

97 Arthur Tansley first coined the term 'ecosystem' in 'The Use and Abuse of Vegetational Concepts and Terms' (1935) 16(3) Ecology 284–307. The definition used here is Tansley's

following descriptions focus mainly on the physical and biological aspects of the marine ecosystems relating to specific types of mineral resources. Currently there are three types of mineral resources on the seabed, the exploration for and exploitation of which are under the control of the international DSM legal regime: polymetallic nodules (manganese nodules), polymetallic sulphides (SMS deposits) and cobalt-rich ferromanganese crusts.[98]

Manganese nodules form at the vast, sediments-covered abyssal plains; the high concentrated nodules occur on the ocean floor at water depths of about 4,000 to 6,000 m; and the nodules of economic interest are localized in the centre of the north central Pacific Ocean, the Peru Basin in the south-east Pacific Ocean and the centre of the north Indian Ocean.[99] Marine life is found both in the soft sediments and on the nodules themselves. To date, the biology associated with manganese nodules has been studied most intensively in the Clarion-Clipperton Zone (CCZ). It is estimated that the studies in the CCZ might be applicable to other abyssal plain habitats.[100] It is also estimated that different nodule regions sustain different levels of particulate organic carbon flux which could affect the levels of species diversity and faunal communities.[101] Nevertheless, it is acknowledged that the threat of nodule mining to biodiversity is still to a large extent unpredictable because of the very limited knowledge of species and their biogeographic distribution within the nodule province.[102]

SMS deposits form on and below the seabed from high temperature hydrothermal fluids emitted by volcanoes along ridges, island arcs and in

as recited from: Hanling Wang, 'Ecosystem Management and Its Application to Large Marine Ecosystem: Science, Law, and Politics' (2004) 35 *ODIL* 41–74, 41.

98 There are other mineral resources in the Area such as the natural gas hydrate and rare earth which are not covered by the current DSM legal regime. Yet this does not mean that they will not be included in the future.

99 Enrico Bonatti and Y. Rammohanroy Nayudu, 'The Origin of Manganese Nodules on the Ocean Floor' (1965) 263(1) *American Journal of Science* 17–39; ISA, 'Brochure – Polymetallic Nodules'; Sven Peterson et al., 'News from the Seabed – Geological Characteristics and Resource Potential of Deep-Sea Mineral Resources' (2016) 70 *Marine Policy* 175–187, 176.

100 SPC-EU Deep Sea Minerals Project, 'Manganese Nodules: A Physical, Biological, Environmental, and Technical Review' (2013) 23. Available at: http://dsm.gsd.spc.int/public/files/meetings/TrainingWorkshop4/UNEP_vol1B.pdf.

101 Ibid., 22.

102 ISA, 'Biodiversity, Species Ranges and Gene Flow in the Abyssal Pacific Nodule Province: Predicting and Managing the Impacts of Deep Seabed Mining', Technical Study No. 3 (2008), 2.

rifted back-arc basins behind subduction zones.[103] In 1977, the US manned submersible *Alvin* discovered deep-sea hydrothermal vents and biological communities living around the vents.[104] The discovery of life in the extreme environment of hydrothermal vents was definitely a revolutionary breakthrough in the field of marine biology.[105] The hydrothermal vents are called chemosynthetic ecosystems because marine life in this habitat uses chemical energy rather than photosynthesis to create organic matter.[106] The discovery of chemosynthetic ecosystems was historic.[107] Since the discovery of chemosynthetic ecosystems, scientific research has been ongoing for more than three decades. Nevertheless, until now there are still critical gaps in knowledge about chemosynthetic ecosystems particularly with respect to the (genetic or demographic) connectivity of populations among sites, the special distribution of benthic fauna at SMS deposits, the resilience of vent and seep systems to cumulative disturbance and the effectiveness of mitigation and restoration strategies.[108]As is exemplified in the Environmental Impact Statement of the Nautilus' copper-gold project, Solwara 1, under development in the territorial waters of Papua New Guinea:

> The need to understand the biology and potential impacts of mining on the hydrothermal vent communities and the surrounding seafloor, where knowledge of the dynamics of recruitment, growth, diversity and

[103] Sven Peterson et al., 'News from the Seabed – Geological Characteristics and Resource Potential of Deep-Sea Mineral Resources' (2016) 70 *Marine Policy* 175–187, 180; Laurent Godet, Kevin A. Zelnio and Cindy L. Van Dover, 'Scientists as Stakeholders in Conservation of Hydrothermal Vents' (2011) 25(2) *Conservation Biology* 214.

[104] Woods Hole Oceanographic Institution: www.divediscover.whoi.edu/ventcd/vent_discovery/.

[105] Ibid.

[106] C.L. Van Dover et al., 'Designating Networks of Chemosynthetic Ecosystem Reserves in the Deep Sea' (2012) 36 *Marine Policy* 378–381.

[107] The historic discovery could to a large extent be attributed to the big theoretical innovations in marine geology, starting from the continental drift theory in 1920s (Alfred Wegener, *The Origin of Continents and Oceans* (John Biram tr, Dover 1966).) to the seafloor spreading theory in 1950s and to the theory of plate tectonics in 1960s (James Kennett, *Marine Geology* (Prentice-Hall 1982) 114–177).

[108] Rachel E. Boschen et al., 'Seafloor Massive Sulfide Deposits Support Unique Megafaunal Assemblages: Implications for Seabed Mining and Conservation' (2016) 115 *Marine Environmental Research* 78–88. Rachel E. Boschen, et al, 'Mining of Deep-sea Seafloor Massive Sulfides: A Review of the Deposits, their Benthic Communities, Impacts from Mining, Regulatory Frameworks and Management Strategies' (2013) 84 *Ocean Coast Management* 54–67, 55; ISA, 'Environmental Management of Deep-Sea Chemosynthetic Ecosystems: Justification of and Considerations for a Spatially-Based Approach', Technical Study No. 9 (2011) 52.

geographic interrelationships is still under development, is one of the key environmental issues for this Project.[109]

In contrast with manganese nodules which form in (the diagenetic growth) or on the sediment (hydrogenous growth), cobalt-rich ferromanganese crusts precipitate onto rock surfaces free of sediment; they are found on the flanks of volcanic seamounts, ridges, guvots and plateauxin at water depths ranging from 400 to 7,000 m.[110] To date, research on the marine environment of cobalt-rich ferromanganese crusts has been conducted mainly on seamounts. 'It is estimated that the distribution of animals varies considerably between areas.'[111] It is also estimated that 'depth, and to a lesser extent, locality, appear to be the main factors determining faunal distribution pattern'.[112] Except that, very little is known about the communities that are found on seamounts, particularly those in the most likely regions for crust exploration and mining.[113]

It follows from the above that each of the three types of mineral resources forms at a different topography of the seabed and is associated with a different biological community. Mineral resources either themselves constitute the habitats for marine life or are closely connected with marine life and their habitats. The issue of the marine environmental impacts of DSM concerns mainly the detrimental impact of mining activities on marine life, species, the biological community and further the overall functioning of ecosystems. However, the gaps in knowledge about marine life constitute the major obstacle for the assessment of the environmental impact of DSM.

[109] Nautilus Minerals Niugini Limited, Environmental Impact Statement (Solwara 1 Project), Executive Summary 2008 (prepared by Coffey Natural Systems, September 2008) Available at: www.nautilusminerals.com/irm/content/pdf/environment-reports/Environmental%20Impact%20Statement%20Executive%20Summary%20(English).pdf.

[110] Sven Peterson et al., 'News from the Seabed – Geological Characteristics and Resource Potential of Deep-Sea Mineral Resources' (2016) 70 *Marine Policy* 175–187, 178; ISA, 'Brochure-Cobalt-Rich Ferromanganese Crusts': www.isa.org.jm/files/documents/EN/Brochures/ENG9.pdf.

[111] The reports of the SPC-EU deep seabed minerals project, 'Cobalt-rich Ferromanganese Crusts: A Physical, Biological, Environmental, and Technical Review', 16. Available at: http://dsm.gsd.spc.int/public/files/meetings/TrainingWorkshop4/UNEP_vol1C.pdf.

[112] ISA, 'Fauna of Cobalt-Rich Ferromanganese Crust Seamounts', Technical Study No. 8 (2011), 72.

[113] ISA, 'Brochure – Cobalt-Rich Crusts'; ISA, 'Fauna of Cobalt-Rich Ferromanganese Crust Seamounts' (2011).

Knowledge about marine life is still in the age of discovery.[114] Until 2000 when the first Census of Marine Life started oceanographers estimated that only 5 per cent of the ocean had been systematically explored for life.[115] The ten-year programme of the Census of Marine Life advanced substantially the knowledge of the diversity, distribution and abundance of marine life.[116] It drew a baseline against which future changes in marine life can be measured. However, it is acknowledged that 'after all its work, the Census still could not reliably estimate the total number of species, the kinds of life, known and unknown, in the ocean'.[117] In the absence of adequate information about marine species, understanding of the functioning of the ecosystems is even poorer, let alone of the question of how ecosystems react to the impact of DSM. As is stated,

> For most deep-sea ecosystems, we lack basic information on species composition and distribution ranges, their natural variability and dynamics, dispersal distance, demographics, connectivity, and the many factors that affect community diversity.[118]

With an anticipation that DSM is heading towards the exploitation phase, the European Union (EU) conducted the Managing Impacts of Deep Sea Resource Exploitation project (MIDAS).[119] MIDAS covered the topics of 'geological and geochemical impacts', 'plumes in a dynamic environment', 'ecotoxicology', 'impacts on species connectivity', 'impacts

[114] First Census of Marine Life 2010: Highlights of a Decade of Discovery, 12. Available at: www.coml.org/highlights-2010.

[115] Ibid., 6.

[116] The Census of Marine Life started in 2000 and ended in 2010. It involved 2,700 marine scientists from more than 80 countries and was at the expenditure of USD 650 million. The Census covered the seas and oceans on a global scale. It found that 'rare species are common' in oceans and in marine habitats 'extreme is normal'. First Census of Marine Life 2010: Highlights of a Decade of Discovery. Available at: www.coml.org/highlights-2010.

[117] Ibid., 3.

[118] Kathryn J. Mengerink et al., 'A Call for Deep-Ocean Stewardship' (2014) 344 *Science* 696–698, 698.

[119] The Managing Impacts of Deep Sea Resource Exploitation project ('MIDAS') is funded under the European Commission's Framework 7 programme, running at a budget of EUR 12 million. The project started on 1 November 2013 and lasted for a period of three years. The final report of the project titled 'Report on the implications of MIDAS results for policy makers with recommendations for the future regulations to be adopted by the EU and the ISA' was submitted on 16 December 2016 (the '2016 Midas Final Report'). The final report is available at: www.eu-midas.net/sites/default/files/deliverables/D9.6_FINAL_lowres.pdf.

on ecosystem function' and 'ecosystem resilience and recovery'. Examination of these topics showed that the environmental impacts of DSM have two levels. First, it has direct impacts which include (1) the mortality of benthic fauna, and (2) the modification or loss of the habitats for benthic living species. The second level of the impacts is the indirect impacts. That is, DSM activities would cause sediment plumes[120] and introduce toxic substances to deep-sea water which may bring about further detrimental effects on (3) the benthic biological community or (4) deep-sea ecosystems. It is acknowledged that the impacts, at both levels, were still poorly understood.

Indeed, although progress was made, the gaps in scientific knowledge were repeatedly acknowledged in the final report of MIDAS.[121] More recently, a group of marine scientists had made an effort to assess more accurately the gaps of scientific knowledge about the deep-sea and the environmental impact of DSM activities by (1) review and synthesis of the published peer-reviewed literature and (2) consultations with DSM stakeholders via questionnaire.[122] It concluded that 'there are few categories of publicly available scientific knowledge comprehensive enough to enable evidence-based decision-making regarding environmental management'.[123] These great gaps of marine scientific knowledge pose a serious obstacle to the making as well as the implementation of international environmental rules in DSM. They made it difficult to answer the following questions: what are the substantive contents of the international environment obligations? What are the concrete criteria to judge whether such obligations are fulfilled or not? All in all, how should DSM participants act against the backdrop of these great gaps in

[120] It states that 'plumes present perhaps the most significant potential source of environmental impact from deep-sea mining'. (Section 3.2.1 of the 2016 MIDAS Final Report).

[121] For instance, in Section 2, it is stated that 'the impacts and effects of mining surrounding the directly mined area are poorly understood', that 'it is not possible at this stage to suggest effective thresholds for density of plumes and the distance of their spread away from the mined areas', and that 'current understanding of ecosystem functioning, recoverability, connectivity and recruitment in the deep sea is limited'. In Section 3.4.10, it is stated that 'baseline knowledge of the deep-sea in general, and in particular the CCZ and mid ocean ridges is still too incomplete to enable reasonable mitigation advice to be given with regard to connectivity and biogeography'. Section 3.6.9 indicates that 'in areas other than active vents, species distributions are poorly known in time and space'. And Section 3.8.3.4 is titled 'Gaps in existing knowledge'.

[122] Diva Amon et al., 'Assessment of Scientific Gaps related to the Effective Environmental Management of Deep-Seabed Mining' (2022) 138 *Marine Policy*.

[123] Ibid.

knowledge? It appears that the ultimate solution to this fundamental problem is to boost marine sciences.[124]

2.5 Conclusions

This chapter examined the governing principle of the international DSM legal regime – the common heritage of mankind, investigating the meaning and nature of the principle. It identified eight elements of the principle in the context of DSM. The concept of CHM in the context of DSM is further compared with the common interest/common heritage of mankind in outer space and common interest of mankind in Antarctica. The comparison shows that they differ but they also share common elements. Moreover, it indicated the close connection between the concept of CHM and a broad trend of international law – community interests. Such a connection is significant because it opens a large intellectual space for the reflection of the principle of CHM. It then zoomed in one element of the principle in particular – marine environmental protection. General observations are made at two levels: It is argued that, at the conceptual level, marine environmental protection in DSM embraces community interests, common concerns of humankind and should be characterized as obligations *erga omnes*. While at the operational level, it indicated that marine environmental protection relies heavily on marine scientific knowledge; yet, there are big unknowns in the current status of marine sciences, which poses a fundamental obstacle in the making and implementation of international environmental law in DSM. In brief, community interests and marine scientific knowledge are two threads running through this entire book.

124 Amon et al. pointed out that 'the greatest scientific challenge facing deep-seabed mining is shortage of monetary and human resources, i.e. number of people who currently have expertise and sufficient funding to carry out research in the deep sea'. Ibid., 15.

3

International Seabed Authority and Its Environmental Mandate

3.1 Introduction

The International Seabed Authority (ISA) is entrusted with the operationalization of the principle of common heritage of mankind (CHM) at the international level. It has already been indicated in Chapter 2 that the ISA plays critical roles in securing the global commons status of the Area and its resources (Articles 137 and 157), the equitable sharing of economic benefits among States (Article 140(2)), the promotion of marine scientific research (Article 143) and the protection of the marine environment (Article 145). This chapter demonstrates the ISA's roles in detail, focusing particularly on its function relating to the protection of the marine environment in deep seabed mining (DSM).

It starts with a brief account of the nature of the ISA (Section 3.2). Then it moves to the main parts of this chapter, discussing the composition, functions and powers and the decision-making procedures of its organs (Section 3.3), and specifically the powers conferred on the ISA with respect to marine environmental protection (Section 3.4). The analyses in Sections 3.3 and 3.4 rely on the text of the UN Convention on the Law of the Sea (UNCLOS) and more importantly on the practice of the ISA since 1996. Finally, this chapter introduces briefly the ongoing development of the Exploitation Regulations within the ISA. Importantly, it highlights that the ISA's in-house scientific capacities are arguably insufficient to fulfil its function concerning marine environmental protection; as a possible solution, it recommends that the ISA's Legal and Technical Commission (LTC) should explore new mechanisms for assessing marine scientific knowledge on a continual basis (Section 3.5).

3.2 Nature of the International Seabed Authority

Article 157(1) of the UNCLOS, being faithfully repeated in the 1994 Agreement, enunciates the nature of the ISA as an international organization entrusted with regulatory powers in DSM. It stipulates that

> [t]he Authority is the organization through which States Parties shall, in accordance with this Part [XI], organize and control activities in the Area, particularly with a view to administering the resources of the Area.

A key to understanding the nature of an international organization lies in its relation with its member States.[1] This is also the case with the ISA. The relation between the ISA and its member States contains two aspects. On the one hand, like any other international organization, the ISA was created by States and the ISA's maintenance and functioning rely on the contribution from, participation and cooperation of its member States.[2] For these reasons, the ISA needs to reflect the interests of its member States with respect to DSM, otherwise its very existence could be threatened.[3] On the other hand, however, once founded, the ISA possesses a separate legal personality independent from its member States. It is the ISA but not its member States that is entrusted with powers and functions and obliged to fulfil the purpose stated in the UNCLOS. Moreover, in the case of failure to fulfil the obligations, it is the ISA itself rather than the member States that would assume responsibility.[4] Specifically, since the Area and its resources are declared as CHM, the ISA is obliged to act for the interests of mankind as a whole. To bring the two aspects together, the nature of the ISA can be phrased as follows: although created by States, the ISA is an autonomous international legal person independent from its member States. In its operation, the ISA must take into consideration the interests of its member States; at the same time, under the principle of CHM, it must act on behalf of mankind as a whole.

Thus, there are two pairs of tension about the ISA: the tension between the ISA's dependence on member States and its autonomous functioning, and the tension between the ISA's representing the interests of member

[1] The tension between international organizations and their member States is an eternal theme of international institutional law. Niels Blokker, 'International Organizations and Their Members: "International Organizations Belongs to All Members and to None" – Variations on a Theme' (2004) 1 *IOLR* 139–161.

[2] The ISA has 168 members (167 member States and one non-State member, the EU), the 2022 Report of the Secretary-General of the ISA, ISBA/27/A/2.

[3] The wording of Article 157(1), the UNCLOS – 'the Authority is the organization through which States Parties shall [. . .]' – reflects this aspect of the relation between the ISA and its member States. Namely, the ISA is the representative of the interests of its member States.

[4] There are, however, exceptional circumstances when member States are required to assume responsibility instead of or together with the ISA. This point will be discussed in Chapter 8.

States and its representing the interest of mankind as a whole. These tensions are reflected particularly in the fulfillment of the ISA's function relating to the protection of the marine environment in DSM. The challenge faced by the ISA is to set and implement adequate standards of environmental protection against the legitimate demands for mineral activities in the Area which include operations and the profitability of the operations. How the ISA takes up this difficult task hinges largely upon the composition, powers and functions and decision-making procedures of its organs and subsidiary bodies, in terms of both law and practice.

3.3 Organs and Subsidiary Bodies

An explanatory note is necessary at the beginning: it is recalled that the setting up and the functioning of the organs and subsidiary bodies of the ISA are based on an 'evolutionary approach'.[5] It is also noted that, with the expanding work and especially the impending exploitation of mineral resources in the Area, the constitution and functioning of the ISA are now under great challenge. In the following discussions, it will indicate specifically what challenges the organs and subsidiary bodies are facing and how they could respond. Special effort will be made to propose and analyse the needed reform of the ISA in order to effectively discharge its environmental mandate in this transitional stage and the upcoming exploitation stage.

3.3.1 The Assembly

The ISA has three principal organs: the Assembly, the Council and the Secretariat, which is a typical trio of a traditional international organization. During the negotiations, the relationship between the Assembly and the Council was at issue.[6] The question was whether the Assembly or the Council would be supreme. Although the supremacy of the Assembly as a decision-making organ was accepted in the final text of the UNCLOS, it was later changed. Article 160(1) of the UNCLOS prescribes that

> [t]he Assembly, as the sole organ of the Authority consisting of all of members, shall be considered the supreme organ of the Authority to

[5] Section 1, paragraph 3, annex to the 1994 Agreement.

[6] The comments the Chairman of the First Committee on the RNST (1976), in Nandan, Lodge and Rosenne (eds.), *United Nations Convention on the Law of the Sea 1982* (2002).

> which the other principal organs shall be accountable as specifically provided for in this Convention.

Article 160 of the UNCLOS empowers the Assembly to establish general policies, approve the rules, regulations and procedures, adopt budget, elect the Secretary-General, members of the Council and members of the Finance Committee and establish subsidiary bodies. However, during the informal consultation process (1990–1994), decision-making was identified as one of the nine issues as problem areas.[7] As a result of that informal consultation process, the 1994 Agreement in essence revokes the supremacy of the Assembly by considerably restricting the exercise of decision-making power of the Assembly. Pursuant to section 3, paragraph 1, Annex to the 1994 Agreement, 'the general policies of the Authority shall be established by the Assembly in collaboration with the Council'. Moreover, under section 3, paragraph 4, 'decisions of the Assembly on any matter for which the Council also has competence or on any administrative, budgetary or financial matter shall be based on the recommendations of the Council'. The provision continues, 'if the Assembly does not accept the recommendation of the Council on any matter, it shall return the matter to the Council for further consideration'. Since the Assembly must consider and cannot deny the recommendations made by the Council but at most return them, the Assembly does not have the final say, thereby losing its supremacy as a decision-making organ of the ISA.

In practice, since its coming into operation the Assembly has faced a persistent problem: the poor attendance of members at its meetings. As it is revealed by the 2013 Report of the Secretary-General of the ISA,

> Between 2000 and 2011, the Assembly had a quorum on only two occasions, namely, in 2004 and in 2008. With the exception of those years, however, attendance has been relatively constant at between 57 and 66 members of the Authority (roughly 40 to 45 per cent of the membership). The lowest attendance was in 2007, when only 57 (36 per cent) of the membership of the Authority attended. With 165 members, a quorum of 83 members is required.[8]

[7] ISA, Introduction to the Secretary-General's Informal Consultations on Outstanding Issues Relating to the Deep Seabed Mining Provisions of the United Nations Convention on the Law of the Sea: Collected Documents (2002).

[8] The 2013 Report of the Secretary-General of the ISA, ISBA/19/A/2, footnote 5.

Thereafter, the attendance figures continued to fluctuate and remained at a low level.[9] In 2018, 82 (out of 168) members attended the annual session of the Assembly, which was considered by the Secretary-General of the ISA as a 'record attendance'.[10] This situation severely weakens the decision-making ability of the Assembly and causes problems concerning the legitimacy of its decisions. Indeed, viewed from both the 1994 Agreement and practice, the Assembly has lost its primary role in the decision-making process. However, it remains to be seen whether the attendance in the Assembly would improve once commercial exploitation commences, and if so, whether the Assembly as the only plenary policy-making organ would exert bigger influence on the development of DSM regime in future.

3.3.2 *The Council*

The Council is the non-plenary policy-making organ of the ISA which plays a pivotal role in directing the development of DSM regime and supervising the operation of the ISA. In theory, the Council as an executive organ shall establish the specific policies in conformity with the general policies established by the Assembly.[11] In practice, however, due to the apparent flaw of the Assembly – its low level of attendance – the Council makes policies and adopts almost all binding decisions independently from the plenary organ. The Council is more like a governing organ than an executive organ. The composition of the Council is special. It comprises the representatives of special interests in combination with those selected on the basis of an equitable geographical distribution. Specifically, the thirty-six members of the Council are divided into five groups, the first four groups represent special interests, while the fifth group reflects the principle of ensuring an equitable geographical distribution. The number of members is divided equally between the first four groups and the last group, with a total of eighteen members in the four groups and an equal number in the last group too.[12] With respect to the election of members, it

[9] The number of participant members was fifty-seven in 2013, sixty-seven in 2014, sixty-two in 2015, eighty-five in 2016, source from: 'Record attendance at Seabed Assembly', *Jamaica Observer*. www.jamaicaobserver.com/news/record-attendance-at-seabed-assembly_139397?profile=1373.

[10] Ibid.

[11] Article 162(1), UNCLOS.

[12] According to section 3, para. 15, Annex to the 1994 Agreement, members of Group A are selected among the States of the biggest consumption or net importation of the mineral

has become an established practice that, as a first step, the Secretariat prepares an informal indicative list of States that would fulfil the criteria for membership in each group.[13]

When it comes to decision-making procedure of the Council, 'as a general rule, decision-making in the organs of the Authority should be by consensus'.[14] In the opinion of the ISA's Secretary-General, consensus is

> [a] finely balanced decision-making mechanism that is intended to safeguard the interests of all States, even though it is apparent that a number of the States represented in the Council have conflicting interests as the States sponsors of contractors with the Authority on the one hand and custodians of the CHM on the other hand.[15]

During the past more than two decades, all decisions of the Council have been made by consensus. Yet, this does not exclude the possibility that other methods, such as vote, would be employed in future. In case that the Council were to make decision by voting, members of the Council would be regrouped for that purpose.

> Each group of States elected under paragraph 15 (a) to (c) shall be treated as a chamber for the purposes of voting in the Council. The developing States elected under paragraph 15 (d) and (e) shall be treated as a single chamber for the purposes of voting in the Council.[16]

resources to be derived from the Area; members of Group B are from the States of the largest investments in preparation for and in the conduct of activities in the Area; members of Group C are from the States of the largest production or net exportation of the categories of minerals to be derived from the Area. The number of members of each of the three groups is four. Group D is composed of six members selected among developing States Parties, representing special interests. While the eighteen members of Group E are selected in light of the principle of ensuring an equitable geographical distribution of seats in the Council as a whole. Members of Group E are elected in accordance with a formula for allocating seats among five regional groups: African Group ten seats; Asia-Pacific Group nine seats; Eastern European Group three seats; Latin American and Caribbean Group seven seats; and Western and Others Group eight. This method, however, brings the total number of members of the Council to thirty-seven. To solve this problem, each regional group other than the Eastern European Group will relinquish a seat in rotation. The regional group which relinquishes a seat will have the right to designate a member of that group to participate in the deliberations of the Council without the right to vote during the period the regional group relinquishes the seat. ISBA/A/L.8, 1996.

13 The composition, relinquishment of a seat and Presidents of Council since 1996 are available at the website of the ISA. –www.isa.org.jm/authority/council-members.

14 Section 3, paragraph 2, Annex to the 1994 Agreement.

15 The 2008 Report of the Secretary-General of the ISA, ISBA/14/A/2, para. 105.

16 Section 3, paragraph 9(a), Annex to the 1994 Agreement.

Importantly, as the adoption of decisions is conditioned on that 'such decisions are not opposed by a majority in any one of the chambers referred to in paragraph 9',[17] 'a vote on any matter can be defeated if the decision is opposed by a majority in any one of the chambers of the Council, regardless of whether there would otherwise be a two-thirds majority in favour of the decision'.[18] It is seen that any three members together in Chamber I (Group A), Chamber II (Group B) or Chamber III (Group C) can paralyze the Council. Such an arrangement gives the *de facto* veto power to members in the first three chambers (groups), thereby making the interests of States who consume, invest or produce (seabed or counterpart terrestrial) minerals a dominating voice in the Council.

The powers and functions of the Council are detailed in Article 162(2) of the UNCLOS and they can be roughly divided into two categories. One category encompasses those relating to 'matters within the mandate of the Assembly upon which the Council is required to make recommendations before the Assembly may act'[19] or 'other matters must be considered sequentially by the Council and the Assembly'.[20] Theoretically, the fulfillment of powers and functions in this category necessitates collaboration between the Council and the Assembly. In practice, the liaison between the Council and the Assembly has been loose. Yet, this has not been an impediment. Because first, as indicated earlier, the Assembly cannot deny the recommendations made by the Council, and second, the Council can adopt and apply provisionally rules, regulations and procedures prior to the approval of the Assembly. The second category comprises the powers and functions the Council may exercise without reference to the Assembly, which in most cases are 'these relate

[17] Section 3, paragraph 5, Annex to the 1994 Agreement.

[18] Satya N. Nandan, Michael Lodge and Shabtai Rosenne (eds.), *United Nations Convention on the Law of the Sea 1982: A Commentary (Vol. VI)* (Martinus Nijhoff 2002) 419.

[19] The powers and functions in this category are described in Article 162, paragraphs 2(b) (election of the Secretary-General); 2(c) (election of the Governing Board and Director-General of the Enterprise); 2(n) (system of compensation or other measures of economic adjustment assistance); 2(o)(i) (equitable sharing of financial and other economic benefits under article 82); 2(t) (membership) and 2(s) (any other questions and matters). Nandan, Lodge and Rosenne (eds.), *United Nations Convention on the Law of the Sea 1982* (2002), 455-456.

[20] The powers and functions in this category are described in Article 162, paragraph 2(o)(ii) (adopt and apply provisionally rules, regulations and procedures); 2(g) (reports of the Enterprise); 2(f) (cooperation with other IOs); 2(h) (annual reports) and 2(r) (annual budget). Ibid.

to the operational activities of the Authority'.[21] The exercise of powers and functions of the second category relies on expertise in various fields relating to DSM. For this reason, the Council has established a subsidiary expert body – the Legal and Technical Commission.

In recent years, with the growing interest in DSM, the Council has gotten in new situations. To begin with, more NGOs have become observers of the ISA[22] whose active participation in the Council sessions is increasingly visible: they make intervention, submit written reports and organize side events alongside the meetings of the Council.[23] Appeals of NGOs for the protection of the marine environment in DSM are growing increasingly stronger. This phenomenon would have far-reaching implications on the future environmental governance of DSM. Secondly, the past few years have also seen a substantial increase of the workload, which has resulted in a change of the frequency of the Council meetings from annual session to two sessions per year since 2018. Thirdly, since the Council relies on expert advice of LTC in deciding on technical problems, the relationship between the Council and the LTC is highlighted. The questions raised are: to what extent the technical subsidiary organ – the LTC – is within the practical control of the principal organ – the Council? How to improve the synergy of the LTC and the Council? Put it in another way, how do science and politics integrate in governing DSM? Answers to these questions are important to the effective functioning of the Council; they are sought in the following subsection.

[21] The powers and functions in this category are described in Article 162, paragraphs 2(a) (supervise and coordinate the implementation of the provisions of Part XI), 2(k) and Section 3, paragraph 11(a), Annex to the 1994 Agreement (approve plans of work), 2(1) (exercise control over activities in the Area), 2(w) (issue emergency orders), and 2(x) (disapprove areas for exploitation by contractors or the Enterprise), ibid.

[22] Pursuant to Article 169 of the UNCLOS, to become observers, NGOs must file applications which need to be approved by the Council, and they must have made arrangements with the Secretary-General of the ISA. Once accepted as an observer, an NGO is entitled to attend meetings of organs of the ISA and make intervention at the meetings; they can also submit written reports. The list of NGO observers is available at: www.isa.org.jm/observers.

[23] For instance, during the 22nd session of the ISA, Deepsea Conservation Coalition held a side event titled 'Environmental Aspects of the ISA Exploitation Regulations' on 11 July 2016. It is common practice that NGOs may organize side events during the annual sessions of an intergovernmental organization at or around the same venue where the annual sessions are held. To do so, prior registration and/or approval might be required. In the case of the ISA, NGOs that wish to hold side events during the annual sessions of the ISA must fill in the 'side event request form' and be selected by the ISA.

3.3.3 *The Legal and Technical Commission*

The Legal and Technical Commission has been set up to provide expert advice to the Council, thereby enabling the latter to act on the basis of the best technical advice available when making decisions on important issues.[24] Purposes and functions determine the composition. Therefore,

> [m]embers of the Legal and Technical Commission shall have the appropriate qualification such as those relevant to exploration for and exploitation and processing of mineral resources, oceanology, protection of the marine environment, or economic or legal matters relating to ocean mining and related fields of expertise. The Council shall endeavour to ensure that the membership of the Commission reflects all appropriate qualifications.[25]

Article 163(2) of the UNCLOS foresees the LTC as having fifteen members but also prescribes that 'if necessary, the Council may decide to increase the size of either Commission giving due regard to economy and efficiency'. In practice, the size of the LTC expanded several times to thirty members as it stands now.[26] Lodge opined that 'the decision [to increase members of the LTC] had been motivated less by the actual or perceived workload of the LTC than by the desire to avoid a vote to accommodate late nominations'.[27] He further observed that 'on no occasion did the Council attempt an assessment of the actual needs of

24 Nandan, Lodge and Rosenne (eds.), *United Nations Convention on the Law of the Sea 1982* (2002).

25 Article 165(1), UNCLOS.

26 The membership of the LTC was increased to twenty-two in 1996 when the LTC was first elected, to twenty-four in 2001 and to twenty-five in 2006. (Considerations relating to the functioning of the LTC: note by the Secretary-General of the ISA, ISBA/16/C/3, 2010.) Since then the size of the LTC had remained at twenty-five (owing to the resignation in 2014 of one member, with no subsequent nomination of a replacement candidate, the membership of the LTC had been at twenty-four from 2014 to 2016. Report of the Secretary-General on the election of members of the LTC, ISBA/23/C/2, 2017) until in 2016 when the Council decided to increase the number of members of the LTC to thirty (for 2016–2021) on a temporary and exceptional basis (Decision of the Council of the ISA relating to the election of members of the LTC, 2016, ISBA/22/C/29, para. 3.) A term for members of the LTC is five years. There have so far been five cycles of the LTC election: the first in 1996 for a period of 1997–2001; the second in 2001 for 2002–2006; the third in 2006 for 2007–2011; the fourth in 2011 for 2012–2016; the fifth in 2016 for 2017–2021. Due to the COVID-19, the fifth cycle five-year term was extended until 31 December 2022. During the 27th session of the Council, election for the sixth cycle (for 2022–2027) is in process.

27 Report of the Secretary-General on the election of members of the LTC, ISBA/23/C/2, 2017, para. 4.

the LTC in terms of the number of members'.[28] However, the sharp increase of the number of members from twenty-five to thirty in 2016 may be a response to the growing workload of the LTC; at least responding to the growing workload may be an unspoken motivation for the behaviour of nominating States.

Now facing the sixth cycle of the election of members of the LTC, the complex issues of the size and composition of the LTC, the nomination and election of its members are under hot debate within the Council.[29] The Council has decided that the size of the LTC for 2022–2026 would be between twenty-five and thirty members.[30] The composition shall be determined on the basis of assessment of the current and future needs for specific areas of expertise by the LTC itself.[31] As to the election of members, it shall take into account the following three elements: expertise, equitable geographical distribution and representation of special interests.[32] In a post commenting the initial draft proposal of a mechanism for the election of LTC members by the Facilitator in April 2020, Singh expressed his basic position that, no matter what mechanism is adopted to converge the three elements, the Council should not convert the LTC 'from a technical and expert advisory body into a political body'.[33] For that consideration, nominating candidates of appropriate

[28] Ibid.

[29] There are decisions by the Council (ISBA/25/C/L.2, 2019; ISBA/26/C/9, 2020 and others). There are also proposals jointly or individually submitted by States, such as, Algeria on behalf of the African Group, and Brazil on behalf of the Latin American and Caribbean States Group (ISBA/25/C/L.2, 2019) and, Australia, Canada, France, Italy, Norway, Spain and the UK (ISBA/26/C/L.2, 2020).

[30] Decision of the Council of the ISA relating to the election in 2021 of members of the Legal and Technical Commission, 2020, ISBA/26/C/9.

[31] Ibid.

[32] Annex: Working paper of the facilitator on the election in 2021 of members of the Legal and Technical Commission, 2020, ISBA/26/C/9. The legal basis for this requirement is Article 163(3) and (4) of the UNCLOS. Yet, understandings of the provision are different between, for instance, Belgium and the Secretary-General of the ISA. For Belgium, the provision refers to the 'regional distribution of seats' (Proposed procedure for the election of members of the Commission submitted by the delegation of Belgium, ISBA/25/C/22, 2019, para. 4), while for the Secretary-General of the ISA the provision simply provides that due account shall be taken of the need for equitable geographical distribution and the representation of special interests, but no specific requirements in relating to regional representation. (Report of the Secretary-General on the election of members of the LTC, 2017, ISBA/23/C/2, para. 7.)

[33] Pradeep Singh, 'Commentary: Latest Developments in the election of members of the LTC', DSM Observer, available at: https://dsmobserver.com/2020/05/commentary-latest-developments-in-the-election-of-members-of-the-ltc/.

qualifications by States on time is crucial; only when the element of expertise is satisfied can the other two elements come into play during the election.

The reason why the election of members of the LTC becomes such a notable event is because 'the LTC occupies a central place within the structure of the ISA'.[34] Functions of the LTC, as laid down in Article 165 (2) of UNCLOS, fall into four broad categories: functions relating to the approval of plans of work (2(b)); functions relating to the supervision of activities in the Area (2(c), (i), (j) and (m)); regulatory functions (2(f), (g)); and functions relating to the assessment of environmental impact of activities in the Area (2(d), (e), (h), (k) and (l)).[35] These functions, albeit of an advisory or recommendatory nature, are closely related to the functions of the Council under Article 162.[36] Put it in another way, the LTC is involved in the policy-making process of the Council, albeit in an advisory capacity. Most of the recommendations of the LTC are so technical in character that members of the Council do not have the needed time and expertise to study them during sessions.[37] Moreover, as will be shown in Section 3.4.2, the decision-making procedural rules also make it difficult for the Council to reject the recommendations of the LTC. In a word, the Council could have little control over the LTC in practice, except the election of its members. This is perhaps another reason why the election of members of the LTC is a big issue for the Council. The fact that the LTC is composed of experts (who take the positions in personal capacities) nominated by States, but not independent experts, may help the Council to maintain a certain level of control of the LTC, which in turn is beneficial to a smooth communication and cooperation between these two organs. Indeed, an effective functioning of the Council requires a synergy of the LTC and the Council.

[34] Final Report of the Periodic Review under Article 154, ISBA/23/A/3, 2017, para. 26.

[35] Nandan, Lodge and Rosenne (eds.), *United Nations Convention on the Law of the Sea 1982* (2002).

[36] Ibid., 477–480. However, the relation between the LTC and the Council changed during the negotiating period. Originally, the powers to issue emergency orders, to disapprove areas for exploitation, to initiate proceedings before SDC and the function of directing and supervising a staff of inspectors were assigned to the LTC, but were transferred to the Council upon the endorsing of a proposal from the United States in 1979.

[37] This is not an unusual phenomenon for functional commissions. For instance, 'Commissions of the UN, such as those on statistics or Narcotic Drugs, operate officially under the supervision of the ECOSOC. In practice, however, they are so technical in character that the ECOSOC has little control over them.' Henry Schermers and Niels Blokker, *International Institutional Law*, 5th edn. (Martinus Nijhoff 2011) Section 422.

The work of the LTC determines, to a large extent, the ISA's ability to fulfil its environmental mandates. Now, the crucial question is: is the LTC fit for the purpose? A look at the practice reveals that the LTC has encountered a series of problems: (a) too heavy workload, (b) absence or low level of involvement of some members, (c) lack of transparency and public participation and (d) the inadequacy of expertise.

In response to the heavy workload, the LTC adjusts the meeting schedule, including increasing the frequency and extending duration of its meetings.[38] However, change of the meeting schedule would not improve the performance of the LTC if its members do not participate or have a low level of involvement. In practice, some members' absence from meetings or inactive involvement has been a problem.[39] There are several factors which discourage members from devoting to the work of the LTC. For instance, serving as members of the LTC is an unpaid but demanding part-time job. Not only do members of the LTC need to invest lots of time and energy in this job, but also the job may generate costs. To tackle the problem of some members' absence from meetings for financial reason, the ISA established the Voluntary Trust Fund for the purpose of defraying the cost of participation of members of the LTC from developing countries.[40] Yet, as it stands now, there seems no way to ease the conflict between the demand of active involvement of members on the one hand and the limited time and energy members could invest in the work with the LTC on the other hand. The performance of the LTC lies with the self-motivated commitment to the Commission by each individual member. Perhaps turning the LTC into a permanent organ is one way out; replacing State-nominated experts with independent experts as members of the LTC might be another. Yet, neither way is practically possible unless relevant provisions of the UNCLOS are revised.

[38] Rule 1, Rules of Procedure of the Legal and Technical Commission provides legal basis for the change of meeting schedule. Before 2013, the LTC held only one session annually; afterwards, the LTC holds two sessions annually, each session lasts for about ten days.

[39] Take the 21st session in 2015 as an example, twenty out of twenty-five members of the LTC attended the meetings, 1/5 members were absent; yet, this attendance rate was considered by the ISA as satisfactory.

[40] The Voluntary Trust Fund was established also for the purpose of defraying the cost of participation of the members of Finance Committee from developing countries for the meetings of the committee, but the money used for support members of the Finance Committee was much less compared to that for support members of the LTC. Considerations relating to the functioning of the LTC: note by the Secretary-General, ISBA/16/C/3, 2010.

The form of meetings of the LTC also becomes a matter of debate. Although rules of the LTC prescribe that 'the meetings of the Commission shall be held in private unless the Commission decides otherwise'.[41] In recent years, the private meetings of the LTC have been subject to growing criticisms for its lack of transparency and public participation.[42] The LTC justifies the privacy of some meetings on the basis of the confidential information of contractors which such meetings involve. Critics do not direct at this justification as such. Yet, they shift the target to more specific issues of the judgment of the confidentiality of information and the burden of proof. It is generally accepted that information relating to marine environmental protection should be regarded as non-confidential. Correspondingly, meetings of the LTC concerning this subject matter shall be held in public, which is an important step for public participation.

Finally, there is the unavoidable problem of the inadequacy of expertise of the LTC. As the LTC acknowledged, 'it was unlikely to be able to provide every type of expertise needed to fulfil its wide remit of work'.[43] Hence, 'when necessary, expertise had been sought outside its members by the Secretariat to bring additional specialized knowledge and skills to its work'.[44] Indeed, the LTC from time to time seeks external consultancy services or incorporates contributions of renowned experts in practice.[45] The global scientific community at large is the ultimate expertise sources. However, there are two conditions to make use of such sources: first, a strong manager to collect and sort out the worldwide expertise resources, and second, a mechanism through which the most needed experts can be sought for. These two conditions can be satisfied by strengthening the

[41] Rule 6, Rules of Procedure of the Legal and Technical Commission, ISBA/6/C/9, 2000. However, Rule 6 also states that the LTC shall take account of the desirability of holding open meetings when it discusses issues of general interest to members of the ISA which do not involve the discussion of confidential information. Furthermore, Rule 53 allows any member of the ISA to send a representative to attend a meeting of the LTC when the LTC considers a matter particularly affecting that member.

[42] Jeff Ardron et al., 'Incorporating Transparency into the Governance of Deep-seabed Mining in the Area beyond National Jurisdiction' (2018) 89 *Marine Policy* 58–66.

[43] Report of the Secretary-General on election of members of the LTC, ISBA/23/C/2, 2017, para. 9.

[44] Ibid.

[45] For example, the 2005 Report of the Secretary-General of the ISA states that 'the Commission also had the benefit of advice from three internationally renowned experts, Dr James R. Hein, Dr Peter Herzig and Dr Kim Juniper', ISBA/11/A/4 and Corr.1, para. 33.

scientific capacity of the Secretariat. Scientific officers within the Secretariat can serve as the contact point connecting the LTC with the outside scientific communities. Additionally, the enhancement of in-house expertise within the Secretariat can provide direct assistance to the LTC. To illustrate this point, the review of annual reports of contractors can be taken as an example. Reviewing annual reports of contractors is one of the main tasks for the LTC. Such a work, however, is too time-consuming to be finished during meetings of the LTC. In practice, members of the LTC do not read the annual reports directly. Instead, they work only on the documents prepared by the Secretariat which contain the key information extracted from the annual reports and the comments given by the scientific officers at the Secretariat.[46] Thus, the preparatory work of the Secretariat is crucial for the work of the LTC with respect to the review of annual reports. In sum, the introduction of external experts and the strengthening of the scientific capacity of the Secretariat could both contribute to complementing the LTC's expertise.

3.3.4 The Secretariat

The Secretariat is one of the three principal and the only permanent organ of the ISA. It is composed of the Secretary-General[47] and staff, which are of an international nature, acting independently from members of the ISA.[48] The ISA is headquartered at Kingston, Jamaica. Owing to the principle of cost-effectiveness and the evolutionary approach to the establishment of the ISA, the Secretariat has continued to be small in size. Since its operation from 1996 to 2017, there has been very little change in the organizational structure of the Secretariat, except for a modest increase in the number of established posts from thirty-

[46] Detailed description on how the review of annual reports submitted by contractors is conducted can be found in: Comments by the Secretary-General on the recommendations contained in the final report on the periodic review of the ISA pursuant to article 154 of the UNCLOS, ISBA/23/A/5/Rev.1, 2017, paras. 10--18.

[47] Satya Nandan (Fiji) served as the first Secretary-General of the ISA from 1996 to 2008, in three consecutive terms. His successor was Nii Allotey Odunton (Ghana), who was elected at the 118th meeting of the Assembly, on 5 June 2008. His first four-year term commenced on 1 January 2009 and was re-elected in 2013 for a second term. In the 22nd session in July 2016, Michael Lodge (the United Kingdom) was elected as the third Secretary-General of the ISA, he took office on 1 January 2017.

[48] Article 168, UNCLOS.

seven to forty-one.[49] The functions of the Secretariat, like a typical administrative organ of an international organization, include representing the ISA, providing administrative support to the other organs and so on.[50] In particular, as a small specialized technical organization, the Secretariat of the ISA also serves as a worldwide information centre for deep sea sciences, policies and mining activities.

In practice, the Secretariat has encountered two main problems. First, owing to the fact that the substantive work of the ISA has become substantially scientific and technical in nature, there is the need to 'strengthen the technical expertise of the secretariat'.[51] Secondly, the number of exploration contracts has grown fast and the task of drafting Exploitation Regulations has been initiated since 2012, which in combination led to a substantially increased workload for the Secretariat. In response to these problems, the transformation of the Secretariat has been under discussion for years.[52] In 2017, the third Secretary-General assumed his office and started to implement a series of organizational changes in the Secretariat.[53]

First, the posts for contract management and database management[54] have been newly added, while some other posts for professionals would be added later. Secondly, descriptions of the functions of each of the four departments have been revised and division of labours among the departments has been adjusted.[55] Thirdly, the internal management has

[49] ISA, 'Restructuring of the Secretariat of the International Seabed Authority', note by the Secretary General, ISBA/23/A/4, 2017, para. 2.

[50] For a general account on the functions of secretariat of international organizations, see Schermers and Blokker, *International Institutional Law* (2011), paras. 442–464.

[51] This point has been reaffirmed repeatedly in the annual reports of the Secretary-General of the ISA. For instances, paras. 65–66 of the 2003 Report and para. 3 of the 2004 Report.

[52] For instance, 'it is anticipated that a proposal will be submitted in 2014 to restructure the Secretariat, possibly to include a contracts management unit'. The 2013 Report of the Secretary-General of the ISA at the 19th session, para. 7.

[53] The assumption of office of the third Secretary-General coincided with the release of the final report of the Article 154 periodic review of the ISA. He adopted an active attitude towards the practical problems identified and recommendations proposed by the Article 154 Review Committee concerning the Secretariat.

[54] In response to a call from the LTC that 'the capacity in assessing, storing and managing data needs to be strengthened' (The 2013 summary report of the Chair of the LTC, ISBA/19/C/14, para. 9), database has been launched and a data manager placed for the maintenance of database.

[55] The four departments are (1) Executive Office of the Secretary-General, (2) Office for Administrative Services, (3) Office of Environmental Management and Mineral Resources (former name was Office for Resources and Environmental Monitoring) and (4) Office of Legal Affairs.

also been changed. This is reflected in the revision of the Staff Regulations,[56] the recommencement of meetings of the senior management team composed of the head of each departments and the Secretary-General, the more transparent planning and implementation of budget of the Secretariat and the enhanced internal communication. Finally, the Secretariat also makes efforts to enhance transparency of the work of the ISA. This work is undertaken by the Documentation and Conference Management Officer, Webmaster/Publications Officer and a newly added post of a Communications Officer. The restructuring of the Secretariat is intended to consolidate and streamline activities and thereby enhancing its efficiency and capacity. Indeed, a Secretariat which is equipped with highly qualified personnel and well managed is essential for the ISA to perform optimally. In order to be kept abreast with the development of DSM, the Secretariat needs to be restructured periodically. As an incidental remark, the internal structure, management and work methods of Secretariat are in effect very much affected by the work ability, style and personality of the Secretary-General. The leadership of the Secretary-General is crucial for the effective functioning of the Secretariat.

The Secretary-General not only leads the Secretariat, but could also assume some duties of the Council. Since around 2019, the question of whether, and if so, to what extent, the Council could delegate its powers and functions to the Secretary-General has been discussed during the drafting process of Exploitation Regulations.[57] Is such a delegation lawful? The answer is affirmative. Article 166(3) of the UNCLOS prescribes that the Secretary-General shall 'perform such other administrative functions as are entrusted to him or her by the Assembly, Council or any subsidiary organ'. This is very similar to Article 98 of the UN Charter which states that 'the Secretary-General [. . .] shall perform such other functions as are entrusted to him by these organs'. Furthermore, it is common practice for an organ to delegate powers and functions, either to another organ within an international organization, or to member states, or to other actors.[58] As the Secretariat of the ISA observed, 'the Council may delegate its functions' and 'it is within the power of the

[56] Decision of the Assembly of the ISA concerning the staff regulations of the Authority, ISBA/23/A/11, 2017. Decision of the Assembly of the ISA concerning an amendment to the staff regulations of the Authority, ISBA/25/A/13, 2019.

[57] Delegation of functions by the Council and regulatory efficiency, note by the Secretariat, ISBA/25/C/6, 2019.

[58] Schermers and Blokker, *International Institutional Law* (2011), section 224.

Council and the Assembly to authorize the functional delegation of ISA through the regulations that they will approve and adopt'.[59]

The 2019 draft Exploitation Regulations contain such a delegation in many provisions. The scope of powers and functions delegated to the Secretary-General covers such matters as 'contracts management', 'monitoring implementation of duties', 'ensuring compliance of the contractors' and 'taking enforcement measures'. These delegations are justified mainly on the need for 'timely action' and 'administrative efficiency'. Indeed, in contrast with the Council and Assembly whose actions and decisions are usually time-lagged, the Secretariat is more fit for the purpose of ensuring an effective administration of activities in the Area. Nevertheless, the delegation would lead to a shift in power and accountability. Then the ensuing question is how to ensure appropriate accountability and good governance of the Secretary-General. Also, the delegation would weaken the roles of member States in the governing DSM activities. In a word, with these changes, the ISA will be more an international administration than a traditional international organization.

3.3.5 The Finance Committee

The Finance Committee was established under section 9, Annex to the 1994 Agreement.[60] It is composed of fifteen members nominated by States and selected by the Assembly, as a subsidiary organ to the Assembly to deal with financial matters. In practice, however, the report of the Finance Committee is submitted to both the Assembly and the Council.[61] This unusual phenomenon could be explained by the revised decision-making rules under the 1994 Agreement which states that decisions by the Assembly on budgetary or financial matters have to be made on the basis of recommendations by the Council.[62] This might also

[59] Delegation of functions by the Council and regulatory efficiency, note by the Secretariat, ISBA/25/C/6, 2019, para. 8.

[60] The requirement of Article 162, paragraph 2(y) of the UNCLOS to establish a subsidiary organ to deal with financial matters shall be deemed to have been fulfilled by the establishment of the Finance Committee in accordance with this section.

[61] For instance, during the 21st session, the report of the Financial Committee was submitted to the Assembly (ISBA/21/A/6) and the Council (ISBA/21/C/15) simultaneously. This resulted in an unusual phenomenon, namely, one document being assigned two different document numbers.

[62] Section 3, paragraph 4, annex to the 1994 Agreement.

be to do with the crippled decision-making ability of the Assembly due to the chronic problem of the low attendance of its members. The Finance Committee works in a similar way as the LTC. The practical problems faced by the two subsidiary bodies are similar too. For instance, they both have the problem of some members' absence from meetings or low level of involvement.[63]

During the first three years of its existence (1995–1997), the administrative expenses of the ISA were met through the UN budget. From 1998 on, expenses were covered by States' contributions.[64] The scale of assessment of the ISA is based on that of the UN, and Japan has been the largest contributor all these years.[65] Budgets adopted for the ISA were very stable from 2000 to 2006, at around USD 10 million for two budgetary years; after 2006, the amount increased moderately year by year.[66] The growing spending is caused, in general, by the substantial increase of workload. Specifically, added costs are generated by an increase of the meeting frequency of the LTC and the Council and by a more active role of the Secretariat. For instance, in recent years, the Secretariat has added new established posts, has sought more frequently for consultancies from external experts, has established and maintained a database, has provided more conference service and has organized more workshops. All of these activities generate additional costs.

3.3.6 The Enterprise and the Economic Planning Commission

In addition to the Assembly, the Council, the LTC, the Secretariat and the Finance Committee, the ISA has two other organs – the Economic

[63] Take the 21st session in 2015 as an example, eleven out of the fifteen members attended the meetings, four members were absent.

[64] Annual budgets in 1995 and 1996 were USD 2,500,000, and in 1997, USD 4,150,500. The budget in 1998 was USD 4,703,900 and in 1999, USD 5,011,700. Jean-Pierre Levy, 'International Seabed Authority: 20 Years, paper submitted at the special session in memory of the 20th Anniversary of the ISA', 2014, 12–13.

[65] Ibid., 14–17.

[66] In 2000, the approved annual budget was USD 5,265,000. Since 2001, it has begun to adopt biennial budgets, the amounts were USD 10,506,400 (2001–2002), USD 10,509,700 (2003–2004), USD 10,800,000 (2005–2006), USD 11,782,400 (2007–2008), USD 12,516,500 (2009–2010), USD 13,014,700 (2011–2012) and USD 14,312,948 (2013–2014), USD 15,743,143 (2015–2016), USD 17,130,700 (2017–2018), USD 18,235,850 (2019–2020), USD 19,411,280 (2021–2022) and USD 22,256,000 (2023–2024). Sources from decisions of the Assembly relating to the budget of the ISA for different financial periods.

Planning Commission (EPC) and the Enterprise – which, however, are still inactive. Under Article 163, the Economic Planning Commission is a subsidiary body to the Council entrusted with making recommendation to the Council in order to accommodate the interests of those developing land-based producer States whose economies have been determined to be seriously affected by the production of minerals from the deep seabed. Pursuant to Article 170, the Enterprise is 'the organ of the Authority which shall carry out activities in the Area directly as well as the transporting, processing and marketing of minerals recovered from the Area'. The Enterprise is commonly understood as the ISA's 'operational arm'. Owing to the prolonged delay in commercial development of DSM, and based on the cost-effectiveness principle and the evolutionary approach in the institutional arrangements, the 1994 Agreement rendered the functions of the Economic Planning Commission to be provisionally performed by the LTC, while functions of the Enterprise were to be carried out by the Secretariat.[67]

In recent years, with a prospect that commercial exploitation is soon to commence, the operationalization of these two organs have been under discussions. With respect to the EPC, the process started in 2020 when the Secretariat of the ISA commissioned the All-Russian Scientific-Research Institute of Mineral Resources to conduct a study.[68] Thereupon, the LTC, the Council and the Secretariat continued to make further progress along the way.[69] The first report of the Secretary-General on 'Operationalization of the Economic Planning Commission' covers the establishment, membership and functions of the EPC, the financial implications for the ISA, as well as the provision of assistance via an economic assistance fund, etc.[70]

As to the Enterprise, in 2012 Nautilus Minerals Inc. proposed to 'enter into negotiations to form a joint venture with the Enterprise for the

[67] Section 1, paragraphs 2, 3 and 4, and Section 2, paragraph 1, annex to the 1994 Agreement.

[68] 'Study of Potential Impact of Polymetallic Nodules Production from the Area on the Economics and Developing Land-based Producers of those Metals which are Likely to be Most Seriously Affected', Report to the ISA, 2020: https://isa.org.jm/files/documents/impactstudy.pdf. The affected metals covered in the study are: copper, nickel, cobalt and manganese.

[69] See the report of the LTC, ISBA/26/C/12, 2021, para. 17 and ISBA/26/C/12_Add.1, 2021, paras. 17–19; the decision of the Council, ISBA/26/C/57, 2021, paras. 15–16.

[70] The report of the Secretary-General on 'Operationalization of the Economic Planning Commission', ISBA/27/C/25, 2022.

purpose of developing eight of the reserved area blocks in the Clarion-Clipperton Zone'.[71] According to section 2, paragraph 2, Annex to the 1994 Agreement,

> Upon the approval of a plan of work for exploitation for an entity other than the Enterprise, or upon receipt by the Council of an application for a joint-venture operation with the Enterprise, the Council shall take up the issue of the functioning of the Enterprise independently of the Secretariat of the Authority.

Although Nautilus' proposal was not accepted by the Council, it did trigger the Council to start considering the issue of 'the independent operation of the Enterprise'. Soon, the issue was studied by the Secretariat and put on the agenda of the LTC.[72] In 2018, the ISA received again an expression of interest to enter into negotiations to form a joint venture with the Enterprise, this time, from the Government of Poland.[73] The proposal gained regional and cross-regional support.[74] In the view of the African Group, the proposal from Poland during the making of Exploitation Regulations sends a strong signal that the timing is ripe for the Enterprise to be launched into a 'formal existence independent of the ISA's Secretariat' and the Council to 'take action to operationalize the Enterprise'.[75] Being supported by over a quarter of the member States of

[71] Report by the Secretary-General on 'Considerations relating to a proposal by Nautilus Minerals Inc. for a joint venture operation with the Enterprise', ISBA/19/C/6, 2013, para. 1.

[72] Issues relating to the operation of the Enterprise, in particular the legal, technical and financial implications for the Authority and for States parties, Note of the Secretariat, ISBA/20/LTC/12, 2014; ISBA/22/LTC/9, 2016.

[73] Report of the Secretary-General on 'Considerations relating to a proposal by the Government of Poland for a possible joint-venture operation with the Enterprise', ISBA/24/C/12, 2018.

[74] Report of the Special Representative of the Secretary-General of the ISA for the Enterprise on the proposal by the Government of Poland for a joint venture with the Enterprise, ISBA/25/C/7, 2019; Report of the Special Representative of the Secretary-General of the ISA on 'Issues relating to the operation of the Enterprise, in particular the legal, technical and financial implications for the ISA and for States parties to the UNCLOS', ISBA/25/C/26, 2019, para. 39.

[75] Request for consideration by the Council of the African Group's operationalization of the 'Enterprise', 6 July 2018, statement before the Council: www.isa.org.jm/files/files/documents/alg-oboag-entp.pdf. For an analysis of the submission made by African Group, see Mehdi Remaoun, 'The International Seabed Authority and the Enterprise: How Africa Is Reinvigorating the Principle of the Common Heritage of Mankind' (2021) 1(1) *Journal of Ocean Governance in Africa*. See also Eden Charles, 'The Enterprise under the 1982 United Nations Convention on the Law of the Sea and the Common Heritage of Mankind', in Alfonso Ascencio-Herrera and Myron H. Nordquist (eds.), *The United*

the ISA, the issue of independent operation of the Enterprise has certainly gained momentum. The LTC stated in 2020 that it was time to consider joint venture with the Enterprise and that an interim director general for the Enterprise should be appointed within the Secretariat of the ISA.[76] The interim director general discussed in 2022 managerial policy options for the administration of the Enterprise and administrative functions of the interim director general during the period from July 2022 to December 2023.[77]

To activate the Enterprise, there are legal, technical as well as financial problems.[78] Here, only the legal aspect will be discussed. From a legal point of view, the Enterprise is a complex, even paradoxical, entity. As it is supposed to be both a contractor and an organ of the ISA and to act both in accordance with and independently from other organs of the ISA. The legal nature of the Enterprise can be revealed by peeling away the three layers of implications.

In the first layer, the Enterprise is an eligible operator, a special type of contractor in the Area. In accordance with Article 153(2) of the UNCLOS, the Enterprise alongside with States, state enterprises or natural or juridical persons sponsored by States are entitled to develop mineral resources in the Area. This is called the 'parallel development system'. The 1994 Agreement revoked the differentiation between the Enterprise and other kinds of operators with respect to conditions for admission and obligations. It is prescribed that

> [t]he obligations applicable to contractors shall apply to the Enterprise. Notwithstanding the provisions of article 153, paragraph 3, and Annex III, article 3, paragraph 5, of the Convention, a plan of work for the Enterprise upon its approval shall be in the form of a contract concluded between the Authority and the Enterprise.[79]

Nations Convention on the Law of the Sea, Part XI Regime and the International Seabed Authority: A Twenty-Five Year Journey (Brill 2022). Both authors from Africa emphasized the operationalization of the Enterprise as a means to apply the principle of CHM.

76 Report of the Chair of the LTC, ISBA/26/C/12, 2020, paras. 37–41.

77 Report of the Special Representative of the Secretary-General of the ISA for the Enterprise, ISBA/27/C/14, 2022.

78 Edwin Egede, Mati Pal and Eden Charles, 'A study related to issues on the operationalization of the Enterprise: legal, technical and financial implications for the International Seabed Authority and for States parties to the United Nations Convention on the Law of the Sea', Technical Report 1/2019 (International Seabed Authority, 2019).

79 Section 2, paragraph 4, Annex to the 1994 Agreement.

Therefore, the Enterprise as a contractor acts on an equal footing with States as contractors or other private contractors.

In the second layer, the Enterprise is an organ of the ISA.[80] In effect, it is exactly due to the Enterprise that the ISA is regarded as a *sui generis* international organization: the only international organization to date that can develop mineral resources in the Area by itself. Pursuant to Article 170(2) of the UNCLOS, the Enterprise shall act in accordance with the general policies of the Assembly and the directives of the Council. This means that the Enterprise is under the direct control of the two decision-making organs, and the purpose of the operation is subject to the purpose of the ISA as a whole, namely to safeguard common heritage of mankind. However, that is the only one aspect of its relationship with the ISA.

The other facet is the third layer of the legal aspect of the Enterprise. 'Albeit within the framework of the international legal personality of the Authority',[81] 'the Enterprise shall enjoy autonomy in the conduct of its operations'.[82] Specifically, the Enterprise assumes obligations and liabilities independent from the ISA, which is reflected in Annex IV of the UNCLOS where it prescribes, 'Nothing in this Convention shall make the Enterprise liable for the acts or obligations of the Authority, or make the Authority liable for the acts or obligations of the Enterprise.'[83] Hence, there is a wall of separation between the Enterprise and the ISA concerning liability. Meanwhile, a wall of separation is also erected between members of the ISA and the Enterprise. Article 3, Annex IV of the UNCLOS prescribes, 'without prejudice to article 11, paragraph 3, of this Annex, no member of the Authority shall be liable by reason only of its membership for the acts or obligations of the Enterprise'.[84] The third

80 Article 158(2), UNCLOS.

81 Article 170(2), UNCLOS.

82 Article 2(2), Annex IV (Statute of the Enterprise), UNCLOS.

83 When talking about the legal personality, obligation and liability of the Enterprise, distinction should be made between that under international law and national law (legal status of the Enterprise within the territory of member states is without controversy) (see Article 13 of Annex IV to the Convention). However, whether the Enterprise, as an organ of the ISA, possesses international personality and therefore can be held liable under international law is arguable. This kind of problem is also faced by some international financial organizations which are subsidiary organs to international organizations. Reference can be made to Schermers and Blokker, *International Institutional Law* (2011), para. 1591.

84 This provision can be seen as a key example of the 'no-liability of member States rule' which is discussed in detail in Chapter 8 of this book.

layer is critical since this is the reason why the discussion of the ISA's liability is divided into two separate parts: the liability of the Enterprise as the contractor (in Chapter 6) and the liability of the ISA as the regulator (in Chapter 8).

With such a *sui generis* nature of the organ, the operationalization of the Enterprise can draw no lessons from practice of any other organs; it will be a matter of trial and error. The independent functioning of the Enterprise is a matter of importance, because, as the African Group noted, 'the Enterprise is the only mechanism by which the vast majority of developing States can participate in activities in the Area' and it is a way to implement the principle of CHM.[85]

3.3.7 *Summary and Comments*

The ISA is a small specialized international organization that is mandated to control activities and administer mineral resources in the Area; meanwhile, through the Enterprise, it can conduct activities in the Area itself. The ISA comprises the following seven organs and subsidiary bodies: the Assembly, the Council, Legal and Technical Commission, Secretariat, Finance Committee, Economic Planning Commission and the Enterprise. Upon completion of the organizational work in the initial years since 1996, it proceeded on to substantive work. They have encountered various practical problems during operations. For the Assembly, the largest problem is the poor attendance at meetings, which jeopardizes its decision-making competence. The two subsidiary bodies – the LTC and the Finance Committee – face similar problem of some members' absence from or passive participation in meetings. To tackle this problem, voluntary trust funds have been set up to subsidize participation of meetings of representatives or expert members from developing countries. Most importantly, since the LTC plays a critical role in the functioning of the ISA, its constitution and operation have been vital issues. In the past more than twenty-five years, the size of the LTC has been expanded several times. But it is criticized for lack of transparency with work and in particular for inadequacy of expertise of its members in dealing with technical problems. In recent years, with the prospect of a soon-to-come exploitation era, the election, work methods and expertise

85 Request for consideration by the Council of the African Group's operationalization of the 'Enterprise', 6 July 2018, statement before the Council: www.isa.org.jm/files/files/documents/alg-oboag-entp.pdf.

inadequacy of the LTC have increasingly become a matter of concern. Against this background, Belgium proposed 'transparency', 'independence' and 'expertise' as the three principles for strengthening environmental scientific capacity of the ISA.[86] The Secretariat, being responsible to support the LTC, needs to strengthen its technical expertise too. The transition to the exploitation era has institutional implications on other organs of the ISA too: the Council doubles its frequency of meetings, and the independent operation of the Economic Planning Commission and the Enterprise is beginning to be taken under consideration. Additionally, along with a rapidly increasing workload and institutional changes, the past years have seen a steady rise in the budget of the ISA too. These findings on the organizational aspect of the ISA should be kept in mind when turning to the powers and obligations of the ISA relating to marine environmental protection since the former constitutes the very physical basis on which the latter can be discussed. The questions to be asked are: is the ISA fit for the purpose? Is the marine environment protected and preserved? And ultimately, is the principle of CHM lived up with?

3.4 Powers and Obligations Relating to Marine Environmental Protection

Section 1, paragraph 5, Annex to the 1994 Agreement lists specifically eleven tasks of the ISA during a period of time 'between the entry into force of the Convention and the approval of the first plan of work for exploitation'. Owing to the fact that exploitation has not yet commenced, discussion of the powers and obligations of the ISA relating to marine environmental protection in this section, in terms of both theory and practice, must be within the scope of those eleven tasks. Second, the exercise of the function of marine environmental protection by the ISA is, in practice, interconnected intricately with the exercise of its other functions, in particular, the functions of administering resources and encouraging and promoting marine scientific research. Because environmental consideration is an integral part of DSM activities and it is impossible to safeguard the marine environment without adequate marine scientific knowledge. Third, powers of the ISA relating to marine environmental protection are at the same time its obligations; albeit

[86] 'Strengthening Environmental Scientific Capacity of the ISA', a non-paper submission by Belgium to the ISA on 22 June 2018.

presenting from a different angle, both powers and obligations are for the purpose of fulfilling the function. This proposition is derived from the belief that 'the finality of international organizations is functional' and that 'functional finality embodies three normative aspects: the authorization aspect, the moderation aspect and the obligation aspect'.[87] Bearing these three points in mind, and based upon the analysis of the structure of the ISA, powers and functions and decision-making procedures of its organs, this section seeks to answer the questions of how the ISA acted (in practice), must or may act (in theory) in order to protect the marine environment in DSM.

3.4.1 Power to Adopt Rules, Regulations and Procedures

Article 145 of the UNCLOS empowers the ISA to adopt appropriate rules, regulations and procedures for the effective protection of the marine environment. However, it is noted that initially this power was not entrusted to the ISA but to States.[88] During the negotiations on the UNCLOS, the designation of power changed from States to the ISA[89] and such a change was eventually endorsed in Article 145 of the UNCLOS. Part XII UNCLOS also addresses the subject matter of marine environmental protection in DSM. Article 209(1) reaffirms the necessity of international rules, regulations and procedures for protecting the marine environment from detrimental effect arising from activities in the Area, making cross-reference to Article 145; it further states that 'such rules, regulations and procedures shall be re-examined from time to time as necessary'. Article 209(2), on the other hand, stipulates that 'states shall adopt laws and regulations', and that 'the requirements of such laws and regulations shall be no less effective than the international rules, regulations and procedures referred to in paragraph 1'. Thus, there is international as well as national norms concerning DSM. Yet, only the adoption of international norms is subject to investigation in this section.

87 Schermers and Blokker, *International Institutional Law* (2011) paras. 16–17.

88 Declaration of Principles Governing the Sea Bed and Ocean Floor, and the Subsoil Thereof, Beyond the Limits of National Jurisdiction, UN GA Resolution 2749 (XXV), adopted on 24 October 1970, para. 11.

89 Nandan, Lodge and Rosenne (eds.), *United Nations Convention on the Law of the Sea 1982* (2002) 194 (Article 28, paragraph (xii)(c), of the ISNT/Part I [1975]).

3.4.1.1 Scope of the Power

In accordance with Articles 145 and 209 of UNCLOS, the scope of the power of the ISA is confined to 'activities in the Area', the meaning of which is defined in Article 1 as 'all activities of exploration for, and exploitation of, the resources of the Area'. Meanwhile, Article 133 defines the term 'resources' as 'all solid, liquid or gaseous mineral resources *in situ* in the Area at or beneath the seabed, including polymetallic nodules'. Taken together, it means the power to adopt rules, regulations and procedures can only be exerted in respect to the exploration for and exploitation of mineral resources in the Area. However, under Article 17, paragraph 2(f), Annex III to the UNCLOS, the scope of the regulatory power relating to marine environmental protection extends to 'shipboard processing immediately above a mine site of minerals derived from that mine site'. In practice, the exercise of such power extends further to cover the prospecting activities in the Area. The three sets of Exploration Regulations adopted by the ISA impose almost the same environmental obligations on prospectors as those on contractors.[90] Considering the broad function of marine environmental protection in DSM and the fact that no objection to the expansion of the power based on either Article 17, paragraph 2(f), Annex III to the UNCLOS or the Exploration Regulations, it is fair to conclude that the scope of the ISA's power to adopt rules, regulations and procedures relating to marine environmental protection is not restricted to the exploration for and exploitation of mineral resources in the Area, but includes other closely related activities like on-board processing and prospecting. However, an open question is whether such a power can be extended further to other activities in the Area which are not directly connected to mining activities, such as bioprospecting and exploitation and use of marine genetic resources.[91]

[90] In the notification of prospecting, the prospector shall submit a satisfactory written undertaking that it will protect marine environment. Data relating to environmental protection shall be transferred along with the notification. The prospector is also required to take preventive measures, applying a precautionary approach and best environmental practices. Furthermore, the prospector 'shall cooperate with the Authority in the establishment and implementation of programmes for monitoring and evaluating the potential impacts of the exploration for and exploitation of polymetallic nodules on the marine environment'. In addition, it is a compulsory obligation for the prospector to submit an annual report to the ISA. The 2013 Exploration Regulation on Nodule (ISBA/19/A/9); the 2010 Exploration Regulations on Sulphides (ISBA/20/A/10); the 2012 Exploration Regulations on Crusts (ISBA/20/A/9).

[91] The topic of marine genetic resources has been under consideration in three fora: Convention on Biological Diversity Conference of Parties; UN Ad Hoc Open-ended

3.4.1.2 Exercise of the Power: Organs and Procedures

Questions then arise as to which specific organs of the ISA are to exercise such power and how. The exercise of the quasi-legislative power by the ISA, as can be inferred from Articles 160, 162 and 165, involves three organs sequentially: the LTC, Council and Assembly. First and foremost, the LTC is to 'formulate and submit to the Council the rules, regulations and procedures' and to 'keep such rules, regulations and procedures under review'.[92] Importantly, the LTC is to 'prepare assessment of the environmental implications of activities in the Area' and take into account 'assessments of the environmental implications of activities in the Area' when formulating or amending rules, regulations and procedures.[93] Also, the LTC may take into account 'views of recognized experts' when making recommendations to the Council on the protection of the marine environment.[94] The draft rules, regulations and procedures and the amendments thereto are then submitted to the Council who will decide whether to adopt and to apply them provisionally.[95] Finally, upon an approval from the Assembly, the rules, regulations and procedures or amendments adopted and provisionally applied by the Council will become definitely effective.[96] It is seen that the LTC plays the most

Informal Working Group to study issues relating to the conservation and sustainable use of marine biological diversity beyond areas of national jurisdiction (BBNJ) (www.un.org/Depts/los/biodiversityworkinggroup/biodiversityworkinggroup.htm); and the annual session of the ISA. Many resolutions have been adopted under the former two fora. In the annual reports of the Secretary-General of the ISA, the issue of the marine genetic resources is touched upon but no conclusion has been reached on the role of the ISA. The ISA participates, makes interventions in the inter-government conferences on BBNJ; it also organizes side events during the conferences. On these occasions, however, the ISA confined itself to introduce objectively what it had done relating to the protection of the flora and fauna (that is, the biodiversity); it seemed not keen to play an active role in the ongoing negotiation BBNJ legal regime. Some scholarly literature, on the other hand, intend to see a more positive role of the ISA in this management of marine genetic resources. See: Lyle Glowka, 'Genetic Resources, Marine Scientific Research and the International Seabed Area' (1999) 8(1) *RECIEL*; Tullio Scovazzi, 'Mining Protection of the Environment, Scientific Research and Bioprospecting: Some Considerations on the Role of the International Sea-Bed Authority' (2004) 19 *IJMCL* 383.

92 Article 165, paragraph 2 (f) and (g), UNCLOS.

93 Ibid.

94 Article 165, paragraph 2(d) and (e), UNCLOS.

95 Article 162, paragraph 2(o)(ii), UNCLOS.

96 Article 160, paragraph 2(f)(ii), UNCLOS. Considering that the draft rules, regulations and procedures and the amendments thereto could become provisionally (but without time limits) effective once the Council adopts them, the role of Assembly in the quasi-legislative process is less important.

critical role in the exercise of quasi-legislative power of the ISA because it is the LTC that is entrusted with formulating draft regulations which form the basis on which the Council and the Assembly may adopt legally binding instruments.

In practice, to date, the ISA has adopted three sets of regulations covering prospecting and exploration for polymetallic nodules, polymetallic sulphides and cobalt-rich ferromanganese crusts.[97] The three sets of Exploration Regulations have the same structure and are very similar in contents. In particular, they encompass a common section which prescribes the environmental obligations of all participants in DSM: the prospector/ contractor, the sponsoring State and the ISA itself. Furthermore, the ISA is currently in the process of drafting regulations for exploitation. Section 3.5 comments preliminarily on that work in respect of environmental protection.

3.4.2 *Issuing Recommendations, Standards and Guidelines*

The LTC not only plays the most critical role in the exercise of quasi-legislative power of the ISA, but also has large influence on contractors through its issuance of recommendations, standards and guidelines. According to the Exploration Regulations,

> [the] LTC may from time to time issue recommendations of a technical or administrative nature for the guidance of contractors to assist them in the implementation of the rules, regulations and procedures of the Authority.[98]

So far, the LTC has issued three sets of Recommendations on the conduct of environmental impact assessment (EIA),[99] the preparation of annual

[97] Regulations on Prospecting and Exploration for Polymetallic Nodules in the Area, 2000 (ISBA/6/A/18), revised in 2013 at the 19th session of the Council (ISBA/19/C/17), approved by the Assembly during the 19th session (ISBA/19/A/9). Regulations on Prospecting and Exploration for Polymetallic Sulphides in the Area, 2010 (ISBA/16/A/12/Rev.1). Regulations on Prospecting and Exploration for Cobalt-rich Ferromanganese Crusts in the Area, 2012 (ISBA/18/A/11). In this book, frequently the three sets of Regulations are collectively referred to as the 'Exploration Regulations'.

[98] Regulation 39, the 2013 Exploration Regulations on Nodules, ISBA/19/C/17.

[99] The LTC has issued Recommendations for the Guidance for the EIA with respect to Polymetallic Nodules in 2001 (ISBA/7/LTC/1/REV.1), one year after the adoption of the 2000 Exploration Regulations on Nodules. The Recommendations have been revised three times: First in 2010 (ISBA/16/LTC/7), after the adoption of the Exploration Regulations on Sulphides. Then in 2013, one year after the adoption of the 2012 Exploration Regulations on Crusts. The 2013 version is a comprehensive set of

reports of the contractor[100] and the designation of Areas of Particular Environmental Interests (APEI) in the Clarion Clipperton Zone (CCZ) by the ISA.[101] According to Brager et al., a careful analysis of these Recommendations 'provides a list of 100 environmental requirements' related to the physical, chemical, geological and, most notably, biological aspects of the marine environment.[102] These documents specify, to a large extent, the environmental requirements of contractors, in particular, with respect to the marine environmental baseline studies as well as the collection, statistical processing, assessment and management of marine environmental baseline data. They also set out the detailed measurements (of currents and particulate matter, water properties, particle flux, etc.) needed to be taken.

The LTC incorporates new knowledge into Recommendations by regular amendments. The Recommendations on EIA is a key example. As explained in the introduction of the 2019 Recommendations on EIA, it is because the marine scientific knowledge keeps developing, in particular, 'recent years have witnessed a revolution in the development of knowledge and technology in deep-sea science' that the LTC updates the 2013 Recommendations on EIA on the basis of 'outputs from workshops and programmes'.[103] Because the Recommendations on EIA place environmental requirements of the contractor on basis of the latest status of marine scientific knowledge and technology, Lodge et al. argued that the Recommendations 'may be regarded as best environmental practice'.[104]

environmental guidelines covering all three kinds of mineral resources (ISBA/19/LTC/8); it retains the structure of the original version. Finally in 2019, the 2013 version was updated and replaced by the document 'Recommendations for the Guidance of Contractors for the Assessment of the Possible Environmental Impacts arising from Exploration for Marine Minerals in the Area' (ISBA/25/LTC/6).

100 Recommendations for the format and structure of annual reports included as an Annex of the Evaluation of the annual reports submitted by contractors, ISBA/8/LTC/2, 2002; Recommendations for the Guidance of Contractors on the Content, Format and Structure of Annual Reports, ISBA/21/LTC/15, 2015.

101 Recommendations on the Designation of Areas of Particular Environmental Interests in the CCZ, ISBA/17/LTC/7, 2011.

102 Stefan Brager, Gabriela Q Romero Rodriguez and Sandor Mulsow, 'The Current Status of Environmental Requirements for Deep Seabed Mining Issued by the International Seabed Authority' (2020) 114 *Marine Policy*.

103 The 2019 Recommendations on EIA, para. 4 and para. 57 of Annex I.

104 Michael Lodge et al., 'Seabed Mining: International Seabed Authority Environmental Management Plan for the Clarion-Clipperton Zone: A Partnership Approach' (2014) 49 *Marine Policy* 66–72, 68.

Presently, when the Exploitation Regulations are under development, the LTC is simultaneously drafting Standards and Guidelines which will constitute an integral part of the exploitation regulatory framework.[105] With regard to the environmental protection, setting environmental performance standards is a top priority task because it is necessary to implement the environmental rules broadly depicted in draft Exploitation Regulations. And these environmental performance standards should be of mandatory nature. Nevertheless, the LTC's setting up of environmental performance standards will face enormous challenges, including but not limiting to the following factors: the inadequacy of environmental data and information, the inability to set precise and quantitative thresholds and trigger points, the nascent nature of the industry and the lack of a well-functioning self-regulatory industry association.[106] It is also thought that the LTC should issue guidelines on environmental management systems and with regard to an environmental assessment framework, etc. Unlike standards, guidelines would be of recommendatory nature and more easily be modified. 'Guidelines will give the regulatory framework the necessary flexibility to be adaptive and responsive to new technology, information and knowledge.'[107]

3.4.3 *Safeguarding the Marine Environment while Administering Activities*

Besides exercising quasi-legislative power by the Council and the Assembly (upon the recommendation of the LTC), and issuing recommendations for guidance by the LTC which aims to assist contractors in implementing their environmental obligations under the Exploration Regulations, the ISA has regulatory powers to ensure contractors' compliance with their environmental obligations.

3.4.3.1 Approval of Plans of Work

The UNCLOS confers the monopolistic power on the ISA in controlling activities and administering resources in the Area at the international level.[108]

[105] Content and development of standards and guidelines for activities in the Area under the Authority's regulatory framework, Note by the Secretariat, ISBA/25/C/3, 2019.

[106] Ibid., para. 18.

[107] Ibid., para. 13.

[108] Articles 153(1) and 157(1), UNCLOS. In comparison with Article 153(1), Article 157(1) omits the phrase 'carry out'. However, it is clear that the ISA can, through its operational

This is the centralized international administration which contains an international licensing system. In accordance with Article 153(3) of UNCLOS, 'Activities in the Area shall be carried out in accordance with a formal written plan of work drawn up in accordance with Annex III and approved by the Council after review by the LTC'. The approval of a plan of work shall be 'in the form of contract'.[109] The question is how this licensing system influences contractors' compliance with its environmental obligations. In accordance with the Exploration Regulations, an applicant must submit, *inter alia*, environmental data and information to the ISA for approval of the plan of work. The data and information will then be reviewed by the LTC. The LTC will make recommendation to the Council on approval of the plan of work only if, in the LTC's opinion, 'the proposed plan of work for exploration will provide effective protection and preservation of the marine environment including, but not restricted to, the impact on biodiversity'.[110] In other words, assuming environmental obligations is a necessary condition for being granted the contract, that is, the licence to carry out activities in the Area. Therefore, by placing environmental requirements as prerequisites for an approval of the plan of work, the ISA has an undeniable power in securing compliance with environmental requirements prior to the commencement of exploration activities. Foreseeably, the same rationale will work at the exploitation stage too.

3.4.3.2 Annual Report Review and Periodic Review

Upon the approval of a plan of work, a fifteen-year contract on exploration will be granted. Thereafter, the ISA has the duty to supervise the implementation of the contract by the contractor, including ensuring the compliance of the contractor with environmental obligations.[111] The most important means is the annual report and review mechanism. The contractor must submit annual reports to the Secretary-General of the ISA; those reports must cover certain information, including information on 'the results obtained from environmental monitoring

arm – the Enterprise – carry out activities in the Area by itself. Therefore, it is advisable to understand Article 157(1) in line with Article 153(1).

109 Article 153(3) and Annex III, Article 11, UNCLOS.

110 Regulation 18 and Annex IV (standard clauses for exploration contract) section 5, the 2013 Exploration Regulations on Nodules, ISBA/19/C/17.

111 As of the 27th session (July 2022), there have been thirty-one exploration contracts in force (nineteen for polymetallic nodules, seven for polymetallic sulphides and five for cobalt-rich ferromanganese crusts) which involve twenty-two contractors, the 2022 Annual Report of the Secretary-General of the ISA, ISBA/27/A/2.

programmes, including observations, measurements, evaluations and analyses of environmental parameters'.[112]

> The objective of the reporting requirements is to establish a mechanism whereby the Authority, through the LTC, can be provided with the information necessary to carry out its responsibilities under the Convention, particularly those relating to the protection of the marine environment from the harmful effects and activities in the Area.[113]

Therefore, it is important for the ISA to make sure that contractors submit annual reports which contain the required environmental data. For the purpose of improving the availability of reliable data, the LTC issued recommendations on annual reports and updated it in light of practice. In the observations of a few members of the LTC, the revised Recommendations made a big progress by requiring contractors to submit raw environmental data in standardized format.[114] They also contend that 'the development of good practices for the annual reporting and data submission by contractors is crucial for the assessment of the role of the ISA as a regulator and its responsibility to ensure the protection of the marine environment'.[115]

At the same time, the LTC, with the assistance from the Secretariat, is entrusted with reviewing those reports. How does the LTC review an annual report submitted by a contractor? First, the Secretariat is required by the LTC to 'undertake a technical evaluation of the reports, which include a detailed analysis of the contractors' activities'.[116] The LTC, in turn, 'establishes a subcommittee to assist the Secretariat in preparing a draft evaluation of the annual reports'.[117] Second, 'the annual reports of contractors are to be made available to members of the Commission through a secure website' in order to enable them to be better prepared for meetings.[118] Third, the LTC is divided into working groups based on different subject matters to review the reports. Take the meeting in July 2013 as an example, when reviewing annual reports, the LTC was divided

[112] Section 10, paras. 1 and 2, Annex IV (the standard clauses for exploration contract) to the 2013 Exploration Regulations on Nodules, ISBA/19/A/9.

[113] The 2004 Report of the Secretary-General of the ISA, ISBA/10/A/3, para. 107.

[114] Pedro Madereira et al., 'Exploration of Polymetallic Nodules in the Area: Reporting Practices, Data Management and Transparency' (2016) 70 *Marine Policy* 101–107, 104. Authors of the article were members of the LTC.

[115] Ibid., 107.

[116] The 2014 Summary Report of the Chair of the LTC, ISBA/20/C/20, para. 6.

[117] The 2002 Report of the Chairman of the LTC, ISBA/8/C/6, para. 5.

[118] The 2014 Summary Report of the Chair of the LTC, ISBA/20/C/20, para. 6.

into four working groups on (a) environmental matters, (b) legal and financial matters, (c) training and (d) technical matters.[119] Finally, the result of the review is conveyed to contractors through the Secretary-General in the form of 'evaluative report'.

Annual reports have been submitted and reviewed since 2002.[120] There have been problems in practices of both the submission, data management and review. With respect to the submission, the failure to submit annual report in a timely manner is one, submission not made in a uniform format is another. In response to these problems, the LTC placed a high value on the timely submission of annual reports by contractors and suggested contractors use a format designed by the LTC for their annual reports in order to facilitate the review. Yet the largest problem is that the LTC found the situation with data submission on the part of contractors and data management on the part of the Secretariat of the ISA unsatisfactory:

> Currently, the completeness of data submission, including metadata and cruise reports, is unsatisfactory. Furthermore, in terms of internal procedures, including data-handling processes and verification, the Authority lacks a centralized application that adequately displays data and allows interrogation.[121]

To address this problem, the Secretariat launched in 2016 and completed in 2019 a data management programme which 'saw the delivery of a fit-for-purpose database and application interface to store the ISA's digital data'.[122] Through this database, the environmental data will be made available to the public. With respect to review,

> Over the years, the system of reviewing the annual reports of contractors has become cumbersome and time consuming both for the secretariat and

[119] The 2013 Summary Report of the Chair of the LTC, ISBA/19/C/14, para. 7.

[120] The 2002 Report of the Chairman of the LTC, ISBA/8/C/6, para. 5.

[121] The 2013 Summary Report of the Chair of the LTC, ISBA/19/C/14, para. 9.

[122] The 2019 Report of the Secretary-General of the ISA, ISBA/25/A/2, para. 66. Prior to the data management programme, the Secretariat operated a Central Data Repository (CDR) system, starting in 2000 (ISBA/9/LTC/3). In 2014, the Secretariat proposed the development of a global deep sea database (the 2014 Summary Report of the Chair of the LTC, ISBA/20/C/20, para. 38). In 2015, the LTC identified the implementation of the database management strategy as a high priority action in the context of the development of the Exploitation Regulations (ISBA/21/C/16, para. 36). In 2016, the LTC considered the initial implementation of database management programme (ISBA/22/LTC/15).

> for the members of the LTC, particularly as the number of annual reports has increased, as well as their length and complexity.[123]

This situation caused that the LTC has been deficient in providing valuable feedback to the contractor. In a word, although both the LTC and the Secretariat have taken measures to address the practical problems with the implementation of the annual report and review mechanism,[124] further efforts are still needed for safeguarding the marine environment.

Periodic review is another mechanism through which the ISA could safeguard the marine environment while administering activities. The fifteen-year tenure for each contract on exploration is divided into three five-year phases. At the end of each phase, there is a periodic review of the implementation of the plan of work jointly conducted by the contractor and the Secretary-General of the ISA.[125] And in light of the review, the contractor shall indicate its programme of activities for the following five-year period, including such adjustments to its previous programme of activities as are necessary.[126] Through this mechanism, the ISA and the contractor can update a contract without amending it since the contractor can adjust the plan of work every five years and such adjustments, once approved by the ISA, are automatically incorporated in the contract. In practice, the Secretary-General of the ISA plays a leading role in the five-year periodic review process.[127] To start with, the Secretary-General initiates the periodic review process by inviting all contractors to submit, in addition to their annual reports, a comprehensive report of the exploration work carried out to date and data and results obtained, including any data not yet supplied to the ISA. Then, the key step is the bilateral discussion between the Secretary-General, or his representative, and each contractor over the implementation of the

[123] Comments by the Secretary-General on the recommendations contained in the final report on the periodic review of the International Seabed Authority pursuant to Article 154 of the United Nations Convention on the Law of the Sea, Report of the Secretary-General, ISBA/23/A/5/Rev.1, 2017, para. 11.

[124] For instance, the LTC provided guidance on the format and structure for annual reports, the standardized data can be entered directly into database. The Secretariat streamlined internal processes for review of annual reports through the establishment of the Contract Management Unit.

[125] Regulation 28, the 2013 Exploration Regulations of Nodules, ISBA/19/C/17.

[126] Ibid.

[127] The periodic review process described below is mainly based on the 2013 Report of the Secretary-General of the ISA on 'Periodic review of the implementation of the plans of work for exploration for polymetallic nodules in the Area', ISBA/19/C/9/Rev.1, paras. 5, 7 and 9.

plan of work. This step is very useful for achieving better communication and understanding between the ISA and the contractor. Following the bilateral discussion, the review process concludes with an exchange of letters between the two parties. Meanwhile, the Secretary-General reports on the period review to the LTC and the Council.[128]

3.4.3.3 EIS Review and Other Means

Among the documents the contractor is required to submit during application for approval of plans of work and annual reporting include a key one – environmental impact statement (EIS); review the EIS is usually conducted by the LTC in the process of approval of plans of work and the review of annual reports. Considering the particular importance of EIA as a tool for environmental protection, EIS review should be singled out. This point will be discussed in detail, in combination with obligations of the contractor to conduct EIA and submit EIS, in Section 4.3.1. Additionally, inspection[129] and instituting legal proceedings against contractors before the SDC[130] are two other means available for the ISA to safeguard the marine environment while administering activities. So far, neither means has been used in practice. Yet, when exploitation starts, it is expected that inspection would become a regulator means to resort[131] to and chances for instituting proceedings would become bigger.

3.4.4 Responding to Environmental Emergencies

In the event of an (risk of) environmental emergency, the ISA's response embodies five aspects. First, once the Secretary-General is aware of an incident (either upon receiving a report from a contractor or on his/her own), he/she shall make it known, in particular, to organs and members of the ISA.[132] This timely notification requirement, being analogous to that in the 1986 Convention on Early Notification of a Nuclear Accident, shall include the provision of relevant information of the incident as early as possible. Secondly, facing (a risk) of environmental emergency, the

[128] Regulation 28(3), the 2013 Exploration Regulations on Nodules, ISBA/19/C/17.
[129] Article 162, paragraph 2(z), UNCLOS.
[130] Article 162, paragraph 2(u), UNCLOS.
[131] Regulations 96–100 of the 2019 draft Exploitation Regulations set out rules about inspection, ISBA/25/C/WP.1.
[132] Regulations 33(1) and 33(2), the 2013 Exploration Regulations on Nodules, ISBA/19/C/17.

LTC may hold a special meeting and non-members of the LTC are allowed to participate in that meeting.[133] Thirdly, the Council may issue emergency orders, including orders for suspension or adjustment of operations, to prevent serious harm to the marine environment, taking into account the recommendation from the LTC.[134] Fourthly, the Secretary-General is empowered to take immediate measures of a temporary nature, pending any action by the Council.[135] Fifthly, if a contractor does not promptly comply with an emergency order, the Council can take practical measures, either by itself or through arrangements with others on its behalf. All these acts and practical measures shall be taken in a timely manner; swift response is critical.

Among the five aspects just described, the Council's decision on whether to issue an Emergency Order, and if so, what the contents of the order are, is the core step. But Emergency Orders can exert a disruptive effect on the operation of DSM activities. Realizing that the contractor may challenge the ISA's Emergency Orders post-facto and seek redress before the SDC, Preller-Borquez suggested that the ISA adopt the sustainable development narrative to provide a strong legal discourse to fend against contractors' challenge.[136] True, as will be shown in Section 4.2.1, sustainable development has become a general environmental principle which integrates environmental and social considerations into economic development. Under the narrative of sustainable development, a restriction on economic development can be reasonably justified on the basis of environmental protection. That is, in our case, an Emergency Order requiring a contractor to adjust, halt or stop DSM operation for the purpose of preventing serious environmental damage is justified under the sustainable development principle.

There is little controversy at the conceptual level that issuance of an Emergency Order for environmental protection is justified. However, practically speaking, the key question is whether there are scientific evidences of (imminent) serious environmental damage. If there are, then the ISA may issue an Emergency Order, requiring the contractor to take preventive measures under the prevention principle; if no

[133] Rule 53(4), Rules of Procedure of the Legal and Technical Commission, 2000.

[134] Article 162, paragraph 2(w) and Article 165, paragraph 2(k), UNCLOS.

[135] Regulations 33(7) and 33(3), the 2013 Exploration Regulations on Nodules, ISBA/19/C/17.

[136] Sebastian Preller-Borquez, 'Integrating Sustainable Development into the Adoption of Emergency Orders for the Protection of the Common Heritage of Mankind and the Marine Environment' (2022) 37 *IJMCL* 73–88.

established scientific evidences but the concern of (imminent) serious environmental damage is not a mere speculation, the ISA could still require the contractor to take measures under the precautionary approach. Both the prevention principle and the precautionary approach are subjacent to the sustainable development principle. Employing either must be conditioned on the results of an evaluation of the impact on the marine environment and monitoring. From a legal perspective, judgment over the correctness in the ISA's determination of the existence of a (risk of) serious environmental damage and the appropriateness of the measure the ISA demands or takes must be made against environmental standards prescribed in Regulations, Standards and Guidelines which are in turn determined as well as confined by the current state of scientific knowledge, technological availability and practical capacity of the contractor.

Owing perhaps to the practical as well as legal requirements which are not easy to be satisfied, as will be argued in Section 4.3.2, the centre for preparing for and responding to environmental emergency is shifted from the ISA to the contractor in the draft Exploitation Regulations. It is expected that the ISA's issuance of Emergency Orders would be done only in exceptional circumstances when the contractor evidently fails to take its role in preparing for and responding to environmental emergency.

3.4.5 *Obligation to Apply the Precautionary Approach*

For the ISA, application of a precautionary approach is a self-imposed obligation. But this self-imposition of obligation did not happen unexpectedly; the Exploration Regulations simply incorporated a rule widely accepted in international environmental law. Section 4.2.3 will examine in detail the historic development, nature and meanings of the precautionary approach/principle as well as its relationship with the prevention principle. Most of those discussions can apply, *mutatis mutandis*, to the ISA, because the rationale underlying the application of a precautionary approach is the same for the ISA as for the sponsoring State. As will be demonstrated in Chapter 4, the precise legal meaning of the precautionary approach is still controversial. Yet, the challenge lies less at the conceptual level than at the practical level. The pivotal question is what measures and procedures different actors take to implement the precautionary approach.

For the ISA to implement the precautionary approach, Jaeckel highlighted (1) the need to set specific conservation objectives, (2) to enhance the level of transparency of and public participation in DSM governance,

(3) the central role for scientific advice (4) and in particular the establishment of 'a procedural framework that enables effective risk assessment and adjustment of risk management measures'.[137] Indeed, a full implementation of the precautionary approach entails procedural, substantive and scientific requirements as well as institutional adjustment of the ISA. It has become an overarching approach/principle that should be considered along with other principles, approaches and obligations.[138]

What's more, the LTC considers that 'the precautionary approach is not so much an approach to scientific assessment but rather a matter of how the EIA translates into effective and acceptable environmental management'.[139] A distinctive way for the ISA to implement precautionary approach is to employ environmental management tools innovated in practice.[140] Specifically, it employs environmental management strategy to set environmental goals and objectives and strategic environmental directions;[141] it employs adaptive environmental management to 'ensure that the management and monitoring of environmental effects is constantly informed by Best Available Scientific Evidence, Best Available Techniques and Best Environmental Practices';[142] and it

[137] ISA, 'The Implementation of the Precautionary Approach by the International Seabed Authority', Discussion Paper No. 5 (March 2017) 8. This document was prepared by Aline Jaeckel, deriving from her book *The International Seabed Authority and the Precautionary Principle: Balancing Deep Seabed Mineral Mining and Marine Environmental Protection* (Brill 2017).

[138] Note by the Secretariat of the ISA on 'The Implementation of the Precautionary Approach to Activities in the Area', ISBA/25/C/8, 2019.

[139] Report of the Chair of the Legal and Technical Commission summarizing stakeholder feedback on phase 1 draft standards and guidelines, ISBA/27/C/2, 2022.

[140] Aline Jaeckel, 'An Environmental Management Strategy for the International Seabed Authority? The Legal Basis' (2015) 30 *IJMCL* 93–119. Jennifer Durden et al., 'A Procedural Framework for Robust Environmental Management of Deep-Sea Mining Projects Using a Conceptual Model' (2017) 84 *Marine Policy* 193–201. Daniel Jones et al., 'Existing Environmental Management Approaches Relevant to Deep-Sea Mining' (2019) 103 *Marine Policy* 172–181.

[141] Technical Study No. 17, 'Towards an ISA Environmental Management Strategy for the Area', 2017. ISA, Decision of the Assembly of the ISA relating to the strategic plan of the Authority for the period 2019–2023, ISBA/24/A/10, 2018. Aline Jaeckel, 'Strategic Environmental Planning for Deep Seabed Mining in the Area' (2020) 114 *Marine Policy*. Verena Tunnicliffe et al., 'Strategic Environmental Goals and Objectives: Setting the Basis for Environmental Regulation of Deep Seabed Mining' (2020) 114 *Marine Policy*.

[142] ISA, Draft guidelines for the preparation of environmental management and monitoring plans, ISBA/27/C/6, 2022, para. 29. Literature on adaptive management, see Neil Craik, 'Implementing Adaptive Management in Deep Seabed Mining: Legal and Institutional Challenges' (2020) *Marine Policy* 114. Aline Jaeckel, 'Deep Seabed Mining and Adaptive

employs regional environmental management to furnish participants with 'a proactive area-based management tool to support informed decision-making that balances resource development with conservation'.[143]

So far, the ISA has gained some practical experience in regional environmental management. In 2012, the ISA established nine areas of particular environmental interests in the CCZ for the purpose of environmental management (CCZ-EMP), without explicit legal authorization.[144] Starting from this pioneer CCZ-EMP, the ISA intends to expand the regional environmental management plans (REMPs) to other deep sea areas. In 2018, the ISA identified the Mid-Atlantic Ridge, the Indian Ocean triple junction ridge and nodule-bearing province and the North-west Pacific and South Atlantic for seamounts as the three priority areas for the development of REMPs.[145] Thereupon, related workshops were convened and in-site investigations and research conducted,[146] and

Management: The Procedural Challenges for the International Seabed Authority' (2016) 70 *Marine Policy* 205–211. Jan McDonald and Megan Stules, 'Legal Strategies for Adaptive Management under Climate Change' (2014) 26 *Journal of Environmental Law* 25–53. Byron K. Williams, 'Adaptive Management of Natural Resources – Framework and Issues' (2011) 92(5) *Journal of Environmental Management* 1364–1353.

143 Report of the Secretary-General on 'Preliminary strategy for the development of regional environmental management plans for the Area', ISBA/24/C/3, 2018, para. 5.

144 The Environmental Management Plan for the Clarion-Clipperton Zone was recommended by the LTC in 2011 (ISBA/17/LTC/7) and decided by the Council in 2012 (ISBA/18/C/22). CCZ-EMP is the first regional-scale environmental management plan for the deep seabed. This plan identifies a network of nine areas of particular environmental interests (APEIs) located along the CCZ, outside of the sites attributed to the contractors or reserved for the ISA. This will enable the establishment of reference data, the evaluation of ecological impacts and the study of potential risks that new technologies in mining extraction might present. Discussions over the establishment of CCZ-EMP see: Michael Lodge, 'Some Legal and Policy Considerations Relating to the Establishment of a Representative Network of Protected Areas in the Clarion-Clipperton Zone' (2011) 26(3) *IJMCL* 463–480; Michael Lodge et al., 'Seabed Mining: International Seabed Authority Environmental Management Plan for the Clarion-Clipperton Zone: A Partnership Approach' (2014) 49 *Marine Policy* 66–72; David Johnson and Maria Adelaide Ferreira, 'ISA Areas of Particular Environmental Interest in the Clarion-Clipperton Fracture Zone' (2015) 30 *International Marine and Coastal Law* 559.

145 Report of the Secretary-General on 'Preliminary strategy for the development of regional environmental management plans for the Area', ISBA/24/C/3, 2018, para. 12.

146 Technical Study No. 22, 'Developing A Framework for Regional Environmental Management Plans for Polymetallic Sulphide Deposits on Mid-Ocean Ridges', 2018. ISA, 'Outcomes of the ISA workshops on REMPs held in 2019' note by the Secretariat, ISBA/26/LTC/2, 2020.

recommendation on a general template for REMPs is being drafted by the LTC.[147] REMPs now occupy a very important place in the environmental regulatory system in DSM: the ISA recognized REMPs as one of the strategic directions for environmental protection in its first strategic plan (2019–2023);[148] States as well as non-State actors were unanimous in REMPs' being a precondition that should be in place before exploitation begins;[149] in the 2019 draft Exploitation Regulations, REMPs are considered as one of the fundamental policies.[150] In a word, there seems to be two reasons why REMPs have become so important: one, it reflects a proactive thinking that is consistent with the precautionary approach; the other, it is a spatial management tool that is consistent with an ecosystem approach.[151]

It is noted, however, that REMPs 'are not themselves legal instruments but rather instruments of environmental policy'.[152] Employing environment management tools focuses on the operational level of the ISA's

147 ISA, Decision of the Council concerning a standardized approach for the development, approval and review of regional environmental management plans in the Area, ISBA/26/C/10, 2020. The decision endorsed the following two joint submissions. 'Procedure for the development, approval and review of regional environmental management plans' submitted by the delegations of Germany and the Netherlands with co-sponsorship by Costa Rica, ISBA/26/C/6, 2020. ISA, 'Proposal for a template with minimum requirements for regional environmental management plans: a proposal for a standardized approach' submitted by the delegations of Germany and the Netherlands with co-sponsorship by Costa Rica, ISBA/26/C/7, 2020.

148 Report of the Secretary-General on 'consideration, with a view to adoption, of the draft strategic plan of the International Seabed Authority for the period 2019–2023', ISBA/24/A/4, 2018, para. 28.

149 See the interventions of participants in the 25th session of the ISA in February 2019.

150 Draft regulation 2, ISBA/25/C/WP.1, 2019. It is also seen that the development of REMPs is closely linked to the contractors' obligations concerning EIS, EMMP and the Closure Plan. Draft regulation 47 (Part IV, section 2): the EIS shall be in accordance with the objectives and measures of the relevant REMP; Draft regulation 48: the EMMP shall be in accordance with the relevant REMP; annex VIII: the Closure Plan shall be prepared and implemented in accordance with the Guidelines and the relevant REMP. ISBA/25/C/WP.1, 2019.

151 In the opinions of Christiansen et al., REMPs are consistent with an ecosystem approach, and an ecosystem approach-based REMP has the potential to bring out an integrated biodiversity conservation and management in the Area and the high seas. Sabine Christiansen et al., 'Towards an Ecosystem Approach to Management in Areas Beyond National Jurisdiction: REMPs for Deep Seabed Mining and the Proposed BBNJ Instrument' (2022) 9 *Frontiers in Marine Science*. See also Roberto Danovaro et al., 'An Ecosystem-Based Deep Ocean Strategy' (2017) 355(6324) *Science* 452–454.

152 ISA, note by the Secretariat on 'Relationship between the draft regulations on exploitation of mineral resources in the Area and regional environmental management plans', ISBA/25/C/4, 2019, para. 4.

exercise of its environmental mandate and the results could be achieved. As deep sea environment is an integral and complex system, the ISA must take a holistic and long-term view with both setting of environmental goals and objectives and employment environment management tools. Durden et al. present an environment management framework that could facilitate gathering and synthesis of environmental information and its use in decision-making throughout the phases of a mining project; they also emphasize that environment management will need to improve as the quantity and quality of data increases and technologies are honed.[153] Undoubtedly, environment management is not a fixed but a dynamic process which requires the ISA to learn and change in the process.

Finally, it should be reminded that an emphasis on environment management tools does not mean a disregard of traditional implementation tools, such as EIA, BAT, BEP, monitoring and mitigation measures. It simply means that the focus has changed from compliance with individual tools at a normative level to comprehensive effect of the employment of tools in its totality. This change reflects a new result-oriented thinking of the ISA with respect to the discharge of its environmental mandate.

3.4.6 Promoting and Encouraging Marine Scientific Research

The exercise or fulfillment of each of the five categories of powers or obligations presented above, however, needs to be based on sound marine scientific knowledge. In other words, marine scientific knowledge is the bedrock upon which the ISA can build and implement the legal regime for marine environmental protection. Although it is certainly true that scientific knowledge is also important for sponsoring States and contractors in fulfilling their environmental obligations, that importance is of particular significance for the ISA since the ISA is entrusted with the function of promoting and encouraging marine scientific research. Article 143(2) of the UNCLOS prescribes that

> [t]he Authority may carry out marine scientific research concerning the Area and its resources, and may enter into contracts for that purpose. The Authority shall promote and encourage the conduct of marine scientific

[153] Jennifer Durden et al., 'A Procedural Framework for Robust Environmental Management of Deep-Sea Mining Projects using a Conceptual Model' (2017) 84 *Marine Policy* 193–201.

> research in the Area, and shall coordinate and disseminate the results of such research and analysis when available.[154]

Promoting and encouraging marine scientific research is a goal and at the same time a necessary tool for the ISA. To date, the primary focus of the substantive work of the ISA, as repeatedly mentioned in almost all the annual reports of the Secretary-General, has been on 'the scientific and technical work necessary to carry out its functions under the Convention and the 1994 Agreement and in particular to promote a better understanding of the potential environmental impact of deep seabed mining, when it takes place'.[155]

Within the ISA, it is the Secretariat which takes actions to discharge the mandate of promoting and encouraging marine scientific research. The Secretariat has explored three ways to do so in practice. First, the ISA participates in some marine scientific research projects or initiatives. For many years, the Kaplan Project (2002–2007) had been the only case. The Kaplan Project was a collaborative project undertaken by the ISA with some contractors with the aim of assessing levels of biodiversity, species range and gene flow in the CCZ abyssal nodule provinces in the Pacific Ocean.[156] However, the past years have seen a few more cases, including the ISA's joining the University of Hawaii to 'establish long-term deep sea observatories as part of a global DOOS system to monitor environmental variables and improve understanding of ecosystem functions in the deep sea'; the ISA's being an official partner in the European 'Joint Programming Initiative-Oceans' project 'MiningImpact 2' (JPI-O MiningImpact 2, 2018–2022); the ISA's commitment to the UN Decade

[154] Article 143(2) should be read in conjunction with Article 143(1), as well as Article 256, of the UNCLOS. Article 143(1) states 'marine scientific research in the Area shall be carried out exclusively for peaceful purposes and for the benefit of mankind as a whole, in accordance with Part XIII'. Therefore, subject to Article 256, Article 143 stresses the principle of CHM and the role of the ISA. In contrast, Article 256 states that 'all States, irrespective of their geographical location, and competent international organizations have the right, in conformity with the provisions of Part XI, to conduct marine scientific research in the Area', so it is 'the freedom to conduct marine scientific research' which is highlighted in Article 256. In the words of the Secretary-General of the ISA, 'Articles 143 and 256 represent a delicate balance between opposing views on whether or not marine scientific research in the Area was to be subject to the jurisdiction and control of the Authority' (the 2002 Report of the Secretary-General, para. 39, ISBA/8/A/5).

[155] For example, the 2007 Report of the Secretary-General, ISBA/13/A/2, para. 83.

[156] ISA Technical Study No. 3, 'Biodiversity, Species Ranges, and Gene Flow in the Abyssal Pacific Nodule Province: Predicting and Managing the Impacts of Deep Seabed Mining', 2008.

of Ocean Science; the ISA's cooperation with UNESCO-IOC; and the ISA's association with the Nippon Foundation-GEBCO Seabed 2030 Project.[157] Among them, the JPI-O MiningImpact 2 is prominent. The project attracts a consortium of thirty partners from scientific institutions and industry, spread out across nine European countries, and the ISA. It follows up on the result of the JPI Oceans pilot action on 'ecological aspects of DSM' (2015–2017) which was terminated in December 2017. It will independently study and comprehensively monitor in real time the environmental impact of an industrial trial on mine manganese nodules on the seafloor which will be conducted simultaneously and independently by the Belgian contractor DEME-GSR in the Belgian and German licence area in the CCZ.[158]

Secondly, the Secretariat established an 'Endowment Fund for Marine Scientific Research in the Area' in 2006.[159] The Fund aims to promote and encourage the conduct of marine scientific research in the Area for the benefit of humankind as a whole, in particular by supporting the participation of qualified scientists and technical personnel from developing countries in marine scientific research programmes and offering the opportunity to participate in training, technical assistance and scientific cooperation programmes. The Fund is administered by the Secretariat. In 2011, an advisory panel was appointed by the Secretary-General to evaluate applications for assistance from the Fund. The Endowment Fund is also one of the key mechanisms for enabling capacity-building in the field of marine scientific research in the deep ocean. However, the training opportunity under the Endowment Fund should be distinguished from that provided by the contractor under contracts. The latter is an obligation of the contractor which aims at

[157] Harald Ginzky, Pradeep Singh and Till Markus, 'Strengthening the ISA's Knowledge-Base: Addressing Uncertainties to Enhance Decision-Making' (2020) 114 *Marine Policy*.

[158] The project aims at delivering new and relevant state of the information and knowledge on future deep-sea nodule mining by (1) 'developing, standardizing and testing monitoring concepts and strategies, (2) investigating the presently poorly-known short and intermediate-term environmental impacts of nodule collection, that in turn feed into the proposition of potential mitigation measures and the development of spatial management plans and (3) developing sound methodologies to assess risks and uncertainties that can be implemented in future regulations and guidelines'. Source: https://miningimpact.geomar.de/.

[159] Resolution establishing an Endowment Fund for Marine Scientific Research in the Area, 16 August, 2006, ISBA/12/A/11. Detailed rules and procedures for the administration and utilization of the Fund were adopted in 2007 (ISBA/13/A/6).

securing equal participation in DSM activities while the former aims to promote scientific research.

Thirdly, the most common way is to organize or sponsor 'expert workshops, seminars and meetings', either on its own or in partnership with member States or other international organizations.[160] In practice, recommendations-issuing of the LTC are almost always preceded by one or several same-topic expert workshop(s); the results of workshops form bases on which recommendations are made. This is especially so when the issue under consideration is about environmental protection. To illustrate this point, a few examples have been cited. For instance, the LTC issued Recommendations on the Guidance on EIA in 2001 on the basis of the findings of the workshop on 'Deep Seabed Polymetallic Exploration: Development of Environmental Guidelines' convened by the Secretariat of ISA in collaboration with Chinese government in Sanya, China, in 1998. Also, the Council decided in 2012 to establish environmental management plan for the Central Pacific Clarion Clipperton Zone (CCZ-EMP) in light of the findings of the workshop to develop CCZ-EMP convened by the Secretariat in Kingston, Jamaica, in 2010. Likewise, the drafting of the three sets of Exploration Regulations all drew on the results of a series of workshops. To some extent, the function of these expert workshops, seminars and meetings is comparable to that of the LTC. Both provide the ISA with experts' views on scientific or technical issues. However, the difference is that views of members of the LTC as a subsidiary organ of the ISA have legal implications, while opinions expressed by experts at a meeting convened by the ISA are, at best, sources of information.

The mandate concerning marine scientific research is not marginal but constitutes an indispensable part to the core functions of the ISA. It is for this reason that the Article 154 Review Committee recommends that 'the Secretary-General should be encouraged to consider how to engage more extensively with the scientific community and deep-sea science projects and initiatives related to the Area'.[161] The Secretary-General fully agreed with this recommendation. Yet, he is realistic about what the Secretariat

[160] This opinion is expressed in almost every Report of the Secretary-General, for instance, the 2002 Report, ISBA/8/A/5, para. 40; the 2004 Report, ISBA/10/A/3, para. 123. See also J-P Levy, 'International Seabed Authority: 20 Years', paper submitted at the special session in memory of the 20th Anniversary of the ISA, 2014, 20.

[161] David Johnson et al., 'Final Report on the Periodic Review of the International Seabed Authority Pursuant to Article 154 of the United Nations Convention on the Law of the Sea', 30 December 2016, Recommendation 6.

can do with a limited budget. In his view, it is impossible for the Secretariat to 'carry out any original scientific research or to organize activities and coordinate results on a global scale'; the most efficient way to use the limited available resources would be seeking to 'leverage extra-budgetary funds to engage with the scientific community and support relevant initiatives'.[162] In contrast with the Secretary-General, some scholars have higher expectations with the Secretariat. Ginzky et al. suggested the ISA build 'a proactive knowledge management system' in the process of developing Exploitation Regulations.[163] Yet, taking a proactive knowledge management approach implies to turn the Secretariat into a global knowledge centre in the field of deep ocean sciences, which in turn would mean a significant reform of the ISA. At the same time, the authors were aware that

> [t]he political will to ensure implementation in order to effectively overcome the existing knowledge gaps is still lacking, as the methods and institutional structures within the ISA to enable and support the active pursuit of knowledge generation and information synthesis have clearly not yet been put in place.[164]

Thus, gaps in marine scientific knowledge would continue to be a persistent problem faced by the ISA in the discharge of its environmental mandates. In the long run, how the ISA is to address this problem will not only affect the capacity but also the legitimacy of its exercise of power. Finally, as an auxiliary point, non-confidential information provided by contractors, in particular, with environmental matters may also be a source of marine scientific knowledge. However, where the dividing line lies between confidential and non-confidential information has been controversial.

To summarize, the ISA has so far fulfilled its function to protect the marine environment in DSM through the exercise and fulfillment of the six categories of powers and obligations; no environmental harm has occurred in practice. However, the real challenge to the ISA will be in the exploitation phase when risks to the marine environment caused by

162 Comments by the Secretary-General on the recommendations contained in the final report on the periodic review of the International Seabed Authority pursuant to Article 154 of the United Nations Convention on the Law of the Sea, Report of the Secretary-General, ISBA/23/A/Rev.1, 2017.

163 Ginzky, Singh and Markus, 'Strengthening the ISA's Knowledge-Base: Addressing Uncertainties to Enhance Decision-Making' (2020).

164 Ibid.

exploitation activities will be much larger in comparison with exploration activities. Against this background, the next section discusses preliminarily environmental regulations for exploitation in the Area. The main tasks are to identify the primary challenge to the ISA and possible ways out.

3.5 Ongoing Development of the Exploitation Regulations

Owing to the anticipation that DSM will enter into the exploitation stage in the near future, in 2011 Fiji made a request to the ISA for the formulation of the Exploitation Regulations.[165] As a response, the ISA started the drafting process in 2012.[166] The drafting process was meant to be completed but got delayed several times, as at the 27th session of the ISA (July 2022), a final draft of the Exploitation Regulations has not yet been adopted.[167] In this section, first the features of the drafting work and changed approach to environmental regulation in the exploitation stage will be highlighted. Next, it is proposed to offer possible ways to overcome the fundamental obstacle of environmental protection in DSM – marine scientific knowledge gaps.

3.5.1 Features of the Drafting Work and Changed Approach to Environmental Regulation

A first feature of the ISA's drafting work on Exploitation Regulations is that it alternates taking the drafting work as a whole with dividing the labours on basis of subject matters. In 2016, the LTC decided to take a 'building block' approach towards the drafting work and the environmental matters were dealt with separately and on a priority basis.[168] But

[165] Statement to the Council by the delegation of Fiji at the 17th session in July 2011, ISBA/17/C/22.

[166] Work plan for the formulation of regulations for the exploitation of polymetallic nodules in the Area: Report of the Secretary-General, ISBA/18/C/4, 2012.

[167] Schedules and deadlines for the adoption of Exploitation Regulations were set twice in 2018 and 2019, but neither was met. The ISA had produced five drafts: zero draft in July 2015, the first draft in 2016, the second in 2017, the third in 2018 and the fourth in March 2019.

[168] Discussion Paper on the Development and Drafting of Regulations on Exploitation for Mineral Resources in the Area (Environmental Matters), 2017. This discussion paper was an important document for the development of environmental rules in Exploitation Regulations and related standards and guidelines. In this book, this document will be referred to as the '2017 discussion paper on environmental matters'.

that approach was soon dropped and all issues of the draft Exploitation Regulations were considered together. However, in 2020, the Council decided to set up three informal working groups to advance discussions on the draft Exploitation Regulations with respect to three categories of subject matters.[169] The environmental matters were again identified as complex and important that need to be discussed separately. A second feature is the inclusion of stakeholder consultations in the drafting process.[170] The ISA launched the first round of stakeholder survey in March 2014. Thereafter several rounds of stakeholder consultations were conducted when new versions of draft Exploitation Regulations were put forward. Indeed, the LTC made a commitment to ongoing stakeholder engagement concerning its discharge of the drafting task.[171] To accurately evaluate the effect of stakeholder consultations, empirical research revolving around the following two questions has to be done: who have participated in the consultation processes as stakeholders? To what extent stakeholders' input were considered by the LTC and/or reflected into the new instruments? It is not to take up this empirical research here. It simply attempts to point out that the inclusion of stakeholder consultation may contribute to a better result of the drafting work, enhance the level of legitimacy of the ISA's exercise of its regulatory power and induce a better compliance with the Exploitation Regulations in the future.

Drafting Exploitation Regulations on environmental matters at this time faces a dilemma that, on the one hand, it is generally agreed that environmental rules should be established before large-scale exploitation activities commence, on the other hand, it is difficult to set out such rules in the absence of practical data and information derived from exploitation activities. What's more, there is a fundamental obstacle for both the

169 The three informal working groups cover the following subject matters: (1) protection and preservation of the marine environment; (2) inspection, compliance and enforcement; and (3) institutional matters (including the role and responsibilities of the various organs of the International Seabed Authority, timelines, recourses to independent expertise and stakeholder participation). A facilitator was designated to each of the three informal working groups. ISBA/26/C/11, 2020.

170 Different versions of draft Exploitation Regulations and the stakeholder consultations can be referred to the ISA at: https://isa.org.jm/mining-code/draft-exploitation-regulations.

171 Report of the Chair of the Legal and Technical Commission on the work of the Commission at its session in 2016, ISBA/22/C/17, para. 53; Report of the Chair of the Legal and Technical Commission on the work of the Commission at its session in 2017, ISBA/23/C/13, annex.

drafting task and the ultimate goal of marine environmental protection: the great gaps in scientific knowledge about the marine environment (the deep sea ecosystems) and the impact of exploitation on the marine environment.[172] For these reasons, it was proposed in 2017 that the environmental regulations should only prescribe general rules, which would be supported and operationalized by technical guidance, guidelines and recommendations.[173] This legislative technique meant to afford stability of environmental regulatory framework but at the same time allow flexibility for accommodating the development of marine sciences and technologies and the increase in practical experience in DSM. The ISA seemed to partly endorse this technique. Upon the completion of the 2019 draft Exploitation Regulations, the LTC started the drafting work on Standards and Guidelines.[174] Whatever their legal status and whenever they will be in place, perhaps no one would deny that 'the standards and guidelines are of eminent importance with regard to the *de facto* level of the protection of the marine environment'.[175] This legislative technique of Regulations supplemented by Standards and Guidelines is the third feature of the drafting work.

On the other hand, the draft Exploitation Regulations seems to demonstrate a move to outcome- or results-based environmental regulation;[176] this point has been shown above when the ISA's employment of management tools to implement the precautionary approach is discussed. The draft Exploitation Regulations seems also to show that the ISA's fulfillment of environmental functions at the exploitation stage would become a more cooperative and consultative process. In particular, the ISA would depend on the cooperation and supply of data and

[172] See Section 2.5.2.

[173] Section 4.7 of the 2017 discussion paper on environmental matters.

[174] The LTC is taking a three-phase approach towards the drafting work. It is agreed that the standards will be legally binding on contractors and ISA, whereas the guidelines will be recommendatory in nature. See https://isa.org.jm/mining-code/standards-and-guidelines.

[175] Comments on the Phase 1 draft standard and guidelines by Germany in 2022.

[176] The ISA stated its preference for outcome- or results-based regulation in 'Content and development of standards and guidelines for activities in the Area under the Authority's regulatory framework', Note by the Secretariat, ISBA/25/C/3, 2019, para. 10. Similarly, literature on US environmental law identified a move from 'rule-based' to 'result-based' approach towards environmental regulation. See Daniel J. Fiorino, 'Rethinking Environmental Regulation: Perspectives on Law and Governance' (1999) 23 *Harvard Environmental Law Review*. Robert Durant, Daniel Fiorino and Rosemary O'Leary (eds.), *Environmental Governance Reconsidered: Challenges, Choices, and Opportunities* (MIT 2004).

information from other participants, their active engagement and the effective communication. This point is well reflected in Regulation 3 of the 2019 draft Exploitation Regulations which embodies general obligations of all participants in DSM to cooperate and of exchange of information. It may suggest a transformation of the role of the ISA and signal a new modality of global environmental governance for the deep sea.

3.5.2 *Continual Assessment of Marine Scientific Knowledge*

As indicated earlier, the environmental regulations to be adopted for exploitation are likely to be at a highly abstract level which will need to be supported and operationalized by technical guidance, guidelines and recommendations. Since issuing technical guidance, guidelines and recommendations falls within the mandate of the LTC and it should be based on sound marine scientific knowledge, the LTC will need to assess the current state of marine scientific knowledge on a continual basis. That will be an extremely large task because the marine sciences cover a broad range of scientific areas. On the other hand, however, the LTC is composed of only thirty members who assume volunteering work and it encounters a practical problem of some members' absence from meetings or inactive involvement; it holds meetings only twice a year, each meeting lasts for about ten days. The contrast between the demand of the task and the scientific ability of the LTC is obvious.

Admittedly, as mentioned in Section 3.3.3, the LTC is assisted by the scientific officers at the Secretariat and sometimes by external consultants appointed by the Secretariat or individual marine scientists. Also, as mentioned in Section 3.4.6, the LTC has benefited from workshops and seminars organized by either the ISA or other institutions. These practices have contributed to filling in the expertise gap of the LTC, enabling it to fulfil its environmental functions. However, since environmental challenges at the exploitation stage will be much more extensive and complex, it is argued that employing the existing practices would be insufficient then. Henceforth, the following paragraphs explore two possible new ways.

One possible way is to cooperate closely with existing scientific bodies related to marine sciences, such as the International Oceanographic Commission of the United Nations Educational, Scientific and Cultural Organization (UNESCO-IOC)[177] and the Joint Group of Experts on the

[177] Established in 1960, now the most influential international institution in the field of marine sciences. The UNESCO-IOC has broad presence at both international and

Scientific Aspects of Marine Environmental Protection (GESAMP).[178] Both the UNESCO-IOC and the GESAMP have been operating successfully for over fifty years: they have attracted a large number of marine scientists to get involved in marine environmental protection at the global level; they also are well connected with governments and international organizations. For these reasons, they are important mechanisms for providing scientific advice that is needed for international policymaking for the purpose of marine environmental protection. Close cooperation with the UNESCO-IOC and the GESAMP would certainly offer the advantage of enhancing the capacity of the ILC in integrating updated marine scientific knowledge. Yet, to make use of this advantage, coordination between the three bodies is necessary.

Another way is to establish a new mechanism similar to the Intergovernmental Panel on Climate Change (IPCC) for the purpose of achieving scientific consensus on marine sciences at the global level.[179] 'The IPCC neither undertakes research itself nor monitors climate data, but rather seeks to assess and evaluate the current state of scientific (and related) knowledge'[180] by assessing the published literature.[181] In so doing, the IPCC aims to demonstrate scientific consensus on climate change. Institutionally speaking, the IPCC is a small body: it is composed

regional levels, and *vis-à-vis* both governments and civil societies. Such broad presence is achieved through many regional subsidiary bodies as well as various partnerships. Source: http://ioc-unesco.org.

178 Established in 1969 under the sponsorship of the UN and specialized agencies within the UN system in order to provide a scientific basis for international governance of the marine environment. Sources: www.imo.org/en/OurWork/Environment/Pages/GESAMP.aspx and www.gesamp.org.

179 The IPCC was set up in 1988 by the World Meteorological Organization (WMO) and UN Environment Programme (UNEP) to provide policymakers with regular assessments of the scientific basis of climate change, its impacts and future risks and opinions for adaption and mitigation. Source: www.ipcc.ch.

180 Duncan French and Benjamin Pontin, 'The science of climate change: a legal perspective on the IPCC' in Michael Faure (ed.), *Elgar Encyclopedia of Environmental Law* (Edward Elgar 2016) 10.

181 IPCC: www.ipcc.ch. To some extent, the following article (with thirty-one authors) seems to demonstrate that a group of marine scientists had made a similar effort like climate change scientists under the IPCC mechanism: they both attempted to assess the status of scientific knowledge by 'assessing published literature'. Of course, the sizes the scientist groups involved in these two issue areas are not comparable. Moreover, besides 'a review and synthesis of the peer-reviewed literature', the group of marine scientists conducted 'consultations with DSM stakeholders via questionnaire', this work method is not adopted by IPCC scientists. Amon et al., 'Assessment of Scientific Gaps related to the Effective Environmental Management of Deep-Seabed Mining' (2022).

of plenary sessions, three working groups and a task force and Secretariat. Yet, the IPCC is at the same time huge in the sense that 'thousands of scientists from all over the world contribute to the work of the IPCC on a voluntary basis as authors, contributors and reviewers'.[182] It is exactly due to the collective labour of thousands of scientists that the output of the IPCC – Assessment Reports – demonstrates the global scientific consensus on climate change. The work of the IPCC is of a scientific nature, but at the same time governments play a 'cradle to grave' role in the assessment of science within the IPCC.[183] Not only do the documents produced by the IPCC need to be reviewed by governments, but also the scientific findings of the IPCC need to be translated into advice.[184] Thus, the IPCC is not only a 'scientific body', but also an 'intergovernmental body'.

Two features of the IPCC mechanism can be identified. First, the broad engagement of scientists at the global level is unparalleled by any other mechanism. It is exactly due to the involvement of a huge number of scientists that the work of the IPCC could be said to demonstrate the global scientific consensus on climate change. Second, the work of the IPCC is of a scientific nature, but providing policymakers with scientific advice is the reason for its existence. Thus, the IPCC mechanism is an exemplary case of close interplay between science and policy. The protection of the marine environment in DSM shares much commonality with the subject matter of climate change: both are global issues that are subject to international governance; international governance relating to both subject matters relies heavily on scientific knowledge; the scientific aspects of both subject matters are complex and demand global scientific consensus at the broadest level. For these reasons, if the IPCC mechanism serves well for international governance of climate change, a mechanism similar to the IPCC could also be valuable for international marine environmental protection in DSM.

It is noted that the LTC must take 'views of recognized experts' into account when making recommendations to the Council on the protection of the marine environment.[185] Considering the limited capacity of the LTC, as well as gaps in marine scientific knowledge, the LTC will

182 Ibid.

183 French and Pontin, *Climate Change Law* (2016) 17.

184 Concretely, the 1000+-page Assessment Report is normally reduced to a few dozen-page Summaries for Policymakers which are scientific advice provided to policymakers.

185 Article 165, paragraph 2 (e), UNCLOS.

need to explore new ways of assessing the current state of marine scientific knowledge on a continual basis. Whether it is through cooperation with existing scientific bodies in the field of marine sciences, or establishment of a new mechanism similar to the IPCC, or by any other means, the demand on the LTC remains unchanged. The LTC should attempt to demonstrate global scientific consensus on marine sciences relating to DSM and, on the basis of this consensus, make recommendations to the Council, and/or provide contractors with guidance. To a large extent, whether the ISA will be able to fulfil its function to protect the marine environment at the exploitation stage depends on whether the LTC will be able to effectively respond to gaps and advances made in marine scientific knowledge.

3.6 Conclusions

As an international organization for operationalizing the CHM principle, the ISA represents the interests of both its member States and humankind as a whole. It is composed of organs and subsidiary bodies, including the Assembly, Council, Secretariat, Legal and Technical Commission, Finance Committee, the Enterprise and Economic Planning Commission. The last two organs are currently under discussion for independent functioning, while the rest have been in operation since 1996 but have encountered practical problems. Now in transition from exploration to exploitation, the question of whether the ISA is fit for the purpose arises.

The ISA is entrusted with the function of protecting the marine environment from the detrimental effects arising out of DSM activities. Six categories of powers and obligations of the ISA with respect to its environmental function are identified. First, the Council and Assembly are empowered to adopt rules, regulations and procedures, while the LTC is entrusted with the drafting work. Second, the LTC is authorized to issue technical and administrative guidance to contractors which, although not legally binding, have significant practical effect. Third, the ISA has a monopolistic power to control over access to DSM by granting contracts, is in charge of reviewing annual reports, including EISs, submitted by the contractor, and is empowered to sending inspector and to initiate judicial proceedings before the SDC, thereby ensuring compliance of the contractor with its environmental obligations. Fourth, the Council is entitled to issue environmental emergency order to the contractor for preventing (risk of) serious environmental damage. Fifth, the ISA has the self-imposed obligations to apply a precautionary approach and best environmental practices. Sixth, the ISA is also obliged to encourage and promote marine scientific research. The LTC, the Secretariat and the Council are the three most important organs for the exercise of these powers and fulfillment of these obligations. Specifically, the LTC is responsible for drafting legal instruments, reviewing applications, providing guidance for contractors and supervising the implementation of contracts by reviewing the annual reports of contractors. The Secretariat is key in managing data and assisting other organs of the ISA, especially the LTC; it also supervises the implementation of contracts. The Council is charged with adopting rules, regulations and procedures, issuing environmental emergency orders and instituting proceedings or requesting an advisory opinion at the SDC.

However, as highlighted in Chapter 2, there are still great gaps in marine scientific knowledge. This poses the greatest challenge for the ISA in fulfilling its function to protect the marine environment, especially once exploitation commences. The ISA is currently drafting the Exploitation Regulations. Once the Exploitation Regulations are adopted and commercial exploitation commences, both the organizational aspect of the ISA and how the ISA exercises its powers and fulfils its obligations will be seriously tested. Undoubtedly, the LTC will play a vital role in operationalizing the Environmental Regulations in the exploitation phase by issuing technical guidance. In so doing, the LTC will need to undertake the difficult task of assessing the current state of marine scientific knowledge on a continual basis. To undertake this task, it is suggested that the LTC could either cooperate with other existing scientific bodies in the field of marine sciences or establish a new mechanism similar to the IPCC.

Whether the ISA will be able to successfully discharge its environmental mandate during exploitation remains to be seen. Nevertheless, the ISA undoubtedly cannot safeguard the marine environment alone. Since the protection of the marine environment is regarded as a community interest, all participants in DSM are under the obligation to protect the marine environment. The next chapter turns to the international environmental obligations of the sponsoring State and the contractor.

4

International Environmental Obligations of the Sponsoring State and Contractor

4.1 Introduction

4.1.1 The Role and Status of the Sponsoring State in a Dual-Track Regulatory System

Before embarking on analysing the contents of international environmental obligations of the sponsoring State, a preliminary question needs to be first taken into consideration: what status does the sponsoring State have and what role does it play *vis-à-vis* the International Seabed Authority (ISA) as the international regulator and the sponsored contractor as the operator in the deep seabed mining (DSM) legal regime?

As demonstrated in Chapter 2, DSM regime is, so far, the only international regime that operationalizes the principle of common heritage of mankind (CHM). Among the eight elements of CHM which together make the regime unique, the international administration of the ISA stands out as a core element. In Chapter 3, the ISA has been presented as one of its kind international organization: not only because the ISA has an operational arm (the Enterprise), but more importantly because it is empowered to make, implement and even enforce rules, regulations and procedures *vis-à-vis* the contractor directly at the international level. This international administration (or regulation) of the ISA over DSM activities might well be considered as an apt example of the 'exercise of international public authority',[1] which is, to some extent, analogous to the exercise of executive power by governments at the national level. However, practically speaking, the ISA is not, and would never be, comparable to any governments (except perhaps those of very few mini-States) owing to its limited finance, facilities as well as human

[1] Armin von Bogdandy, Matthias Goldmann and Ingo Venzke, 'From Public International to International Public Law: Translating World Public Opinion into International Public Authority' (2017) 28(1) *EJIL* 115–145.

resources. There exists a huge chasm between the legal and practical powers of the ISA which cannot be bridged by itself.

The solution lies in States Party to the UN Convention on the Law of the Sea (UNCLOS), in particular the sponsoring States, as backup.[2] To use a metaphor of Archimedes' principle, one could view the UNCLOS as the long lever in the hands of the ISA while the sponsoring States the fulcrum on which to place the lever, by the lever and fulcrum the ISA shall move the (potential) contractor, thereby controlling the seabed. Article 139 of UNCLOS prescribes clearly that 'States Parties shall have the responsibility to ensure that activities in the Area [...] shall be carried out in conformity with this Part'. Then, Article 153, paragraph 2(b) and Article 4, Annex III to the UNCLOS establish a 'sponsorship' mechanism through which the specific sponsoring State Party that shall assume the 'responsibility to ensure' compliance of the contractor under Article 139 is pinpointed. More specifically, Exploration Regulations prescribe that: an applicant for a contract must submit to the ISA a certificate of sponsorship which shall describe the basic information of both the applicant and the sponsoring State, ascertain their legal connection (by 'nationality' or 'effective control') and declare the sponsoring State's recognition of its 'responsibility to ensure' under the abovementioned three provisions. In the opinion of the SDC,

> The purpose of requiring the sponsorship of applicants for contracts for the exploration and exploitation of the resources of the Area is to achieve the result that the obligations set out in the Convention, a treaty under international law which binds only State Parties thereto, are complied with by entities that are subjects of domestic legal systems.[3]

The SDC continued to explain that

> [t]he role of the sponsoring State is to contribute to the common interest of all States in the proper implementation of the principle of the common heritage of mankind by assisting the Authority and by acting on its own

[2] When the sponsoring State is itself with low practical capacity (for instance, the Pacific Small Island Developing States), it would not be able to serve as a meaningful backup to the ISA. In this situation, it seems that the purpose of sponsorship mechanism is defeated.

[3] ITLOS, Advisory Opinion of 1 February 2011 (Case No. 17), para. 75. Note: the SDC's explanation over the purpose of 'sponsorship' (para. 75) was strikingly similar to that of the function of 'obligation to ensure' (para. 108). In my opinion, 'sponsorship', like 'flag' or 'registration', is meant to ascertain a legal connection between entities and States, thereby making it easier to pinpoint the State(s) that shall assume due diligence obligation, while 'obligation to ensure' refers to the due diligence obligation itself. It seems that the SDC mixed up the two things.

> with a view to ensuring that entities under its jurisdiction conform to the rules on deep seabed mining.[4]

These clarifications sent out three messages: first, although only the ISA is assigned explicitly as the trustee of CHM in the Area, States are not exempted from shouldering this burden. Secondly, the sponsoring State makes its contribution to safeguarding the CHM by ensuring compliance of its sponsored contractor. Thirdly, the sponsoring State plays roles at both international and national levels: At the international level, the sponsoring State shall assist the ISA[5]; at the national level, it functions as the regulator *vis-à-vis* its sponsored contractor.[6] It is worth noting that these two roles are interconnected since the sponsoring State assists the ISA in ensuring compliance of the contractor mainly through establishing and implementing a national regulatory system within its own jurisdiction. This parallel existence of international and national regulations makes DSM regime a dual-track regulatory system.

What is the relationship between the two tracks of regulation? It is argued that the international regulation centred on the ISA should be of primary status, while national regulation presided by the sponsoring State should be subordinate and complementary, since the subject matter of DSM is legally internationalized. It is worth recalling what Jenks once observed:

> In such fields as aviation, safety of life at sea, postal relations, quarantine regulations and telecommunications, however, the international and national rules have in many cases become indistinguishable for practical purposes to the extent of national services being operated on the basis of international manuals of regulations. In such cases we are confronted with a practical consolidation of the detailed content of the international and national legal systems which represents a new factor of major importance in the relationship between international and municipal law.[7]

Deep seabed mining is very similar to those five issue areas identified by Jenks in the sense that they are all highly international. Very likely, 'a practical consolidation of the detailed content of the international and national legal

[4] ITLOS, Advisory Opinion of 1 February 2011 (Case No. 17), paras. 76 and 226.

[5] The last sentence of Article 153(4) of the UNCLOS stipulates that 'States Parties shall assist the Authority by taking all necessary measures necessary to ensure such compliance in accordance with article 139'.

[6] Article 4(4), Annex III to the UNCLOS prescribes that '[t]he sponsoring State or States shall, pursuant to article 139, have the responsibility to ensure, within their legal systems, that a contractor so sponsored shall carry out activities in the Area in conformity with the terms of its contract and its obligation under this Convention'.

[7] C. Wilfred Jenks, *The Common Law of Mankind* (Stevens 1958) 37.

systems' would be the situation for DSM too. That is, the substantive legal requirements for a contractor will be essentially the same under the international and national laws. However, the difference is that while the ISA can exercise international regulation *vis-à-vis* the contractor directly, the international organizations in those five issue areas[8] have to rely on their member States respectively for the implementation of the international rules, regulations and procedures. Therefore, although sharing a commonality of dual (international and national) legal systems, the practical problem of potential duplication with respect to regulatory burden and liability of the operator occurs only in the field of DSM.[9] To avoid duplication necessitates cooperation, coordination or clear division of labour between the ISA and the sponsoring State as regulators. Xiangxin Xu regarded the sponsoring State as the 'secondary regulator' and argued that 'a sponsoring state should focus on monitoring and enforcement in its national legislation for the purpose of assisting the ISA'.[10] This opinion is compatible with the idea of this book that the sponsoring State should serve as a backup to the ISA in practical realm where the latter has inherent weaknesses and may often find its limits. Such an understanding of the role and status of the sponsoring State necessarily leads to an emphasis on the consistency in international environmental obligations between the sponsoring State and the ISA and on obligations of the sponsoring State to assist and cooperate with the ISA. Also, it would entail an integral reading of obligation of the contractor at the national level in conjunction with that at the international level.

4.1.2 Structure

Section 4.2 focuses on international environmental obligations of the sponsoring State. It is noted that, unlike the ISA and the contractor which base their legal obligations only on *lex specialis* of DSM regime, there exists a body of applicable general and customary international (environmental)

[8] They are International Civil Aviation Organization (ICAO), International Maritime Organization (IMO), Universal Postal Union (UPO), World Health Organization (WHO) and International Telecommunication Union (ITO).

[9] This problem has been identified and discussed at international level as well as in the related national laws of Tonga (Tonga Seabed Minerals Act 2014), Nauru (International Seabed Minerals Act 2015) and Germany (Seabed Mining Act of 6 June 1995).

[10] Xiangxin Xu, *Responsibility to Ensure: Sponsoring States' Environmental Legislation for Deep Seabed Mining and China's Practice* (Brill 2021); Xiangxin Xu and Guifang (Julia) Xue, 'Potential Contribution of Sponsoring State and Its National Legislation to the Deep Seabed Mining Regime' (2021) 13(19) *Sustainability*.

law developed through longtime State practice. While acknowledging *lex specialis derogat legi general*, this section attaches importance to the examination of applicable customary and general international (environmental) law because that contributes to expounding on the meaning of corresponding legal requirements under *lex specialis* DSM regime. It is perhaps for this reason that the Seabed Disputes Chamber (SDC) relied on customary and general international (environmental) law when clarifying international (environmental) obligations of the sponsoring State, in particular on the 'responsibility to ensure', in its 2011 Advisory Opinion.[11] In Duncan French's words, there were 'rich pickings of [sustainable] principles and general international law' in the SDC's 2011 Advisory Opinion.[12] Section 4.3 turns to international environmental obligation of the contractor. Since private entities or persons are traditionally not regarded as subjects of public international law, nor does public international law deal with the commercial activities of States, the legal basis for the international environmental obligations of the contractor cannot be found in general international law but in *lex specialis* of DSM regime only. National laws of the sponsoring States may also prescribe environmental obligations for their sponsored contractors respectively. Yet, since this book focuses on the international level, the discussion in this section is based only on the international DSM legal regime.

4.2 International Environmental Obligations of the Sponsoring State

Since the Stockholm Declaration of 1972, important international environmental principles, rules and procedures have emerged, developed and

[11] Commentary notes on the SDC's 2011 Advisory Opinion see: David Freestone, 'Responsibilities and obligations of States Sponsoring Persons and Entities with respect to Activities in the Area' (2011) 105(4) *AJIL* 755–760. Gunther Handl, 'Responsibilities and Obligations of States Sponsoring Persons and Entities with respect to Activities in the Area' (2011) 20(2) *RECIEL* 208. Ilias Plakokefalos, 'Seabed Disputes Chamber of the International Tribunal for the Law of the Sea: Responsibilities and Obligations of States Sponsoring Persons and Entities with respect to Activities in the Area' (2012) 24(1) *Journal of Environmental Law* 133–143. Jianjun Gao, 'The Responsibilities and Obligations of the Sponsoring States Advisory Opinion' (2013) 12(4) *Chinese JIL* 771–786. Hui Zhang, 'The Sponsoring State's "Obligation to Ensure" in the Development of the International Seabed Area' (2013) 28(4) *IJMCL* 681–699.

[12] Duncan French, 'From the Depths: Rich Pickings of Principles of Sustainable Development and General International Law on the Ocean Floor – the Seabed Disputes Chamber's 2011 Advisory Opinion' (2011) 26(4) *IJMCL* 525–568.

partly or fully crystallized. These principles, rules and procedures, by which the sponsoring State is basically bound, are interconnected; they give rise to a set of international environmental obligations of the sponsoring State. This section will analyse the environmental legal requirements of States under the sustainable development principle, the principle of prevention, the precautionary approach[13] and environmental impact assessment (EIA). Special attention will be paid on the extent general principles and rules appropriate to the DSM context. Additionally, sponsoring States' obligation to cooperate with the ISA is discussed in the end.

4.2.1 The Overarching Principle of Sustainable Development

The principle of sustainable development sets the keynote for discussions of environmental protection in the utilization of natural resources, DSM is just one of the examples.[14] Sustainable development is defined as development 'that meets the needs of the present without compromising the ability of future generations to meet their own needs'.[15] This definition emphasizes the intergenerational equity in exploiting the Earth as a resource.[16] In the specific case of DSM, since mineral resources are non-renewable the utilization of which by some necessarily deprives others of its utilization, hence, intergenerational equity may not mean that each generation is in an equally advantageous position in harvesting those minerals.[17] Rather, it would mean that exploiting deep seabed mineral

[13] There is debate on whether the concept of precaution should be interpreted as 'approach' or 'principle'. In Peel's opinion, there are small differences between the two in textual analysis. Yet they provide a legal language for expressing political differences in risk attitude and regulatory approach in the face of the common problem of scientific uncertainty (see Jacqueline Peel, 'Precaution – A Matter of Principle, Approach or Process?' (2004) 5(2) *MJIL* 483). On the other hand, it is also noted that the precautionary approach is very often used interchangeably with the precautionary principle. What really matters is the meaning and the way to materialize the idea of precaution in practice, rather than the choice of terminologies. In this book, the 'precautionary approach' and the 'precautionary principle' are used interchangeably.

[14] About the development and legal meaning of the principle of sustainable development, see Nico Schrijver, *The Evolution of Sustainable Development in International Law: Inception, Meaning and Status* (Martinus 2008).

[15] Report of the World Commission on Environment and Development: Our Common Future (Brundtland Report), 1987, UN Doc. A/RES/42/187.

[16] Otto Spijkers, 'Intergenerational Equity and the Sustainable Development Goals' (2018) 10(11) *Sustainability* 3836.

[17] But it is still required that mineral extraction should be carried out as economically as possible because mineral resources are in general geologically scarce.

resources by our generation should not result in leaving a seriously damaged deep sea environment to our descendants. This refers to another dimension of the concept of sustainable development – the need to reconcile economic development with protection of environment – which was not embodied in Brundtland Report's definition[18] but was revealed by the International Court of Justice (ICJ) in its 1997 judgment of the *Gabcikovo-Nagymaros Project* case.[19] As would be agreed by everyone, almost all activities that bring economic benefits leave environmental footprints, and in reality, to gain certain economic benefits, the choice made is not between activities with risk and those without but between activities with risks of different levels. In the specific case of DSM, where to set the standard of environmental protection depends on the desirability of the goal of economic and social development brought by DSM and the availability of alternative mining activities with lesser risks.[20]

The overarching principle of sustainable development is closely linked to the principle of prevention and the precautionary principle/approach since all of them have at their core the tension between economic development on the one hand and environmental protection on the other. Thus, it is not surprising that most legal instruments which prescribe the principle of prevention or the precautionary principle/approach also state sustainable development as a goal; the other way around, the legal instruments which declare a goal of sustainable development also require application of the principle of prevention and the precautionary principle/approach.[21] Naturally, preventive and precautionary measures, such as environmental impact assessment, best

[18] Iris Borowy, *Defining Sustainable Development for Our Common Future: A History of the World Commission on Environment and Development (Brundtland Commission)* (Routledge 2014).

[19] ICJ, *Gabčíkovo-Nagymaros Project (Hungary/Slovakia)*, Judgment of 25 September 1997, para. 140.

[20] One should be reminded that terrestrial mining has for a long time been regarded as one of the most notorious environmentally devastating industries around the world. If DSM proves to be a potentially more environmentally friendly alternative to terrestrial mining, this would serve as a justification for DSM.

[21] There are many examples of this aspect. For instance, the 1990 Ministerial Declaration on Sustainable Development in the ECE Region, the 1990 Declaration on Environmentally Sound and Sustainable Development in Asia and the Pacific, the 1990 Ministerial Declaration of the Second World Climate Conference, he 1995 Global Programme of Action for Protection of the Marine Environment from Land-Based Activities and the 2002 New Delhi Declaration of the ILA.

available technologies (BATs) and best environmental practices (BEPs), also play an important role in achieving the goal of sustainable development. Taken together, international environmental law (IEL) that imposes a set of environmental obligations on the sponsoring State can be divided into three levels. At the highest level is the principle of sustainable development, which sets the overarching goal of environmental protection. In the middle are the principle of prevention and the precautionary principle/approach, which prescribe general legal obligations. At the lowest level are EIA, BATs and BEPs, the practical rules and procedures for implementing the principles of prevention and precaution and for achieving the goal of sustainable development.

Due to the knowledge gap in the deep sea environment and DSM's impact on the marine environment, the precautionary principle/approach is of special importance because it deals particularly with the question of how to respond when there is scientific uncertainty. O'Riordan and Cameron commented more than two decades ago:

> Our contention is that precaution will not explode onto the environmental stage sweeping out cost benefit analysis, risk assessment, strict liability and EIA into heavily weighted antagonistic devices against development and change. Rather it will seep through the pores of decision-making institutions and the political consciousness of humanity by stealth.[22]

Having been 'seeping through' for a period of nearly three decades, the precautionary principle/approach has indeed substantively changed our views towards the relation between economic development and environmental protection. Nowadays, the idea of precaution has been firmly established in laws, although the precautionary principle/approach as a legal norm is still troubled by the diverse interpretations of its meaning and difficulties in its application. When the subject of DSM emerged within the UN in the 1960s and was included in the UNCLOS in the 1980s, the idea of precaution was not even spoken of. Yet now, not only has the precautionary principle/approach been expressly incorporated into the Exploration Regulations and will certainly appear in the to-be-adopted Exploitation Regulations, but the interpretation of the precautionary principle/approach should also keep pace with developments in general IEL. Undoubtedly DSM is and will be regulated with increasing precaution when commercial exploitation commences. Yet, before going

[22] Timothy O'Riordan and James Cameron (eds.), *Interpreting the Precautionary Principle* (Earthscan 1994) 26.

into details of the precautionary approach, it is better to first discuss the departure point and the most well-settled principle of IEL – prevention.

4.2.2 *Obligation of Prevention*

4.2.2.1 Conventional Bases and the SDC's Clarification

As the UNCLOS 'forms an integral whole',[23] the conventional bases for international environmental obligations of the sponsoring State in DSM are not confined to Part XI, but to the UNCLOS as a whole, including in particular Part XII. Article 192 pins down the general obligation of States (including sponsoring States) 'to protect and preserve the marine environment'. Article 193 fully acknowledges Principle 21 of the 1972 Stockholm Declaration.[24] While Article 194(1) is interpreted as a reflection of the principle of prevention, which stipulates that

> [s]tates shall take, individually or jointly as appropriate, all measures consistent with this Convention that are necessary to prevent, reduce and control pollution of the marine environment from any source, using for this purpose the best practicable means at their disposal and in accordance with their capacities, and they shall endeavour to harmonize their policies in this connection.

In similar words, Article 194 (2) reads,

> States shall take all measures necessary to ensure that activities under their jurisdiction or control are so conducted as not to cause damage by pollution to other States and their environment [. . .].

From these provisions it is clear that the sponsoring State, as a State Party to the UNCLOS, is obliged to apply the principle of prevention. In doing so, the sponsoring State must take preventive measures. And to adequately discharge its obligation of prevention, the sponsoring State must demonstrate that it has 'the best practicable means at its disposal' within its domestic system to manage and control its sponsored contractor in order to prevent DSM activities from causing marine environmental damage. Such a requirement, however, is not to guarantee that damage will not be caused by the sponsored contractor. This is the so-

[23] 'A Constitution for the Oceans' – Remarks by Tommy T. B. Koh of Singapore President of the Third United Nations Conference on the Law of the Sea of 10 December 1982.

[24] Article 193 of the UNCLOS stipulates that 'States have the sovereign rights to exploit their natural resources pursuant to their environmental policies and in accordance with their duty to protect and preserve the marine environment'.

called due diligence obligation. It means that if acts of the sponsoring States meet a standard of due diligence then it fulfils its obligation of prevention and hence can be exempted from liability even if environmental damage occurs.

It is noted that in the 2011 Advisory Opinion, the SDC identified not Part XII but Article 139 (1) in Part XI of the UNCLOS as the legal basis for due diligence obligations of States Parties in the context of DSM.[25] Article 139 (1) stipulates that

> [s]tates Parties shall have the responsibility to ensure that activities in the Area, whether carried out by States parties, or state enterprises or natural or juridical persons which possess the nationality of States Parties or are effectively controlled by them or their nationals, shall be carried out in conformity with this Part [. . .].

The SDC then elaborated on the function, nature and feature of the sponsoring State's 'responsibility to ensure' compliance of its sponsored contractor under Article 139 (1).[26] As to the function, in the SDC's view, the sponsoring State's 'responsibility to ensure' establishes a mechanism through which related rules of the UNCLOS became effective for sponsored contractors.[27] A key step for establishing such a mechanism is that the sponsoring State must incorporate or translate international DSM legal framework into its national legal system. For this reason, national legislation is a crucial means for the sponsoring State to fulfil its obligation under Article 139 (1) of the UNCLOS.[28] With respect to the nature, the SDC considered that the sponsoring State's 'responsibility to ensure' is 'obligation of conduct' and 'due diligence obligation', that is, 'an obligation to deploy adequate means, to exercise best possible efforts, to do the utmost, to obtain this result'.[29] The SDC continued to explain that the standard of 'due diligence' must change along with the changed level of technological development and that of risks of the activities themselves. As it was stated,

25 Article 139(1) covers the obligations of sponsoring States to ensure the contractor conforms to, such as, the production policy, financial requirement, requirement of safety operation, environmental protection requirement in the context of DSM and so on. This coverage is broader than Articles in Part XII which cover only the environmental obligations of States.

26 ITLOS, Advisory Opinion of 1 February 2011 (No. 17 case), paras. 103 to 120.

27 Ibid., para. 108.

28 Ibid., para. 218 and Annex III, Article 4(4), UNCLOS.

29 Ibid., para. 110.

> The content of "due diligence" obligations may not easily be described in precise terms. Among the factors make such a description difficult is the fact that "due diligence" is a variable concept. It may change over time as measures considered sufficiently diligent at a certain moment may become not diligent enough in light, for instance, of new scientific or technological knowledge. It may also change in relation to the risks involved in the activity. [. . .] the standard of due diligence has to be more severe for the riskier activities.[30]

The 'responsibility to ensure' under Article 139 may have a different scope of application from obligation of prevention under Article 194; yet, insofar as the sponsoring State's environmental obligation is concerned, their legal implications are the same. Under either provision, the sponsoring State is required to assume an obligation of prevention for the purpose of protecting the marine environment. In effect, this requirement flows not only from the UNCLOS but also from the principle of prevention as a general and customary IEL which forms the cornerstone upon which the edifice of IEL is built.[31] A brief account of the development of this principle is helpful for a deeper understanding of international environmental obligations of states as a whole.

4.2.2.2 The Principle of Prevention as Customary and General International Environmental Law

The International Law Commission's (ILC's) 2001 Draft Articles on Prevention constituted a cumulative result of the development of the most basic norm for international environmental protection over the years: it started from the 'no harm principle' originated in the seminal *Trail Smelter* case,[32] to 'Principle 21' of the 1972 Stockholm Declaration, 'Principle 2' of the 1992 Rio Declaration ('Principle 21/2') and the many subsequent treaties, policy instruments and consistent state practices that endorsed Principle 21/2,[33] and eventually to the principle of prevention codified by the ILC. Over the course of development, the principle of

[30] Ibid., para. 117.

[31] Leslie-Anne Duvic-Paoli, *The Prevention Principle in International Environmental Law* (CUP 2018).

[32] *Trail Smelter* case (*United States v. Canada*), awards on 16 April 1938 and 11 March 1941, UNRIAA, Vol. III, 1905–1982, 1965.

[33] The 1972 Stockholm Declaration and the 1992 Rio Declaration, as international policy instruments, are not legally binding in themselves. However, as a commentary emphasizes, 'the Stockholm and Rio Conferences contributed to creating a global consensus on basic principles of international environmental law and led, directly and indirectly, to the conclusion of numerous global and regional environmental agreements'. Dinah Shelton,

prevention had gradually taken shape and firmly gained a customary and general international law status.[34] Three points with the development of this basic norm merit to be highlighted: first, it redirects States from a 'right-based' (emphasizing States' sovereign right over its natural resources) to a 'duty-based' (emphasizing States' duty to ensure activities causing no harm) legal discourse regarding development and environmental protection.[35] Second, it extends the geographical scope of application of the norm from a transboundary context to including the global commons as well. This change is a part of the broad trend of 'community interest' in international law as identified in Chapter 2.[36] Third, it presents a transformation from a passive obligation of States to 'ensure no harm' to a more active obligation to 'take all appropriate measures' to prevent or minimize damage or risk.[37]

The ILC's work on the 2001 Draft Articles on Prevention clarifies the nature and substantive content of prevention obligation of States and the criterion to determine the fulfillment of such obligation. In a nutshell, the ILC's clarifications can be summarized as follows: the obligation of prevention of States is 'obligation of conduct' (as opposed to 'obligation of result') by nature, that is, what it requires is not to guarantee the non-occurrence of environmental damage but to endeavour to avoid the occurrence.[38] The standard used to determine whether a State has sufficiently endeavoured to discharge its obligation is due diligence. For this reason, the obligation of prevention is also called 'due diligence obligation'. In applying the standard of due diligence, the key is to see whether

'Stockholm Declaration (1972) and Rio Declaration (1992)', MPEPIL (article last updated 2008).

[34] ICJ, *Legality of the Threat and Use of Nuclear Weapons*, Advisory Opinion of 8 July 1996, para. 29. PCA, *Award of 24 May 2005 on Iron Rhine Railway Arbitration (Belgium v. the Netherlands)*, para. 59. ICJ, *Judgment of 20 April 2010 on Pulp Mills on the River Uruguay (Argentina v. Uruguay)*, para. 101.

[35] Nico Schrijver, *Sovereignty over Natural Resources: Balancing Rights and Duties* (CUP 1997).

[36] Yet, just like mechanisms for implementing community interests are weak points of international law, procedural rules for States to discharge their obligation of prevention in the global commons context are weak points of international environmental law too. Probably partly for this reason, the ILC's 2001 Draft Articles on Prevention covered only transboundary environmental damage, but left out the issue of environmental damage to the global commons.

[37] Article 3 of the 2001 Draft Articles on Prevention.

[38] ILC Report, A/48/10, 1993, para. 122; Report of the Working Group, Commentary to Draft Article 4, para. (4), UN Doc. A/CN.4/L.533 and Add. 1, 1996; commentary to Article 3 of the 2001 Draft Articles on Prevention, para. (7).

the conduct of the State is proportionate with the degree of risk involved in the activity.[39] The ILC also reminded that the standard of due diligence must change with time and keep abreast of technological changes and scientific development.[40] In the field of IEL, the substantive content of obligation of prevention is that States should take preventive measures. What specific preventive measures to take is up to the State, but they are mainly in the forms of domestic legislation and enforcement mechanism.[41] Additionally, when determining whether a State has fulfilled its obligation of prevention, the different economic and technological capacities between States can be taken into account, which means that States are left with discretion in deciding what preventive measures to take in accordance with their own capacities but such discretion is restricted.[42]

4.2.2.3 Appraisal

It is seen that the SDC's interpretation of 'responsibility to ensure' of the sponsoring State in the context of DSM is perfectly compatible with the ILC's clarification about the obligation of prevention of States. They demonstrate a consistent understanding of States' due diligence obligation. It should be noted that 'by itself, due diligence is simply a standard used across the many disparate fields of international law to evaluate state compliance with various international legal obligations'.[43] The reasons why the due diligence standard is so broadly employed, as explained by the ILA Study Group on Due Diligence, are, first of all, because of the lack of uniformity in the standard of conduct, and secondly, the flexibility and adaptability of the due diligence standard.[44]

39 In the commentary to Article 3 of the 2001 Draft Articles on Prevention, discussions on due diligence are found in paragraphs (8) to (18). See also the commentary to draft Article 4, para. (10) of the 1996 Report; Commentary to articles in general, para. (2) of the 2001 Draft Articles on Prevention.

40 Commentary to Article 3 of the 2001 Draft Articles on Prevention, para. (11).

41 Commentary to Article 3 of the 2001 Draft Articles on Prevention, para. (10); the Sixth Report of the Special Rapporteur, Julio Barboza, A/CN.4/428 and Add. 1, 1990, Draft Article 16.

42 ILC Report, A/48/10, 1993, para. 123; Commentary to Draft Article 4, para. (12). Report of the Working Group. UN Doc. A/CN.4/L.533 and Add. 1, 1996.

43 Julian Aguon and Julie Hunter, 'Second Wave Due Diligence: The Case for Incorporating Free, Prior, and Informed Consent into the Deep Sea Mining Regulatory Regime' (2018) 38(3) *Stan. Envtl. L. J.* 1–55, 8. The same idea is also expressed by the International Law Association (ILA) in the first report of the ILA's Study Group on Due Diligence in International Law, 7 March 2014.

44 The second report of the ILA's Study Group on Due Diligence in International Law, July 2016, 2, 3 and 47.

Owing exactly to these features, it is anticipated that, had a dispute about whether a sponsoring State has fulfilled its obligation of prevention arose in the future, the substantiation of the standard of 'due diligence' would become the focal point of controversy. As can be inferred from Section 4.2.4, a State's fulfillment of its due diligence obligation is well associated with that of its obligation concerning EIA, since EIA is considered as a necessary tool to implement the prevention principle. It would not be wrong to predict that the benchmark of due diligence will become increasingly higher. As it is observed,

> [N]umerous advances in international environmental law suggest that the normative content of due diligence is steadily expanding, imposing ever higher duties and obligations on states and non-state actors respecting the protection of the marine environment.[45]

As a step forward, some proposed to read more procedural elements (for instance, the 'free, prior and informed consent of States') into the due diligence standard and suggested the coming of a 'second wave of due diligence'.[46] Considering the dynamic nature of its content, determination on what is 'due diligence' needs to be made when a case is brought forward.

4.2.3 *Obligation to Apply the Precautionary Approach*

4.2.3.1 Incorporation of the Precautionary Approach in DSM Regime and the SDC's Clarification

Unlike the principle of prevention, the precautionary approach does not appear in the UNCLOS; it was incorporated in DSM legal regime by the ISA in its Regulations.[47] The three sets of Exploration Regulations have a common provision as follows:

> In order to ensure effective protection for the marine environment from harmful effects which may arise from activities in the Area, the Authority

[45] Julian Aguon and Julie Hunter, 'Second Wave Due Diligence: The Case for Incorporating Free, Prior, and Informed Consent into the Deep Sea Mining Regulatory Regime' (2018) 38(3) *Stan. Envtl. L. J.* 1–55, 8.

[46] Ibid.

[47] UNCLOS did not include the precautionary approach since the precautionary approach emerged after adoption of the UNCLOS.

> and sponsoring States shall apply a precautionary approach, as reflected in principle 15 of the Rio Declaration, and best environmental practices.[48]

The Exploration Regulations simply transposed Principle 15 of the 1992 Rio Declaration. Yet, that was a meaningful step, because as the SDC indicated:

> The provisions of the aforementioned Regulations transform this non-binding statement of the precautionary approach in the Rio Declaration into a binding obligation. The implementation of the precautionary approach as defined in these Regulations is one of the obligations of sponsoring States.[49]

The SDC elaborated the meaning of Principle 15 of the 1992 Rio Declaration in the 2011 Advisory Opinion. First of all, it pointed out two restrictive factors with respect to application of the precautionary approach.

> It should be noted that while the first sentence of Principle 15 seems to refer in general terms to the "precautionary approach," the second sentence limits its scope to threats of "serious or irreversible damage" and to "cost-effective" measures adopted in order to prevention "environmental degradation."[50]

The import of these restrictions reflects the consideration of a balance between environmental protection and economic and social development. Secondly, the SDC also recognized the different capacities of States which would affect their application of the precautionary approach. The SDS held,

> Moreover, by stating that the precautionary principle shall be applied by states "according to their capabilities," the first sentence of Principle 15 introduces the possibility of differences in application of the precautionary approach in light of the different capabilities of each state.[51]

It is noted that, as just shown above, the ILC also held that the different capabilities of States in terms of economy and technology should be taken into account when determining whether they had fulfilled their obligations of prevention. Considering that the substantive requirements

[48] Regulation 31 (2) of the 2013 Regulations on Nodules, Regulation 33 (2) of the 2010 Regulations on Sulphides and the 2012 Regulations on Crust.

[49] ITLOS, Advisory opinion of 1 February 2011 (case No. 17), para. 127.

[50] Ibid., para. 128.

[51] Ibid., para. 129.

under the principle of prevention and the precautionary approach are in essence the same, namely, to take preventive/precautionary measures, it is understandable that the disparity in capabilities of States should also be taken into account when applying the precautionary approach. On the other hand, the discretion left to States in application of the precautionary approach is restricted, just like that for the principle of prevention.

The SDC considered the sponsoring State's obligation to apply the precautionary approach as a 'direct obligation', distinct from the obligation of due diligence.[52] But at the same time, the SDC pointed out the link between the two obligations. It indicated that

> [t]he precautionary approach is also an integral part of the general obligation of due diligence of sponsoring States, which is applicable even outside the scope of the Regulations. [. . .] This obligation applies in situations where scientific evidence concerning the scope and potential negative impact of the activity in question is insufficient but where there are plausible indications of potential risks. A sponsoring State would not meet its obligation of due diligence if it disregarded those risks. Such disregard would amount to a failure to comply with the precautionary approach.[53]

Thus, in the view of the SDC, the precautionary approach is closely connected to the principle of prevention. By applying the precautionary approach, the threshold for taking preventive measures lowers, and the standard of due diligence becomes stricter. In practice, application of the precautionary approach and of the principle of prevention overlap to a large extent.

However, unlike the well-established principle of prevention, the precautionary approach is a latercomer and its legal meaning and status are still unsettled, which pose challenges to its application in practice. The clarification of the SDC on Principle 15 of the 1992 Rio Declaration, albeit helpful, is not enough. The following subsection will further elaborate on the nature and meaning of the precautionary approach, and its relationship with the principle of prevention in a broader context of IEL.

4.2.3.2 The Precautionary Approach/Principle in International Environmental Law

The idea of precaution is by no means unfamiliar to human beings. However, the idea was expressed in a legal term only recently. At the

[52] Ibid., para. 125.
[53] Ibid., para. 131.

international level, it is generally acknowledged that the precautionary approach made its debut at the Second International Conference on the Protection of North Sea in 1987.[54] Five years later, the precautionary approach found its solemn presence in Principle 15 of the 1992 Rio Declaration, which states that

> [i]n order to protect the environment, the precautionary approach shall be widely applied by States according to their capabilities. Where there are threats of serious or irreversible damage, lack of full scientific certainty shall not be used as a reason for postponing cost-effective measures to prevent environmental degradation.

In less than fifteen years, there were at least fifty-three treaties and forty-four non-binding international instruments and decisions which incorporated the precautionary approach.[55] The wide acceptance in a large number of treaties and international instruments prompted States to claim for the relevance and application of precautionary approach in judicial cases.[56] However, the ICJ was reluctant to apply the precautionary approach/principle, while the International Tribunal for the Law of the Sea (ITLOS) stopped short of applying it. Neither of them clarified the legal meaning of the precautionary approach in international proceedings. A number of scholarly articles in this respect have been published, the gist of which is presented below.

[54] International Conferences on the Protection of the North Sea, Ministerial Declarations – the London Declaration (1987). Source from OSPAR website, available at: www.ospar.org/site/assets/files/1239/declarations_compilation_1995.pdf.

[55] Arie Trouwborst, *Evolution and Status of the Precautionary Principle in International Law* (Kluwer 2002). Note, however, this phenomenon of 'precaution spotting' was criticized, for example, by Elizabeth Fisher, 'Precaution, Precaution Everywhere: Developing a Common Understanding of the Precautionary Principle in the European Community' (2002) 9 *MJECL* 7–28.

[56] Before the ICJ, examples included New Zealand's argument in the 1995 *Nuclear Tests* case (para. 5), Hungary and Slovakia's endorsement in the 1997 *Gabcikovo-Nagymaros Project* case (para. 113), Argentina's contention for a reversal of burden of proof under the requirement of precaution in the 2010 *Pulp Mills* case (para. 160) and the arguments of both Australia and New Zealand in the 2013 *Whaling in the Antarctic* case (Memorial of Australia (Volume I) on 9 May 2011, paras. 4.87–4.90, Written observations of New Zealand on 4 April 2013, paras. 73–75). Before the ITLOS, the precautionary approach was also invoked in three cases in the provisional measures procedure on the basis of Article 290 of the UNCLOS. Examples included Australia and New Zealand's request in the 1999 *Southern Bluefin Tuna* cases (paras. 1 and 8), the appeal for recognizing the customary international law status of the precautionary principle by Ireland in the 2001 *MOX* case (paras. 97–98) and Malaysia's argument in the 2003 *Land Reclamation* case (para. 74).

If 'science is the linchpin around which environmental law is organized',[57] then the precautionary approach is the new development of environmental law in response to the limitation of science. Indeed, the precautionary approach 'unfolds around the scientific uncertainty'.[58] On the other hand, while the precautionary approach recognizes the limitation of science,

> [t]he precautionary principle does not reject science, but it does rest on the recognition that physical sciences do not always provide all the answers, that social sciences and even the humanities are also valid sources of information and decision making, and that concerns based on common fears are also relevant.[59]

The precautionary approach implies a combination of science and value. There is no doubt that policymaking should be science-based. However, when science fails or reaches its limits, policies can only be made on the basis of a value judgment. Here policymakers must rely on social sciences, humanities and even the common sense of humans in making a value judgment. Thus, 'one of the most important contributions of the precautionary principle is that it implies a new division of labour between scientists and political decision-makers'.[60] In light of the statements above, it seems that the primary function of the precautionary approach is to address the question of how policymakers should behave in a situation when science faces a high level of uncertainty. However, the answer the precautionary approach gives is very general: it simply points out a direction for policymakers, that is, precaution. What specific obligations the precautionary approach entails depend on interpretation.

Indeed, 'one of the greatest problems of the precautionary principle as a policy tool is its extreme variability in interpretation'.[61] A literal reading of the formulation in Principle 15 of the Rio Declaration could lead to the

[57] Nicolas De Sadeleer, 'The Principles of Prevention and Precaution in International Law: Two Heads of the Same Coin?' In Malgosia Fitzmaurice, David Ong and Panos Merkouris (eds.), *Research Handbook on International Environmental Law* (Edward Elgar 2010) 185.

[58] Ibid.

[59] Jon van Dyke, 'The Evolution and International Acceptance of the Precautionary Principle', in David Caron and Harry Scheiber (eds.), *Bringing New Law to Ocean Waters* (Martinus Nijhoff 2004) 337.

[60] Minna Pyhala, Anne Brusendorff and Hanna Paulomaki, 'The Precautionary Principle', in Malgosia Fitzmaurice, David Ong and Panos Merkouris (eds.), *Research Handbook on International Environmental Law* (Edward Elgar 2010) 213.

[61] Ibid., 211.

conclusion that the precautionary approach requires 'not to postpone action' in a situation of scientific uncertainty. Yet, according to Bodansky, the precautionary approach could also function as 'a license to act' or, in the strongest version, as 'a duty to act'.[62] This demonstrates the different ways to interpret the precautionary approach and correspondingly the distinct legal effects each interpretation entails. Similarly, David Freestone identified three possible interpretations of the obligations under the precautionary approach:

> It is clear that the precautionary principle covers a very wide range of possible obligations and actions. In its weakest formulations (such as that in the Bergen Declaration) it would be difficult to distinguish from the preventive principle which is already well known to international environmental law. At its strongest it can be seen as a reversal of the normal burden of proof, as in the Oslo Convention Prior Justification Procedure, so that a potential actor must prove that his activity will not cause harm before it can be sanctioned. The more common understanding of the principle appears to lie somewhere between these extremes.[63]

Therefore, the nature of the precautionary approach is as a policy tool to deal with a specific situation of scientific uncertainty. Although it has been included in many legal instruments, the legal meanings of the precautionary approach are contestable. There are different interpretations with respect to the specific obligations that the precautionary approach entails.

Despite the variability in interpretation, two basic legal elements of the precautionary approach can be identified. The first is the 'threshold of damage' which should be crossed in order to trigger the application of the precautionary approach.[64] For instance, the threshold of 'threats of

[62] According to Bodansky, the three interpretations (not to postpone action, a licence to act and a duty to act in a situation of scientific uncertainty) demonstrate the three functions that the precautionary principle serves. See Daniel Bodansky, 'Deconstructing the Precautionary Principle', in David Caron and Harry Scheiber (eds.), *Bringing New Law to Ocean Waters* (Martinus Nijhoff 2004) 383–386.

[63] David Freestone, 'The Precautionary Principle', in Robin Churchill and David Freestone (eds.), *International Law and Global Climate Change* (Graham & Trotman 1991) 30.

[64] See James Cameron and Juli Abouchar, 'The Precautionary Principle: A Fundamental Principle of Law and Policy for the Protection of the Global Environment' (1991) 14(1) *B.C. Int'l & Comp.* 1–21; Elizabeth Fisher, 'Precaution, Precaution Everywhere: Developing a Common Understanding of the Precautionary Principle in the European Community' (2002) 9 *MJECL* 7–28; Daniel Bodansky, 'Deconstructing the Precautionary Principle', in David Caron and Harry Scheiber (eds.), *Bringing New Law to Ocean Waters* (Martinus Nijhoff 2004), etc.

serious and irreversible damage' is a built-in element of the definition of the precautionary approach in Principle 15 of the 1992 Rio Declaration. Bodansky proposed three relevant factors in considering such a threshold: the severity of the potential harm, the likelihood or evidence of that harm and the source of the harm.[65]

The theoretical as well as practical problem, however, lies in the question of who should prove that the threshold is (or is not) crossed. This is the legal issue of the allocation of the burden of proof. There are opinions for[66] and against[67] the reversal of burden of proof. In fact, the cases mentioned above epitomize this controversy. Generally the respondents were not opposed to the applicability of the precautionary approach in itself, but they argued against the claim by the applicants that the application of the precautionary approach implied a reversal of burden of proof. The respondents also drew attention to the threshold of damage.[68] As is well known, allocation of the burden of proof is a critical legal device for distributing legal risk in proceedings, especially in cases where evidence is insufficient. Allocation of burden of proof is of particular significance to application of the precautionary approach since the precautionary approach is applied exactly in a situation of scientific uncertainty, namely, insufficient evidence. If the burden of proof is allocated to those proposing to undertake a potentially risk-generating activity, it means the credit is given to the environment. Vice versa, if the burden of proof is not reversed, then the credit is given to those proposing to change the environment. To whom the credit is given is a matter of value choice. However, if the value of the environment prevails, then the reversal of burden of proof is the necessary choice. It means that those proposing to undertake a potentially risk-generating activity must prove the 'harmlessness' (below the threshold) of the activities. Of course, to prove 'harmlessness' one also has to rely on scientific evidence. It

65 Daniel Bodansky, 'Deconstructing the Precautionary Principle', in David Caron and Harry Scheiber (eds.), *Bringing New Law to Ocean Waters* (Martinus Nijhoff 2004) 387–389.

66 For instance, Pyhala, Brusendorff and Paulomaki commented that 'the precautionary principle embodies reversal of the burden of proof' (2010, 213); Bodansky stated that some formulations to articulate substantive elements of a precautionary approach include shifting the burden of proof (2004, 390).

67 For instance, in the 2010 *Pulp Mills* case, the ICJ held that 'it does not follow that it [the precautionary approach] operates as a reversal of the burden of proof' (para. 164).

68 For instance, argument of Japan in the 2014 *Whaling in the Antarctic* case, Counter-memorial of Japan on 9 March 2012, paras. 9.33 and 9.34.

reminds us once again of the argument of van Dyke that to apply the precautionary principle, 'science is not ignored, but its role has changed, and the burden of persuasion is shifted'.[69]

If the threshold of damage is crossed, precautionary measures should be taken. This is the second basic element of the precautionary approach. As indicated by Schrijver,

> In practice the operation of the precautionary principle implies a number of precautionary measures, such as the application of best available technologies (BATs), best environmental practices (BEPs) and the development of environmental quality standards. Important for the application of the precautionary principle is also the obligation to conduct an "environmental impact assessment" (EIA) which has now become standard procedure in many states.[70]

It can be seen that the precautionary measures under the precautionary principle are not, as such, different from the preventive measures under the principle of prevention. The difference lies only in the conditions for their application, namely, the different level of the threshold of damage and whether a reversal of burden of proof is employed. There is indeed a strong connection between the precautionary approach and the principle of prevention.

The precautionary approach was promulgated as a response to the inadequacy of the principle of prevention. Since the application of the principle of prevention requires the (enhanced) ability to trace the chain of causation,[71] while science is not always certain about the causal link between activities and the environmental impacts. The principle of prevention becomes inapplicable where science fails, it is in this sense that it is inadequate. In the pioneering article written in 1989, shortly after the Bergen Conference, Lothar Gundling indicated that 'precautionary action' is a more stringent form of preventive environmental policy.[72]

[69] Jon van Dyke, 'The Evolution and International Acceptance of the Precautionary Principle', in David Caron and Harry Scheiber (eds.), *Bringing New Law to Ocean Waters* (Martinus Nijhoff 2004) 378.

[70] Nico Schrijver, 'The Status of the Precautionary Principle in International Law and Its Application and Interpretation in International Litigation', in Jean Pierre Cot (ed.), *Le procès international: liber amicorum Jean-Pierre Cot* (Bruylant 2009) 250–251.

[71] The 2001 ILC Draft Articles on Prevention, commentary to the Articles in general, para. (2).

[72] Lothar Gundling, 'The Status in International Law of the Principle of Precautionary Action', in David Freestone and Ton Ijlstra (eds.), *The North Sea: Perspectives on Regional Environmental Co-operation* (Graham & Trotman 1990) 26.

James Cameron and Juli Abouchar observed that the precautionary approach is 'an extension of Principle 21'.[73] In the 2001 Draft Articles on Prevention, the ILC commented that preventive measures are required under both the principle of prevention and the precautionary approach.[74] As David Freestone indicated, the precautionary approach in the weakest formulation can hardly be distinguished from the principle of prevention.[75] In sum, the precautionary approach overlaps with the principle of prevention. The former can be seen as both a part and a new development of the latter.

Yet, the problem with the precautionary approach is the diverse interpretation of its meaning which makes obligations flow from it uncertain. This might account for why judicial institutions are still reluctant to apply the precautionary approach. It might also explain why, despite having been incorporated into such a large number of international instruments and 'having received widespread support by the international community', its legal status still 'continues to evolve'.[76] Indeed, opinions about the question of whether the precautionary principle/approach has gained a status of customary international law (CIL) are divided. Nonetheless, this unsettled question does not matter that much since in most cases the precautionary principle is applied as 'a matter of treaty law'.[77] Or because the precautionary approach is incorporated in other positive legal sources like the Exploration Regulations in the DSM case.

4.2.3.3 Appraisal

Back to the sponsoring State in the context of DSM, undoubtedly, it is obliged to apply the precautionary approach. However, the precautionary approach simply provides general guidance to policymakers in the situation of scientific uncertainty. The largest problem is the variable

[73] James Cameron and Juli Abouchar, 'The Status of the Precautionary Principle in International Law', in David Freestone and Ellen Hey (eds.), *The Precautionary Principle and International Law: The Challenge of Implementation* (Kluwer 1996).

[74] The 2001 ILC Draft Articles on Prevention, commentary to Article 3, para (14).

[75] David Freestone, 'The Precautionary Principle', in Robin Churchill and David Freestone (eds.), *International Law and Global Climate Change* (Graham & Trotman 1991) 30.

[76] Philippe Sands, Jacqueline Peel, Adriana Fabra, and Ruth MacKenzie (eds.), *Principles of International Environmental Law* (CUP 2012) 222, 228.

[77] Nico Schrijver, 'The Status of the Precautionary Principle in International Law and Its Application and Interpretation in International Litigation', in Jean Pierre Cot (ed.), *Le procès international: liber amicorum Jean-Pierre Cot* (Bruylant 2009) 150.

interpretations of its meaning. Can a sponsoring State apply it according to its own interpretation? A negative answer is preferable because DSM is not only internationalized as a subject matter but also subject to international regulation as activities. This would imply a unifying interpretation of the precautionary approach via sponsoring States' following the ISA. Then the next question is: is there an international consensus about the meaning of the precautionary approach in the field of DSM? Up until now, perhaps the answer is still a 'no'.[78] As shown in the Introduction chapter of the book, at the moment, some are trying to 'boycott' DSM while others support a 'go-ahead', both camps endorse the precautionary approach and can partly justify their claims on its basis. Owing to the lack of consensus of its meaning, it would be more difficult to claim for a sponsoring State's breach of the precautionary approach than that of the principle of prevention. The precautionary approach overlaps with the principle of prevention. The main difference between them lies in the fact that while the principle of prevention is based on reactive thinking, the precautionary approach calls for proactive thinking. Nonetheless, the most difficult part of the precautionary approach is less at the conceptual level than at the implementation level. The next section thus turns to analyse the most commonly recognized tool for implementation of the precautionary approach and the principle of prevention – environmental impact assessment.

4.2.4 Obligation concerning Environmental Impact Assessment

4.2.4.1 Conventional Bases and the SDC's Clarification

The UNCLOS requires States to conduct EIA; three Articles are of relevance. Article 206 states,

> When states have reasonable grounds for believing that planned activities under their jurisdiction or control may cause substantial pollution of or significant harmful changes to the marine environment, they shall, as far

[78] See ISA, Draft regulations on exploitation of mineral resources in the Area – Parts IV and VI and related Annexes, prepared by the Facilitator, Raijeli Taga, of the Informal Working Group on the protection and preservation of the marine environment, ISBA/27/C/IWG/ENV/CRP.1, 2022. 'It is noted that a proposal was made to specify, in the paragraph related to Rio Principle 15 that "where information is uncertain or inadequate, the Authority shall favour caution and environmental protection." The proponent is invited to clarify if this is aimed at elaborating on the concrete application of Rio Principle 15 or if this is an additional requirement.'

> as practicable, assess the potential effects of such activities on the marine environment and shall communicate reports of the results of such assessments in the manner provided in article 205.

Under Article 204, States are required to monitor those activities during their operation. In the meanwhile, both Articles 206 and 204 refer to Article 205. According to Article 205, the State is obligated to make public the information gained from EIA and the monitoring programme to all States either by publishing or providing the information to competent international organizations. The sponsoring State, as State Party to the UNCLOS, must observe obligations of EIA in the three Articles.

In the specific context of DSM, the Exploration Regulations embody the obligation of the sponsoring State with respect to EIA.[79] And the SDC clarified such an obligation in its 2011 Advisory Opinion. First, the SDC recognized the inherent connection between EIA and the obligation of prevention:

> [Regulations] establish a direct obligation of the sponsoring State concerning EIA, which can also be read as a relevant factor for meeting the sponsoring State's due diligence obligation.[80]

Second, the SDC concurred with the ICJ, acknowledged the customary international law status of EIA:

> It should be stressed that the obligation to conduct an EIA is a direct obligation under the Convention and a general obligation under customary international law.[81]

Third, taking the *Pulp Mills* case of the ICJ as a precedent, the SDC held that

> [t]he Court's reasoning in a transboundary context may also apply to activities with an impact on the environment in an area beyond the limits of national jurisdiction; and the Court's reference to "shared resources" may also apply to resources that are the common heritage of mankind.[82]

What the SDC elaborated reflects a general understanding of EIA in existing IEL. EIA is recognized as a tool or a procedure to implement both the principle of prevention and the precautionary approach. It has to be employed to protect the environment, whether in global commons

[79] Regulation 31(6) of the 2013 Exploration Regulations on Nodules, ISBA/19/A/9; Regulation 33(6) of the Exploration Regulations on Sulphides (ISBA/16/A/12, 2010) and Crust (ISBA/18/A/11, 2012).

[80] ITLOS, Advisory Opinion of 1 February 2011 (case No. 17), para. 142.

[81] Ibid., para. 145.

[82] Ibid., para. 148.

or in a transboundary context. However, what SDC failed to bring forward is the question of whether rules of transboundary EIA can fit completely to EIA in the context of global commons like the Area.

4.2.4.2 Transboundary EIA in International Environmental Law

The 1991 Convention on Environmental Impact Assessment in a Transboundary Context (the Espoo Convention) is the only comprehensive treaty dedicated exclusively to transboundary EIA to date.[83] The principle of prevention constitutes the foundation, the logical starting point from which the procedures of EIA developed. EIA is defined as 'a national procedure for evaluating the likely impact of a proposed activity on the environment'.[84]

> The main emphasis of the [Espoo] Convention is centered in the creation of two kinds of procedural rules: those rules which obligate the contracting States to reform their national EIA systems in order to provide a basis for the transnational EIA system and those rules which oblige the contracting State to ensure that the potentially affected State, and its population, can participate in the transnational EIA procedure.[85]

The contents of the Espoo Convention can be divided into two parts: the establishment of a national EIA system,[86] and the operating of a national EIA in a transboundary context.[87]

[83] Adopted under the auspices of the UN Economic Commission for Europe on 25 February 1991, entered into force on 10 September 1997; 45 parties as at 30 July 2022. The Espoo Convention comprises twenty articles and seven appendices, appendices attached form an integral part of the convention. Since the Espoo Convention only requires EIA at a project level, to fill in the gaps, Protocol on Strategic Environmental Assessment (SEA) was adopted in 2003. The Protocol requires its parties to evaluate the environmental consequences of their official draft plans and programmes. SEA is undertaken much earlier in the decision-making process than project EIA. The Protocol also provides for extensive public participation in government decision-making in numerous development sectors.

[84] Article 1(vi) of the Espoo Convention.

[85] Timo Koivurova, 'The Transnational EIA Procedure of the Espoo Convention' (1997) 8 *FinnishYBIL* 161–199.

[86] For a contracting Party to the Espoo Convention, the establishment of a national EIA system must meet the minimum standards regarding (1) the screening system (that is, the scope of an EIA), (2) the contents of an EIA, (3) the control of an EIA and (4) public participation during a transboundary EIA.

[87] Procedures of how a national EIA system is to be applied in a transboundary context are detailed in Articles 3 to 7. The sequence of these five Articles reflects the five phases of the application of a transboundary EIA.

The 2001 Draft Articles on Prevention is another important legal instrument on transboundary EIA. It embodies a set of procedural Articles[88] revolving around Article 7 which prescribes 'risk assessment' (including EIA) as follows:

> Any decision in respect of the authorization of an activity within the scope of the present articles shall, in particular, be based on an assessment of the possible transboundary harm caused by that activity, including any environmental assessment.

It is clearly seen that the ILC put much effort on stipulating EIA procedures in an instrument on the principle of prevention. The second Special Rapporteur Babarzo gave his reasons for doing so. He said,

> In the absence of any procedures, the participation of the presumed affected state was not assured, and consequently there would be neither any guide for measures of prevention nor any criteria by which the affected state or states could determine whether any preventive measure had been taken. The role of prevention in the draft articles would then be seriously diminished.[89]

For this reason, EIA is considered as the procedural corollary of the principle of prevention.[90]

The 2001 Draft Articles on Prevention and the 1991 Espoo Convention are so far the two most important international instruments on transboundary EIA; the contents of the former were influenced by the latter. Both instruments recognized the value of EIA procedures for protection of the environment. Although there is no global convention on transboundary EIA, some common issues and concerns of

[88] Articles 8 (notification the result of an EIA), 9 (consultation), 12 (exchange of information) and 13 (public participation) of the 2001 Draft Articles on Prevention.

[89] ILC Report, A/44/10, 1989, para. 382. However, the importance of the procedures was not without disagreement within the ILC. Initially, the first Special Rapporteur stipulated procedural rules in the reports. Then, the question of whether the procedural rules should be retained in the draft articles arose. In the end, the second Special Rapporteur chose to formulate general procedural articles with much flexibility in their application. Upon this choice, articles on the procedural rules were retained in the following reports.

[90] See Olufemi Elias, 'Environmental Impact Assessment', in Malgosia Fitzmaurice, David Ong and Panos Merkouris (eds.), *Research Handbook on International Environmental Law* (Edward Elgar 2010), 227; John Knox, 'The Myth and Reality of Transboundary Environmental Impact Assessment' (2002) 96(2) *AJIL* 291, 295–296; John Knox, 'Assessing the Candidates for a Global Treaty on Transboundary Environmental Impact Assessment' (2003) 12 *N.Y.U. Envtl. L. J.* 153–168, 154; and Kees Bastmeijer and Timo Koivurova (eds.), *Theory and Practice of Transboundary Environmental Impact Assessment* (Martinus Nijhoff 2008) 7.

transboundary EIA can be identified from existing EIA instruments. Angela Cassar and Carl Bruch identify seven common elements of transboundary EIA in practice as follows: (1) who prepares a transboundary EIA? (2) screening; (3) scoping; (4) preparation of a draft transboundary EIA; (5) publication and public review of a draft transboundary EIA; (6) final transboundary EIA and formal approval/denial; and (7) monitoring and appeals.[91] Kees Bastmeijer and Timo Koivurova identify the most important three elements as below: (1) the threshold for transboundary EIA; (2) the questions of how and to what extent the information contained in the EIA report will be used by the decision-maker; and (3) the importance of institutionalization for supervising compliance with EIA procedures.[92]

Like the precautionary approach/principle, EIA has also been invoked by States in international proceedings. In effect, very often states invoked EIA together with the precautionary approach in the same cases. Unlike the precautionary approach/principle, however, (judges of) courts and tribunals endorsed, applied and elaborated EIA. Most prominently, in its 2010 judgment of the *Pulp Mills* case, the ICJ declared:

> EIA as a requirement under general international law where there is a risk that the proposed industrial activity may have a significant adverse impact in a transboundary context, in particular, on a shared resource.[93]

This statement was reaffirmed by the SDC in its 2011 Advisory Opinion and in the ICJ's 2015 judgment on cases between Nicaragua and Costa Rica as well.[94]

To summarize, upon development and application for thirty-five years, EIA has become an indispensable tool for international environmental protection. Inherently, EIA is considered as a procedural corollary of the principle of prevention as well as one of the critical tools to implement the precautionary approach. States' obligation concerning EIA has by now firmly established in international law. No State will

[91] Angela Cassar and Carl Bruch, 'Transboundary Environmental Impact Assessment in International Watercourse Management' (2003) 12 *N.Y.U. Envtl. L. J.* 169, 220–232.

[92] Kees Bastmeijer and Timo Koivurova (eds.), *Theory and Practice of Transboundary Environmental Impact Assessment* (Martinus Nijhoff 2008).

[93] *Pulp Mills on the River Uruguay (Argentina v. Uruguay), Judgment, I.C.J. Reports 2010*, p. 14. para. 204.

[94] *Certain Activities Carried Out by Nicaragua in the Border Area (Costa Rica v. Nicaragua)* and *Construction of a Road in Costa Rica along the San Juan River (Nicaragua v. Costa Rica), Judgment, I.C.J. Reports* 2015, p. 665. paras. 101, 146.

argue against the necessity of EIA when industrial activities that risk causing environmental damage are involved. However, the questions of whether a specific activity is risky and whether a State has adequately fulfilled its obligation concerning EIA would be debatable matters,[95] and no binding global EIA convention is available for determining these matters. The 1991 Espoo Convention, 2001 Draft Articles on Prevention, judicial practices and scholarly work could provide lexicon for such a debate. Yet, final decision would certainly need to take into account the special circumstance in each specific case and be based on *lex specialis*, if available.

4.2.4.3 Appraisal: EIA in the Area Deviating from Procedural Rules of Transboundary EIA

Deep seabed mining are in general considered as inherently risky, if not ultrahazardous, industrial activities. Undoubtedly, EIA is a prerequisite in DSM context. The question for sponsoring States' obligation concerning EIA should then focus on the adequacy of their fulfillment of the obligation. Are there criteria for such a determination? Lingjie Kong asserted that the EIA provisions of the UNCLOS are 'rudimentary and unelaborated' which are 'incapable of safeguarding environmental sustainability'.[96] He then suggested competent organizations may adopt new rules on EIA in forms of agreements and guidelines to supplement and develop the UNCLOS; he also proposed the contents of EIA rules by drawing mainly on the 1991 Espoo Convention and the 2001 ILC's Draft Article on Prevention.[97] It is noted that in DSM context, first, the Legal and Technical Commission (LTC) of the ISA has issued EIA guidelines; and second, ISA's Exploration Regulations requires the sponsoring State to cooperate with the ISA in the establishment and implementation of EIA and monitoring programmes. The Area and mineral resources in it as the global commons administered by the ISA makes the sponsoring State's obligation concerning EIA deviate from requirements of States under transboundary EIA rules.

[95] Alan Boyle, 'Developments in the International Law of Environmental Impact Assessments and their Relation to the Espoo Convention' (2012) 20(3) *RECIEL* 227–231.

[96] Lingjie Kong, 'Environmental Impact Assessment under the United Nations Convention on the Law of the Sea' (2011) 10 *Chinese JIL*, 651–669.

[97] Ibid., the contents of EIA rules include: (1) screening in marine EIA, (2) scope and contents of marine EIA reports, (3) public participation in marine EIA, (4) interstate notification and consultation in marine EIA, (5) final decision and (6) post-project monitoring of marine EIA.

How does EIA in the global commons distinguish from transboundary EIA?[98] Let us first look at an example of EIA in the global commons – EIA in the Antarctic Treaty area. According to Annex I to the 1991 Protocol on Environmental Protection to the Antarctic Treaty (EIA Annex to the 1991 Protocol), proposed activities in the Antarctic could be subject to three levels of assessment, depending on their potential impacts on the environment. Specifically, any proposed activities in the Antarctic Treaty Area are to be assessed at the preliminary stage; if the assessment shows that there is a minor or transitory impact or more than minor or transitory impact, then an Initial Environment Evaluation (IEE) or Comprehensive Environment Evaluation (CEE) must be considered at the second or the third stage.

Both Consultative Parties to the Antarctic Treaty and the Antarctic Treaty Consultative Meeting (ATCM) play roles in the EIA procedure in Antarctica.[99] First, Consultative Parties should have national legislation in place which includes procedures and guidelines for the preparation of EIAs in the Antarctic.[100] To enhance the effectiveness of the Consultative Parties' fulfillment of the obligation, the ATCM adopted EIA Guidelines.[101] Second, Consultative Parties are obliged to exchange information on EIA with other Parties.[102] In this respect, the ATCM adopted 'EIA: Circulation of Information'.[103] Third, during a CEE, national authorities should review the draft CEE, make comments and make decisions on the basis of the consideration of the final CEE. The draft

[98] Warner examined initiatives of global EIA and Strategic Environmental Assessment (SEA) in areas beyond national jurisdiction (ABNJ) as well as the role of sectoral environmental assessment in ABNJ. However, he did not touch upon the differences between EIA in ABNJ and that in a transboundary context. See Robin Warner, 'Oceans beyond Boundaries: Environmental Assessment Frameworks' (2012) 27(2) *IJMCL* 481–499.

[99] Committee of Environmental Protection (CEP) was established under Article 12 of the 1991 Protocol. The ATCM normally acts in light of the advice of CEP with the subject matter of environmental protection.

[100] Guidelines for Environmental Impact Assessment in Antarctica, Resolution 1(1999) ATCM XXIII – CEP II, Lima, adopted on 4 June 1999.

[101] Ibid. The document was revised twice: Resolution 4 (2005) ATCM XXVIII – CEP VIII, Stockholm, adopted on 17 June 2005 and Resolution 1 (2016) at ATCM XXXIX – CEP XIX, Santiago, adopted on 1 June 2016.

[102] Article 6 of the EIA Annex to the 1991 Protocol.

[103] EIA: circulation of information, Resolution 6 (1995) ATCM XIX, Seoul, adopted on 19 May 1995; upon the establishment of the Secretariat of the Antarctic Treaty, the document was revised by Resolution 1 (2005) ATCM XXVIII – CEP VIII, Stockholm, adopted on 17 June 2005.

CEE should be considered by the ATCM upon the advice of the Committee of Environmental Protection. Fourth, upon completion of a CEE, the Consultative Parties should review activities carried out, record any changes to the activities and report to the Parties on the outcomes; the ATCM provided guidance to the Consultative Parties in this respect.[104] It is seen that the obligation of a Consultative Party concerning EIA is not towards another State but to the other Consultative Parties collectively.[105] This is the most critical difference between EIAs in the Antarctic and transboundary EIAs.[106] Another difference is the fact that in a transboundary context, States notify and consult each other directly, while in the Antarctic context, the ATCM plays important roles in providing guidance for EIA, circulation of information and review of the draft CEE.

Since the Area and the Antarctic are both considered as the global commons, EIA in the context of DSM shares much similarity with EIA in the Antarctic. First, the sponsoring State's obligation is directed towards the States Parties to the UNCLOS collectively, or towards the international community as a whole in light of the principle of CHM. Second, the ISA plays important roles in the EIA procedure. Especially, the roles played by the ISA in the context of DSM are much larger than the ATCM in the Antarctic. As analysed in Chapter 3 of this book, the ISA is the representative of both the collective interests of the States Parties to the UNCLOS and the common interests of mankind, and it functions as a centralized administrator with respect to DSM. For this reason, it is the ISA rather than the sponsoring State that plays the dominant role in the EIA procedure at the international level. The ISA provides guidance to the contractor on conducting an EIA; it also establishes and implements the monitoring programme, while the sponsoring State and the contractor must cooperate with the ISA in

[104] Procedures for Comprehensive Environmental Evaluation follow-up, Resolution 2 (1997) ATCM XXI, Christchurch, adopted on 30 May 1997.

[105] This is the obligation *erga omnes partes*. Arguably, it might also be seen as the obligation *erga omnes* because the Antarctic gains the status of global commons and the obligation is towards the international community as a whole.

[106] It is noted that during the ILC's work on international liability, some members of the ILC pointed out that if the 'global commons' were to be included in the scope of the topic, procedures should be applicable to situations in which the whole of the international community was considered to be affected and harmed. (ILC Report, A/44/10, 1989, para. 379). Owing exactly to this consideration, the ILC has confined the scope of its work to the transboundary context, while the environmental damage that occurs in the global commons is excluded.

monitoring and implementing the EIA programme, especially through the establishment of 'impact reference zones' and 'preservation reference zones'.[107] The relationship between the ISA and the sponsoring State in the context of DSM is distinct from that between the affected State and the State of origin in a transboundary context. While the latter is an equal relationship between sovereign States, the former is an unequal relationship between an international organization and its member State, or between the 'international community' and a State. While EIAs in a transboundary context must follow a principle of equitable balance of interests between States concerned,[108] EIAs in the context of DSM are for the common interests of the international community as a whole in the protection of the marine environment.

In a word, owing to the different subjects involved, the different nature of legal relationships between the subjects and the different governing principles, the procedures for EIA designed in a transboundary context as exemplified in the 1991 Espoo Convention and the 2001 Draft Articles on Prevention are not suitable in the DSM context.[109] For the sponsoring State's obligation concerning EIA, two points are highlighted here. First, the sponsoring State may implement the EIA guidelines issued by the ISA by endorsing, translating or incorporating them into its national law. As shown in the beginning of this chapter, DSM legal regime embodies a dual-track regulatory system, it is neither necessary nor desirable for the sponsoring State to issue EIA guidelines in disregard of the ISA's. Second, the sponsoring State's obligation to cooperate with the ISA in the establishment and implementation of EIA and monitoring programmes is mandatory and of importance. Craik highlighted the 'duty to cooperate' as a dimension of EIA.[110] The next subsection will further discuss the sponsoring State's obligation to cooperate in a broader sense.

[107] Regulation 31(6) of the 2013 Exploration Regulations on Nodules (ISBA/19/A/9), Regulation 33(6) of the 2010 Exploration Regulations on Sulphides (ISBA/16/A/12/Rev.1) and the 2012 Exploration Regulations on Crust (ISBA/18/A/11).

[108] Article 9 of the 2001 Draft Articles on Prevention requires the States concerned to seek solutions based on an equitable balance of interests; Article 10 lays down the factors involved in an equitable balance of interests.

[109] These are the procedures for notification, exchange of information, consultation and public participation.

[110] Neil Craik, 'The Duty to Cooperate in The Customary Law of Environmental Impact Assessment' (2020) 69(1) *International and Comparative Law Quarterly* 239–259.

4.2.5 Obligation to Cooperate

In contrast with the sponsoring State's 'obligation to assist' the ISA which is associated with the unique dual-track regulatory system in DSM regime, its 'obligation to cooperate' is based not only on the DSM legal regime but also general international law. Moreover, the obligation to cooperate may involve a wider range of subjects. That is, a sponsoring State may not only be required to cooperate with the ISA, but with others as well, including the contractor, other States, other competent international organizations and entities. Finally, the obligation to cooperate is of particular importance to international environmental protection and especially that in the Area as a global commons.

Within the DSM legal regime, the sponsoring State is specifically required to cooperate with the ISA and the contractor in 'the establishment and implementation of programmes for monitoring and evaluating the impacts of deep seabed mining on the marine environment' under Exploration Regulations.[111] Under the 2019 draft Exploitation Regulations that obligation covers a wider subject-matter. In addition to a general provision on 'duty to cooperate and exchange of information' in Regulation 3 which covers a wide range of specific issues, Regulations 53(2) and 75(5) highlight the duty to cooperate in making plans for and responding to environmental incidents and in auditing and inspecting activities of the contractor at the enforcement stage, respectively.[112]

Article 197 of the UNCLOS imposes on States the obligation of cooperation on a global or regional basis for the protection and preservation of the marine environment, directly or through competent international organizations. Principle 7 of the Rio Declaration pronounces that 'States shall co-operate in a spirit of global partnership to conserve, protect and restore the health and integrity of the Earth's ecosystem.'[113] The ITLOS indicated in the *MOX* case that 'duty to cooperate is a fundamental principle in the prevention of pollution of the marine environment under Part XII of the Convention and general international

[111] Regulation 31(6) of the 2013 Exploration Regulations on Nodules (ISBA/19/A/17); Regulation 33(6) of the 2010 Exploration Regulations on Sulphides (ISBA/16/A/12/Rev.1) and the 2012 Exploration Regulations on Crust (ISBA/18/A/11).

[112] The 2019 draft Exploitation Regulations, ISBA/25/C/WP.1.

[113] Ileana M. Porras, 'The Rio Declaration: A New Basis for International Cooperation', in *Greening International Law* (Routledge 1993).

law'.[114] In effect, nowadays any discussions about the utilization, preservation and protection of shared/common natural resources or heritage would be incomplete if the legal issue of States' duty to cooperate were not covered.[115] The duty to cooperate for the purpose of international environmental protection both attests and gives further impetus to the shift from 'international law of coexistence' to 'international law of cooperation' initially proposed by Friedmann in the 1960s.[116] Such a shift is tied to the trend of the development of international law towards community interests as demonstrated in Chapter 2. The DSM legal regime based on the principle of CHM not only brings that trend to a new height but more importantly transforms the ideal to a reality. Within this terrain to cater to community interests, States' duty to cooperate is both essential and mandatory. Yet, the concrete contents of the sponsoring State's duty to cooperate will have to be specified in future practice alongside the progress of DSM.

4.3 International Environmental Obligations of the Contractor

Like the ISA and the sponsoring State, the contractor is required by the Exploration Regulations to comply with the principle of prevention, applying the precautionary approach and the best environmental

114 ITLOS, *MOX Plant (request for provisional measures)*, Order of 3 December 2001, para. 82.

115 Oran R. Young, *International Cooperation: Building Regimes for Natural Resources and the Environment* (Cornell University Press 1989). Neil Craik, 'The Duty to Cooperate in International Environmental Law: Constraining State Discretion Through Due Respect' (2021) Yearbook of International Environmental Law. With respect to the general duty to cooperate in international water law, see Christina Leb, 'Implementation of the General Duty to Cooperate' in Stephen McCaffrey, Christina Leb and Riley Denoon (eds.), *Research Handbook on International Water Law* (Edward Elgar 2019). With respect to duty to cooperate on the high seas, see Margaret Young and Sebastian Sullivan, 'Evolution through the Duty to Cooperate: Implications of the Whaling case at the International Court of Justice' (2015) 16 *MJIL* 311; and Murray, 'Strengthening Regional Fisheries Management – An Analysis of the Duty to Cooperate' (2011) 9(2) *New Zealand Journal of Public and International Law* 223–245. With respect to cooperation in outer space, see Shengli Jiang, Yun Zhao, 'China's National Space Station: Opportunities, Challenges, and Solutions for International Cooperation' (2021) 57 *Space Policy*. With respect to duty to cooperate for protecting world cultural heritage, see Michail Risvas, 'The Duty to Cooperate and the Protection of Underwater Cultural Heritage' (2013) 2(3) *Cambridge Journal of International and Comparative Law* 562–590.

116 Wolfgang Friedmann, *The Changing Structure of International Law* (Stevens & Sons 1964).

practices.[117] Moreover, the contractor is required to conduct an EIA, to cooperate with the ISA and the sponsoring State in the establishment and implementation of a monitoring programme[118] and to report the result of the monitoring programme.[119] Additionally, the contractor has also obligations in preparing for and responding to an environmental emergency.[120] Finally, as the ISA shifts to a results-based regulatory approach featured with environmental management, the contractor will also be imposed with environmental management obligations during the exploitation stage.

Three explanatory notes are necessary. First, since at the international level the principal legal relationship is between the ISA and the contractor, obligations of the contractor are correlative to the regulatory powers and obligations of the ISA. To avoid repetition, as an obligation was discussed in detail in Chapter 3, then the corresponding part in this section will be succinct, and vice versa. Second, the obligations of contractors can derive from either international law or the contract signed between them and the ISA; they are of different nature but their contents are almost the same because most of the legal requirements under the UNCLOS, the 1994 Agreement and the Regulations are incorporated into contracts. Third, this section refers frequently to draft Exploitation Regulations as well as phase 1 Standards and Guidelines, since a forward-looking attitude is adopted here, and it is believed that, once adopted, they will become the primary legal bases for international environmental obligations of the contractor.

4.3.1 *Obligations to Conduct EIAs and Submit EISs*

Insofar as environmental protection is concerned, the most important obligation of the contractor is to conduct EIAs. Section 1, paragraph 7 of the Annex to the 1994 Agreement requires that 'an application for

117 Regulation 31(5) of the 2013 Exploration Regulations on Nodules (ISBA/19/A/17); Regulation 33(5) of the 2010 Exploration Regulations on Sulphides (ISBA/16/A/12/Rev.1) and the 2012 Exploration Regulations on Crust (ISBA/18/A/11).

118 Ibid.

119 Regulation 32(2) of the 2013 Exploration Regulations on Nodules (ISBA/19/A/17); Regulation 34(2) of the 2010 Exploration Regulations on Sulphides (ISBA/16/A/12/Rev.1) and the 2012 Exploration Regulations on Crust (ISBA/18/A/11).

120 Regulation 33 of the 2013 Exploration Regulations on Nodules (ISBA/19/A/17); Regulation 35 of the 2010 Exploration Regulations on Sulphides (ISBA/16/A/12/Rev.1) and the 2012 Exploration Regulations on Crust (ISBA/18/A/11).

approval of a plan of work shall be accompanied by an assessment of the potential environmental impacts of the proposed activities'. The Exploration Regulations further clarify the data and information that should be contained in an environmental impact statement (EIS) accompanied with the application for approval of a plan of work as follows:

(a) A description of the programme for oceanographic and environmental baseline studies [. . .], including, but not restricted to, the impact on biodiversity, of the proposed exploration activities [. . .];
(b) A preliminary assessment of the possible impact of the proposed exploration activities on the marine environment;
(c) A description of proposed measures for the prevention, reduction and control of pollution and other hazards, as well as possible impacts, to the marine environment.[121]

The same contents are repeated in standard clauses for the exploration contract, therefore making it also a contractual obligation for contractors.[122] Because the impact on the marine environment is assessed against the baseline of the environment, to conduct an EIA, first, the contractor must 'gather baseline data and to establish an environmental baseline'.[123] Recognizing the importance of baseline knowledge as a prerequisite for effective EIAs, Christiansen et al. proposed the quality criteria of a robust environmental baseline.[124] And the LTC identifies environmental baseline as a priority issue for its Phase 1 Standards and Guidelines for exploitation activities.[125] Then, the contractor must monitor the change of the environment continuously during and after the DSM activities. Likewise, the LTC provides practical guidance for contractors on conducting EIAs by issuing Recommendations for exploration activities, and

[121] Regulation 18 of the 2013 Exploration Regulations on Nodules (ISBA/19/A/17); Regulation 20 of the 2010 Exploration Regulations on Sulphides (ISBA/16/A/12/Rev.1) and the 2012 Exploration Regulations on Crust (ISBA/18/A/11).

[122] Section IV, Annex II to 2013 Exploration Regulations on Nodules (ISBA/19/A/17), the 2012 Exploration Regulations on Crust (ISBA/18/A/11) and the 2010 Exploration Regulations on Sulphides (ISBA/16/A/12/Rev.1).

[123] Regulation 32(1) of the 2013 Exploration Regulations on Nodules (ISBA/19/A/17); Regulation 34(1) of the 2010 Exploration Regulations on Sulphides (ISBA/16/A/12/Rev.1) and the 2012 Exploration Regulations on Crust (ISBA/18/A/11).

[124] Sabine Christiansen, Stefan Brager and Aline Jaeckel, 'Evaluating the Quality of Environmental Baselines for Deep Seabed Mining' (2022) 9 *Frontiers in Marine Science* 898711.

[125] Draft Guidelines for the Establishment of Baseline Environmental Data, ISBA/27/C/11, 2022.

Standard and Guidelines for exploitation activities.[126] In order to keep abreast of technological developments, such Recommendations, Standard and Guidelines must be subjected to periodical review. Also, to ensure the continuity between exploration and exploitation, the Standard and Guidelines on EIA must be consistent with Recommendations.

The EIA practice of exploration contractors had been by and large unknown to the public. Because EISs, if there were, were normally included in the application files and annual reports of contractors which were not disclosed to the public and the review process of the LTC was done privately. However, the situation changed in 2018 when two contractors, Global Sea Mineral Resources (GSR) and Federal Institute for Geosciences and Natural Resources (BGR), submitted EISs concerning equipment and technological testing activities. For the first time, EISs of contractors were published by the ISA on its website.[127] In 2020, another EIS submission by the Ministry of Earth Sciences (MoES), Government of India was disclosed to the public too.[128] These three published EISs share a common conclusion that 'due to the small spatial and temporal scale of the testing activity, no serious harm will be caused' to the seafloor environment or at any depth within the water column.[129] It is noted that the 2019 version of Recommendations for Guidance on EIA includes 'testing of collection systems and equipment' as one of the activities

[126] For EIA at the exploration stage, 'Recommendations for the guidance of contractors for the assessment of the possible environmental impacts arising from exploration for marine minerals in the Area' ('EIA Recommendation'), ISBA/25/LTC/6/Rev.2, 2019. For EIA at the exploitation stage, 'Draft standard and guidelines for the environmental impact assessment process', ISBA/27/C/4, 2022. 'Draft guidelines for the preparation of environmental impact statements', ISBA/27/C/5, 2022.

[127] GSR and BGR EISs of 2018 are available at the official website of the ISA: www.isa.org.jm/environmental-impact-assessments.

[128] The Ministry of Earth Sciences (MoES), Government of India submitted an EIS to the ISA in January 2020 for the purpose of a deep sea mining system trial in the Central Indian Ocean Basin in 2021. The EIS is available at: https://moes.gov.in/content/deep-sea-mining-system-trials-moes.

[129] BGR's testing activities were conducted in an area of 100 * 900 m at a water depth of around 4,100 m over a time period of maximally four days. GSR's testing activities were conducted in a small area of approximately 0.1 km^2 at a water depth of around 4,400 m over a time period of maximal four days. MoES' testing activities are planned to be conducted in an area with 0.8 m width and maximum 1000 m length and collected nodules from sediment layer down to 15–30 cm, at a water depth of around 5,100 m for a period of nine days.

'requiring environmental impact assessment'.[130] Admittedly, the impacts of testing activities are not comparable to that of large-scale commercial exploitation activities, these three EISs have demonstrated that the guidance of the LTC can be instrumental to consistent EISs among contractors. The contents of the abovementioned three published EISs are to a large extent compatible with the EIS templates annexed to various versions of the draft Exploitation Regulations,[131] although the EIS template to be issued by the LTC would likely be of a recommendatory nature.[132]

Based upon an analysis of the EISs of BGR and GSR in 2018, and in particular, the EIAs by seabed miners at the national level, Clark et al. came to a negative conclusion concerning the effectiveness of EIAs in the industry of seabed mining.[133] In spite of the suggestions for improvement of the effectiveness of DSM EIAs in the future, there is, in a sense, no immediate remedy because 'EIA preparation and the development of environmental management plans are almost by definition working in a knowledge-poor situation, with many gaps in information for risk assessment, and high uncertainty.'[134] Hence, from a scientific point of view, the quality of EIAs could only be enhanced progressively along with the advancement of marine sciences and technologies.

Besides marine sciences and technologies, it has been much debated that the EIA procedure would also affect the effectiveness of EIAs. Durden et al. depicted an ideal EIA process as containing screening, scoping and assessment phases, along with the development of an environmental management plan (EMP) and considered that 'the existing [DSM] regulations present only a portion of a robust EIA process'.[135] They also argued that an ideal EIA process should include not only regulatory review, but also external review by experts and stakeholder consultation with respect to which the current DSM EIA process is

130 EIA Recommendation, ISBA/25/LTC/6/Rev.2, 2019. Section VI(B) (b).

131 Draft Environmental Impact Statement template, ISBA/23/LTC/CRP.3*, 2017; ISBA/24/LTC/WP.1/Add.1, 2018; and ISBA/25/C/WP.1, 2019.

132 'Draft guidelines for the preparation of environmental impact statements', ISBA/27/C/5, 2022.

133 Malcolm Clark, Jennifer Durden and Sabine Christiansen, 'Environmental Impact Assessment for Deep-Sea Mining: Can We Improve Their Future Effectiveness?' (2020) 114 *Marine Policy* 1–9.

134 Ibid., 2.

135 Jennifer Durden et al., 'Environmental Impact Assessment Process for Deep-Sea Mining in "the Area"' (2018) 87 *Marine Policy* 194–202, 195.

inadequate. This view echoed Laura Lallier and Frank Maes' criticism.[136] They contended that the very nature of ISA as an international organization, in particular 'the meeting cycle of the ISA organs', may present a challenge to the inclusion of independent expert review and public participation mechanisms in EIA process.[137] Similarly, Durden et al. considered the institutional capacity of the ISA at its present state as too limited to address its numerous environment management tasks, including the implementation a robust EIA process.[138] Secondly, Lallier and Maes argued that 'one of the challenges of setting up an EIA framework is to design an adequate review procedure that guarantees well-informed decision-making'.[139] Likewise, Durden et al. contended that the ISA should make more efforts to integrate EIA into decision-making process.[140] Clark et al. were of the same opinion that 'the ultimate goal of EIA effectiveness is decision-making'.[141] Thirdly, Durden et al. regarded the questions of how to address scientific uncertainty[142] and to detail requirements for all phases of an EIA process[143] as other challenges faced by the ISA, specifically, the LTC.

The above criticisms concentrate mostly on the lack of external expert review and public participation procedures in the review process of an DSM EIA. If these criticisms were true because EIA reports submitted by contractors were reviewed by the LTC in private in the beginning, they cannot be true for the review of the EISs submitted by BGR and GSR in 2018 where external expert review[144] and public participation

[136] Laura Lallier and Frank Maes, 'Environmental Impact Assessment Procedure for Deep Seabed Mining in the Area: Independent Expert Review and Public Participation' (2016) 70 *Marine Policy* 212–219.

[137] Ibid., 218.

[138] Jennifer Durden et al., 'Environmental Impact Assessment Process for Deep-Sea Mining in "the Area"' (2018) 87 *Marine Policy* 194–202, 200, 201.

[139] Laura Lallier and Frank Maes, 'Environmental Impact Assessment Procedure for Deep Seabed Mining in the Area: Independent Expert Review and Public Participation' (2016) 70 *Marine Policy* 212–219, 213.

[140] Durden et al., 200.

[141] Malcolm Clark, Jennifer Durden and Sabine Christiansen, 'Environmental Impact Assessment for Deep-Sea Mining: Can We Improve Their Future Effectiveness?' (2020) 114 *Marine Policy*, 7.

[142] Durden et al., 200.

[143] Ibid.

[144] The EISs submitted to the Secretary-General of the ISA were first under preliminary review by technical officers within the Secretariat, then sent to 'two internationally recognized external experts' for further evaluation in the form of peer review before it is subjected to the evaluation of the LTC. ISA, Review of EIA for the testing of collector components in the exploration area, note by the Secretariat, ISBA/25/LTC/4, 2019.

procedures[145] were employed. In the draft Exploitation Regulations, the EIA process is further strengthened, which is featured by greater transparency, public participation and inclusiveness. For instance, environmental plans submitted by an applicant for approval of plans of work should be published on the website of the ISA (transparency) for comments of stakeholders (public participation); such comments shall be taken into account by the LTC in its review process and reflected in its report as well as in its recommendations to the Council (inclusiveness).[146] It is acknowledged by the ISA that 'a more formalized and transparent approach to the use and engagement of independent experts merits consideration'.[147] In this regard, many questions are involved: the topics subject to independent review, the selection of qualified experts, the weight accorded to independent expert advice and the coordination between this new mechanism with the exercise of powers by the Secretariat and the LTC of the ISA, etc.[148] Introducing independent reviewers alongside the LTC has benefits but generate new problems too. For instance, what would the contractor do if independent reviewers and the LTC hold different or even opposite views towards its EIS?

There is close interplay between the review of EISs by the LTC (and stakeholders) and the conduct of EIAs by the contractor. For one thing, the reviewers (the LTC and other possible external reviewers) and the EIA doers (applicants and contractors) should follow the same (minimal) standard as described in the Regulations and LTC's Recommendations, Standards and Guidelines. For another, how an EIS is reviewed would have great implications on the way an EIA is conducted and the contents and quality of an EIS.[149] Hence, the effectiveness of an EIA is determined by both the substantive requirement (on the basis of scientific progress)

145 The sponsoring States, Belgium and Germany, respectively organize consultative procedures to allow the public to comment on the EISs and the sponsored contractors to respond to these comments. They also make these comments available for the public online. Ibid.

146 Regulation 11 (publication and review of the Environmental Plans), Part II (applications for approval of plans of work in the form of contracts), Draft Regulations on Exploitation of mineral resources in the Area, prepared by the LTC, ISBA/25/C/WP.1, 2019.

147 Consideration of a mechanism and process for the independent review of environmental plans and performance assessments under the regulations on exploitation of mineral resources in the Area, Note by the Secretariat, ISBA/25/C/10, 2019.

148 Ibid.

149 The purpose of the EIS is to document and report the results of the EIA, Regulation 47 of the 2019 Draft Exploitation Regulations.

and the procedural design, by both the conduct and review processes, and by the involvement of both contractors, regulatory body (the ISA) and possibly the public (expert community and the general public).

4.3.2 Obligations to Prepare for and Respond to Environmental Emergencies

In addition to fulfilling the obligation to conduct an EIA on a regular track, equally important for the contractor is to fulfil the requirements in an environmental emergency. According to Exploration Regulations, first of all, much should be done in advance, at a pre-incident phase. To start with, the contractor is required to be equipped with adequate 'financial and technical capability' in order to 'comply promptly with emergency orders'.[150] In addition, prior to the commencement of testing of collecting systems and processing operations, the contractor must 'provide the Council with a guarantee of its financial and technical capability to comply promptly with emergency orders or to assure that the Council can take such emergency measures'.[151] Moreover, before the commencement of its programme of activities under a exploration contract, the contractor is required to submit contingency plans.[152] Secondly, when an incident has occurred or threatens to occur, the contractor is under the obligation to report to the ISA promptly[153] and to comply with emergency orders issued by the Council and immediate measures of a temporary nature issued by the Secretary-General.[154] Thirdly, in case the contractor does not promptly comply with the emergency orders and take measures, the Council shall take reasonable measures.[155] In this

[150] Regulation 21(3)(c) of the 2013 Exploration Regulations on Nodules (ISBA/19/A/17), Regulation 23 (3) (c) of the 2012 Exploration Regulations on Crust (ISBA/18/A/11) and the 2010 Exploration Regulations on Sulphides (ISBA/16/A/12/Rev.1).

[151] Regulation 33(8) of the 2013 Exploration Regulations on Nodules (ISBA/19/A/17), Regulation 35 (7) of the 2012 Exploration Regulations on Crust (ISBA/18/A/11) and the 2010 Exploration Regulations on Sulphides (ISBA/16/A/12/Rev.1).

[152] Section 6.1, Annex IV to the Exploration Regulations.

[153] Regulation 33(1) of the 2013 Exploration Regulations on Nodules (ISBA/19/A/17), Regulation 35 (1) of the 2012 Exploration Regulations on Crust (ISBA/18/A/11) and the 2010 Exploration Regulations on Sulphides (ISBA/16/A/12/Rev.1). Detailed contents of the report are listed in Section 6.2, Annex IV to all three sets of Exploration Regulations.

[154] Section 6.3, Annex IV to the Exploration Regulations.

[155] Regulation 33(7) of the 2013 Exploration Regulations on Nodules (ISBA/19/A/17), Regulation 35 (7) of the 2012 Exploration Regulations on Crust (ISBA/18/A/11) and the 2010 Exploration Regulations on Sulphides (ISBA/16/A/12/Rev.1).

situation, the contractor must reimburse the ISA; monetary penalties may also be imposed on the contractor.[156]

In the draft Exploitation Regulations, the contractor shall 'reduce the risk of incidents as much as reasonably practicable' during exploitation.[157] And the contractor shall discontinue exploitation activities in case such activities would be likely to cause an incident.[158] 'Incident', insofar as environment is concerned, means an event or sequence of events which cause(s) 'serious harm to the marine environment'.[159] It should be distinguished from the acceptable environmental impacts of normal operation of DSM. More importantly, the contractor is required to prepare 'Emergency Response and Contingency Plans' and maintain the capability to implement such plans throughout the mining life cycle.[160] The LTC has issued Standard and Guidelines on the preparation and implementation of Emergency Response and Contingency Plans.[161]

Comparing the environmental emergency provisions in the Exploration Regulations and those in the 2019 draft Exploitation Regulations, the most notable difference is that, in the former, the 'emergency order' issued by the Council of the ISA plays a central role, while in the latter, it is the 'Emergency Response and Contingency Plan' of the contractor. This shifting of centre from the ISA to the contractor in dealing with environmental emergency may be explained by the following facts. On the one hand, States acknowledge that 'the current functionality of the Council and restrictive nature of its working methods is not conductive to taking urgent action that may be required in future'.[162] On the other, the contractor is both in a better position (as the operator) and with better capability (with technologies and facilities) than the ISA in preparing for and responding to an environmental emergency.

156 Section 6.4, Annex IV to the Exploration Regulations.

157 Regulation 32 of the 2019 draft Exploitation Regulations, ISBA/25/C/WP.1.

158 Regulation 33 of the 2019 draft Exploitation Regulations, ISBA/25/C/WP.1.

159 Schedule (use of terms and scope) annexed to the 2019 draft Exploitation Regulations, ISBA/25/C/WP.1.

160 Regulation 53 of the 2019 draft Exploitation Regulations, ISBA/25/C/WP.1. Annex V of the draft Regulations details on the contents of an Emergency Response and Contingency Plan.

161 Draft Standard and Guidelines for the Preparation and Implementation of Emergency Response and Contingency Plans, ISBA/27/C/12, 2022.

162 David Johnson et al., 'Periodic Review of the International Seabed Authority pursuant to UNCLOS Article 154' Final Report, 30 December 2016, 32.

The contractor, however, does not develop an Emergency Response and Contingency Plan on its own. Rather, the Plan is developed 'in junction with other international organisations, flag states, coastal states and sponsoring States and other entities that have relevant jurisdictional competence with regard to specific components of the plan'.[163] And such a Plan shall be developed in light of the Good Industry Practice (GIP), best available scientific evidence (BASE) and best available technologies (BATs).[164] With the advancement of marine sciences and technologies, and the change of practice of maritime mining industries, the Emergency Response and Contingency Plan shall correspondingly be kept under review and revised. In effect, the contractor should be constantly alert to environmental incident because DSM is inherently a highly risky activity. Thus, EISs of contractors shall include 'incident reporting' which outlines how incidents will be reported and managed. Also, the Emergency Response and Contingency Plans are incorporated into the contractors' environmental management system (EMS). In a word, the legal obligation of the contractor with respect to environmental emergency is interconnected with that of conducting EIAs, submitting EISs and maintaining an environmental management system.

4.3.3 Environmental Management and Monitoring Obligations

Under the Exploration Regulations, the contractor is required to establish a programme to monitor and report on the likely effects of exploration activities on the marine environment.[165] The same requirement of running a monitoring programme is found in the draft Exploitation Regulations too. Additionally, at the very beginning of the development of the Exploitation Regulations, it is stated that the ISA will require the contractor to submit and implement an EMP alongside the required EIS.[166] Later on, the draft Exploitation Regulations requires the contractor to implement and maintain an environmental management system while carrying out the exploitation activities.[167] It is seen that

[163] Annex V of the 2019 Draft Exploitation Regulations, ISBA/25/C/WP.1.
[164] Regulation 53 of the 2019 Draft Exploitation Regulations, ISBA/25/C/WP.1.
[165] Regulation 32 of the 2013 Exploration Regulations on Nodules (ISBA/19/C/17), Regulation 34 of the 2012 Exploration Regulations on Crust (ISBA/18/A/11) and the 2010 Exploration Regulations on Sulphides (ISBA/16/A/12/Rev.1).
[166] ISA, 'Developing a Regulatory Framework for Mineral Exploitation in the Area – Stakeholder Engagement', March 2014, para. 18.
[167] Regulation 46 of the 2019 draft Exploitation Regulations, ISBA/25/C/WP.1.

an applicant must submit an environmental management and monitoring plan (EMMP) to the ISA when applying for the approval of a Work of Plan for Exploitation. An EMMP provides details of the applicant's EMS and environmental policy[168] and must include a description of 'the planned monitoring program'.[169] The purpose of an EMMP is to 'manage and confirm that environmental effects meet the environmental quality objectives and standards for the mining operation'.[170] It is thus seen that the requirements of environment monitoring and EMS are component measures for implementing an EMMP.

An EMS is originally designed by the International Organization for Standardization (ISO)[171] as 'a framework that helps an organization achieve its environmental goals through consistent review, evaluation, and improvement of its environmental performance'.[172] The 2019 draft Exploitation Regulations endorses ISO 14001. With an intention to help the contractor to fulfil the ISA's environmental regulatory requirements in a systematic manner, the phase 1 draft Standard and Guidelines on the development and application of EMSs details on the leadership and policy, core processes and support of the contractor in developing and applying EMS in the specific context of DSM.[173] The draft Standard and Guidelines shows that the requirement of EMS is voluntary, has a focus on the internal governance of the contractor and embodies an all-embracing process that is connected to all other environmental requirements of the contractor.

Indeed, the substantive contents of obligations concerning EMS are to a large extent self-determined by the contractor. Some commentators expressed their concern over the situation of 'relying on contractors to define environmental metrics' and the EMS processes being 'contractor driven'.[174] Such a concern would be relieved for the following two

168 Annex VII to the 2019 draft Exploitation Regulations, paragraph 2(d), ISBA/25/C/WP.1.

169 Ibid., paragraph 2(g).

170 Regulation 48 of the 2019 draft Exploitation Regulations, ISBA/25/C/WP.1.

171 ISO 14001 family 'environmental management': www.iso.org/iso-14001-environmental-management.html.

172 United States Environmental Protection Agency, 'learn about environmental management systems', available at: www.epa.gov/ems/learn-about-environmental-management-systems.

173 Draft Standard and Guidelines on the Development and Application of Environmental Management Systems, prepared by the Legal and Technical Commission, ISBA/27/C/7, 2022.

174 Report of the Chair of the Legal and Technical Commission summarizing stakeholder feedback on the phase 1 draft standards and guidelines, ISBA/27/C/2, 2022, para. 20.

considerations. First, the 'contractor' should refer not to an individual contractor but to all contractors collectively, which means that the efficiency of EMS of each contractor need to be evaluated at the industrial level. Admittedly, the nascent nature of the industry poses a significant challenge to the environmental management evaluation. Still, the operators in the industry are arguably in better position than the ISA to tackle this challenge, as it is the industry that accumulate experience at the front-line exploitation operations and thus can adjust the environmental management in response to the changed situation in the most timely manner. Second, the contractor's obligation to implement and maintain an EMS must be read in conjunction with all other environmental requirements imposed on it, including that of EIA, EIS, environmental baseline, EMMP, closure plan, emergency response and contingency plan. The contractor's obligation to implement and maintain an EMS must also be read in conjunction with the ISA's environmental management strategies, goals and tools, such as regional environmental management plans (REMPs).[175] In other words, this obligation does not exist in isolation but as a part of a package deal, the big picture is the context that constitutes an inherent restraint to the interpretation of each component obligation. For this reason, allowing the contractor to substantiate the obligation concerning EMS would not be problematic.

As to the environmental monitoring programmes, they should include proposals for areas to be set aside and used exclusively as impact reference zones (IRZs) and preservation reference zones (PRZs).[176] IRZs and PRZs are areas 'representative of the environmental characteristics of the Area' that are both located in contract areas. What differentiates the two is the fact that IRZs are designated in mining areas and they will be used for assessing the effect of each contractor's activities on the marine environment, whereas in PRZs there will be no mining activity to ensure representative and stable biota of the seabed in order to assess any changes in the flora and fauna of the marine environment.[177] Jones et al. regard the approach used for allocating and assessing IRZs and PRZs as important for determining the environmental impacts that can

175 Relationship between the draft regulations on exploitation of mineral resources in the Area and regional environmental management plans, ISBA/25/C/4, 2019, para. 7.

176 Article 31(6) of the 2013 Exploration Regulations on Nodules (ISBA/19/A/17), Regulation 33 (6) of the 2012 Exploration Regulations on Crust (ISBA/18/A/11) and the 2010 Exploration Regulations on Sulphides (ISBA/16/A/12/Rev.1).

177 ISA, 'Design of IRZs and PRZs in Deep-Sea Mining Contract Areas', Briefing Paper 02/2018.

be measured and managed.[178] They attempt to provide scientific guidance for establishing these reference zones for polymetallic nodule mining by identifying eleven key considerations.[179] At the moment, as pilot mining activities are likely to start soon, it seems that the designation of IRZs and PRZs becomes an imminent burden on the shoulder of the contractor. IRZs and PRZs for the contractor, like areas of particular environmental interest (APEIs) for the ISA, are area-based management tools (ABMTs).[180] Yet, the designation of IRZs and PRZs by the contractor is at a claim-area scale, while that of APEIs by the ISA is at a regional level. In spite of the difference, they are functionally complementary to each other and should be taken together when assessing the environmental impacts of DSM activities. This is consistent with the requirement that when establishing a monitoring programme, the contractor shall cooperate with the ISA. Besides designation of IRZs and PRZs in the contract areas, the contractor could also set up monitoring stations.[181] Additionally, like the EMS, the monitoring obligation is also interlinked with other environmental obligations of the contractor. For instance, the EIA, environmental risk assessment (ERA) and mitigation measures are used to prepare the detailed monitoring plans within the EMMP.

4.3.4 *Obligation to Apply the Highest Standards of Environmental Protection*

The contractor is required to apply the highest standards of environmental protection at the exploitation stage. This is reflected by the frequent appearance of a few terms like best available scientific evidence (BASE), best available technologies (BATs), best environmental practices (BEPs) and Good Industry Practice (GIP) in the draft Exploitation Regulations. The advantage of including these flexible terms is obvious: they can automatically adapt to the future development of scientific knowledge, technologies and practices relating to DSM. On the other

[178] Daniel Jones et al., 'Environmental Considerations for Impact and Preservation Reference Zones for Deep-Sea Polymetallic Nodule Mining' (2020) 118 *Marine Policy.*

[179] Ibid.

[180] ABMTs have become key mechanisms for the protection of marine environment in respect to subject matters such as the fishery management in the high seas, the conservation of biological diversity in area beyond national jurisdiction (BBNJ) as well as DSM in the Area.

[181] Annex VII to the 2019 draft Exploitation Regulations (ISBA/25/C/WP.1) describes illustrative contents of an EMMP which include monitoring.

hand, however, even though definitions of these terms are given in the draft Exploitation Regulations,[182] they are difficult to be applied due to their inherent vagueness and fluidity. Standards for what is 'good' or 'best', if there are, cannot be predetermined once and for all, but must be determined and redefined along with the development of DSM activities.

Questions are: who is to set and update periodically the standards? Should these standards be voluntary or compulsory? Past experience shows that an industry could either self-regulate or be regulated by public authorities or resort to a mixed employment of these two ways. Among the many factors that determine which way to take, the level of matureness of the industry is important. With respect to DSM, owing to 'the nascent nature of industry' and 'the lack of an industry association equivalent to, for example, the International Association of Oil and Gas Producers',[183] self-regulation by the DSM industry is not the case at the moment.[184] It has been the LTC of the ISA that sets and updates Recommendations, Standards and Guidelines for the performance and process of the DSM activities of contractors.[185] Nonetheless, the factors that discourage self-regulation of the DSM industry and two other factors – 'the current levels of data and information' and 'the ability to set precise and quantitative thresholds and trigger points' – pose significant challenges to the standards-setting work of the LTC.[186] Indeed,

[182] Schedule 1 of the 2019 draft Exploitation Regulations, ISBA/25/C/WP.1. Explanatory notes on these terms were given by the Secretariat of the ISA: 'Key terms: distinguishing between good industry practice and best practices under the draft regulations on exploitation of mineral resources in the Area', ISBA/25/C/11, 2019.

[183] ISA, 'Content and Development of Standards and Guidelines for Activities in the Area under the Authority's Regulatory Framework' Note by the Secretariat, ISBA/25/C/3, 2018, para. 18.

[184] The International Marine Minerals Society (IMMS)'s Code for Environmental Management of Marine Mining' was an exceptional example (originally adopted by the IMMS on 2 November 2001, revised on 21 August 2009 and submitted to the ISA (ISBA/16/LTC/2, 2010). However, this Code only described a set of high-level-of-abstract principles and guidelines that are voluntary and meant to be complementary to the ISA's instruments.

[185] Gerber and Grogan suggested 'any required guideline standards for GIP and BEP are explicitly restricted to only those formally adopted, endorsed or issued by the ISA' and the ISA should provide 'prescriptive and dedicated procedural documents'. Leonardus Gerber and Renee Grogan, 'Challenges of Operationalising Good Industry Practice and Best Environmental Practice in Deep Seabed Mining Regulation' (2020) *Marine Policy* 1–6, 4 and 5.

[186] ISA, 'Content and Development of Standards and Guidelines for Activities in the Area under the Authority's Regulatory Framework' Note by the Secretariat, ISBA/25/C/3, 2018, para. 18.

setting standards against a background of a great gap in knowledge and experience is a seriously challenging job, no matter who is to take it.

As to the legal status of the instruments produced by the LTC, theoretically, the LTC's Recommendations are not binding. Yet, it would be hard for the contractor to challenge their applicability in practice. After all, the contractor is required expressly to apply BEP and there is no alternative source to show what BEP is other than the LTC's Recommendations. Lodge et al. argued that Recommendations of the LTC is a short name for BEP.[187] However, if the industry produces (voluntary) standards as it gets mature in the future, this would lend power to the contractor to challenge the applicability of the LTC's Recommendations, or even to claim for a phase-out of the LTC in this respect. For the exploitation stage, now the mainstream opinion is that the LTC's Standards will be obligatory while its Guidelines recommendatory. However, Guidelines might be presumptively applied to the contractor just like Standards, except that the application of the former may be subject to rebuttals of the contractor while the latter do not. Moreover, with the changing scientific knowledge, mining technology and practice, the dividing line between environmental requirements of a compulsory nature and that of recommendatory nature may shift too. There might be a dynamic twilight zone when it comes to the contents of international environmental obligations of the contractor. This ambiguity not only opens a big room for arguments but also poses a substantive obstacle to the establishment of international environmental liability of the contractor. Realizing the ambiguities concerning the contents of the international environmental obligations of the contractor, delegation of Germany proposed that the ISA should have 'normative environmental thresholds' available as the minimum controlling line of environmental quality.[188]

Additionally, it is recalled that BATs and BEPs have long been considered as tools to implement the precautionary principle/approach. Practice shows that, in the application of BATs and BEPs, one must take into account the economic feasibility as well as practicalities. That is, the technology or environmental practice to be applied must be practically

[187] Michael Lodge et al., 'Seabed Mining: International Seabed Authority Environmental Management Plan for the Clarion-Clipperton Zone: A Partnership Approach' (2014) 49 *Marine Policy* 66–72, 68.

[188] Normative Environmental Thresholds for Deep-Seabed Mining, submitted by the delegation of Germany, ISBA/27/C/30, 2022.

reasonable and cost-effective. It means that the superlative word 'best' cannot be read in an absolute sense but subject to restrictions. It also means that a certain degree of discretionary rights and self-regulation of operators are inevitable. This situation adds another layer of difficulty in the application of these highest standards of environmental protection.

4.3.5 Other Environmental Obligations

There are other environmental obligations imposed on the contractor. First, mining discharges during exploitation operations are in principle prohibited unless permitted or for the safety of the vessel, installation and human life in times of emergency.[189] This subject matter falls within the scope of the Convention on the Prevention of Marine Pollution by Dumping of Wastes and Other Matter (the 1972 London Convention) and the 1996 London Protocol. It is expected that the ISA will draw on the 1972 London Convention and the 1996 London Protocol when it issues standards or guidelines in this respect, thereby making the existing substantive legal requirements concerning dumping at sea applicable to the contractor. Secondly, the contractor is required to make closure plan and conduct post-closure monitoring during exploitation stage.[190] In particular, restoration and rehabilitation is common closure practice in terrestrial mining. Admittedly, the regulation of DSM would certainly draw on the experience of that of territorial mining. Yet, the two kinds of mining activities have very different operating environments and marine ecosystems are much less understood than territorial ecosystems. The practice in offshore mining or the oil industry might be able to offer more valuable lessons for the regulation of DSM. Yet, again the deep seas and oceans are much less understood in comparison with offshore waters. In a word, the pioneer nature of DSM industry makes the contractor's obligation concerning closure subject to a high level of uncertainty. Thirdly, the contractor must also cooperate with the ISA in the establishment and implementation of monitoring programmes and in the response mechanism for an environmental emergency. The contractor fulfils its obligation of cooperation by submitting annual reports, transferring data and information, notification of an environmental incident,

[189] Regulation 50, the 2019 draft Exploitation Regulations, ISBA/25/C/WP.1.

[190] Regulations 59–61 and Annex VIII, the 2019 draft Exploitation Regulations, ISBA/25/C/WP.1.

etc. Fourthly, as a reasonable requirement under the general principle of contract law in all legal systems, the contractor must fulfil its contractual obligations stemming from exploration and exploitation contracts in good faith. Finally, the contractor is obligated to comply with administrative orders, instructions and notices issued by the ISA or its delegates,[191] as well as the decisions of the SDC or other dispute-settlement bodies.

4.4 Conclusions

The DSM regime embodies a dual-track regulatory system where the ISA plays the primary role as the international regulator and the sponsoring State assumes a secondary regulatory role. Sustainable development has become an overarching principle which directs the discourse of environmental protection in natural resources utilization, marine environmental protection in DSM is such an example. Subjacent to this principle, there are general international environmental principles and rules that are also endorsed or incorporated in the *lex specialis* of DSM. Section 4.2 elaborated the sponsoring States' obligation of prevention, obligation to apply the precautionary approach, obligation concerning EIA and obligation to cooperate stemmed from those principles and rules. Additionally, it indicated that the substantiation of the standard of due diligence would be the focal point if a breach of obligation of prevention of a sponsoring State is alleged; while failure of the sponsoring State in applying the precautionary approach would be more difficult to prove because a consensus on the legal meaning of the precautionary approach is still to be achieved at the international DSM community. With respect to obligation concerning EIA, it is argued that, while the same rationale, EIA in a context of global commons deviates significantly from transboundary EIA in procedural rules. In contrast with transboundary EIA where consultation, notification and negotiation between States is at the core, for EIA evaluation in DSM, the ISA occupies a central place, while the sponsoring State is suggested to endorse the EIA guidelines issued by the LTC and cooperate with the ISA. Finally, the obligation to cooperate is essential for implementing the principle of CHM in DSM, including in particular, for marine environmental protection in the Area.

[191] Reference can be made to discussion over the regulatory liability of the contractor in Chapter 7 of this book.

Section 4.3 focuses on international environmental obligations of the contractor to conduct EIAs and submit EISs, to prepare for and respond to environmental emergencies, on environmental management and monitoring and to apply the highest environmental standards. The contractor has been required to conduct EIAs and submit EIA reports from the very beginning, following recommendations issued by the LTC. However, it was not until recent years when information on EIA practice began to be open to the public, and external expert review and public participation began to be introduced into the EIA review process. This improvement of EIA procedures affects the way an EIA is conducted by the contractor and its quality as well. With respect to environmental emergencies, the contractor is obliged to prepare itself in terms of finance, technology and management prior to an incident; when an incident has occurred or threaten to occur, the contractor shall respond swiftly in accordance with its environmental emergency plans and comply with emergency orders and/or immediate measures if they are given by the ISA. Notably, it is argued that the 2019 draft Exploitation Regulations shows a weight-shift from the ISA to the contractor in response to environmental emergencies. During daily operation of DSM, the contractor shall maintain environmental monitoring and management plan and system. While environmental monitoring has the focus on the establishment of reference zones (including IRZ and PRZ) and data collection, environmental management requirement focuses on the internal governance of the contractor. Yet, both tools aim at facilitating the contractor to meet environmental performance standards and goals. As to environmental standards, it appears that the contractor is required to meet the highest standards. At the moment, the LTC takes up the challenging work of defining such standards by issuing Standards and Guidelines. However, one should realize that the environmental standards are of a dynamic nature, correspondingly, the instruments issued by the LTC shall be flexible and updated periodically. In any case, however, the minimum controlling line of environmental quality seems to be needed.

At last, let us consider, first, the sponsoring State is supplementary to the ISA with respect to international environmental regulation. Second, some general international environmental law applicable to the sponsoring State may apply *mutatis mutandis* to the ISA and/or the contractor too, or at least, could contribute to interpreting special environmental rule in DSM context or serve as a reference point. Third, the international environmental obligations of the ISA and the contractor are closely correlated to each other, Chapter 4 should be read in conjunction with Chapter 3. Moreover, the pioneering and nascent nature of DSM and the considerable unknowns about the marine environment constitute the fundamental challenges to not only the exercise of regulatory powers of the ISA and the sponsoring States but also the interpretation of the content of the environmental obligations of the contractor.

5

Definition and Measure of Marine Environmental Damage

5.1 Introduction

The subject matter of environmental protection revolves around the concept of environmental damage. As seen in Chapter 4, the purpose of the principle of prevention and the precautionary approach is to prevent the occurrence of environmental damage, and the purpose of the requirement of EIA is to ascertain whether a proposed activity would cause potential environmental damage and, if so, to estimate the extent of that damage. As is shown in the discussion of the International Law Commission's (ILC's) work on international liability, a salient point that distinguishes the notions of state responsibility and liability is that, while 'damage' is not a constituent element for state responsibility, 'environmental damage' is the common triggering element of environmental liability. Thus, it is necessary to define and measure environmental damage in order to establish and implement international environmental liabilities in the context of deep seabed mining (DSM). Discussions on the definition and measure of marine environmental damage in this chapter constitute an integral part of liabilities discussed in Chapters 6 and 8. It equally forms an integral part of alternative regimes of insurance and environmental compensation fund (ECF) discussed in Chapter 7.

However, defining environmental damage is not an easy task and measuring environmental damage is even more challenging in practice. This chapter deals with these difficult but at the same time unavoidable tasks. Section 5.2 clarifies the definitions of 'marine environment' and 'marine environmental damage' in the context of DSM. Since under the ISA's Exploration Regulations only 'serious harm to the marine environment' is compensable, that is, the liability threshold, Section 5.3 takes the question of how to determine the threshold level of environmental damage for triggering liability. Thereafter, Sections 5.4–5.6 address the question of how to measure environmental damage. Owing to the fact that so far no practice exists in the context of DSM, lessons will have to be learnt from experiences in other contexts, including the practice of International Oil Pollution Compensation (IOPC) under the Civil Liability and Fund conventions, the United Nations Compensation Commission (UNCC) 'F4' claims, the related legislative practice in the United States and EU laws, as well as the discussions on liability and redress on damage to biological diversity in the context of the Convention on Biological Diversity (CBD). To some extent, these experiences can serve as precedent, or at least reference points, for the measure of damage to the marine environment in the context of DSM. On the basis of the analyses in Sections 5.4–5.6, a general pattern for the measure of environmental damage is arrived at and applied in the context of DSM in Section 5.7.

5.2 'Marine Environmental Damage': A Broad Definition with Threshold Requirement

To define 'marine environmental damage', one must first define what 'marine environment' is. The Exploration Regulations adopted by the International Seabed Authority (ISA) define 'marine environment' as follows:

> 'Marine environment' includes the physical, chemical, geological and biological components, conditions and factors which interact and determine the productivity, state, condition and quality of the marine ecosystem, the waters of the seas and oceans and the airspace above those waters, as well as the seabed and ocean floor and subsoil thereof.[1]

This definition has several salient characteristics. First of all, it is in essence a scientific definition. In practice, the determination of whether damage to the marine environment has occurred would involve scientific expertise in multiple areas, such as marine physics, marine chemistry, marine geology and marine biology. Secondly, it adopts an ecosystem approach. Namely, it concerns primarily the integral function of the marine ecosystem as a whole. This feature will have strong implications for the issue of reparation of the marine environmental damage. For instance, the aim of restoration would be to restore overall ecological functioning rather than one specific component of the marine ecosystem. Thirdly, due largely to the ecosystem approach, the ISA defines marine environment broadly: it covers not only bodies of water but also the airspace above and the seafloor under the water. On this aspect, similarity can be found in 'the Antarctic environment or dependent or associated

[1] Common Regulation 1, paragraph 3(c) of the Exploration Regulations.

ecosystems' used by the Antarctic Treaty System, in particular the 1988 Convention on the Regulation of Antarctic Mineral Resource Activities (CRAMRA),[2] the 1991 Environmental Protocol and the 2005 Annex to the 1991 Environmental Protocol. Apparently, the Antarctic environment or dependent or associated ecosystems covers a geographic area greater than Antarctica. Partly due to this reason, Burmester considered the definition of environmental damage in the 1988 CRAMRA 'notable for its expansive coverage'.[3] In a word, the 'marine environment' is defined broadly, from an ecosystem perspective and, in essence, as a scientific matter in the DSM legal regime.

The United Nations Convention on the Law of the Sea (UNCLOS) does not define the term 'marine environmental damage' or 'damage to the marine environment' but 'pollution of the marine environment'. It is prescribed that

> '[p]ollution of the marine environment' is the introduction by man, directly or indirectly, of substances or energy into the marine environment, including estuaries, which results or is likely to result in such deleterious effects as harm to living resources and marine life, hazards to human health, hindrance to marine activities, including fishing and other legitimate uses of the sea, impairment of quality for use of sea water and reduction of amenities.[4]

Although the term 'pollution of the marine environment' is primarily used in Part XII, considering that the UNCLOS is an integral package, the definition above is applicable to the DSM regime too.

The ISA uses the phrase 'serious harm to the marine environment' rather than 'damage to the marine environment' or 'pollution of the marine environment'. In the Exploration Regulations,

> 'serious harm to the marine environment' means any effect from activities in the Area on the marine environment which represents a significant adverse change in the marine environment determined according to the rules, regulations and procedures adopted by the Authority on the basis of internationally recognized standards and practices.[5]

[2] Article 1(15), the 1988 CRAMRA.

[3] Henry Burmester, 'Liability for Damage from Antarctic Mineral Resource Activities' (1989) 29 *VaJIntlL* 621–660, 633.

[4] Article 1, para. 1(4), UNCLOS.

[5] Decision of the Council of the ISA relating to amendments to the Regulations on Prospecting and Exploration for Polymetallic Nodules in the Area and related matters, ISBA/19/C/17, 22 July 2013. Regulation 1, para. 3(f).

Here, the ISA adds a requirement of threshold to the definition of marine environmental damage. This is not new. The requirement of threshold appears also in the definitions of environmental damage in other environmental protection and liability regimes. For instance, when discussing the definition of 'damage to biological diversity', the group of experts *ad hoc* appointed by the COP-CBD noted that 'a mere change in the state of biological diversity might not necessarily constitute damage. To constitute damage, the change had to result in an adverse or negative effect and it should be measurable'.[6] In effect, almost all human activities involving natural resources will inevitably leave footprints (mostly detrimental impacts) on nature. If there is no requirement of a threshold pertaining to the definition of 'environmental damage', it would be tantamount to a denial of any human activities. Thus, the requirement of a threshold pertaining to the definition of 'environmental damage', as the ISA did in the Exploration Regulations, is more reasonable. As a result, only those DSM activities that have a significant adverse impact on the marine environment may incur international liability.

Indeed, setting a threshold level of environmental damage for triggering environmental liability is very common in treaty practices.[7] For instance, in the 1988 CRAMRA, environmental damage means the impact on the Antarctic environment or ecosystem that goes beyond that which is negligible or which has been assessed and judged to be acceptable.[8] Stated conversely, liability will not arise if damage is considered as negligible or acceptable. For other instances, the 1991 Convention on Environmental Impact Assessment in a Transboundary Context covers only the 'significant adverse transboundary environmental impact'.[9] Under the 1997 Convention on the Law of the Non-navigational Uses of International Watercourses, parties have the obligation not to cause 'significant harm'.[10] In the 1991 UNECE

[6] Liability and Redress in the context of Paragraph 2 of Article 14 of the Convention on Biological Diversity – synthesis report on technical information relating to damage to biological diversity and approaches to valuation and restoration of damage to biological diversity, as well as information on national/domestic measures and experiences, UNEP/CBD/COP/9/20/Add.1, 2008. para. 107.

[7] The examples referred to in this section are drawn mostly from the research done by the ILC, see commentary to Principle 2 of the 2006 Draft Principles, Para. (1), footnote 326. However, one should be aware that in some environmental liability regimes, a threshold of environmental damage is not required. The UNCC compensation system is such an example.

[8] Articles 1(15) and 4(2) of the 1988 CRAMRA (not in force).

[9] Article 2(1) and (2) of the 1991 Espoo EIA Convention.

[10] Article 7 of the 1997 Non-navigational Uses of International Watercourses (not in force).

Convention on the Transboundary Effects of Industrial Accidents, 'hazardous activity' covers only those generating hazardous substance in quantities at or in excess of the threshold quantities.[11] In the 2008 Expert Group's report in the context of the CBD, 'the issue of thresholds of significance of the damage' is included as one of the guidances with respect to the definition of 'damage to biological diversity'.[12] In the 2000 EC White Paper on Environmental Liability, it is stated:

> Not every change to the quality or quantity of natural resources should be qualified as damage and give rise to liability. For the well-functioning of the liability regime, it might be beneficial to identify threshold criteria below which the responsible party will not be liable.[13]

The ILC embraced 'significant' as the threshold criteria regarding environmental damage in the 2001 Draft Articles on Prevention and the 2006 Draft Principles. It made important clarifications to the word 'significant'. First, 'significant' refers to something more than 'detectable' but need not be at the level of 'serious' or 'substantial'.[14] Specifically, there should be a real detrimental effect on the environment and that detrimental effect must be susceptible of being measured by factual and objective standards.[15] Moreover, 'the term "significant", while determined by factual and objective criteria, also involves a value determination which depends on the circumstances of a particular case and the period in which such determination is made'.[16]

Like the ILC, the ISA adopts 'significant' as the threshold criterion: it defines 'serious marine environmental damage' as 'a significant adverse change in the marine environment'. Following the clarification of the ILC, the determination of whether the threshold has been crossed involves examination on two aspects. On the factual aspect, marine environmental damage caused by DSM needs to be determined against

[11] Article 1(b) of the ECE Convention on the Transboundary Effects of Industrial Accidents.

[12] UNEP/CBD/COP/9/20/Add.1, 2008. para. 5(h).

[13] COM (2000) 66 final, 9 February 2000. Annex III (Liability for ecological damage and assessment of ecological damage), 47.

[14] Commentary to Article 2 of the 2001 Draft Articles on Prevention, para. (4); commentary to Principle 2 of the 2006 Draft Principles, para. (2).

[15] Ibid.

[16] Commentary to Article 2 of the 2001 Draft Articles on Prevention, para. (7) and; commentary to Principle 2 of the 2006 Draft Principles, para. (3).

the baseline condition of the marine environment. In this connection, it merits reiterating that the contractor is required to conduct environmental baseline studies, to collect baseline data and to establish the baseline condition of the marine environment. The establishment of the baseline condition of the marine environment is a prerequisite for determining whether a marine environmental damage above the threshold has occurred.[17] This refers to not only a general scientific understanding of the deep-sea environment, but also a consideration of the special features of the abyssal plains where manganese nodules are collected, the active and inactive hydrothermal vents where seafloor massive sulphides are extracted and the seamounts where cobalt-rich crusts are removed. Levin et al. focused on the special features of these targeted ecosystems in determining 'significance' of the predicted environmental impacts of DSM.[18] They also acknowledged that major knowledge gaps concerning habitat distribution, ecosystem structure and function posed challenges to that determination.[19] On the value determination aspect, two related questions are considered here. First, who determines whether the threshold has been crossed? Second, what is the rationale underlying the requirement of a threshold? In reply to the first question, according to the Exploration Regulations, the legal basis for the determination is 'the rules, regulations and procedures adopted by the Authority on the basis of internationally recognized standards and practices'.[20] Since it is the ISA which exercises regulatory power, it is therefore the ISA which determines whether the threshold has been crossed. As to the second question, the ILC revealed the rationale behind the requirement of threshold. It is said that 'the threshold is designed to

[17] In fact, the baseline condition of the marine environment is the converging point which connects several important issues of the environmental aspect of the DSM legal regime: the obligation to conduct prior EIA, the measurement of the environmental damage and the restoration as a means of remediation. The importance of baseline information should not be underestimated. One of the main tasks of the LTC of the ISA is to provide guidance for collecting baseline information and to review submission of baseline information in the annual reports of the contractor. However, the problem in practice has been that the baseline information submitted by the contractor so far is of low scientific value for reasons such as the very small sample size. For this reason, the LTC constantly urges the contractor to collect better baseline information.

[18] Lisa Levin et al., 'Defining "Serious Harm" to the Marine Environment in the context of Deep-seabed Mining' (2016) 74 *Marine Policy* 245.

[19] Ibid., 248.

[20] Common Regulation 3(f), Exploration Regulations.

prevent frivolous or vexatious claims'.[21] In the case of DSM, the threshold can be a flexible tool in the hands of the ISA to adjust the balance between environmental protection and development of the DSM industry. If the threshold did not exist, it would be hard to imagine that any mining operations could be conducted in the Area since mining activities inevitably exert adverse effects, to varying extents, on the marine environment. That would be tantamount to a ban on DSM activities. Therefore, the fundamental rationale behind the idea of threshold in the DSM regime is the balancing of two conflicting interests: development of the DSM industry and protection of the marine environment. This type of balancing should be distinguished from the balancing of economic interests between countries in a transboundary context. Taking the two aspects together, the interpretation of the threshold of environmental damage should be based on the objective marine environmental damage determined against the baseline environmental condition and also in accordance with the DSM policy of the ISA.

The above conceptual clarification on the definition (including the threshold level) of marine environmental damage is necessary but not enough. To ascertain the content of liabilities, the payment by insurance companies and the distribution of environmental compensation fund all necessitates measure of the marine environmental damage in a relatively precise term. The remainder of the chapter thus turns to this task. It attempts to identify methods for measuring environmental damage and to propose a number of heads of compensable marine environmental damage in DSM, by drawing on experience in other contexts and taking into account the particularities of DSM activities and the DSM legal regime.

5.3 Measure of Marine Environmental Damage in DSM: Drawing on Experience of the International Oil Pollution Compensation Funds

So far, at the international level, the International Oil Pollution Compensation Funds (the IOPC Funds) have been the only permanent compensation mechanism for damage to the marine environment, which have been operating successfully for several decades. This section

[21] Commentary to Principle 2 of the 2006 Draft Principles on the Allocation of Loss in the case of Transboundary Harm Arising out of Hazardous Activities (the '2006 Draft Principles'), para. (1).

conducts an enquiry into the IOPC Funds' continuous practice pertaining to the assessment of oil pollution damage, that is, marine environmental damage caused by oil pollution during oil shipping. The purpose of doing so is to see whether, and if so to what extent, that practice can provide valuable lessons for the measure of marine environmental damage caused by DSM activities.[22]

5.3.1 *Definition of 'Pollution Damage'*

Under the International Convention on Civil Liability for Oil Pollution Damage of 1969 (the 1969 CLC),

> 'pollution damage' means loss or damage caused outside the ship carrying oil by contamination resulting from the escape or discharge of oil from the ship, wherever such escape or discharge may occur, and includes the costs of preventive measures and further loss or damage caused by preventive measures.[23]

The term is defined in such general wording that it leaves broad room for divergent interpretations in the practice of the 1971 IOPC Fund (the 1971 Fund) since it began operations in 1978. Taking a position that 'a uniform interpretation of the definition of pollution damage was essential for the functioning of this regime' and that 'the definition should deal explicitly with the problem of compensation for damage to the marine environment as such', a new definition of pollution damage was adopted in the 1984 Protocol.[24] Under the 1984 Protocol, 'pollution damage' is defined as:

22 This section relies heavily on the following database built and maintained by the IOPC Funds. http://documentservices.iopcfunds.org/.

23 Article 1(6) of the 1969 CLC (adopted on 29 November 1969, entered into force on 19 June 1975; being replaced by the 1992 Protocol which was adopted on 27 November 1992 and entered into force on 30 May 1996). This definition was incorporated into the International Convention on the Establishment of an International Fund for Compensation for Oil Pollution Damage of 1971 in its origin. (the '1971 Fund Convention' adopted on 18 December 1971, entered into force on 16 October 1978; Protocols to the 1971 Fund Convention were adopted in 1976 and 1984, but were superseded by the 1992 Protocol; the 1971 Fund Convention ceased to be in force from 24 May 2002. However, the 1971 Fund was not dissolved until 2014.)

24 Mans Jacobsson and Norbert Trotz identified these two reasons for amending the definition of 'pollution damage' during the 1984 Diplomatic Conference in 'The Definition of Pollution Damage in the 1984 Protocols to the 1969 Civil Liability Convention and the 1971 Fund Convention' (1986) 17(4) *JMLC* 467–491, 481–482.

(a) loss or damage caused outside the ship by contamination resulting from the escape or discharge of oil from the ship, wherever such escape or discharge may occur, provided that compensation for impairment of the environment other than loss of profit from such impairment shall be limited to costs of reasonable measures of reinstatement actually undertaken or to be undertaken;
(b) the costs of preventive measures and further loss or damage caused by preventive measures.[25]

The 1984 Protocol never entered into force. But the new definition of pollution damage under the 1984 Protocol is incorporated into the 1992 Protocol. In comparison, the new definition of pollution damage maintains the basic content of the old definition in the 1969 Civil Liability Convention and the 1971 Fund Convention. However, the phrase 'compensation for impairment of the environment other than loss of profit from such impairment shall be limited to costs of reasonable measures of reinstatement actually undertaken or to be undertaken' is newly added. It should be noted, however,

> [t]he new wording of the definition was not in any way intended to widen the concept. The Diplomatic Conference which adopted the 1984 Protocol based its deliberations on the policy of the IOPC Fund and the principles developed by the IOPC Fund Assembly and Executive Committee as regards the admissibility of claims and the interpretation of the definition of pollution damage as worded in the original text of the Convention. The Diplomatic Conference adopted the modified wording of this definition in order to codify the interpretation of the definition as developed by the IOPC Fund.[26]

Indeed, the new definition simply reflected the practice of the IOPC Funds. It made clear that damage to the marine environment as such was embodied in the term pollution damage. In light of this, claims for marine environmental damage were admissible in principle under the 1971 Fund.

5.3.2 *Criterion for Admissibility of Claims for Marine Environmental Damage*

In the very first case of the 1971 Fund, the *Antonio Gramsci* incident occurred in the USSR in 1979, the USSR claimed an amount calculated

[25] Article 2(6) of the 1984 Protocol to amend the International Convention on Civil Liability for Pollution Damage; the same definition is adopted in Article 1(6) of the 1992 CLC (adopted on 27 November 1992, entered into force on 30 May 1996).

[26] IOPC Funds decision document, 71FUND/EXC.28/6 add.1, 2 October 1991, para. 6.4.

through a mathematical model for ecological damage. The 1971 Fund rejected straightforwardly the claim for the reason that

> the Conventions did not allow damages to be quantified through the use of a mathematic model, leaving aside the specific aspects and factors of a particular incident such as the location of the incident, the resources at risk, the composition of the oil, and its fate in the marine environment. Pollution damage claims should be based on quantifiable losses which can be positively attributed to a particular incident.[27]

In dealing with this case, the 1971 Fund was not confronted with the issue of admissibility of ecological damage as such. Yet, it presented its strong opposition to the use of a mathematical model as the quantification method of pollution damage. To make this position public, the Assembly of the 1971 Fund unanimously adopted the No. 3 resolution in 1980. The resolution confirmed that 'the assessment of compensation to be paid by the IOPC Fund is not to be made on the basis of an abstract quantification of damage calculated in accordance with theoretical models'.[28] This resolution is further clarified by the 1981 Working Group as follows: 'a claimant is entitled to compensation under the Civil Liability Convention and the Fund Convention only if he had suffered quantifiable economic loss'.[29] The above two documents established the criterion for determining the admissibility of claims for compensation, namely being economically quantifiable. This criterion relates in particular to claims for compensation for environmental damage because this type of claim usually encounters the problems of whether it is possible and, if so, how to quantify the environmental damage.

After the 1979 *Antonio Gramsci* incident, the 1971 Fund dealt with several other cases where their position on the admissibility of claims for environmental damage was reiterated and/or further clarified. Following the 1985 *Patmos* incident, the Italian government filed claims relating to damage to the marine environment. Yet, it neither indicated the kind of damage nor provided any documentation explaining how the amount had been calculated.[30] Following the 1987 *Antonio Gramsci* incident, the

[27] Para. 4 of Consideration of certain aspects of the term 'pollution damage' (Article 1.2 Fund Convention), FUND/A/ES.1/9, 8 August 1980.

[28] Annex I to the record of decisions of the Assembly, FUND/A/ES.1/13, 8 October 1980.

[29] 71FUND/A.4/10, Annex, 15 July 1981, paras. 18–19.

[30] 71FUND/EXC.16/4, 22 September 1986, para. 2.19. The Italian Government admitted during the proceedings that 'proof of the extent of the ecological damage could not be given by documents or by witnesses'. It requested the Court to set up a technical committee to establish that damage had been suffered.

Estonian authorities also filed claims relating to damage to the marine environment for an amount calculated by the same method as the USSR did following the 1979 *Antonio Gramsci* incident. In both cases, the 1971 Fund reiterated its position expressed in the 1980 No. 3 Assembly Resolution and the 1981 Working Group Report and consequently denied the claims.

In the 1991 *Haven* case, the director of the 1971 Fund clarified the criterion of admissibility. He divided environmental damage into 'quantifiable elements' and 'unquantifiable elements' and deemed that only the quantifiable elements of environmental damage can be admitted. He further elaborated on what the 'quantifiable elements' are. As he put it,

> It should first be noted that the IOPC Fund does not reject all types of claims for compensation resulting from damage to the marine environment. The IOPC Fund accepts claims which, in accordance with the terminology used in the present document, relate to "quantifiable elements" of damage to the marine environment, for example:
>
> (a) reasonable costs of restoration of the damaged environment; and
> (b) loss of profit (income, revenue) resulting from damage to the marine environment suffered by persons who depend directly on earning from coastal or sea-related activities, e.g. loss of earnings suffered by fishermen or by hoteliers and restaurateurs at seaside resorts.[31]

In the meanwhile, he reaffirmed that

> [o]n the other hand, the IOPC Fund has consistently taken the position that claims relating to unquantifiable elements of damage to the environment cannot be admitted.[32]

The director emphasized that the compensation under the 1971 Fund is 'compensatory' by its nature, which should be distinguished from payment of a punitive nature. As a corollary, he considered, it implies that economically unquantifiable damage falls outside the scope of coverage of the 1971 Fund. This understanding of the nature of compensation and its implications is similar to that of the ILC as reflected in the 2001 Articles on State Responsibility (the 2001 ASR). When commenting on Article 36 of the 2001 ASR, the ILC clarified the meaning of compensation as follows:

[31] FUND/EXC.30/2, 29 November 1991, para. 8.3.

[32] Ibid., para. 8.4.

> The function of article 36 is purely compensatory, as its title indicates. Compensation corresponds to the financially assessable damage suffered by the injured State or its nationals. It is not concerned to punish the responsible State, nor does compensation have an expressive or exemplary character. Thus, compensation generally consists of a monetary payment, though it may sometimes take the form, as agreed, of other forms of value.[33]

It can be seen that in spite of the fact that the IOPC legal regime is labelled as private law while the general rules of State responsibility are public law, they share a similar understanding about the nature of compensation. On the basis of the similar understanding, they impose a similar requirement for the compensability of damage, that is, 'being economically quantifiable' or 'being financially assessable'. In practice, the IOPC Funds have compensated three heads of pollution damage: costs of preventive measures, costs of reinstatement measures and costs of post-spill environmental impact studies.

5.3.3 *Costs of Preventive Measures*

As shown above, the definitions of 'pollution damage' explicitly embody the costs of preventive measures. The director of the 1992 Fund further explained that

> [a]lthough the definition of 'pollution damage' limits compensation for impairment of the environment to losses of an economic nature and costs of reinstatement, in the Director's view practically all preventive measures taken to prevent environmental damage should be admissible in principle for compensation, since they would also have a direct or indirect economic benefit.[34]

Under the Civil Liability Conventions, 'preventive measures' mean 'any reasonable measures taken by any person after an incident has occurred to prevent or minimize pollution damage'.[35] In turn, 'incident' is defined originally as 'any occurrence, or series of occurrences having the same origin, which causes pollution damage'.[36] It was without controversy that costs of reasonable measures to prevent or mitigate pollution damage after a spill has occurred was covered. However, views were varied in the

[33] ILC, Commentary to Article 36 of 2001 Articles on State Responsibility, para. (4).
[34] 92FUND/A.11/24, 29 September 2006, para. 3.5.
[35] Article 1(7) of both the 1969 and 1992 CLC.
[36] Article 1(8) of the 1969 CLC.

beginning on the question of 'whether the Civil Liability and the Fund Conventions cover expenses for preventive measures taken before an actual spill of persistent oil has occurred or in cases where no spill of persistent oil occurs at all'. A positive answer was given by the Assembly of the 1971 Fund in October 1981, when the No. 6 resolution was adopted.[37] Consequently, the 1992 CLC revised the definition of 'incident' as 'any occurrence, or series of occurrences having the same origin, which causes pollution damage or creates a grave and imminent threat of causing such damage'.[38] The inclusion of the costs of pre-spill and precautionary preventive measures in the 1992 CLC provides a basis for claims in cases such as *Santa Anna*. In this case, the director of the 1992 Fund considered that there existed a 'grave and imminent threat' of pollution damage of the grounding of the unladen tanker because the bunker was still on board. Consequently, he affirmed that claims for the costs of such measures as mobilizing oil combating equipment and refloating the ship were admissible in light of the 1992 CLC.[39] The criterion for admissibility of claims for costs of preventive measures is, the same as that for reinstatement measures, reasonableness. Specifically, two factors need to be considered: first, preventive measures should be objectively reasonable under the circumstances existing at the time they are taken. Second, the costs of the measures should be reasonable, and not disproportionate to the likely benefits in the form of the expected reduction in loss or damage that would have resulted from those measures.[40] Above all, 'when considering the reasonableness of preventive measures account should be taken of the potential environmental damage that could be caused if the measures were not taken'.[41]

5.3.4 *Costs of Reinstatement Measures*

The 1992 definition of 'pollution damage' expanded to include the costs of reasonable measures of reinstatement. There are two requirements for the compensability of this head of environmental damage. First, the reinstatement measures have to be reasonable. The criterion of

[37] 71FUND/A.4/10/1, October 1981, Annex III.
[38] Article 1(8) of the 1992 CLC.
[39] 92FUND/EXC.1/7, October 1998, para. 3.3.
[40] 92FUND/A.11/24, 29 September 2006, para. 3.2.
[41] 92FUND/A.11/35, 27 October 2006, para. 26.23.

reasonableness in the context of oil pollution is clarified by the IOPC Funds as follows:

> A reasonable measure of reinstatement should aim to bring the damaged site back to the same ecological state that would have existed had the oil spill not occurred, or at least as close to it as possible (i.e. to re-establish a healthy biological community in which the organisms characteristic of that community prior to the spill are present and are functioning normally).[42]

Thus, in the opinion of the IOPC Funds, the reasonableness of the measures is determined not by themselves but by their effects on the recovery of the ecological functions of the environment. Second, the measures must be actually undertaken or are to be undertaken. There are two situations. For one situation, the measures have already been undertaken. Here, the costs of the measures are fixed, so are their effects on the recovery of the environment. For the other situation, since the measures are still to be taken, the costs of the measures are not fixed. In the latter situation, it is required that the claimants provide a practical plan for the reinstatement programme which must be approved by the IOPC Funds. With increasing experience, the IOPC Funds further elaborated on the criterion of reasonableness of reinstatement measures in the revised Claims Manual of 2002 as follows:

The measures should be likely to accelerate significantly the natural process of recovery;
The measures should seek to prevent further damage as a result of the incident;
The measures should, as far as possible, not result in the degradation of other habitats or in adverse consequences for other natural or economic resources;
The measures should be technique feasible;
The costs of the measures should not be out of proportion to the extent and duration of the damage and the benefits likely to be achieved.[43]

Through these specific elements, claims for the costs of reinstatement measures have become more predictable in practice.

[42] 92FUND/A.7/29, Annex I, 18 October 2002.
[43] 92FUND/A.7/29, Annex I, 18 October 2002. The 2000 version of Claims Manual was revised in 2002.

5.3.5 *Costs of Post-spill Environmental Impact Studies*

The Claims Manual of 2002 not only clarified on 'reasonable measures of reinstatement' but also included a new head of environmental damage – the costs of post-spill environmental impact studies – which was not embodied in the 1992 definition of 'pollution damage'.[44] The purpose of post-spill environmental impact studies 'is to establish the precise nature and extent of environmental damage and to determine whether or not reinstatement measures are necessary and feasible'.[45] Hence, it is the goal of reinstating the damaged environment that explains the reason of existence for post-spill environmental impact studies. Interestingly, at almost the same time as the inclusion of post-spill environmental impact studies into the IOPC system, the UNCC 'F4' Panel was reviewing and deciding on claims for the costs of monitoring and assessing environmental damage. Although the names differ, post-spill environmental impact studies in the IOPC system and monitoring and assessment of environmental damage in the UNCC system are in essence the same. For this reason, argumentation with respect to one applies *mutatis mutandis* to the other. In Section 5.4, it is argued that the costs of monitoring and assessing environmental damage should be treated as an independent head of environmental damage in the UNCC's 'F4' claims. With no need to repeat the same reason, it is equally argued that the costs of post-spill environmental impact studies should be considered as an independent head of environmental damage in the context of the IOPC system. Nevertheless, there are differences in the operation of the two compensation systems. Most prominently, within the IOPC system, several subjects are involved in post-spill environmental impact studies. They are the claimants, the shipowners, the shipowners' insurers and the IOPC Fund. Among them, the Fund plays the most important role in deciding whether to initiate the studies and the planning of the studies. The Fund also pays attention to avoiding duplicating work among the different subjects. In contrast, within the UNCC system, the claimant plays the sole role in deciding whether and how to conduct the monitoring and assessment, which are subject to the review of the 'F4' Panel afterwards.

44 92FUND/A.7/29, Annex I, 18 October 2002.
45 Ibid.

5.3.6 *Lessons for the Measure of Marine Environmental Damage in DSM*

Through examination, it is seen that the term 'pollution damage' defined by the Civil Liability Conventions and the Fund Conventions embodies damage to the marine environment *per se*. Correspondingly, the IOPC Funds not only compensate for claimants' loss of economic benefits through marine environmental damage but also compensate for damage to the marine environment *per se*. However, the compensability of the environmental damage *per se* is qualified. According to the consistent interpretation by the IOPC Funds, claims for environmental damage *per se* are admissible only if the losses are economically quantifiable; non-quantifiable losses are excluded. In the practice of the IOPC Funds, three heads of environmental damage – the costs of preventive measures, the costs of reinstatement measures and the costs of post-spill environmental impact studies – are considered as economically quantifiable and thus compensable.

The lesson from the practice of IOPC Funds can thus be succinctly summarized in the following four points: (1) damages to the marine environment *per se* are compensable, (2) compensability of marine environmental damage is qualified, (3) a cost-based method is adopted for the measure of marine environmental damage, (4) there are three kinds of costs that are considered as compensable heads of environmental damage in practice. To what extent the measure of environmental damage in DSM can learn from that lesson? With respect to the first point, since the IOPC Funds have already attested the statement with its longtime practice, there is no reason why it cannot retain its validity in other contexts, including the DSM.

With respect to the second point, the question is: should the criterion of 'being-economically-quantifiable' be applied in the DSM context as well? To answer the question, one needs first to understand why such a limitation to the compensability of marine environmental damage is imposed in the IOPC context, and then find out whether similar underlying rationale exists in DSM context or not. So why the IOPC imposed such a limitation? One practical reason might be that the inclusion of economically non-quantifiable environmental damage would increase the uncertainty and unpredictability of the measure of environmental damage in practice. Yet, the fundamental reason in my view is because the IOPC legal system was established for the purpose of compensating for human victims of oil pollution.[46] The compensability of environmental damage is justified not on the value of the environment *per se* b on its connection with the economic loss of persons. This is in stark contrast with the mostly victimless situation of DSM. Owing to the remoteness of the deep sea and the common heritage of mankind (CHM) nature of the Area, it is much less likely for persons to suffer economic loss through marine environmental damages caused by DSM. This means, marine environmental damage in DSM would, to a lesser extent, be connected to economic loss of persons. They are pure environmental damages that could not be expressed in economic terms. If these pure environmental damages be left uncompensated in DSM just as in the IOPC context, then there would be a greater gap in the DSM compensation regimes. Schoenbaum regards that the IOPC system takes 'the unduly restrictive approach' towards the concept of environmental damage.[47] Huguenin, Donlan and Paterson comment that

> [t]he IOPC Fund framework relies on definitions of environmental damage that are substantially narrower than those developed by the F4 Panel, and limits the use of valuation techniques despite their general acceptance in the peer-reviewed literature and inclusion in other natural resource damage frameworks.[48]

These are criticisms about the limited coverage of marine environmental damages in IOPC. If the rationale for DSM compensation mechanism is not victim-centred like the IOPC, then the measure of marine environmental damage in DSM should not be confined only to those 'economically quantifiable', rather, it could draw on practices in other contexts in this respect, such as, that of the 'F4' Panel of UNCC to be examined in the next section.

With respect to the third point, as is shown above and will also be shown in the following sections, the cost-based method is widely adopted as the primary method for the measure of environmental damage because

[46] The purpose is shown in the preamble, paragraph 3 of the 1992 CLC as being 'convinced of the need to ensure that adequate compensation is available to persons who suffer damage caused by pollution resulting from the escape or discharge of oil from ships'.

[47] Thomas Schoenbaum, 'Environmental Damages in Common Law: An Overview', in Michael Bowman and Alan Boyle (eds.), *Environmental Damage in International and Comparative Law* (OUP 2002).

[48] Michael Huguenin, Michael Donlan, Alexandra Van Geel and Robert Paterson, 'Assessment and Valuation of Damage to the Environment' in Cymie Payne and Peter Sand (eds.), *Gulf War Reparations and the UN Compensation Commission: Environmental Liability* (OUP 2011).

of its convenience and also because it can secure a high level of certainty and predictability. With no exception, the cost-based method can be used as the primary method for the measure of marine environmental damage in DSM too. Then the next question naturally follows: what kinds of costs count? This turns to the fourth point. The question is whether the three kinds of costs addressed to by the IOPC Funds can also be used as heads of marine environmental damage in the DSM context. Very likely: yes. Here again, practices in other contexts examined below will show that these three kinds of costs are common compensable heads of environmental damage. And an extended question arises: beside preventive measures, reinstatement measures and post-incident impact studies, are there other measures taken to respond to (the risk) of environmental damage in DSM that would also generate compensable costs? Precise answers to these questions are hard to give until practice in DSM commences and cumulates. However, from the lesson of IOPC Funds, to assess the compensability of these costs, measures taken must be subject to the test of 'reasonableness'. Considering the longtime successful experience, the practice of IOPC Funds serves as a very important reference point.

5.4 Measure of Marine Environmental Damage in DSM: Drawing on Experience of the 'F4' Claims before the United Nations Compensation Commission

The United Nations Compensation Commission was an ad hoc compensation mechanism for damage caused by the Kuwait-Iraq conflict in 1991.[49] Claims for environmental damage and the depletion of natural resources are reviewed and decided by 'F4' Panel of Commissioners of the UNCC (the 'F4' claims).[50] In dealing with 'F4' claims, the UNCC, like the IOPC Funds needed to deal with the measure of environmental damage. This section investigates the practice of the UNCC 'F4' claims pertaining to the measure of the marine environmental damage caused by the Kuwait-Iraq conflict. The purpose of doing so, the same as in the previous section, is to see whether, and if so to what extent, that practice

[49] UN Doc. S/RES/687 (1991), para. 16. The recommendations of UN Secretary-General: UN, the Report of the Secretary-General Pursuant to Paragraph 19 of Resolution 687 (1991), Security Council Resolution 692 (1991): S/22559, 2 May 1991. UN Doc. S/RES/692 (1991), para. 3.

[50] The 'F4' Panel of Commissioners was composed of Thomas Mensah, Jose Allen and Perter Sand who were appointed by the Governing Council of UNCC at its thirtieth session held from 14 to 16 December 1998.

can provide valuable lessons for the measure of the marine environmental damage caused by DSM activities.[51]

5.4.1 Claims and Payment for Direct Environmental Damage

The Security Council Resolution 687 (1991) on the Kuwait-Iraq conflict lays down the legal foundation for international liability of Iraq for, *inter alia*, environmental damage. It is stated in the Resolution that '[the Security Council] reaffirms that Iraq [. . .] is liable under international law for any direct loss, damage, including environmental damage and the depletion of natural resources, [. . .,] as a result of Iraq's unlawful invasion and occupation of Kuwait [. . .]'.[52] The Governing Council decision 7 provided the principal guidance in determining payment for 'the direct environmental damage and the depletion of natural resources' as follows:

> This will include losses or expenses resulting from:
>
> (a) Abatement and prevention of environmental damage, including expenses directly relating to fighting oil fires and stemming the flow of oil in coastal and international waters;
> (b) Reasonable measures already taken to clean and restore the environment or future measures which can be documented as reasonably necessary to clean and restore the environment;
> (c) Reasonable monitoring and assessment of the environmental damage for the purpose of evaluating and abating the harm and restoring the environment;
> (d) Reasonable monitoring of public health and performing medical screenings for the purposes of investigation and combating increased health risks as a result of the environmental damage; and
> (e) Depletion of or damage to natural resources.[53]

It is in light of this guidance that the 'F4' Panel set out to work. To start with, the Panel subdivided the 'F4' claims into five installments, with the claims for the expenses resulting from monitoring and assessment activities (the 'M&A claims') as the first installment;[54] the claims for expenses

[51] This section has been written by relying heavily on the database built by the UNCC. www.uncc.ch/sub-category-f4-claims-environmental-damage.

[52] UN Doc. S/RES/687 (1991), para. 16.

[53] UNCC Governing Council, Criteria for additional categories of claims, UN Doc. S/AC.26/1991/7/Rev.1, 17 March 1992, para. 35.

[54] Report and recommendations made by the Panel of Commissioners concerning the First Instalment of 'F4' claims, UN Doc. S/AC.26/2001/16, 22 June 2001 (the 'first F4 report, 2001').

incurred for measures to abate and prevent environmental damage (the 'abatement and prevention claims') as the second;[55] the claims for expenses resulting from measures to clean and restore the environment (the 'restoration claims/ primary restoration') as the third[56] and fourth;[57] and claims for loss of the use or value of the resources (the 'claims for loss of natural resources without commercial value/compensatory restoration' or 'pure environmental damage') as the fifth.[58] The sequence of these installments was not made at random but intentional. The M&A claims were given the priority to be reviewed first since the Panel considered the results of M&A activities might be helpful in reviewing and assessing the substantive claims.[59] The claims in the other four installments, being regarded as substantive claims *vis-à-vis* the M&A claims, were reviewed sequentially in light of their relative reliance on the results of M&A activities. Abatement and prevention claims were considered to rely on the results of M&A activities the least, therefore, were reviewed first after completion of the first installment. Afterwards, primary restoration and compensatory restoration claims were reviewed.

5.4.2 *Costs of Monitoring and Assessment Activities*

Two legal issues were critical to the M&A claims: the evidentiary requirement and its independent status. In light of paragraph 35(c) and (d) of Governing Council decision 7, the compensability of expenses of M&A activities as such was not problematic. However, what was unclear was the evidentiary requirement for the M&A claims. The Panel clarified this

55 Report and recommendations made by the Panel of Commissioners concerning the Second Instalment of 'F4' claims, UN Doc. S/AC.26/2002/26, 3 October 2002 (the 'second F4 report, 2002').

56 Report and recommendations made by the Panel of Commissioners concerning the Third Instalment of 'F4' claims, UN Doc. S/AC.26/2003/31, 18 December 2003 (the 'third F4 report, 2003').

57 Report and recommendations made by the Panel of Commissioners concerning Part One of the Fourth Instalment of 'F4' claims, UN Doc. S/AC.26/2004/16, 9 December 2004. Report and recommendations made by the Panel of Commissioners concerning Part Two of the Fourth Instalment of 'F4' claims, UN Doc. S/AC.26/2004/17, 9 December 2004 (the 'fourth F4 report, 2004').

58 Report and recommendations made by the Panel of Commissioners concerning the Fifth Instalment of 'F4' claims, UN Doc. S/AC.26/2005/10, 30 June 2005 (the 'fifth F4 report, 2005').

59 This idea derives from paras. 38–40 of the first F4 report, 2001. It includes six claimant countries, 107 claims, and the total compensation claimed is USD 1,007,412,574 (para. 4 of the report).

point. First, it rejected the opinion that environmental damage should be proven with certainty in this category of claims. As it was said,

> The Panel does not consider that conclusive proof of environmental damage is a prerequisite for a monitoring and assessment activity to be compensable in accordance with paragraph 35 of Governing Council decision 7. In the view of the Panel, the purpose of monitoring and assessment is to enable a claimant to develop evidence to establish whether environmental damage has occurred and to quantify the extent of the resulting loss.[60]

Meanwhile, it excluded any situation in the other extreme by saying that

> [h]owever, the Panel is of the view that compensation should not be awarded for monitoring and assessment activities that are purely theoretical or speculative, or which have only a tenuous link with damage resulting from Iraq's invasion and occupation of Kuwait.[61]

Then, the Panel established 'a sufficient nexus' standard[62] and suggested several considerations which should be taken into account when assessing the appropriateness of the M&A activities.[63] The assessment of the appropriateness of the M&A activities was made by reviewing their scientific and technical merits. Furthermore, the Panel also reviewed the reasonableness of the costs for the M&A project.[64] In sum, on the issue of the compensability of the M&A claims, the evidentiary standard was not 'certainty' but 'a sufficient nexus' between the M&A activities and the environmental damage or risk of damage. The Panel evaluated the strength of that nexus by assessing the appropriateness of the M&A activities and the reasonableness of the costs in each specific circumstance. The value of the information obtained from the M&A activities to substantive claims, in particular, with the issues of 'identifying environmental damage and depletion of natural resources' or 'taking preventive or remedial measures', also had an influence on the compensability of the M&A claims.[65]

As to the status of the M&A claims, first of all, it should be noted that the M&A claims were related to the substantive claims. As the Panel indicated,

[60] The first F4 report, 2001, para. 30.
[61] Ibid, para. 31.
[62] Ibid.
[63] Ibid.
[64] Ibid., para. 55.
[65] Ibid., para. 35.

> Most of the monitoring and assessment claims are related to substantive claims for environmental damage and depletion of natural resources because the claimants expect to use information obtained from the monitoring and assessment activities to support their substantive claims.[66]

In the 'F4' practice, owing to the fact that by the time M&A activities started, substantive claims had already been submitted, 'amendment of [substantive] claims based on the results of monitoring and assessment activities' during the review process of the third, fourth and fifth installments became a common phenomenon.[67] The legitimacy of these post-submission amendments was challenged by Iraq, but the Panel found it appropriate to receive and consider these amendments for the reason that

> [t]he possibility that the amounts claimed might increase or decrease in the light of data and information obtained from monitoring and assessment activities is implicit in the decision of the Governing Council to authorize separate funding for monitoring and assessment activities prior to the review of related substantive claims.[68]

The most substantial problem with regard to the constant amendment of the substantive claims was that it would be unfair to the respondent in terms of procedures. As the Iraqi expert consultant team complained,

> Iraq's advisory team was expected to respond to claims submitted without this proper procedure being followed and was obliged to respond to a moving target throughout as monitoring and assessment data were submitted to retrospectively support that claims.[69]

Although the Panel was not unaware of this procedural flaw, it justified its position on the substantive aspects. In the view of the Panel, the usefulness of data generated from the M&A activities to the related substantive claims provided sufficient justification for the acceptance of amendments to the latter. On the other hand, despite its usefulness, the review of the M&A claims could not predetermine the related substantive claims.

66 Ibid., para. 36.

67 Larraine Wilde, 'Scientific and Technical Advice – the Perspective of Iraq's Experts', in Cymie Payne and Peter Sand (eds.), *Gulf War Reparations and the UN Compensation Commission: Environmental Liability* (OUP 2011). Evidence can be found in the third F4 report, 2003, paras. 30–32; Part I of the fourth F4 report, 2004, paras. 34–36; the Part II of the fourth F4 report, 2004, paras. 32–33; and the fifth F4 report, 2005, paras. 33–35.

68 The third F4 report, 2003, para. 32.

69 Larraine Wilde, 'Scientific and Technical Advice – The Perspective of Iraq's Experts', in Cymie Payne and Peter Sand (eds.), *Gulf War Reparations and the UN Compensation Commission: Environmental Liability* (OUP 2011).

> The Panel stresses that its recommendations on monitoring and assessment claims do not in any way prejudge its findings on related substantive claims that it may review subsequently. Each substantive claim will be reviewed on its own merits on the basis of the evidence presented to support it.[70]

Nevertheless, the close connection between the M&A activities and the substantive claims was not tantamount to a denial of the independent status of the M&A claims *vis-à-vis* the related substantive claims. According to the Panel, failing to generate useful evidence for supporting the substantive claims did not by itself make the expenses of M&A activities not or less compensable.[71] Similarly, Elias observed that 'the final outcome of the claim for actual environmental damage does not determine the compensability of the M&A costs'.[72] Furthermore, Elias dwelled on the deeper question of why the expense of M&A activities as an independent head of damage was needed. He opined,

> But perhaps the ultimate justification for having the costs of monitoring and assessment as an independent head of liability is, then, that it facilitates the task of reinstating the environment where the prime concern is its restoration in the public interest, rather than the mere settling of a dispute or series of disputes in a bilateral/adversarial context. The aim is not merely to compensate the claimants for injury suffered, but rather to restore the environment.[73]

Taken together, it would be reasonable to conclude that, although being related to the substantive claims, the expense of M&A activities was an independent head of damage, and its compensability was judged on its own merit.

5.4.3 *Costs of Preventive Measures*

Claims for expenses resulting from abatement and prevention of environmental damage in the second installment had the highest successful ratio among the four heads of environmental damage: about 81.5 per

[70] The first F4 report, 2001, para. 36.

[71] This was implicated in para. 32 of the first F4 report, 2001.

[72] Olufemi Elias, 'The UN Compensation Commission and Liability for the Costs of Monitoring and Assessment of Environmental Damage', in Malgosia Fitzmaurice and Dan Sarooshi (eds.), *Issues of State Responsibility before International Judicial Institutions* (Hart 2004) 235.

[73] Ibid.

cent of the amount of compensation claimed was approved by the Panel.[74] The reason was perhaps that the causal link was much less complex in this installment. Just as the Panel observed,

> The question of Iraq's liability for environmental damage resulting from parallel or concurrent causes is not at issue [in the second instalment] since there is well-documented evidence showing that the massive oil release, oil fire and a large number of mines and ordnance are caused by Iraq.[75]

However, it should be noted that the scope of preventive measures under the UNCC regime was much narrower when compared with those in the IOPC system. Under the IOPC system, apart from measures to prevent or minimize environmental damage, measures to prevent or minimize pure economic loss are also considered as preventive measures. For instance, measures taken immediately after the 1993 *Braer* incident to limit damage to the reputation of Shetland salmon were considered as falling within the definition of preventive measures.[76] Such a difference can be attributed to the fact that the concept of 'pollution damage' within the IOPC system is broader than 'environmental damage' in the UNCC regime in the sense that while pure economic loss was an important category of 'pollution damage' in the former, that was not the case in the latter. By contrast, the two compensation systems were consistent on the head of costs of reinstatement/ restoration measures.

5.4.4 *Costs of Restoration Measures*

The Panel clarified two important points with respect to the claims for the expenses of restoration measures in the third and fourth installments. First, the Panel pointed out that the goal of reinstatement measures was 'to restore the environment to the pre-invasion conditions'. As was formulated,

> With respect to the claims in the third 'F4' instalment, the appropriate objective of remediation is to restore the damaged environment or resources to the condition in which it would have been if Iraq's invasion and occupation of Kuwait had not occurred.[77]

[74] The claimed amount was USD 872,760,534 and the amount recommended by the Panel was USD 711,087,737. The second F4 report, 2002, para. 347.

[75] The second F4 report, 2002, paras. 26–27.

[76] IOPC Funds, 71FUND/EXC.35/10, 8 June 1993, para. 3.4.22.

[77] The third F4 report, 2003, paras. 44 and 47.

Secondly, to judge whether the costs of a reinstatement measure were compensable, the main standard was whether that measure was 'reasonably necessary' to achieve that goal. The Panel continued to clarify the specific meaning of the goal and standard mentioned above as follows:

> The panel considers that, in assessing what measures are 'reasonably necessary to clean or restore' damaged environment, primary emphasis must be placed on restoring the environment to pre-invasion conditions, in terms of its overall ecological functioning rather than on the removal of specific contaminants or restoration of the environment to a particular physical condition.[78]

This was the most important clarification of the goal and standard of restoration. Through the clarification, it was clear 'the overall ecological functioning of the environment' was the core consideration of restoration. Thus, the restoration of 'the overall ecological functioning of the environment' should become the fundamental criterion for determining the necessity of any restoration measures.

The goal and standard of restatement measures were the same in the IOPC and UNCC compensation systems. Both hold that the restoration should aim at bringing the damaged environment back to the pre-invasion/pre-spill condition and, in doing so, emphasis should be placed on the overall ecosystem functioning rather than the components of the environment. Both hold that the measures proposed should be reasonably necessary to achieve that goal and, for practical guidance, specific criteria in judging the reasonableness are given. However, there was a big difference. Pure environmental damage was a head of environmental damage under the UNCC 'F4' claims which do not have a counterpart in the IOPC compensation system.

5.4.5 *Pure Environmental Damage*

In the fifth installment, the Panel opined that neither the phrase 'depletion of or damage to natural resources' in paragraph 35 (d) of Governing Council decision 7, nor the term 'environmental damage' used in Security Council Resolution 687 (1991) can be read in such a way as excluding 'pure environmental damage', that is, damage to environmental resources that have no commercial value.[79] At the same time, the

[78] Ibid., para. 48.

[79] The fifth F4 report, 2005, S/AC.26/2005/10, paras. 52, 55.

Panel pointed out that claims for pure environmental damage may go beyond reimbursement of expenses incurred or to be incurred to remediate or restore the damaged resources.[80] Incidentally, the Panel commented that general international law did not exclude compensation for pure environmental damage either.[81] This position was in line with the ILC's opinion as follows:

> However environmental damage will often extend beyond that which can be readily quantified in terms of clean-up costs or property devaluation. Damage to such environmental values (biodiversity, amenity, etc. – sometimes referred to as "non-use values") is, as a matter of principle, no less real and compensable than damage to property, though it may be difficult to quantify.[82]

Having found that the claimants were entitled to claim for losses of natural resources without commercial value beyond the costs of reinstatement measures, the next question was how to prove and further to assess these losses. In the fifth installment, the claimants relied on statistical evidence and calculations and employed certain methodologies.[83] For instance, Habitat Equivalency Analysis (HEA) was employed to assess the loss of ecological services of the resources. The Panel thus had to determine whether the statistical evidence, calculations and methodologies were acceptable. The Panel made the following three general observations on this issue.

First, the Panel observed that

> [i]nternational law does not prescribe any specific and exclusive methods of measurement for awards of damages for internationally wrongful acts by States. The general rule is to restore what has been damaged to integrity or, if this is not possible, to provide an equivalent for it. The overall criterion is always the effective reparation for the wrongful act.[84]

Therefore, in the absence of specific rules on the methods of measurement, the Panel had to make decisions by exercising its own discretion on the basis of the effective reparation principle.

Second, although recognizing the 'inherent difficulties in attempting to place a monetary value on damaged natural resources, particularly

80 Ibid., para. 52.
81 Ibid., para. 58.
82 ILC, the 2001 ASR with commentary, commentary to Article 36, para. 15.
83 The fifth F4 report, 2005, S/AC.26/2005/10, para. 72.
84 Ibid., para. 80.

resources that are not traded in the market',[85] the Panel stated that 'these potential difficulties are not a sufficient reason for a wholesale rejection of these methodologies, or for concluding that their use is contrary to international law principles'.[86] However, in practice, it was very hard for claimants to prove the occurrence of and to assess pure environmental damage, through the employment of theoretical methodology, to the extent that satisfied the Panel. And such a failure would lead to the rejection of the claims. In fact, a mere 0.5 per cent of the amount of compensation claimed in the fifth installment was approved by the Panel.[87]

Third, although acknowledging the losses of natural resources without commercial value as a head of environmental damage, the Panel took the position that this head of environmental damage was subsidiary to the costs of reinstatement measures. As it was explicitly stated in the following Extract:

> Remediation measures for damaged resources should focus on primary restoration, in terms of the restoration of ecological functioning. Consequently, compensatory restoration measures should be considered only where there is sufficient evidence that primary restoration will not fully compensate for any identified losses.[88]

For this reason, reinstatement measures are called 'primary restoration' while compensation to pure environmental damage is called 'compensatory restoration'.

5.4.6 *Lessons for the Measure of Marine Environmental Damage in DSM*

The UNCC legal regime enumerated four heads of environmental damage which were dealt with by the 'F4' Panel in five installments.[89] They are the costs of M&A activities, the costs of preventive measures, the costs of reinstatement measures and pure environmental damage.

[85] Ibid., para. 81.
[86] Ibid.
[87] The amount claimed for compensation was USD 49,936,562,997; the amount approved by the Panel was USD 252,028,468. The fifth F4 report, 2005, S/AC.26/2005/10, para. 777.
[88] Ibid., para. 82.
[89] One should be aware that 'paragraph 35 of Governing Council decision 7 should be considered as providing guidance regarding the types of activities and events that can result in compensable losses or expenses, rather than a limitative enumeration of such activities or events.' The second F4 report, 2002, para. 22.

Among these four heads, the first three are comparable to the three heads of environmental damage in the IOPC context. But the last one – pure environmental damage – is only accepted by the UNCC 'F4' Panel but not by the IOPC Funds. However, owing to the difficulties in proving and assessing pure environmental damage, only a very low rate (0.5 per cent) of the amount claimed was approved by the Panel in practice. In addition, the Panel was of the opinion that compensation for pure environmental damage is secondary to reinstatement. Indeed, overall, the assessment of environmental damage, in particular, the valuation of the pure environmental damage, is an underdeveloped area in international law. As observed by Kazazi, '[T]here is hardly any direct international precedent for valuation of similar [pure] environmental losses in international law.'[90] However, he continued,

> There are relatively developed systems in some municipal laws, including the US and Canada, that may help the Panel; but it will be for the Panel to decide whether and to what extent these domestic principles are applicable and what is the best approach for evaluating the environmental claims.[91]

The primary lesson the measure of environmental damage in DSM may learn from the experience of UNCC 'F4' claims is the inclusion of pure environmental damage. Reasons for such an inclusion had been expounded by the Panel; they can equally make sense in the DSM context too. Likewise, difficulties faced by the claimants and the Panel in evaluating pure environmental damage would very likely appear in the DSM context too. Consequently, if pure environmental damage is to be included, then it will lead to a higher level of uncertainty and unpredictability in the measure of marine environmental damage in DSM. In this respect, one should further draw on relevant practice at national level. A second lesson the practice of UNCC 'F4' Panel can provide is that, when a claim for compensation includes several heads of environmental damage, a judicial or administrative body may deal with it in sequence: the costs of monitoring and assessment measures/the costs of post-incident impact studies should be dealt with first. Finally, the practice of UNCC 'F4' Panel had demonstrated two additional points that are of value to the measure of environmental damage in DSM. Namely, the

[90] Mojtaba Kazazi 'Environmental Damage in the Practice of the UN Compensation Commission', in Michael Bowman and Alan Boyle (eds.), *Environmental Damage in International and Comparative Law* (OUP 2002) 121.

[91] Ibid.

costs of reinstatement measures should be taken as the most important head and compensation for the costs of preventive measures is relatively easy to be implemented in practice.

5.5 Measure of Marine Environmental Damage in DSM: Drawing on the US and EU Laws and Discussions in the Context of the Convention on Biological Diversity

The investigation into the practices of the IOPC Funds and the UNCC 'F4' Panel has shown that the measure of environmental damage relies mainly on a cost-based method. Since pure environmental damage cannot easily be assessed, it is either not included (by the IOPC Funds) or only compensated at a very low ratio in terms of the account claimed (by the UNCC 'F4' Panel). This section continues the inquiry into other contexts: relevant US and EU laws, as well as discussions in the drafting process of the liability and redress protocol to the Convention on Biological Diversity.

5.5.1 Natural Resources Damage Assessment in US Law

In the United States, the Comprehensive Environmental Response, Compensation, and Liability Act of 1980 (the 1980 CERCLA or Superfund) was the first statute at US federal level which dealt with the measure of natural resources damages.[92] Yet, prior to the adoption of the 1980 CERCLA, there was the *Zoe Colocotroni* case in which the measure of environmental damages was the core issue.[93] In that case, 'in essence the question faced by the court was: in the absence of statutory instruments, how should a court assess damages for harm to non-commercial living natural resources?'[94] The federal district court held that 'restoration or replacement costs provided the best measure of the quantum of damage'.[95] When the case was brought before the federal court of appeals, the defendants argued for 'the diminution in value rule' while the plaintiff adhered to 'the cost of restoring rule'. The court of appeals ruled that damages should not be limited by the diminution in [market]

[92] 42 U.S.C. §§ 9601, et seq.

[93] *Commonwealth of Puerto Rico et al., v. the Ss Zoe Colocotroni*, U.S. Court of Appeals for the First Circuit – 628 F.2d 652 (1st Cir. 1980).

[94] Kevin Grady, '*Commonwealth of Puerto Rico v. SS Zoe Colocotroni*: State Action for Damage to Non-Commercial Living Natural Resources' (1980) 9(2) *B.C. Envtl. Aff. L. Rev.* 397–429, 415.

[95] Ibid., 416.

value; it upheld 'the theory of recovery' of the district court. Moreover, the court of appeals further elaborated on the cost of restoring rule by adding restrictive conditions for its application. To begin with, the restoration cost should be feasible, without grossly disproportionate expenditures.[96] Also, there should be 'a practicable plan for actual restoration'.[97] This position was very similar to the practice of the IOPC with respect to compensation in relation to cost of reinstatement measures discussed above.

The 1980 CERCLA prescribed the measure of environmental damages in the form of a statute. Pursuant to Section 107(f)(1) of the 1980 CERCLA, 'the measure of damages [. . .] shall not be limited by the sums which can be used to restore or replace such resources'. Yet, it was not clear what measure of damages beyond the restoration costs could be. On this point, reference can be made to the Oil Pollution Act of 1990 (the 1990 OPA).[98] In accordance with Section 1006(d)(1) of the 1990 OPA,

> The measure of natural resource damages under section 1002(b)(2)(A) is –
>
> (A) the costs of restoring, rehabilitating, replacing, or acquiring the equivalent of, the damaged natural resources;
> (B) the diminution in value of those natural resources pending restoration; plus
> (C) the reasonable cost of assessing those damages.

To facilitate the implementation of the above two statutes, two sets of regulations were adopted at the federal level which provided specific guidance on the operation of the Natural Resources Damage Assessment (NRDA). One was prescribed by the Department of the Interior (DOI) under the 1980 CERCLA (the 1986 DOI NRDA regulations),[99] the other by the Department of Commerce's National Oceanic and Atmospheric Administration (NOAA) under the 1990 OPA (the 1996 NOAA regulations).[100]

The two statutes assign public trustees to protect the environment, including NRDA.[101] The public trustees' measure of environmental

[96] Ibid., 424.
[97] Ibid.
[98] Oil Pollution Act (OPA) (33 U.S.C. §§ 2701, et seq.)
[99] The U.S. Department of the Interior, Natural Resource Damage Assessment 'Type A' and 'Type B' Regulations, based on the 1980 CERCLA, 1986. 43 C.F.R. 11.
[100] The U.S. Department of the Interior, 15 C.F.R. 990.
[101] 33 U.S.C. §§ 2706(e)(2). Importantly, the NRDA by the public trustees should be taken as a 'rebuttable presumption' in any administrative or judicial proceedings. That is,

damages on behalf of the public is inclusive; it captures social losses too. Specially, public trustees can not only claim for (A) the restoration costs (called 'primary restoration') but also (B) the interim loss (called 'compensatory restoration') as well as (C) the cost of assessment. On the operational level, pursuant to the two regulations, NRDA practice revolves around the restoration planning process. In the observation of Jones, the US law embodies a 'restoration-based measure of damages' approach.[102] This differs saliently from the IOPC compensation system where the core is the reimbursement of claimants' economic losses rather than the restoration of the damaged environment. Claims for interim loss are acceptable in the United States but not before the IOPC Funds. In this respect, the US law and practice is comparable to claims for pure environmental damage before the UNCC 'F4' Panel. Yet, what distinguish them is the fact that relatively well accepted methods for measuring ecological losses are developed and applied in practice in the United States but not before the UNCC 'F4' Panel. For example, Baker et al. has recently introduced a Habitat-Based Resource Equivalency Method (HaBREM) as an advanced method developed on the basis of the methods of the Habitat Equivalency Analysis (HEA) and Resource Equivalency Analysis (REA) to measure the loss ecological services of habitats.[103] Indeed, when addressing compensation for interim loss, a service-to-service approach may be considered before resorting to the monetary valuation approach. And above all, in the United States, restoration must always be considered with priority. These US features and experience with NRDA had big influence on the related EU law.

5.5.2 *Remediation of Environmental Damage in EU Law*

At the EU level, the 1993 Green Paper on Remedying Environmental Damage was the earliest effort to deal with the issue of environmental

unless effectively rebutted by opposing evidence, the NRDA by the public trustees should be accepted as legal fact during administrative or judicial proceedings.

102 Carol Adaire Jones, 'Compensation for Natural Resource Damages from Oil Spills: A Comparison of US Law and International Conventions' (1999) 11(1) *International Journal of Environment and Pollution* 86–107.

103 Mary Baker et al., 'Restoration Scaling Approaches to Addressing Ecological Injury: The Habitat-Based Resource Equivalency Method' (2020) 65 *Environmental Management* 161–177. It is described in this paper that HaBREM integrates REA's reproducible injury metrics and population modelling with HEA's comprehensive habitat approach to restoration.

liability (the 1993 Green Paper).[104] In 2000, the European Commission presented the White Paper on Environmental Liability (the 2000 White Paper).[105] Annex 3 to the 2000 White Paper was titled 'Liability for Ecological Damage and Assessment of Ecological Damage'. As stated in the Annex,

> The measure of damages under the proposed EU liability regime as regards natural resource damage should be the cost of restoring, rehabilitating, replacing, or acquiring the equivalent of the damaged natural resources, including compensation of interim losses and reasonable costs of assessing damage. Compensation should only be used for restoration purposes and be aimed at returning natural resources and services to their baseline condition.[106]

The 2004 Environmental Liability Directive (the 2004 ELD) reflected the content in Annex 3 to the 2000 White Paper.[107] In accordance with the 2004 ELD, there are three categories of environmental remediation: primary remediation, complementary remediation and compensatory remediation. Primary remediation restores the damaged natural resources and/or services to, or towards, baseline condition; complementary remediation provides a similar level of natural resources and/or services (preferably the 'resource-to-resource' or the 'service-to-service' equivalence approach) where the damaged natural resources and/or services do not return to their baseline condition; and compensatory remediation is undertaken to compensate for the interim loss of natural resources and services pending recovery.[108]

It is noted that the terms of 'primary restoration' and 'compensatory restoration' are used in both the US and EU legal systems. Under both legal systems, with regard to environmental remediation, primacy was accorded to restoration of the damaged environment to/towards the baseline condition. Meanwhile, they also acknowledged the compensability of interim loss. One is also reminded that when dealing with the UNCC 'F4' claims, the Panel also employed the terms 'primary

[104] COM(93) 47 final,14 May 1993.
[105] COM(2000) 66 final, 9 February 2000.
[106] Ibid., the Annex was prepared by Edward H. P. Brans and Mark Uilhoorn.
[107] Directive 2004/35/CE of the European Parliament and of the Council of 21 April 2004 on environmental liability with regard to the prevention and remedying of environmental damage.
[108] Annex II (Remedying of Environmental Damage) to the 2004 ELD.

restoration' and 'compensatory restoration'. It might be reasonable to infer that the 'F4' Panel was influenced by the practice in the US and EU legal systems. Additionally, the US and EU experience might further extend its influence to the development of environmental liability regimes at the international level. The liability and redress regime in the context of the Convention on Biological Diversity is such an example.

5.5.3 Liability and Redress in the Context of the Convention on Biological Diversity

Establishing a liability and redress regime in the context of the Convention on Biological Diversity[109] involves, among others, the following three key issues: damage to biological diversity, restoration and the valuation of damage to biological diversity.[110] At its eighth meeting in 2006, the Conference of Parties (COP) to the CBD adopted Decision VIII/25 which provided the options of valuation tools.[111] The Decision emphasizes the concept of total economic value (TEV) which endorses the compensability of 'both the direct and indirect use value as well as non-use value of ecosystem services'.[112] It proposes a number of valuation tools, including stated-preference techniques, cost-based approaches and benefits transfer.[113] Yet, stated-preference techniques are the only techniques that are able to capture non-use values.[114] At the ninth COP of the CBD in 2008, the Group of Legal and Technical Experts on Liability and Redress (the 'Group') submitted a synthesis report which examined these three issues (the 2008 synthesis report).[115]

[109] Owing to the lack of consensus regarding the details of a liability regime during the negotiating period, the issue of 'liability and redress, including restoration and compensation, for damage to biological diversity' was not included in the Convention on Biological Diversity (the '1992 CBD') but left for future consideration. Article 14(2), CBD (adopted on 5 June 1992, entered into force on 29 December 1993).

[110] There are other issues also under discussion, including the necessity of liability and redress regime and the choice between state responsibility and state liability. See Convention on Biodiversity Convention. www.cbd.int/liability.

[111] Application of tools for valuation of biodiversity and biodiversity resources and functions, UNEP/CBD/COP/DEC/VIII/25, 2006.

[112] Ibid., 4.

[113] Ibid., 4–5.

[114] Ibid., 5.

[115] Liability and Redress in the Context of Paragraph 2 of Article 14 of the Convention on Biological Diversity: Synthesis report on technical information relating to damage to biological diversity and approaches to valuation and restoration of damage to biological

While the 2008 synthesis report had its special characteristics concerning the definition of damage to biological diversity, with regard to the approaches to restoration, it followed the laws in the US and EU systems and the practice of UNCC 'F4' claims. The report proposed three categories of restoration measures which were exactly the same as those in the 2004 ELD: primary, complementary and compensatory restorations. Also, it accorded primacy to primary restoration, just like the US, the EU and UNCC practice concerning 'F4' claims. When it comes to the approaches of valuation, the 2008 synthesis report indicated that the costs of restoration should be the basic valuation method. This displayed the close relationship between the approaches to restoration and the approaches to valuation of environmental damage.

5.5.4 Lessons for the Measure of Marine Environmental Damage in DSM

Three valuable lessons may be drawn from the US experience on NRDA and others. Most saliently, measure of marine environmental damage in DSM may also adopt a restoration-based approach that embodies inclusive (accepting claims for interim loss) and comprehensive (including primary, complementary and compensatory restoration) measures of environmental damage. In this respect, it is seen that the EU law, UNCC 'F4' claims and decisions as well as discussions over the liability and redress issue in the context of the 1992 CBD may also be influenced by the US laws and practice. Secondly, the US law empowers public trustees to ensure remediation to the damaged environment for public interests by proposing restoration planning and taking other measures and steps. Considering the remoteness and the CHM status of the Area and its resources, modelling on the US public trustees practice would be preferable to environmental damages claims by individual States or entities. It is suggested that the ISA serves as the international public trustee when it comes to remediation to the damaged marine

diversity, as well as information on national/domestic measures and experiences, Bonn, 19–30 May 2008, UNEP/CBD/COP/9/20/Add.1. The Group was established at COP 6 by Decision VI/11 in 2002; it met for the first time in Montreal, Canada from 12 to 14 October 2005. The Group submitted a report at COP 8 in 2006 (UNEP/CBD/COP/8/27/Add.3), some of the content of which was briefly reviewed in the 2008 synthesis report.

environment in the Area. Finally, methodologies for measuring non-use value of the environment developed and applied during the longtime practice concerning NRDA in the United States may be useful for measuring environmental damage in the DSM context.

5.6 A Two-Step Pattern for the Measure of Marine Environmental Damage in DSM

Taking together the lessons learnt from practices of the IOPC and the UNCC compensation systems, the relevant laws and practice in the US and EU legal systems and discussions in the context of CBD, it is suggested that, first, pure environmental damages or interim losses of non-use value of the deep-sea environment should be compensable in the DSM context. Secondly, DSM should adopt a restoration-based measure of marine environmental damage. The concept of 'restoration' consists of both 'primary restoration' and 'compensatory restoration'. 'Compensatory restoration' involves two approaches to the measure of interim lost service of the deep-sea environment: service-to-service approach and valuation approach. Thirdly, at the operational level, environmental damage can be measured as the costs of primary and compensatory restoration projects and other actions plus monetary compensation to pure environmental damage or interim loss. When environmental damage occurs, normally monitoring and assessment measures will be conducted to ascertain the existence of that environmental damage, preventive measure taken to mitigate environmental damage and, if feasible, reinstatement measures taken to restore the damaged environment (primary restoration) or equivalency provided to replace the damaged resource (service-to-service approach). In some cases, post-incident studies will also be initiated. Activities generate costs. In these situations, the measure of environmental damage is relatively easy because damage is already expressed in monetary term. However, if actions or projects are not taken, the easy monetary indicator – costs – for the measure of environmental damage is not available. There, the problem of how to evaluate pure environmental damage or interim loss arises. Hence, a two-step pattern for measuring environmental damage to be applied in the context of DSM is suggested. That is, to use a cost-based method as the basic method, while valuation of pure environmental damage or interim loss is secondary.

5.6.1 *Applying a Cost-Based Method as the First Step*

As demonstrated in Chapter 2, the primary environmental concern with DSM activities is damage to benthic biological communities (that is, deep sea organisms, species, biodiversity) and marine ecosystems. Are there actions and measures in response to damage to benthic communities and marine ecosystems which generate costs? The answer is affirmative. Take some illustrative examples: in the situation of an environmental emergency, actions could be taken or arranged by the ISA if a contractor does not promptly comply with an emergency order. In this case, the costs caused by these emergency actions are a form of environmental damage that must be compensated by the contractor. These costs of response measures can be analogous to the preventive costs under the IOPC and the UNCC compensation systems. For another instance, to determine whether a certain DSM activity has disturbed the benthic community to such an extent that the damage is beyond acceptable level, it would involve intense scientific studies that generate costs. This type of costs might be analogous to post-spill environmental impact studies under the IOPC compensation system and the expenses of M&S activities under the UNCC compensation system. For yet another instance, measures undertaken or to be undertaken to recover disturbed benthic communities or rehabilitate ecosystems after DSM activities might also generate costs. This type of costs might be equal to the costs of reinstatement/restoration in the IOPC and the UNCC compensation systems. The examples taken here are certainly not exhaustive.

The Exploration Regulations and draft Exploitation Regulations endorse partially a cost-based method for measuring environmental damage. It is expressly prescribed in the Standard Clauses for Exploration Contract[116] and Draft Standard Clauses for Exploitation Contract[117] that 'the contractor shall be liable for the actual amount of any damage, including damage to the marine environment, [. . .] including the costs of reasonable measures to prevent or limit damage to the marine environment'. Meanwhile, the proposed environmental compensation fund is for the purpose of funding, among others, the costs of preventive and other remedial measures uncompensated under liability regimes, restoration and rehabilitations, as well as related research.[118]

[116] Article 16.1 of Annex IV to Exploration Regulations, ISBA/19/17, 2013.

[117] Article 7.1 of Annex X to the 2019 draft Exploitation Regulations, ISBA/25/C/WP.1.

[118] Regulation 55, the 2019 draft Exploitation Regulations, ISBA/25/C/WP.1.

5.6.2 Valuation of Pure Environmental Damage or Interim Loss as the Second Step

In the existing legal parlance, valuation (a process of monetarization) of environmental damage is seen from an economic perspective. In practice, economists serve in environmental litigations as expert witnesses or expert consultants to assist lawyers and judges with respect to valuation of pure environmental damage or interim loss. The discussion here will not venture into the field of economics. Yet, it is necessary to have a general knowledge of how the valuation works. First of all, how is the environmental value defined in economics? According to Hanley, economics defines the environment as valuable in two senses: (1) the direct impacts on the utility to individuals; and (2) the impacts on production.[119] Since the impacts of the environment on production are rarely discussed in environmental liability regimes, the focus here is only on the impacts of environmental changes on the utility to individuals. The utility of the environment is divided into two categories: environmental values which depend on actual use of the environment are referred to as 'use values'; while those do not depend on actual use are 'non-use/existence values'. Since one cannot measure utility itself, two key devices have been invented. They are the 'maximum willingness to pay (WTP)' and the 'minimum willingness to accept compensation (WTAC)'. The most commonly used indicator of both the WTP and WTAC is the market price. However, environmental values are usually unpriced by the market place.

Then, what kinds of environmental values are regarded as recoverable? Only the use values or including both the use and non-use values? Whether it is the consumptive value or does it also include the non-consumptive value? In this respect, the *Ohio v. United States Department of the Interior* is a highly relevant case.[120] In this case, in response to the petitions of state governments and environmental groups against 'the

[119] Nick Hanley, 'The Economic Value of Environmental Damage', in Michael Bowman and Alan Boyle (eds.), *Environmental Damage in International and Comparative Law* (OUP 2002). See also Nick Hanley and Clive Spash, *Cost-Benefit Analysis and the Environment* (Edward Elgar 1993).

[120] US, *880 F.2d 432, 1989*. This is a judicial review case before the U.S. Court of Appeals for the District of Columbia Circuit. Comments on this case, see Pilar Okun, 'The Revised Natural Resource Damage Assessment Rule: Computation for Compensation and Restoration', (1992) 70 *WULQ* 959.

lesser of' rule of the 1986 DOI NRDA Regulations,[121] the court upheld the recoverability of both the use and non-use values of the environment and denied the market prices as the only indicator of environmental values. It concluded that

> [w]e hold that the regulation limiting damages recoverable by government trustees for harmed natural resources to 'the lesser of' (a) the cost of restoring or replacing the equivalent of an injured resource, or (b) the lost use value of the resource is directly contrary to the clearly expressed intent of Congress and is therefore invalid. We also hold that the regulation prescribing a hierarchy of methodologies by which the lost use value of natural resources may be measured, which focused exclusively on the market values for such resources when market values are available, is not a reasonable interpretation of the statute.[122]

Certainly, the example above is a case within the US legal system. It does not have direct implications for international law. However, it does express clearly that market values should not be the exclusive way of measuring the use value of the environment. For those use values which are not reflected in the market price and for the non-use values, one has to resort to alternative valuation methodologies, the most commonly used include the following four: the contingent valuation methodology (CVM), the choice experiment methodology, the travel cost methodology and the hedonic pricing methodology. Among them, the first two methodologies are based on the stated preferences of the reviewees, while the latter two are based on revealed preferences drawn from the actual behaviour of individuals. In Schoenbaum's view, however, these methodologies are all highly controversial.[123] In spite of the controversy and criticisms, the CVM is actually broadly employed in practice within the US legal system.[124] As early as in 1989, Cross already indicated that 'contingent valuation is a convenient, direct measure for assessing any particular type of natural resource damage, and because researchers now

[121] The rule requires the trustee to select the 'lesser of' these costs as the measure of damages. Section 11.35(b)(2) of the 1986 DOI NRDA Regulations.

[122] US, *880 F.2d 432, 1989*, para. 3.

[123] Thomas Schoenbaum, 'Environmental Damages in the Common Law: An Overview', in Michael Bowman and Alan Boyle (eds.), *Environmental Damage in International and Comparative Law* (OUP 2002) 220.

[124] The contingent valuation methodology seeks to establish the value of a resource by asking a sample of the population what, hypothetically, they would be willing to pay to preserve it, and then multiplying the value obtained by the number of households in a geographic area deemed relevant.

have considerable experience using contingent valuation, it is gaining credibility'.[125] Nonetheless, this does not mean that the CVM automatically has a general influence for the application. The acceptance of each valuation methodology needs to be judged in each case, taking into account the specific circumstances. It is recalled here that the 'F4' panel of the UNCC was of the opinion that

> [the method] should be accepted only after the Panel has satisfied itself that the extent of damage and the quantification of compensation claimed are appropriate and reasonable in the circumstances of each claim.[126]

Similar comments were also made by the International Court of Justice (ICJ) in its judgment of 2 February 2018: first, 'international law does not prescribe any specific method of valuation for the purpose of compensation for environmental damage', and secondly, 'it is necessary to take into account of the specific circumstances and characteristics of each case'.[127]

From the analysis above, the CVM might be one possible applicable method. Yet, as expressed by the report in the context of CBD, placing a value on pure damage is novel and it requires further consideration.[128] In particular, the great gaps in scientific knowledge about the marine biological community and marine ecosystems would add further uncertainty and difficulty to the task. This situation is the same in the context of DSM as in the context of the CBD. As the report in the context of the CBD stated,

> Assessing and valuing such adverse or negative effects with regard to variability would require an in-depth understanding of the interdependencies between the structure and diversity of biotic communities and the functioning of ecosystems. However, this understanding is still limited and fragmented, which impedes the assignment of both ecological levels of importance (that is, of ecological value) to variability as such, as well as the assignment of economic values.[129]

[125] Frank Cross, 'Natural Resource Damage Valuation', (1989) 42(2) *Vand. L. Rev.*, 269–341, 315. The shortcomings of the contingent method are of course also discussed in the article. Criticisms are that this method is entirely hypothetical, uncertain and it produces only speculative results.

[126] UNCC, the fifth F4 report, 2005, para. 81.

[127] *Certain Activities Carried Out by Nicaragua in the Border Area (Costa Rica v. Nicaragua), Compensation, Judgment, I.C.J. Reports 2018*, p. 15, para. 52.

[128] UNEP/CBD/COP/9/20/Add.1, 2008, para. 105(c).

[129] UNEP/CBD/COP/9/20/Add.1, 2008, para. 107.

Considering the controversy over the valuation methods, one might doubt whether it is practicable and above all desirable to include pure environmental damage or interim loss within the coverage of marine environmental damage in DSM. Rao was of the opinion that the phrase 'actual amount of any damage' in Article 22, Annex III to the UNCLOS implied that the measure of marine environmental damage should be confined only to 'quantifiable damages and not to extend it to speculative or theoretical calculations (following the example of the IOPC Funds)'.[130] That means only the cost-based method can be used to measure marine environmental damage. However, as the SDC stated, 'neither the Convention nor the relevant Regulations specify what constitutes compensable damage, [. . .]'.[131] This statement, although made when discussing the liability of the sponsoring State, was also true concerning the contractor. In the absence of a definite prescription on this point in the DSM legal regime, the question of whether to adopt a broad or limited interpretation concerning heads of marine environmental damage remains a matter of interpretation in future practice.

5.7 Conclusions

The ISA defines 'marine environment' broadly and imposes a threshold requirement to the definition of 'marine environmental damage' in DSM, that is, 'serious harm' to the marine environment. In determining whether such a threshold has been crossed, one must assess the factual situation on the one hand (that is, scientific investigation into the deep-sea ecosystems and assess the detrimental impacts of mining activities) and do a value judgment on the other (namely, weighing the value of environmental protection against that of the development of the DSM industry).

Determining the existence of 'marine environmental damage' is not easy, measuring it is an even more difficult task. This chapter deals mainly with the latter task. The principal question is how DSM could draw lessons from experience concerning the measure of environmental damage in different contexts. It is found that what DSM could learn from the long-term successful practice of the IOPC Funds is a cost-based method

[130] The first report (subtopic on international liability) of Rao, 2003, UN. Doc. A/CN.4/531, para. 69.

[131] ITLOS, Advisory Opinion of 1 February 2011 (case No. 17), para. 179.

regarding the measure of marine environmental damage. The UNCC 'F4' claims share much similarity with the IOPC practice regarding the categorization of costs as heads of environmental damage. Yet, they differ in one significant point: while the IOPC Funds do not consider pure environmental damage compensable, UNCC 'F4' Panel does. In this respect, it is suggested that DSM should follow the practice of UNCC 'F4' Panel in order to have a comprehensive and inclusive coverage of marine environmental damage. In the United States, natural resources damage is measured not only by cost of assessment, costs of restoration projects for returning the damaged natural resources to their previous condition (primary restoration) or for replacing the damaged natural resources (service-to-service/resource-to-resource compensatory restoration), but also measured by monetary compensation for interim losses of ecological services (value-to-value compensatory restoration). It is thus said that the United States takes a restoration-based approach. The US law concerning NRDA is characterized with a comprehensive and inclusive coverage, and there are rich practices about measuring non-use value of natural resources. The US law and practice heavily influenced the EU law; that influence further extends to the international level, including the liability and redress discussions under the CBD and perhaps also the UNCC 'F4' claims. These existing experiences could certainly provide valuable lessons to DSM regime too. In the context of DSM, ISA is responsible for safeguarding the marine environment, this is similar to the designation of public trustees in the United States. The ISA should then secure that both use and non-use values of the damaged marine environment are covered, that restoration should be accorded with primacy.

Taking the existing experience analysed above together, it is suggested that, at the operational level, a two-step pattern can be applicable in the context of DSM. For the first step, the measure of marine environmental damage caused by DSM activities should rely primarily on the cost-based method. The costs are those that might be incurred by taking preventive measures, restoration measures, assessment measures, etc. In case that damaged marine environment cannot be restored or replaced, as a second step, monetary compensation for pure environmental damage and interim loss must be done. There, valuation methods, such as the contingent valuation method, may be used to measure the non-use value of the marine environment. Yet, valuation methods are subject to a higher level of controversy than cost-based method.

The following chapters turn to the liability regimes and alternative compensation regimes. They demonstrate that (marine) environmental damage constitutes the common triggering element for the establishment of international environmental liabilities of the contractor,[132] the sponsoring State[133] and the ISA.[134] Moreover, the definition and measure of environmental damage are the basis upon which reparation or compensation can be made.

[132] Article 22, Annex III to the UNCLOS, the first sentence. It states that 'the contractor shall have responsibility or liability for any damage arising out of wrongful acts in the conduct of its operations [. . .]'.

[133] Article 139 of the UNCLOS. It states that 'without prejudice to the rules of international law and Annex III, article 22, damage caused by the failure of a State Party or international organization to carry out its responsibility under this Part shall entail liability'.

[134] Article 22, annex III to the UNCLOS, the second sentence. It states that 'similarly, the Authority shall have responsibility or liability for any damage arising out of wrongful acts in the exercise of its powers and functions [. . .]'.

6

International Environmental Liability of the Contractor

6.1 Introduction

Pursuant to Article 22, Annex III (basic conditions of prospecting, exploration and exploitation), of the United Nations Convention on the Law of the Sea (UNCLOS):

> The contractor shall have responsibility or liability for any damage arising out of wrongful acts in the conduct of its operations, account being taken of contributory acts or omissions by the Authority. [. . .] Liability in every case shall be for the actual amount of damage.

This article is incorporated in the common Section 16, Annex IV (standard clauses for exploration contract) of the Exploration Regulations. These provisions are the fundamental legal bases upon which the international environmental liability of the contractor is to be discussed.

The main issues to be dealt with in this chapter include the establishment and the implementation of the international environmental liability of the contractor. For the establishment of liability, two issues need to be considered: (1) the primacy of liability of the contractor to that of the sponsoring State and the International Seabed Authority (ISA) and the underlying reason accounting for it (Sections 6.2 and 6.3), and (2) the conditions for the establishment of liability (Section 6.4). The implementation of liability embodies (3) the remediation of marine environmental damage, that is, the forms and content of liability (Section 6.5), and (4) the invocation of liability or claim action against the contractor which involves mainly procedural rules (Section 6.6). It also incidentally deals with the special issues of the Enterprise as the contractor and States as contractors (Section 6.7).

6.2 Channelling Liability to the Contractor

Channelling liability (primarily) to the owner of the facilities or the operator is a common feature shared by all existing environment-related liability instruments[1] except the 1972 Space Treaty.[2] Not differently, the Seabed Disputes Chamber (SDC) declared that liability for environmental damage arising from deep seabed mining (DSM) activities mainly rests on the contractor rather than on the sponsoring State.[3] Under the DSM legal regime, the contractor is the person who signs the contract with the ISA. This is the person in legal control of DSM activities, who is not necessarily the person operating DSM activities from a factual perspective. Liability for the operation of DSM is channelled only to the contractor. As it is stipulated,

> The Contractor shall be liable for [...] those of its employees, subcontractors, agents and all persons engaged in working or acting for them in the conduct of its operations under this contract [...].[4]

This stipulation makes the identification of the liable person easier. At the same time, it also provides an incentive for the contractor to strengthen its control over or management of its employees,

1 For example, in the three treaties under the auspices of the IMO in the field of shipping/carriage by sea (the 1992 CLC, the 2001 Bunkers' Convention and the 2010 HNS), the shipowner is held liable at the first tier. In all other civil liability regimes, the operator is held liable. For instance, the Paris Convention on Third Party Liability in the Field of Nuclear Energy (adopted on 29 July 1960, entered into force on 1 April 1968, amended by the 1964 Protocol (entered into force on 1 April 1968), the 1982 Protocol (entered into force on 7 October 1988), and the 2004 Protocol (not yet entered into force)); Convention on the Liability of Operators of Nuclear Ships (adopted on 25 May 1962, not yet in force); Vienna Convention on Civil Liability for Nuclear Damage (adopted on 21 May 1963, entered into force on 12 November 1977, as amended by the 1997 Protocol (entered into force on 4 October 2003)); Lugano Convention on Civil Liability for Damage Resulting from Activities Dangerous to the Environment (adopted on 8 March 1993, not yet in force; it is not expected that this Protocol will ever enter into force); Protocol on Liability and Compensation for damage resulting from transboundary movements of hazardous wastes and their disposal (adopted on 10 December 1999, not yet in force; it is not expected that this Protocol will ever enter into force); Annex VI to the Protocol on Environmental Protection to the Antarctic Treaty – Liability Arising from Environmental Emergencies (adopted on 17 June 2005, not yet in force).

2 As it is said that 'with the exception of the question of liability for damage caused by space objects, all other multilateral conventions have channelled liability to a private entity under the jurisdiction of a state party through a strict liability system'. Guido Fernando Silva Soares and Everton Vieira Vargas, 'The Basel Liability Protocol on Liability and Compensation for Damage Resulting from Transboundary Movements of Hazardous Wastes and Their Disposal' (2002) 12(1) *YIntlEnvL* 69–104, 75.

3 ITLOS, Advisory Opinion of 1 February 2011 (case No. 17), paras. 199–200.

4 Section 16(1), Annex IV to the 2013 Exploration Regulations on Nodules (ISBA/19/A/17), 2012 Exploration Regulations on Crust (ISBA/18/A/11) and 2010 Exploration Regulations on Sulphides (ISBA/16/A/12/Rev.1).

subcontractors, agents and others. In this respect, it is noted that, in some existing civil liability treaties, 'the operator' is defined as the person who exercises control over the dangerous activity[5] and that, in most existing civil liability treaties, the liability is channelled only to the operator.[6] The explanatory report to the 1993 Lugano Convention elucidates that

> [a]ttaching liability to the person in control of the activity which caused the damage has the advantages that it is easy to trace the person liable, that overlapping liabilities are avoided, and that it is easier for an insurance company to assess the risk and insure that risk.[7]

Two specific issues relating to channelling liability to the contractor need to be noted here. First, channelling liability has a temporal dimension. Considering the delayed effects of DSM activities on the marine environment, the Exploration Regulations include a provision as follows:

> The contractor shall continue to have responsibility for any damage arising out of wrongful acts in the conduct of its operations, in particular damage to the marine environment, after the completion of the exploration phase.[8]

Therefore, liability of the contractor does not necessarily terminate at the same time as the end of the contract. However, implementing liability after the end of the contract might face additional difficulties. For instance, the (former) contractor might cease to exist or be subject to legal division, merger or other rearrangements. These changes would make identification of the liable party a complex task. Furthermore, with the end of contract, the ISA loses its control over the (former) contractor. Here, the role of the former sponsoring State comes into the picture. As is known, the (former) sponsoring State has jurisdiction or control over the (former) sponsored contractor, and

5 For example, Article 6(1), Lugano Convention, 1993. 'The operator in respect of a dangerous activity mentioned under article 2, paragraph 1, sub-paragraphs a to c shall be liable for the damage caused by the activity as a result of incidents at the time or during the period when he was exercising the control of that activity.'

6 There is an exception: in the 1999 Basel Protocol, the liability might be channelled to the notifier, the exporter, the importer and the disposer of hazardous wastes according to particular situations. Namely, there is a multiplicity of alternatives for imposing liability. Guido Fernando Silva Soares and Everton Vieira Vargas, 'The Basel Liability Protocol on Liability and Compensation for Damage Resulting from Transboundary Movements of Hazardous Wastes and Their Disposal' (2002) 12(1) *YIntlEnvL* 69–104, 87–88. Also in the three treaties concerning shipping by sea under the auspices of the IMO, liability is imposed primarily on the shipowner.

7 Explanatory report to the 1993 Lugano Convention, para. 8.

8 Regulation 30 of the 2013 Exploration Regulation for Nodules, ISBA/19/C/17.

that jurisdiction or control continues even when the sponsorship ends. Thus, it is expected that the former sponsoring State will be in a stronger position to implement liability of a former contractor in the post-contract situation.[9]

Another issue is joint liability or several liabilities. Pursuant to Section 22, Annex IV to the Exploration Regulations, rights and obligations of the contractor are transferrable.[10] The question is who will be liable if damage to the marine environment is detected after the transfer of rights and obligations. Pursuant to Section 22.2 of the standard clauses for exploration contract, the proposed transferee 'shall assume all of the obligations of the Contractor'. Does this mean that the successor to the contract will be liable for any damage that occurs after they take over the contract, including damage caused by their predecessor? Before answering, an analogy can be made to some existing civil liability treaties. For instance, according to Article 3(1) of the 1977 London Convention, 'when the incident consists of a series of occurrences, liability for pollution damage arising out of each occurrence shall attach to the operator of the installation at the time of that occurrence'.[11] In line with this logic, one can argue that liability of the former contractor should not be borne by their successor. However, the situation becomes complex if the subject who causes the damage cannot be identified with precision. In this situation, should only the successor be liable or should both be held jointly liable? The answer is not that clear. Yet another possible situation that would give rise to the issue of joint liability or several liabilities could be that operators might sign the contract jointly with the ISA. In this situation, should these operators be held jointly or severally liable? Here, by drawing again on the 1977 London Convention,[12] the answer would be that if a joint operation caused damage to the marine environment, then all the contractors will be jointly or severally liable.

[9] This is a very specific example to demonstrate that the ISA and the sponsoring State need to cooperate with each other in fulfilling their roles as the administrators or regulators within the DSM legal regime.

[10] The transfer of rights and obligations of the contractor under the contract shall be subject to the consent of the ISA. Section 22, Annex IV (standard clauses for exploration contract) to the 2013 Exploration Regulations on Nodules (ISBA/19/A/17), 2012 Exploration Regulations on Crust (ISBA/18/A/11) and 2010 Exploration Regulations on Sulphides (ISBA/16/A/12/Rev.1).

[11] For instance, Article 3(1) of the 1977 London Convention: 'when the incident consists of a series of occurrences, liability for pollution damage arising out of each occurrence shall attach to the operator of the installation at the time of that occurrence'.

[12] Article 3(2) of the 1977 London Convention states that 'where an installation has more than one operator they shall be jointly and severally liable'.

Turning back to the main line of channelling of liability to the contractor, it is noted that the SDC endorsed the primacy of the liability of the contractor as opposed to the contractor's sponsoring State. However, the SDC made this statement by simply referring to Article 22, Annex III, UNCLOS, without any explanation. It is argued in this chapter that there is an accepted but unstated principle which serves as the theoretical basis for the statement of the SDC, namely the polluter-pays principle.

6.3 The Polluter-Pays Principle

The polluter-pays principle was first enunciated at the international level in the 1972 OECD Council Recommendation, which reads:

> The principle to be used for allocating costs of pollution prevention and control measures to encourage rational use of scarce environmental resources and to avoid distortions in international trade and investment is the so-called Polluter-Pays Principle. This principle means that the polluter should bear the expenses of carrying out the above-mentioned measures decided by public authorities to ensure that the environment is in an acceptable state. In other words, the cost of these measures should be reflected in the cost of goods and services which cause pollution in production and/or consumption. Such measures should not be accompanied by subsidies that would create significant distortions in international trade and investment.[13]

This formulation is based on economic theory and concepts. As Nicolas de Sadeleer commented, the principle has its origin in the theory of externality in economics,[14] and Sanford Gaines observed that

> [t]he polluter-pays principle began as a simple expression of two economic concepts: that efficiency in environmental management required internalization of costs in the producer, and that equity in international trade required all countries to follow the efficiency principle uniformly.[15]

Since only a portion of the costs are allocated to the polluter, the idea that the polluter should assume the costs is only partially materialized. That

[13] The 1972 OECD Council Recommendation on Guiding Principles concerning International Aspects of Environmental Policies, C(72) 128 (final), OECD, 1972.

[14] Nicolas de Sadeleer, *Environmental Principles – From Political Slogans to Legal Rules* (OUP 2002) 21.

[15] Sanford Gaines, 'The Polluter-Pays Principle: From Economic Equity to Environmental Ethos' (1991) 26(3) *TexIntlLJ* 463–496, 495.

is, the Organisation for Economic Co-operation and Development (OECD) adopted the polluter-pays principle narrowly. With small modifications, the principle as articulated above was then reaffirmed in the subsequent recommendations of the OECD.[16]

Closely following the step of the OECD, the European Community incorporated the polluter-pays principle into its secondary legislation.[17] Within the European Community the polluter-pays principle 'began to lose its purely economic meaning'.[18] There, the interrelationship between the polluter-pays principle and civil liabilities was detected: the polluter-pays principle was regarded as the fundamental principle upon which civil liabilities were built. In particular, the principle was frequently invoked to justify a strict liability regime. To illustrate, the statement in the preamble of the 2004 Environmental Liability Directive (the 2004 ELD) can serve as a key example:

> The prevention and remedying of the environmental damage should be implemented through the furtherance of the 'polluter-pays' principle, as indicated in the Treaty and in line with the principle of sustainable development. The fundamental principle of this Directive should therefore be that an operator whose activity has caused the environmental damage or the imminent threat of such damage is to be held financially liable, in order to induce operators to adopt measures and develop practices to minimize the risks of environmental damage so that their exposure to financial liabilities is reduced.[19]

[16] C(74) 223 (final), OECD, 1974; C(89) 88 (final), OECD, 1989; C(91) 177 (final), OECD, 1991.

[17] Examples can be found in Nicolas de Sadeleer, *Environmental Principles – From Political Slogans to Legal Rules* (OUP 2002): Recommendation 75/436/Euratom, ECSC, EEC of 3 March 1975 regarding cost allocation and action by public authorities on environmental matters; The Waste Framework Directive in 1991; Council Directive 92/43/EEC on the conservation of natural habitats and wild fauna and flora; The 1993 EC Green Paper on remedying environmental damage; Article 10 of Directive 1999/31/EC on waste landfill; the 2000 EC White Paper on Environmental Liability; Article 9 of Directive 2000/60/EC in the field of water policy; Article 130R(2) of the Single European Act (SEA) states that 'action by the Community relating to the environment shall be based on the principle that the polluter should pay'; The 1992 Porto Agreement creating the European Economic Area (EEA) also states that 'action by the Contracting Parties relating to the environment shall be based on the principle that the polluter should pay'.

[18] Sanford Gaines, 'The Polluter-pays Principle: From Economic Equity to Environmental Ethos' (1991) 26(3) *TexIntlLJ* 463–496, 495.

[19] European Parliament and Council *Directive 2004/35/CE* of 21 April 2004 on environmental liability with regard to the prevention and remedying of environmental damage, preamble, para. 2.

The influence of the principle was certainly not confined to Europe. Globally speaking, Principle 16 of the 1992 Rio Declaration states that

> [n]ational authorities should endeavor to promote the internalization of environmental costs and the use of economic instruments, taking into account the approach that the polluter should, in principle, bear the cost of pollution, with due regard to the public interest and without distorting international trade and investment.[20]

This statement constitutes a recognition of the polluter-pays principle which has already found its place in treaty practice. It also created momentum for further incorporation of the principle into treaties, either in their preambles or the operational provisions.[21] Here, similar to secondary legislation within the European Community, the polluter-pays principle is closely related to civil liability, in particular, strict civil liability regimes.[22]

Within the International Law Commission (ILC), upon inclusion of civil liability in the topic of international liability in 1990, the polluter-pays principle and its relationship with civil liabilities was explored in the two surveys undertaken by the Secretariat of the ILC in 1995 and 2004. The Secretariat stated that, although not necessarily, civil liability is

[20] UN Doc. A/CONF 151/26(Vol. 1), 1992.

[21] See Nicolas de Sadeleer, *Environmental Principles – From Political Slogans to Legal Rules* (OUP 2002). Examples of the polluter-pays principle's inclusion in the preambles of treaties include: the 1980 Athens Protocol for the Protection of the Mediterranean Sea against Pollution from Land-based Sources and Activities; the 1990 OPRC Convention; the 1992 Helsinki Convention on the transboundary effects of damage resulting from activities dangerous to the environment; the 1993 Lugano Convention on civil liability for damage resulting from activities dangerous to the environment; and the 2000 London Protocol on preparedness, response and co-operation to pollution incidents by hazardous and noxious substances. Examples of the polluter-pays principle's inclusion in the operative provisions of treaties include: the 1985 ASEAN Agreement on the conservation of nature and natural resources; the 1991 Convention on the protection of the Alps; the 1992 proto Agreement to establish the EEA; the 1992 OSPAR Convention; the 1992 Helsinki Convention on the protection and use of transboundary watercourses and international lakes; the 1992 Helsinki Convention on the protection of the marine environment of the Baltic Sea area; the 1994 Convention on Co-operation for the protection and sustainable use of the Danube River; the 1976 Barcelona Convention for the protection of the Mediterranean Sea against pollution; the 1996 London Protocol to the Convention on the prevention of marine pollution by dumping of wastes and other matter; and the 1998 Rotterdam Convention on the protection of the Rhine.

[22] For instance, the 1993 Lugano Convention considers 'the desirability of providing for strict liability' and 'the polluter-pays principle', preamble, para. 7.

considered as one of the methods to implement the polluter-pays principle.[23] It also stated that

> [t]he polluter-pays principle was developed first in a legal context by OECD in 1972. This principle is different from the principle of the operator's liability provided for in many civil liability conventions. However, new approaches to the principle seem to accentuate its remedial function, which is also extant in civil liability regimes.[24]

In the 2006 Draft Principles, 'the Commission considers the polluter-pays principle as an essential component in underpinning the present draft principles to ensure that victims that suffer harm as a result of an incident involving a hazardous activity are able to obtain prompt and adequate compensation'.[25] Boyle commented that 'the ILC Draft Principles represent an application of the polluter-pays principle in its most developed form'.[26] In effect, a comparison between the ILC's 2006 Draft Principles and the 1972 OECD Recommendation reveals clearly that the main function[27] of the polluter-pays principle has changed drastically during a span of thirty-five years. While in the 1972 OECD Recommendation, the implementation of the polluter-pays principle is meant to encourage rational use of scarce environmental resources and to avoid distortions in international trade and investment, in the 2006 ILC Draft Principles, the implementation of the polluter-pays principle is aimed to ensure prompt and adequate compensation to victims of transboundary damage and to preserve and protect the environment in the event of transboundary damage, especially with respect to mitigation of damage to the environment and its restoration or reinstatement.

[23] Secretariat of the ILC, Survey of liability regimes relevant to the topic of international liability for injurious consequences arising out of acts not prohibited by international law, 1995, UN Doc. A/CN.4/471, para. 130; 2004, A/CN.4/543, para. 337.

[24] Secretariat of the ILC, Survey of liability regimes relevant to the topic of international liability for injurious consequences arising out of acts not prohibited by international law (international liability in case of loss from transboundary harm arising out of hazardous activities), 2004, UN Doc. A/CN.4/543, para. 261. See also para. 285: 'these new approaches [EU Directive 2004/35/CE] seem to demonstrate a willingness to give the polluter-pays principle a remedial and compensatory function'.

[25] ILC, General Commentary of the 2006 Draft Principles, para. (2).

[26] Alan Boyle, 'Polluter Pays' MPEPIL (last updated in March 2009), para. 14.

[27] De Sadeleer considered that the polluter-pays principle has four functions as follows: economic integration function; redistribution function; preventive function; and curative function. Nicolas de Sadeleer, *Environmental Principles: From Political Slogans to Legal Rules* (OUP 2002).

Thus, although initially having a purely economic meaning (emphasizing the internalization of external costs of production from an economic perspective), the polluter-pays principle has evolved into a principle that embodies liability and compensation components (emphasizing the remedial effect on the victim and the environment). That development demonstrates a close relationship between the polluter-pays principle and civil liability. On the one hand, the polluter-pays principle provides theoretical justification for assigning liability primarily to the operator. The ILC's turning its focus from State liability to liability of the operator is such a case in point. On the other hand, civil liability has turned into an important means to implement the polluter-pays principle.[28]

However, it should be noted that it is neither practical nor desirable to fully implement the polluter-pays principle through civil liability regimes. Full implementation of the polluter-pays principle is not practical for two reasons. To start with, there are ambiguities in the content of the polluter-pays principle. Who exactly does 'the polluter' refer to? How much should the polluter pay exactly, and for what? A short answer to the first question is that 'the concept of polluter has evolved'.[29] Indeed, 'the polluter' is such a flexible term that a list of candidates for the term must be updated constantly. Simply having a look at several descriptive terminologies of the polluter-pays principle, namely the 'beneficiary-pays principle', 'polluter responsibility principle', the 'user pay principle', 'producer responsibility', 'extended polluter responsibility', illustrates the various meanings of who the polluter is.[30] A similar answer can be given to the second question. As the 2004 ILC Survey indicated, 'the precise contours and breadth of the polluter-pays principle are unclear. It has different interpretations in different contexts'.[31] Also, Schwartz stated that 'like the "polluter", the content of the costs to be borne or paid as an effect of the polluter-pays principle has also diverged considerably and continues to expand to meet the environmental challenges of modern economic activities'.[32] The

[28] Other means to implement the polluter-pays principle could include taxation, charging fees and monetary penalty, etc.

[29] Priscilla Schwartz, 'The Polluter-Pays Principle', in Malgosia Fitzmaurice, David Ong and Panos Merkouris (eds.), *Research Handbook on International Environmental Law* (Edward Elgar 2010), 247.

[30] Ibid, 248.

[31] ILC Survey, 2004, UN Doc. A/CN.4/543, para. 283.

[32] Priscilla Schwartz, 'The Polluter-Pays Principle', in Malgosia Fitzmaurice, David Ong and Panos Merkouris (eds.), *Research Handbook on International Environmental Law* (Edward Elgar 2010), 248.

indications of the likely costs to be borne by polluters include not only the costs arising from preventive and remedial measures which are normally under the coverage of liability, but also the costs to do with human health as well as social costs and so on.[33] This broad level of flexibility in the meaning of both 'the polluter' and 'the costs' leaves significant room for interpretation in implementation of the polluter-pays principle. On the other hand, civil liability is not able to fully implement the polluter-pays principle either. As Boyle puts it,

> The extent to which civil liability makes the polluter pay for environmental damage depends on a variety of factors. If liability is based on negligence, not only does this have to be proved, but harm which is neither reasonably foreseeable nor reasonably avoidable will not be compensated and the victim or the taxpayer, not the polluter, will bear the loss. Strict liability is a better approximation of the polluter-pays principle, but not if limited in amount, as in internationally agreed schemes involving oil tankers or nuclear installations.[34]

Johnston took a similar position,

> Thus, the lesson from US experience with environmental liability under CERCLA is that while liability may indeed generate some strong incentives to avoid liability, on balance *ex post* environmental liability may be a very expensive and often counterproductive instrument for environmental protection. Thus the polluter pays principle is likely to continue to be of quite limited practical significance.[35]

Nor is full implementation of the polluter-pays principle desirable. The ILC's conceptual evolution from civil liability to allocation of loss strongly illustrates this point. Under the concept of allocation of loss, broader actors than the operator are involved in the compensation mechanism, which marks an evident departure from the polluter-pays principle. Boyle and others were very right to observe that 'none of the [loss allocation] schemes follows the polluter-pays principle in full. Instead the burden of major losses is borne partly by the operator, partly

[33] Priscilla Schwartz, 'The Polluter-Pays Principle', in Malgosia Fitzmaurice, David Ong and Panos Merkouris (eds.), *Research Handbook on International Environmental Law* (Edward Elgar 2010), 249.

[34] Patricia Birnie, Alan Boyle and Catherine Redgwell, *International Law and the Environment*, 3rd edn. (OUP 2009) 324.

[35] Jason Johnston, 'Is the Polluter-Pays Principle Really Fundamental? An Economic Explanation of the Relative Unimportance of Environmental Liability and Taxes in the US Environmental Law', in Michael Faure, Han Lixin and Shan Hongjun (eds.), *Marine Pollution Liability and Policy: China, Europe and the US* (Kluwer 2010) 119.

by the industry or state concerned, and beyond that it falls on the innocent victim, or must be recovered in interstate claims'.[36] However, one should be very careful not to go too far to claim that the concept of allocation of loss is tantamount to a rejection of the polluter-pays principle. When turning from civil liability to allocation of loss, the ILC did reject the idea that the 'polluter-pays' should be the sole criterion, yet it acknowledged that the 'polluter-pays' served as the primary criterion of the allocation of responsibility for environment protection. Here, attention is called to the contention that the polluter-pays principle 'expresses a fundamental moral judgment about the allocation of responsibility for environment protection in complex societies'.[37]

To conclude, the polluter-pays principle was introduced initially in the field of economic competition law, focusing on the internalization of costs. Later, the scope of its application was expanded to liability regimes. Many civil liability treaties and international legal instruments referred to the polluter-pays principle as a theoretical basis. In turn, civil liability became a means of implementing the polluter-pays principle. On the basis of this examination of the development of the polluter-pays principle, it is clear why in the context of DSM it is the contractor who will assume primary international environmental liability, not the sponsoring State and also not the ISA. At the same time, one is also reminded that it is neither practical nor desirable to fully implement the polluter-pays principle through liability of the operator. When liability of the operator is not adequate in achieving the goal of prompt and adequate compensation to victims and preservation of the environment, room should be open for the involvement of actors other than the operator. Here the theoretical basis for the discussion goes beyond the polluter-pays principle. Chapter 7 will look at mechanisms for allocation of loss in the context of DSM under the rubric of 'insurance' and 'environmental compensation fund'. Yet, before moving to that point, let us first look into the conditions for establishing international environmental liability of the contractor.

[36] Patricia Birnie, Alan Boyle and Catherine Redgwell, *International Law and the Environment*, 3rd edn. (OUP 2009) 317.

[37] Sanford Gaines, 'The Polluter-Pays Principle: From Economic Equity to Environmental Ethos' (1991) 26(3) *TexIntlLJ* 495.

6.4 Establishment of International Environmental Liability of the Contractor

6.4.1 Environmental Damage

The establishment of international environmental liability of all categories of participants in DSM, including the contractor, is preconditioned on the existence of environmental damage. To satisfy this condition, the core task is to define and measure environmental damage. Nonetheless, as is shown in Chapter 5, defining and measuring environmental damage is a difficult task which constitutes the first hurdle to be crossed in the process of establishing liability.

6.4.2 Internationally Wrongful Acts of the Contractor

6.4.2.1 Interpretation of 'Internationally Wrongful Act'

In accordance with the UNCLOS and the Exploration Regulations, liability of the contractor is conditioned on the wrongful acts of the contractor. It is noted that the ILC expounded on 'internationally wrongful act' in the commentary to the 2001 Articles on State Responsibility (ASR). The term has three layers of meaning. First, there is a breach of an international obligation. Second, the benchmark for deciding whether there is a breach is international law, not domestic law. Third, 'in determining whether given conduct constitutes a breach, the principal focus will be on the primary obligation concerned'. A major question is whether the ILC's interpretation of internationally wrongful acts of the State can be applied to the contractor by analogy? This question can be broken down into three specific questions. First, it is well-known that, when approaching the topic of State responsibility, the ILC made a critical distinction between primary and secondary rules, and the ILC restricted its task exclusively to the secondary rules. Is it appropriate to follow that approach to deal with international environmental liability of the contractor in this chapter? Second, is it international law or domestic law that serves as the benchmark for deciding the issue of international environmental liability of the contractor? Third, is a mental element of 'fault' required in determining the 'wrongfulness' on the part of the contractor? These three questions are each dealt with in turn.

As to the first question, the key is that secondary rules are about the legal consequences of the breach of primary obligations. The distinction between primary and secondary rules is an analytical tool at a very abstract construction level; it can apply to different subjects, whether States or private entities. Thus, if the requirement of 'wrongful acts' of the contractor is interpreted as 'the breach of its obligations' and liability of the contractor is about the legal consequences of that breach, then liability of the contractor as the subject matter of this chapter belongs to the secondary rules.[38]

With respect to the second question, as has already been analysed in previous chapters, the DSM legal regime is international law *sui generis* for the very reason that it includes non-State actors, the ISA and the contractor as full-fledged participants. As far as the contractor is concerned, in light of Article 153 UNCLOS, the Enterprise, States and state enterprises or natural or legal persons are eligible to explore and exploit the mineral resources in the Area. At the international level, Annex III to the UNCLOS lays down the basic conditions of prospecting, exploration and exploitation, the three sets of Exploration Regulations and the contracts that prescribe obligations of the contractor. At the same time, national legislation of sponsoring States can also give rise to obligations of the contractor. However, it is stressed here that the question of whether the contractor has breached its international obligation will be determined by the international DSM legal regime only. Whether a breach can be identified under the domestic law of its sponsoring State is irrelevant. This is 'the characterization of an act of the contractor as internationally wrongful'.[39]

As regard the third question, it is noted that terms like 'fault-based liability', 'non-fault liability' and 'liability without fault' are commonly used in civil liability regimes and the related literature. For instance, Article 5 of the 1999 Basel Protocol defines fault-based liability as follows:

> Any person shall be liable for damage caused or contributed to by his lack of compliance with the provisions implementing the Convention or by his wrongful intentional, reckless or negligent acts or omissions.

From this wording, it seems that apart from the conduct, the mental dimension, as reflected in the words 'intentional', 'reckless' and

[38] This research follows the fundamental approach adopted by the ILC on State responsibility, making a distinction between primary and secondary rules. One advantage of doing so is that by separating liability from the issue of obligation, it places the liability regime in a relatively neutral and stable position: the liability regime is not subject to changes to primary rules which determine the international obligations of the contractor.

[39] The expression is modelled on Article 3 of the ICL's 2001 ASR.

'negligent', should also be analysed when determining the existence of 'fault'.[40] In contrast, the UNCLOS does not employ the term 'fault', nor does it include the wording 'intentional, reckless or negligent'; the terminology it uses is 'wrongful acts (or omissions)'. Here, reference can again be made to the ILC's 2001 ASR. When confronted with the question of 'whether fault constitutes a necessary element of the internationally wrongful act of a State', the ILC commented that

> [t]his is certainly not the case if by 'fault' one understands the existence, for example, of an intention to harm. In the absence of any specific requirement of a mental element in terms of the primary obligation, it is only the act of a State that matters, independently of any intention.[41]

It is reasonable to infer that this clarification of 'fault' can also be applied to the contractor in the context of DSM. As analysed in Chapter 4, the international environmental obligations placed on the contractor include obligations to apply the precautionary principle, take preventive measures, establish an environmental baseline, assess and monitor environmental impact, report an environmental emergency, submit annual reports, cooperate with the ISA and so on. All of them are requirements of acts; the mental element of the contractor is irrelevant when determining fulfillment of these obligations.

Thus, the ILC's interpretation of the term 'internationally wrongful acts' in the 2001 ASR can apply, by analogy, to the contractor. By 'wrongful acts', Article 22, Annex III to the UNCLOS means not the requirement of a mental element of 'fault' of the contractor, but the objective criterion of 'the breach of the primary obligations'. Therefore, to determine whether the contractor has committed wrongful acts is to examine the actual conduct of the contractor against the requirements of the primary obligations. To do so, the focus will be on the primary obligations prescribed in the international DSM legal regime.

6.4.2.2 In Contrast to Strict Liability

The very requirement of 'wrongful act' makes the international environmental liability of the contractor in the context of DSM different from all existing civil liability treaties, since the latter all adopted strict liability of

[40] Article 5 of the 1999 Basel Protocol defines fault-based liability as follows: 'any person shall be liable for damage caused or contributed to by his lack of compliance with the provisions implementing the Convention or by his wrongful intentional, reckless or negligent acts or omissions'.

[41] Commentary to Article 2 of the 2001 ASR, para. (10).

the operator for environmental damage arising from hazardous activities. To understand this point, it is necessary to examine why the standard of strict liability was adopted.

The adoption of strict liability in civil liability treaties is relatively new and was influenced strongly by the trend of strict liability at a national level.[42] In domestic jurisdictions, fault-based civil liability is the general rule;[43] strict liability is an exception and it emerged later. The fundamental change from fault-based to strict liability, of course, did not happen without reasons. The Legal and Technical Commission (LTC) considered that there are five factors which have influenced the development of strict liability in domestic law.[44] With respect to the area of environmental protection, the third factor considered by the ILC is of particular relevance. The ILC stated that 'strict liability has been imposed based on the utility of an activity to society as a whole in comparison with its potential harm to individuals'.[45] For the same reason, strict liability for environmental damage is adopted in civil liability treaties. As a key example, the 1993 Lugano Convention explained that 'the Convention aims at providing for the possibility for adequate compensation for damage resulting from activities which are dangerous to the environment'[46] and 'in order to ensure adequate compensation for damage, the Convention provides for strict liability, i.e. liability irrespective of fault and subject to a limited number of exemptions'.[47]

[42] ILC, the 2004 Survey, para. 113.

[43] It is said that 'contemporary international law and municipal law generally provide for the injurious consequences of harm to lie where they fall, unless the occurrence of harm is imputable, in the sense of wrongful conduct, to the source of the harm: *ubi jus, ibi remdium* (only a violation of a right creates a right to redress)'. Rene Lefeber, *Transboundary Environmental Interference and the Origin of State Liability* (Kluwer 1996), 1–2. Also, it is stated that 'the generally accepted rule in domestic jurisdiction is that damage lies where it falls, unless it originates with the wrongful conduct of a person (fault-based civil liability)'. The submission to the 21st session of the ISA by the delegation of the Netherlands, 2015, ISBA/21/C/13.

[44] ILC, the 2004 Survey, paras. 29–112. Five factors are examined in the 2004 Survey: the first factor is the 'nature' of the thing or activity causing the damage (para. 29–33). The second factor is the type of economy in which the activity takes place (para. 34–43). The third factor involves the inherent risk of the modern industrial activity (para. 44–55). The fourth (para. 56–68) and fifth factors (para. 69–112) are the judicial and codification efforts in respect of hazardous activities, respectively.

[45] ILC, the 2004 Survey, para. 44.

[46] Explanatory report to the 1993 Lugano Convention, para. 6.

[47] Ibid., para. 7.

The functions of liability, according to Lefeber, are three: preventive function, corrective function and reparative function.[48]Apparently, strict liability cannot perform a corrective function because, while the corrective function implies 'a violation of the law', the concept of strict liability completely abandons the idea of fault or wrongful acts or omission concerning the person. And although the preventive function of strict liability can be reflected in, for instance, the 1993 Lugano Convention,[49] the main focus here is the reparative function of the liability regime. The question is whether strict liability and fault-based liability perform the reparative function differently. A short answer is 'yes'. In effect, it is owing exactly to the practical advantage of strict liability in fulfilling the reparative function that the standard of liability shifted from fault-based to strict liability.

Most prominently, resorting to the strict liability standard relieves the plaintiff from the heavy burden of proving the wrongfulness of the defendant, and thus expedites the claim process. This practical advantage plays a central role in justifying adoption of strict liability for environmental damage. As the ILC commented,

> Activities involving risk call for the strict liability that has become widespread in national legislation for reasons which are well known, including the need for an expeditious process that dispenses with the need for demonstration of a breach of an obligation or fault. In international law, the same arguments have been used to establish the civil liability of the private party in conventions on which we have provided frequent comments throughout our reports.[50]

A similar observation is,

> It is well-known that the traditional fault-based system of liability in international law has suffered the influence of an evolving domestic legal system of states that is a result of the industrial revolution. This outcome was the consequence of the recognition of the inevitability of dangers and harms inherent to industrial development and an expeditious way of coping with it.[51]

[48] Rene Lefeber, *Transboundary Environmental Interference and the Origin of State Liability* (Kluwer 1996), 1 and 313.

[49] It is stated that 'the purpose of this rule is to encourage the operator to adopt all useful preventive measures to avoid damage'. Explanatory report to the 1993 Lugano Convention, para. 51.

[50] ILC, the tenth report of Barboza, 1994, UN. Doc. A/CN.4/459, para. 42.

[51] Guido Fernando Silva Soares and Everton Vieira Vargas, 'The Basel Liability Protocol on Liability and Compensation for Damage Resulting from Transboundary Movements of Hazardous Wastes and Their Disposal' (2002) 12(1) *YIntlEnvL* 69–104.

Indeed, proving the fault or wrongfulness of the operator of a certain hazardous activity in modern industries might be very difficult and time-consuming. By diverting the standard of liability from fault-based to strict liability, this obstacle is removed for good.

Besides, it is also said that 'strict liability is a better approximation of the polluter-pays principle [than the fault-based liability]'.[52] Yet, that statement is followed immediately by a vital 'but': 'but not if limited in amount'.[53] The existing civil liability treaties which adopt strict liability normally include such limitations as well as exemptions; there is a general pattern among these treaties. First, these treaties all include a general statement of strict liability which, in the most simplified way, could be condensed to the following sentence: the operator shall be liable for damage or loss caused by its activities.[54] Second, strict liability of the operator subjects to exemption. There are those situations where the operator can be exonerated from liability which include armed conflicts, natural disaster, the fault of a third party and so on.[55] Third, there is a limitation of liability, that is, being limited to an amount of compensation.[56] It is seen that strict liability of a company with an exemption

[52] Patricia Birnie, Alan Boyle and Catherine Redgwell, *International Law and the Environment*, 3rd edn. (OUP 2009), 324.

[53] Ibid.

[54] See Article 3 of the 1960 Paris Convention; Article 2(1) of the 1963 Vienna Convention; Article 3(1) of the 1977 London Convention; Article 6(1) of the 1993 Lugano Convention; Article 3(1) of the 2001 Bunker Convention; Article 4 of the 1999 Basel Protocol; Article 7 of the 2010 HNS Protocol and so on.

[55] See Article 9 of the 1960 Paris Convention; Article 3(3), (4) and (5) of the 1977 Seabed Mineral Resources Convention; Article 8 of the 1993 Lugano Convention; article 4(5) of the 1999 Basel Protocol; Article 3(3) and 3(4) of the 2001 Bunker Convention; article 5(1) of the 1992 CLC; Article 8 of the 2003 Kiev Protocol; Article 9 of the 2010 HNS Convention. Two exceptions are Article 4(1) of the 1963 Vienna Convention, where it stipulates 'the liability of the operator for nuclear damage under this Convention shall be absolute', and Article 2(1) of the 1962 Nuclear Ships Convention where, similarly, the operator of a nuclear ship is held absolutely liable for the nuclear damage. In these two exceptions, the operator cannot be exempted from liability under such situations as [...], but they can be exempted in respect of a nuclear incident directly due to an act of war, hostilities, civil war or insurrection (Article 8 of the 1962 Nuclear Ships Convention). And they are not wholly or partially liable if the damage is the nuclear damage resulting wholly or partially from an act or omission done with the intent to cause damage by the individual who suffered the damage (Article 2(5) of the 1962 Nuclear Ships Convention).

[56] See Article 7 of the 1960 Paris Convention; Article 5 of the 1963 Vienna Convention; Article 6 of the 1977 London Convention; Article 5(3) of the 1992 CLC; Article 12 of the 1999 Basel Protocol; paragraph 5 of the preamble of the 2001 Bunker Convention states that strict liability is linked to an appropriate limitation of the level of that liability; Article 9 of the 2010 HNS Convention. A special article to do with limitation of liability is Article

and limitation of liability does not necessarily implement the polluter-pays principle to a larger extent than fault-based liability. Thus, it seems that the main advantage of strict liability over fault-based liability lies in its practical implication: the adoption of strict liability makes the goal of compensating the innocent victim and for environmental damage easier to achieve in the claim process.

In contrast to strict liability, the choice of 'wrongfulness' as the standard of liability of the contractor in the context of DSM has at least three legal and practical implications. First, because of the requirement of 'wrongful acts', it is of utmost importance to clarify, as clearly as possible, the content of the international environmental obligations imposed on the contractor within the DSM legal regime. Equally important, the criterion against which to determine fulfillment of these obligations should be specified. Second, taking into consideration the heavy burden of proving the wrongful acts or omissions of the contractor in its DSM activities, the claim process might stumble and become protracted, which is a large procedural obstacle. Third, if, in the end, the wrongful acts or omissions of the contractor cannot be proven by the plaintiff, then there is no liability of the contractor, even if environmental damage has occurred. A legal gap then appears. These three implications mean that the establishment and implementation of international environmental liability of the contractor in the DSM legal regime in practice will be very difficult. Realizing these difficulties, the African Group suggested that

> [t]he ISA should include a strict liability standard for contractors. A causation-based standard, as opposed to a fault-based standard, will help to ensure that remedy is available, should any harm be caused. It can also incentivize risk reduction efforts, which is important in a context where the harm may be irreversible.[57]

In spite of the practical conveniences such a suggestion would imply, the ISA cannot change the standard for liability of the contractor from 'wrongfulness' to 'strictness' unless an amendment to Article 22 of the

5(3) of the 1992 CLC, where it stipulates that 'for the purpose of availing of the benefit of limitation provided for in paragraph 1 of this Article the owner shall constitute a fund for the total sum representing the limit of his liability with the Court or other competent authority of any one of the Contracting States in which action is brought'. The EU Directive 2004/35/CE does not establish liability limits, nor does it contain a system of compulsory insurance.

[57] ISA, 'Recommendations on legal liability' submitted by the African Group, ISBA/25/C/25, July 2019, para. 5(e).

UNCLOS is made in that direction. Craik suggested the ISA develop new approaches to liability to better address the particular demands associated with DSM too.[58] But again one should always keep in mind that what the ISA could do must be consistent with what is already written down in the UNCLOS and the 1994 Agreement. Specifically, there will be no room for strict liability of the contractor as long as Article 22 of the UNCLOS is not amended. Yet, the ISA's not acting against the UNCLOS does not mean that it could not devise mechanisms to supplement the existing legal framework. By this it refers to the alternative regimes to liability to be discussed in the next chapter of this book.

6.4.3 *Causal Link between Environmental Damage and Wrongful Acts*

The phrase 'arising out of' in Article 22, Annex III to the UNCLOS indicates the third condition for establishing international environmental liability of the contractor, namely proof of the causal link between the marine environmental damage and the wrongful acts of the contractor. First of all, a subtlety related to causation needs to be clarified. It is noted that for establishing strict liability, it is the causation between the damage and the activity that needs to be proven. For establishing liability based on wrongful acts, such as liability of the contractor in the context of DSM, the causation required is between the damage and the wrongful acts. The causal link in the latter situation is more complicated since there are two pairs of causal links to be proven simultaneously. That is, the causal link between the operation of DSM activities and the marine environmental damage as well as the causal link between wrongful acts of the contractor and the marine environmental damage (attribution). However, the separation of these two pairs of causal links is only at a conceptual level. In practice, the proof of causation between damage and wrongful acts will automatically confirm causation between damage and activity since wrongful acts as an abstract concept cannot be separated from concrete activities. Hence, proving these two pairs of causal links is one single process. Moreover, in practice, the issue of proof of causation can even be merged with the issue of measuring damage. The practice of UNCC 'F4' claims is such a case in point: the UNCC Governing Council

58 Neil Craik et al., 'Determining the Standard for Liability for Environmental Harm from Deep Seabed Mining Activities' CIGI, Liability Issues for Deep Seabed Mining Series Paper No. 2, October 2018, 1.

solved the problem of proof of 'the directness' (causal link) by laying down 'the head of environmental damage'.[59]

Two important questions relating to the issue of causation are examined here: can this causation be presumed? If not, what is the standard of proof of causation? Among all the existing civil liability treaties, only the 1993 Lugano Convention and the 2010 HNS Convention[60] provide some guidance in answering these questions. Judicial practice at the EU level also sheds some light on these issues. Article 10 of the 1993 Lugano Convention states that when considering evidence of a causal link, the court will take due account of the increased danger of causing such damage inherent in the dangerous activity. Very importantly, the explanatory report clarifies that 'the Convention does not create a true presumption of a causal link'.[61] Yet, at the EU level, for instance in the *ERG and Others* case,[62] the ECJ ruled that, in cases involving diffuse pollution, the use of presumptions in determining causation between activities and pollution/environmental damage is allowed; however, the authority must have plausible evidence capable of justifying its presumption.[63] It seems that international civil liability treaties do not allow a presumption of the causation between damage and hazardous activities. While at the EU level such a presumption is permissible to a certain extent. However, it is doubtful whether the experience at the EU level can be of reference or precedence value to liability regimes at the international level. Turning to the context of DSM, it is important to note that when dealing with liability of the sponsoring State, the SDC rejected the idea that the causation between damage and the wrongful acts of the sponsoring State can be presumed; it has to be proven.[64] In a similar vein, it seems proper to argue that the causal link between marine

[59] There, the issues of 'the directness' and 'the head of environmental damage' are merged into one question: what kind of 'environmental damage and the depletion of natural resources' will be regarded as a direct result of Iraq's unlawful invasion and occupation of Kuwait? (for further explanation, see Section 5.4).

[60] International Convention on Liability and Compensation for Damage in connection with the Carriage of Hazardous and Noxious Substances by Sea (HNS), adopted on 3 May 1996, not in force, superseded by 2010 Protocol, adopted on 30 April 2010, not yet in force (the '2010 HNS Convention').

[61] Explanatory report to the 1993 Lugano Convention, para. 63.

[62] ECJ, Case C-378/08, Judgment of 9 March 2010. The case Involving the European Parliament and Council *Directive 2004/35.*

[63] Ibid., paras. 56–57.

[64] ITLOS, Advisory Opinion of 1 February 2017 (case No. 17), para. 182.

environmental damage and the wrongful acts of the contractor cannot be presumed either.[65]

If causation must be proven, the ensuring issue is the standard of proof. Here, reference can be made again to the 1993 Lugano Convention which states that the standard of proof of causation is related to the risk involved in the activities. And in the 2011 Advisory Opinion, the SDC contended that the content of 'due diligence' obligations of the sponsoring State is related to the risk involved in the activities.[66] At first glance, it seems that the standard of proof of causation and the content of due diligence obligations are two unrelated subject matters. However, they have a connecting factor – the risk involved in the activities. This is an important revelation: the legal framework on environmental protection, including the primary rules on environmental obligations and the secondary rules of environmental liability regimes, is built on the very basic notion of risk involved in the hazardous activities. Since the risk varies with different activities and changes with time, the standard of proof of causation also varies and changes, just like the content of due diligence obligations.[67] That means the standard of proof of causation could be lower if the risk is higher, or be higher if the risk is lower; the requirement of due diligence could be stricter if the risk is higher, and looser if the risk is lower. Additionally, Article 14(3)(b) of the 2010 HNS Convention uses 'the reasonable probability' as the standard of proof of causation. Although one should bear in mind that this standard of proof of causation is used for payment by the HNS Fund, it could be of reference value to the establishment of a liability regime.

To summarize, there are three conditions – environmental damage, internationally wrongful act of the contractor and causal link between the environmental damage and wrongful act – which must be met cumulatively in order to establish the international environmental liability of the contractor. Since the condition of environmental damage is dealt with in Chapter 5, this section focuses on the conditions of wrongful act and causal link. The analysis shows that determination of wrongfulness on the part of the contractor must focus on the objective conduct of the contractor and the environmental obligations imposed on the contractor under the international DSM legal regime; the psychological element such as 'fault' is irrelevant. The causal link between the environmental

[65] The presumption of causal link between damage and wrongful acts of the contractor should be distinguished from the presumption of 'wrongfulness' of the contractor.

[66] ITLOS, Advisory Opinion of 1 February 2017 (case No. 17), para. 117.

[67] Ibid.

damage and wrongful acts cannot be presumed but must be proven, and the standard of proof of causation is related to the risk of the activities. In practice, to satisfy none of the three conditions is an easy task. These difficulties constitute the main obstacles for establishing international environmental liability of the contractor. In effect, as will be shown in Chapter 8, similar difficulties are faced equally by the sponsoring State and the ISA while establishing their respective liabilities. The difficulties in crossing these hurdles invite doubt as to the effectiveness of the liability regimes for environmental damage. As Johnston pointed out,

> Economics teaches that the effectiveness of *ex post* liability as a tool of environmental regulation depends primarily upon: (1) the ability to identify and trace causation and thus hold polluters liable for the harm that they have caused; and (2) the ability to accurately measure and then assess natural resource damages. Defects in either establishing causation or assessing damages can cause an environmental liability regime to either undeter or overdeter.[68]

6.5 Forms and Contents of Liability: Remediation of Marine Environmental Damage

Article 22, Annex III to the UNCLOS includes a statement 'liability in every case shall be for the actual amount of damage' which constitutes the legal basis for the forms and contents of liability of the contractor. The key is to interpret the phrase 'the actual amount of damage'. In the case of environmental protection, this is the task of measuring the environmental damage, the topic which has already been taken up in the previous chapter. Here it is simply to note that the phrase should not be interpreted narrowly as referring only to monetary compensation. The primary objective of liability regimes for environmental damage is to restore the damaged environment. This objective determines that restoration in any case should be the primary form of liability. As already pointed out, environmental damages caused by DSM refers mainly to damages to deep-sea marine biodiversity and ecosystems. Niner et al. argued that DSM is doomed to cause biodiversity loss and such a loss cannot be truly offset in the sense that lost biodiversity and ecosystems

[68] Jason Johnston, 'Is the Polluter-Pays Principle Really Fundamental? An Economic Explanation of the Relative Unimportance of Environmental Liability and Taxes in the US Environmental Law', in Michael Faure, Han Lixin and Shan Hongjun (eds.), *Marine Pollution Liability and Policy: China, Europe and the US* (Kluwer 2010) 116.

services cannot be replicated.[69] However, restoration should not be equated with replication of the lost biodiversity or ecosystems; rather, 'ecological restoration' is meant to return a degraded ecosystem 'to its historic trajectory, not its historic condition'.[70] In particular, with this understanding, heed should be paid to the resilience of ecosystems. The Society for Ecological Restoration stated that restoration practitioners do not 'carry out the actual work of ecosystem recovery' but 'create the conditions needed for recovery', that is, they are to assist the natural recovery of ecosystems.[71] Thus, restoration is a joint effort of both humans and nature. Additionally, for the joint effort to manifest its effect (or failure), the passage of time is a necessary element. Taken together, it is found that restoration is a combined effect of human effort, recovery capacity of the nature and the passage of time as such. In other words, restoration as a form of remediation is a process which requires relevant actors to decide whether, when and how to assist the nature to recover over time. In practice, decision on whether to initiate or accelerate a restoration process need to take into consideration a mix of factors, including the conditions of the ecosystems themselves, economic viability, technological feasibility, societal pressure and others.[72] Insofar as the deep sea is concerned, owing to the nascent nature of DSM industry, the not-yet commencement of exploitation activity and the great knowledge gap about the deep-sea ecosystems, none of the abovementioned parameters for decision on restoring damaged environment caused by DSM is clear at the moment. It is only estimated that ecological restoration in deep sea would be much costly, more difficult and take longer time compared with that in the land and shallow water contexts.[73] Bear this point in mind, it is better to have a realistic expectation about the practicability of restoration as a form of liability in the DSM context. That being said, the uncertain prospect about restoration at the moment should not be an *a priori* reason for stopping exploitation activities in advance. Rather, it only implies that exploitation activities should be

[69] Ardron Niner et al., 'Deep-Sea Mining with No Net Loss of Biodiversity: An Impossible Aim' (2018) 5 *Frontiers in Marine Science* 53.

[70] See the definition of 'ecological restoration' proposed by the Society for Ecological Restoration. www.ser-rrc.org/what-is-ecological-restoration/.

[71] Ibid.

[72] C.L Van Dover et al., 'Ecological Restoration in the Deep Sea: Desiderata' (2014) 44 *Marine Policy* 98. Authors in this article demonstrated a set of socio-economic, ecological and technological decision parameters for ecological restoration.

[73] Ibid.

conducted in a precautionary manner, and that when the time comes decision on restoration should be made through a transparent procedure, by broad stakeholders and on the basis of a wide range of considerations.

Besides restoration, there are other forms of remediation. Here, special attention is drawn to Annex II to the 2004 European Liability Direction of the EU which stipulates a comprehensive remediation framework for environmental damage. Considering the uniqueness of deep sea ecosystems, resorting to the complementary remediation – providing equivalent resources and ecosystem services – would be very unlikely. When it is decided that the damaged environment is irreversible and restoration impossible, compensatory remediation can be undertaken to compensate for pure environmental damage or interim loss. As to the content of the liability, it depends on how the environmental damage is measured. And as demonstrated in the previous chapter, in the absence of well-established methods for measuring environmental damage, the content of liability has to be determined on a case-by-case basis.

6.6 Implementation of International Environmental Liability of the Contractor

The implementation of international environmental liability of the contractor involves the following questions: who (the claimant) is entitled to invoke liability of the contractor before which institution or jurisdiction (the forum)? On what legal basis (the applicable law) can the dispute settlement body make its decision which is valid and enforceable within what jurisdictions (the validity and enforcement of final decision)? Clear answers can be given to these questions: the ISA as a party to the contract is entitled to invoke international environmental liability of the contractor before the Seabed Disputes Chamber.[74] On the grounds of the UNCLOS, the 1994 Agreement, the Regulations and the contract, the SDC can make its final decision on the international liability of the contractor which will be valid and enforceable within States Parties to the UNCLOS.

This differs from implementation of civil liability of the operator under all existing civil liability treaties. Under these civil liability treaties, implementation of liability for environmental damage requires that: (a) actions for compensation be instituted by the victim before national courts (normally of the State of origin), and (b) judgments be recognized

[74] Article 187(c) UNCLOS; Section 25.1 of Annex IV (the standard clauses of an exploration contract), the Exploration Regulations.

and enforced in other States. Apparently, this type of implementation is of a transnational nature: It involves foreign elements (including the foreign claimant and the recognition and enforcement of judgments in a foreign country), but both the applicable law and the dispute settlement regime are at a national level. The approach adopted in these existing civil liability treaties could be called the 'traditional civil liability approach'.[75] The UNCLOS endorses the traditional civil liability approach through Article 235(2) which prescribes that

> [s]tates shall ensure that recourse is available in accordance with their legal systems for prompt and adequate compensation or other relief in respect of damage caused by pollution of the marine environment by natural or juridical persons under their jurisdiction.

Turning back to the context of DSM, the SDC states,

> Another direct obligation that gives substance to the sponsoring State's obligation to adopt laws and regulations within the framework of its legal system is set out in article 235, paragraph 2, of the Convention.[76]

To elaborate this point, the SDC continued,

> This provision applies to the sponsoring State as the State with jurisdiction over the persons that caused the damage. By requiring the sponsoring State to establish procedures, and, if necessary, substantive rules governing claims for damages before its domestic courts, this provision serves the purpose of ensuring that the sponsored contractor meets its obligation under Annex III, article 22, of the Convention to provide reparation for damages caused by wrongful acts committed in the course of its activities in the Area.[77]

Thus, the SDC was of the opinion that the traditional civil liability approach was also applicable in the context of DSM.[78] Indeed, under the existing legal framework, international environmental liability of the

[75] Thomas Mensah, 'The Civil Liability and Compensation for Environmental Damage in the 1982 Convention on the Law of the Sea', in the Hamburg Lectures on Maritime Affairs, 2007 & 2008, 4. According to Mensah, the 'civil liability approach' means that actions are taken before national judicial systems; it involves three legal issues, namely the competent courts, applicable law and mutual recognition and enforcement of judgments.

[76] ITLOS, Advisory Opinion of 1 February 2011 (case No. 17), para. 139.

[77] Ibid., para. 140.

[78] Article 23(2) of the 2016 *Law of the People's Republic of China on Exploration for and Exploitation of Resources in the Deep Seabed Area* prescribes civil liability of the contractor. However, this is a rare example. National laws mainly focus on the administrative liability of the contractor for non-compliance with the regulatory requirements.

contractor can be implemented at both the national level (invoked before the national court on the basis of the national law of the sponsoring State) and international level (invoked before the SDC in light of UNCLOS, Regulations or contracts).

The question is whether such a parallel existence of two avenues of implementation is desirable. Insofar as international liability of the contractor for damage to the marine environment *per se* caused by activities in the Area is concerned, a negative answer is preferable. It is argued that international environmental liability of the contractor is preferably implemented at the international level only for the following reasons. First, as already stated above, pursuant to the standard clauses of the exploration contract, any disputes concerning the interpretation and application of the contract are subject exclusively to the compulsory dispute settlement mechanism in Part XV. If the SDC has exclusive jurisdiction, how could an action be launched before a national court at the same time? Second, even if claims for damage can be initiated before domestic courts, the problem is who is entitled to do so. It is well-known that damage to the environment *per se* is mostly a 'victimless' situation, yet traditional civil liability remedies are 'victim-centred' mechanisms. Undoubtedly, it would not be suitable to use a 'victim-centred' mechanism to deal with a 'victimless' situation. Third, even if the traditional 'victim-centred' civil liability mechanism can be adapted to accommodate the 'victimless' situation of damage to the environment *per se*, for instance, to assign a public agency to act on behalf of human beings for the damaged environment, the traditional civil liability approach has its inherent drawbacks which also casts doubt on whether it is appropriate to use this approach in the context of DSM. As Thomas Mensah observed,

> A major drawback [of the civil liability approach] is the absence of a widely recognized judicial system to deal with conflicting claims from victims of different nationalities. Civil liability conventions generally reserve jurisdiction over disputes under the conventions to the national courts of the states parties to the conventions. This means that important issues, such as the existence or otherwise of liability for damage and the level of compensation that is appropriate for the damage, are left for final determination by the courts of the country or countries in which the damage was caused or in the state in which the claimant chooses to bring the claim for compensation.[79]

[79] Thomas Mensah, 'The Civil Liability and Compensation for Environmental Damage in the 1982 Convention on the Law of the Sea', in the Hamburg Lectures on Maritime Affairs (2007 & 2008), 6.

Mensah further dwelled on the drawback of implementing civil liability exclusively at national level. He saw two large problems: one is unequal treatment of different claimants and the other is inconsistency in the assessment of and compensation for environmental damage in different countries.[80]

One might reasonably speculate that one of the reasons for the internationalization of the dispute settlement mechanism in the international DSM regime was exactly to overcome these drawbacks of the traditional civil liability approach. By conferring the right to participate in proceedings before the SDC on States, the ISA and (potential) contractors alike, the problem of *locus standi* is solved. And by conferring compulsory jurisdiction on the SDC, the assessment of and compensation for environmental damage is unified automatically. In effect, when carefully examining the contents of Article 187, it would be hard to imagine that any disputes between participants in DSM concerning liability of the contractor would fall out of the scope of the SDC's compulsory jurisdiction. It is thus concluded that the parallel existence of implementation methods at international and national levels weakens the international mechanism designed in Section 5 of Part XI and places an unnecessary burden on the sponsoring State.

Therefore, it is argued that, owing to the internationalization of the DSM regime and the institutionalization of the dispute settlement mechanism relating to activities in the Area, the traditional civil liability approach, in particular its procedural aspect, should be disregarded, and that Article 235(2) of UNCLOS should not be applicable in the context of DSM. The role of the sponsoring State in this respect should be to secure the enforcement of the final decision of the SDC, rather than to 'establish procedures, and, if necessary, substantive rules governing claims for damages before its domestic courts'. Tara Davenport also found the *status quo* of the double-tier fora for liability claims unsatisfying; correspondingly, three alternative options were proposed: (1) channelling the majority of claims to the SDC and excluding claims to national courts, (2) maintaining the SDC's jurisdiction and harmonizing national legislation and (3) establishing a new administrative mechanism for determining liability.[81] Among these three options, the first one is

[80] Ibid., 6–7.

[81] Tara Davenport, 'Responsibility and Liability for Damage Arising Out of Activities in the Area: Potential Claimants and Possible Fora' CIGI, Liability Issues for Deep Seabed Mining Series Paper No 5, February 2019.

consistent with the position of this book, the second one encounters a problem of the uneven development of national laws and a question of who is to take up the work of harmonization of national laws, while the third one is of the least practical possibility. Weighing the pros and cons of each option, it seems that Davenport inclined to consider the first option as the most preferable one too.[82]

6.7 Special Liability Issues: The Enterprise as Contractor and States as Contractors

All contractors should be treated on an equal footing with respect to the international environmental obligations and liabilities in DSM; no privileges are accorded to the Enterprise or States as opposed to private contractors. This position is in line with the explanation as follows:

> Among the specific concerns of industrialized States in relation to the Enterprise was the perception that the Enterprise would be given more favorable terms of contracts over private contractor. The [1994] Agreement, therefore, makes it clear that notwithstanding the provisions of article 153, paragraph 3 a plan or work for the Enterprise shall be in the form of a contract between the Enterprise and the Authority and that all obligations applicable to contractors shall apply to the Enterprise. That would also cover, for example, obligations relating to the protection and preservation of the marine environment.[83]

Also, the Commentary states that

> [t]he objective of article 13 appears to be to ensure that the Enterprise is placed on an equal footing with other entities engaged in similar commercial activities.[84]

Thus, the international environmental obligations and liabilities of the contractor discussed above are applicable to all kinds of contractor. However, there are some special issues emanating from the different nature of the Enterprise and States in comparison with the private contractor. And these special issues are related to implementation of liability.

[82] Additionally, Davenport proposed to expand the personal jurisdiction of the SDC to cover non-participants to DSM.

[83] Myron Nordquist, Satya Nandan, Shabtai Rosenne and Michael Lodge (eds.), *United Nations Convention on the Law of the Sea 1982: A Commentary*, (Vol. VI) (Martinus Nijhoff 2002) 765.

[84] Ibid., 818.

6.7.1 The Enterprise as Contractor

The key question concerning the Enterprise in this section is whether the Enterprise can assume international environmental liability independent from the ISA. A preliminary positive answer could be given by referring to the following provision:

> Nothing in this Convention shall make the Enterprise liable for the acts or obligations of the Authority, or make the Authority liable for the acts or obligations of the Enterprise.[85]

To further explain this answer, the following paragraphs undertake a theoretical analysis. The ILC expresses unambiguously that the legal personality of an organization is a precondition of the international responsibility of that organization.[86] Following the ILC's line of thought, if the Enterprise is to assume international environmental liability, then it must have an international legal personality of its own. Now, the question above can be transformed to the question of whether the Enterprise, as an organ of the ISA, possesses an independent international legal personality. This is a tricky question since it seems that the UNCLOS embodies contradictory messages.

First, Article 170(2), UNCLOS makes it clear that 'the Enterprise shall, within the framework of the international legal personality of the Authority, have such legal capacity as is provided for in the Statute set forth in Annex IV'. From this provision, it seems that the Enterprise, as an organ within the ISA, attaches its personality to that of the ISA. On the other hand, however, it is equally clear that the Enterprise can act in its own name at both national and international levels. Here, it is necessary to distinguish the legal personality of the Enterprise within the States Parties' national legal systems from the international legal personality. In accordance with Article 13(1), Annex IV (the Statute of Enterprise) UNCLOS, the Enterprise shall have legal personality at national level. As it is stated, 'to enable the Enterprise to exercise its functions, the status, privileges and immunities set forth in this article shall be accorded to the Enterprise in the territories of States Parties'.

85 Article 2(3), Annex IV (Statute of the Enterprise) to the UNCLOS.

86 ILC, 'Draft Articles on the Responsibility of International Organizations, with commentaries' in Yearbook of the International Law Commission, 2011, Vol. II, Part Two. Commentary to Article 2(a) (the definition of 'international organization').

From the next paragraph, in particular subparagraph (a), it can be deduced that the Enterprise must also possess legal capacities/personality at the international level. As is prescribed,

> The Enterprise shall have such legal capacity as is necessary for the exercise of its functions and the fulfilment of its purposes and, in particular, the capacities:
>
> (a) to enter into contracts, joint arrangements or other arrangements, including agreements with States and international organizations;
> (b) to acquire, lease, hold and dispose of immovable and movable property;
> (c) to be a party to legal proceedings.

By way of illustration, to carry out activities in the Area, the Enterprise for example must sign a contract with the ISA. Here, the Enterprise and the ISA are the two parties to the contract. Yet, as another example, according to Article 187(c) of the UNCLOS, the SDC shall have compulsory jurisdiction over 'disputes between parties to a contract, being State Parties, the Authority or the Enterprise, state enterprises and natural or juridical persons referred to in article 153, paragraph 2(b)'. If a dispute over the contract arises between the Enterprise and the ISA, the Enterprise is entitled to appear before the SDC as a party to the dispute. From both the provisions and the two specific examples, it can be seen that the legal capacities/personality of the Enterprise at the international level is beyond doubt. Therefore, it seems that the Enterprise possesses legal personality at both international and national levels.

Second, Article 2(2), Annex IV to the UNCLOS emphasizes that 'subject to paragraph 1, the Enterprise shall enjoy autonomy in the conduct of its operations'. 'Autonomy' means 'the state of existing or acting separately from others' or 'the quality or state of being self-governing'.[87] In the case of the Enterprise, enjoying autonomy on the one hand means the Enterprise can act independently from the ISA. The concept of 'autonomy' is strongly related to the notion of 'legal personality' since what legal personality implies is exactly the capacity to act independently. On the other hand, however, there are restrictions on the autonomy of the Enterprise. It is noted that the Enterprise enjoys autonomy only 'in the conduct of its operations'. According to Article 170(1) UNCLOS, the operations of the Enterprise include 'carrying out activities

[87] Merriam-Webster English Dictionary. www.merriam-webster.com/dictionary/autonomy.

in the Area directly, as well as the transporting, processing and marketing of minerals recovered from the Area'. This restriction on the autonomy of the Enterprise bears similarities to the notion of 'functional personality' in the theory of international organization law.[88] The autonomy of the Enterprise is further restricted under the second sentence of Article 170(2), UNCLOS and Article 2(1), Annex IV to the UNCLOS which require that

> [The Enterprise] shall act in accordance with the Convention and the rules, regulations and procedures of the Authority, as well as the general policies of the Assembly and the directives of the Council.

It should be noted, however, that the ISA is not to give direct instructions on how the Enterprise should act in any specific occasion during its operations. The Enterprise has its own institutional structure.[89] The Governing Board of the Enterprise shall direct the operations of the Enterprise.[90] In addition, 'the funds, assets and expenses of the Enterprise shall be kept separate from those of the Authority'.[91] Moreover, the Enterprise is even accorded with separate privileges and immunities from the ISA in the territories of the States Parties.[92] Thus, subjecting the Enterprise to the control of the ISA in some aspects does not as such constitute a denial of the legal personality of the Enterprise. The purpose of the ISA's supervision over the operations of the Enterprise, through the general policies of the Assembly and Council, is to make sure that the Enterprise gives effect to the principle of common heritage of mankind (CHM). It is thus concluded that, despite these restrictions, the autonomy of the Enterprise stands. In order to secure that the Enterprise can act independently, it is treated as a separate legal person from the ISA in terms of institutional structure, finance and privileges and immunities.

88 The personality of the international organization is considered as 'functional' because the personality of the international organization is limited by the scope of the functions conferred on the organization. Thus, functional personality is limited, which is in contrast to unlimited personality, such as the international personality of the State.

89 Article 4, Annex IV to the UNCLOS prescribes that 'the Enterprise shall have a Governing Board, a Director-General and the staff necessary for the exercise of its functions'.

90 Article 4, Annex IV to the UNCLOS.

91 Article 11(4), Annex IV to the UNCLOS.

92 Article 13, Annex IV (Statute of the Enterprise) and Articles 176–183 of the UNCLOS.

In addition, the Enterprise is by nature a commercial entity.[93] The following two articles of the Statute of the Enterprise reflect this idea. Article 1(3), Annex IV to the UNCLOS stipulates that

> [i]n developing the resources of the Area pursuant to paragraph 1, the Enterprise shall, subject to this Convention, operate in accordance with sound commercial principles.

Article 12(7), Annex IV to the UNCLOS states,

> Only commercial considerations shall be relevant to its decisions, and these considerations shall be weighed impartially in order to carry out the purposes specified in article 1 of this Annex.

On the other hand, however, the ISA as a whole is an international administrative body. The completely different nature of the Enterprise and the ISA as a whole gives rise to tension that needs to be released. It was proposed that 'the Enterprise shall have international legal personality and such legal capacity as may be necessary for the performance of its functions and the fulfilment of its purposes'.[94] Although such wording was not adopted in the UNCLOS, the idea of conferring international legal personality on the Enterprise as a way to release the tension arising from the different nature of the Enterprise and of the ISA as a whole still makes sense.

To summarize, although the provisions analysed above give seemingly contradictory messages, the prevailing messages are that (a) the Enterprise is entrusted with the legal capacities to act on its own at both national and international levels; (b) the Enterprise enjoys autonomy in the conduct of its operations; and (c) conferring international legal personality on the Enterprise is a proper way to release the tension arising from the different nature of the Enterprise and of the ISA as a whole. On those bases, it arrives at the conclusion that the Enterprise as an organ of the ISA has international legal personality. Therefore, the

[93] From the very beginning when the 'Enterprise' was first proposed by 13 Latin American and Caribbean countries in a 45-article working paper in 1971, the Enterprise was considered as an entity of commercial character. International Seabed Authority, *Legislative History of the "Enterprise" under the United Nations Convention on the Law of the Sea and the Agreement relating to the Implementation of Part XI of the Convention*, 2002. p. VI, para. 5 (the 'Legislative History of the "Enterprise"').

[94] The Revised Single Negotiating Text in 1976, A/CONF.62/WP.8/Rev.1/Part 1, 6 May 1976. 'Legislative History of the "Enterprise,"' 100.

Enterprise can assume international environmental liability independent of the ISA.

The Enterprise within the ISA is a specific illustration of the question raised in the well-known *International Institutional Law*, which states that

> [a] problem concerning the international legal personality of international organizations that has not yet been resolved in doctrine, and for which different solutions have been found in practice, is the issue of the (in) divisibility of international legal personality. Is it only the organization as a whole that has such personality, or is it possibly individual organs within the organization as well?[95]

It seems that the situation with the Enterprise provides the answer that its international legal personality is divisible, and organs within the organization could also possess international legal personality.[96] However, one should be fully aware that the situation of the Enterprise is very unique, and the answer it provides cannot be generalized.

6.7.2 States as Contractors

Article 6(5) of Annex VI (Liability Arising from Environmental Emergencies) to the Protocol on Environmental Protection to the Antarctic Treaty (the 2005 Antarctic Liability Annex)[97] prescribes that liability of a State operator shall not affect the sovereign immunity of 'its warships, naval auxiliaries, or other ships or aircraft owned or operated by it and used, for the time being, only on government non-commercial service'. Moreover, owing to state immunity, a State operator cannot be sued in foreign countries. Thus, invocation of liability of a State operator is bound to follow different procedures from invocation of liability of a non-State operator. Pursuant to Article 7(4) and (5) of the 2005 Antarctic Liability Annex, liability of a Party as State operator could only be resolved by the procedures of enquiry, arbitration and the Antarctic Treaty Consultative Meeting.

Turning to the context of DSM, the questions are: does the State contractor enjoy immunities? Should the State contractor be treated

[95] Henry Schermers and Niels Blokker, *International Institutional Law*, 5th edn. (Martinus Nijhoff 2011), para. 1575.

[96] In effect, the Enterprise within the ISA is not the only example, there are other examples such as the European Investment Bank within the EU, and the UNDP within the UN.

[97] Adoption on 14 June 2005, not in force.

differently from the Enterprise and the private contractor when it comes to the procedure for dispute settlement over the issue of liability? These two questions are interrelated. To answer these questions, the key is to understand the concept of jurisdictional immunities of States and their property and the dispute settlement mechanisms under the international DSM legal regime. Jurisdictional immunities of States and their property[98] are based on the concept of sovereign equality of States under international law and the principle of *par in parem non habet imperium.* The issue of immunities of States and their property can be invoked as opposed to 'the jurisdiction of the courts of another State'; this issue arises only in the horizontal legal relationship between States. Thus, in the context of DSM, if liability of a State contractor is invoked before the courts of another State, the issue of the immunities of the State and its property would arise. However, the immunities cannot be invoked before an institution of an international character. Since the dispute settlement mechanisms stipulated in Part XI of the UNCLOS are all of an international character, and the Seabed Disputes Chamber, international commercial arbitration chamber or any other international special chamber has exclusive, compulsory jurisdiction over disputes arising from DSM activities, the answers to the questions above are clear. First, a State contractor cannot invoke its immunity before international DSM dispute settlement bodies. Therefore, second, within the international DSM dispute settlement mechanisms, the State contractor should be treated equally with the Enterprise and private contractor.

6.8 Conclusions

To sum up, the main part of this chapter is the establishment, content and implementation of international environmental liability of the contractor. It identifies three constituent elements for establishing international environmental liability of the contractor, namely internationally wrongful acts of the contractor, environmental damage and the causal link between the wrongful acts and the environmental damage. In particular, environmental damage is not only the prerequisite element for establishing liability but relates to the content of liability.

International environmental liability of the contractor shares similarities with civil liability regimes established in existing international treaties. The

[98] ILC, United Nations Convention on Jurisdictional Immunities of States and their Property, 2004, A/RES/59/38, Article 1.

most salient common feature is that both liability systems are based on the polluter-pays principle and that the operator assumes primary liability for environmental damage. This feature sets international environmental liability of the contractor apart from liability of the sponsoring State and of the ISA. Yet, international environmental liability of the contractor cannot fit completely within existing international civil liability regimes. There are significant distinctions. From a substantive perspective, the establishment of liability of the contractor requires a necessary condition of internationally wrongful acts on its part, while the existing international civil liability regimes commonly adopt the strict liability standard. From a procedural perspective, implementation of international liability of the contractor operates at an international level, while liability of the operator under existing international treaties is implemented at a national level. That is, the former is international in nature while the latter is transnational. For these features, international environmental liability of the contractor is *sui generis*; it has to be considered within the specific international DSM legal regime.

As to special liability issues of the Enterprise as contractor and States as contractors, it is argued that the Enterprise has an international legal personality independent from the ISA and thus can assume liability independently. It is also argued that implementation of liability of the contractor should operate at an international level only and that a State contractor cannot claim immunity of the State and its property when it comes to implementation of liability.

7

Alternatives to International Environmental Liability of the Contractor

7.1 Introduction: A Paradigm Shift from Civil Liability to Other Regimes

From the discussions in Chapters 5 and 6, it is seen that (1) there are significant practical difficulties in establishing and implementing international environmental liability of the contractor, and (2) even if liability is established and well implemented, there could be gaps in compensation for environmental damage under the current liability regime. Against this background, this chapter explores other regimes of compensation for environmental damage (Sections 7.2 and 7.3) and a new type of regulatory liability (Section 7.4).

Faure and Verheij distinguish three phases concerning the issue of compensation for environmental damage: in the first phase, the issue of compensation was considered a problem of the public at large; in the second phase, the polluter-pays principle justified a shift towards liability of the polluter/operator; and in the third phase, owing to discovery of the limits of applying private law solutions to environmental damage, that is, civil liability regimes, there was a tendency to shift to new solutions.[1] However, Faure and Verheij admitted that the process of the new shift in the third phase is still evolving and has not yet come to an end. It is also not clear at this time what direction the shift will take.[2]

Once again, let us turn back to the conceptual evolution of liability within the International Law Commission (ILC's) work on the topic of international liability. It was exactly due to the awareness of the limits of liability regimes that the ILC eventually turned to the idea of allocation of loss. Under the scheme of allocation of loss as depicted in the 2006 Draft Principles, compulsory insurance or financial security is required in

[1] Michael Faure and Albert Verheij (eds.), *Shifts in Compensation for Environmental Damage* (Springer 2007) 1–2.

[2] Ibid.

order to reinforce the liability of the operator and compensation funds are designed to fill in the gaps left by liability regimes. This new way of thinking focuses mainly on adequate and prompt compensation for the victims. Another new approach which was hinted at in the ILC's 2006 Draft Principles but not fully explored is an administrative approach to liability of the operator. Interestingly, this approach was later adopted in the 2010 Nagoya-Kuala Lumpur Supplementary Protocol on Liability and Redress to the Cartagena Protocol on Biosafety (the 2010 Supplementary Protocol). In this chapter, these alternatives to liability regime are explored, with the particular purpose of seeing how they can be used to overcome the various difficulties in establishing international environmental liability of the contractor discussed in Chapter 6.

7.2 Compulsory Insurance or Financial Security Schemes

The deep seabed mining (DSM) legal regime also embodies the ideas of compulsory insurance or financial security and compensation fund. Pursuant to the standard clause of the exploration contract, 'the Contractor shall maintain appropriate insurance policies with internationally recognized carriers, in accordance with generally accepted international maritime practice'.[3]Thus, taking out an insurance policy is a compulsory obligation of the contractor.[4] In effect, the requirement of compulsory insurance is a common feature of most existing civil liability instruments. In the area of nuclear energy, Article 10 of the 1960 Paris Convention, Article 3(2) of the 1962 Nuclear Ships Convention and Article 7 of the 1963 Vienna Convention are good examples. There are examples in other areas as well, such as Article 8 of the 1977 Seabed Mineral Resources Convention, Article 12 of the 1993 Lugano convention, Article 14 of the 1999 Basel Protocol and

[3] Section 16(5), Annex IV to the Exploration Regulations.

[4] Besides the existing Exploration Regulations, the 'zero draft' of the Exploitation Regulations also includes the same requirement of taking out insurance on the contractor. See in particular Section 8 of Annex VII to the first working draft of the Exploitation Regulations and standard contract terms on exploitation for mineral resources in the Area. Available at: www.isa.org.jm/files/documents/EN/Regs/DraftExpl/Draft_ExplReg_SCT.pdf.

The draft was discussed in the LTC and the Council of the ISA during the 22nd session in July 2016.

Article 11 of the 2003 Kiev Protocol.[5] In the international maritime area, since the introduction of the 1969 International Convention on Civil Liability for Oil Pollution Damage (the 1969 CLC), compulsory insurance or requirements for financial security for maritime liabilities was no longer an internal matter for shipowners.[6] Over the years, compulsory insurance or the requirement of financial security has been developed as established maritime practice. The most important treaties are the 1992 Civil Liability Convention (CLC), the 2001 Bunker Oil Convention and the 2010 Hazardous and Noxious Substances (HNS) Convention, all adopted under the auspices of the International Maritime Organization (IMO).

The 2001 Bunker Oil Convention and the 2010 HNS Convention are modelled on the 1992 CLC. For that reason, these three treaties resemble each other in almost all aspects of liability, including channelling, standards, limits of liability and the requirement of compulsory insurance or financial security. Article 7 of the 1992 CLC, article 7 of the 2001 Bunker Oil Convention and article 12 of the 2010 HNS Convention provide the legal basis for the insurance or financial security requirement for the shipowner in each liability regime, with similar wording. They share some eminent common characteristics. To start with, they adopt the wording of 'shall be required to' which indicates that the obligation to take out insurance or to provide other financial security is compulsory. Second, there are conditions for the compulsory obligation to take out insurance or to provide other financial security. Condition one: the ship has to be registered in a contracting State; condition two (only for oil shipping), the gross tonnage must be above a certain threshold (more than 2,000 in the 1992 CLC, more than 1,000 in 2001 Bunker Oil Convention); condition three, there must be a limit to the liability of the shipowner.[7] Third, they are highly flexible concerning the form of

[5] The requirement of taking out compulsory insurance or financial security has not been put into practice in these areas since these treaties are not in force.

[6] Erik Røsæg, 'Compulsory Maritime Insurance' (2000) Marlus 258 SIMPLY 1.

[7] The insurance or other financial security is, in the 1992 CLC, 'in the sum fixed by applying the limits of liability prescribed in Article V, paragraph 1 to cover his liability for pollution damage under this Convention'; in the 2001 Bunker Oil Convention, 'in an amount equal to the limits of liability under the applicable national or international limitation regime, but in all cases, not exceeding an amount calculated in accordance with the Convention of Limitation of Liability for Maritime Claims, 1976, as amended'; while in the 2010 HNS Convention, 'in the sums fixed by applying the limits of liability prescribed in article 9, paragraph 1, to cover liability for damage under this convention'.

financial security. Fourth, they lay down detailed requirement for the compulsory insurance certificate. These requirements include the language, formality, contents and the carrying on board of the certificate. In all of these three conventions, the content of a certificate must include three categories of information: (1) information about the ship, including the name of the ship, distinctive numbers or letters, IMO identification number, port of registry, name and address of the shipowner; (2) information about the insurance or security, including type of security, duration of security, the name and address of the insurer(s) and/or guarantor(s); and (3) information about the authority issuing the certificate, including the name of the State (information about the specific competence of the authority is desirable), the title and name of the issuing or certifying official, the issuing date and place and the expiry date of the certificate.[8] Fifth, direct action against the insurer or financial security provider is allowed.[9] According to Zhu,

> The direct action right under the Bunkers Convention is more than a right to enforce a claim directly as a way of avoiding procedural complexity and expenses. It is mainly to ensure that prompt and effective compensation is available to pollution victims.[10]

In accordance with Røsæg,

> A pivotal point of compulsory insurance is to secure that funds actually are available to compensate victims. This is generally achieved by a right of direct action: the victim can bring action against the insurer.[11]

It is noted that the contractor in the context of DSM is required to take out compulsory insurance in accordance with 'generally accepted international maritime practice'. Hence, the features of compulsory maritime insurance demonstrated above should be taken into particular consideration. On top of that, it is necessary to first ask: why is compulsory insurance or other financial security needed in liability regimes? There are various answers. One opinion is that compulsory insurance or other financial security functions as a reinforcement to strict liability. As the

[8] Pursuant to annexes to the 1992 CLC and 2001 Bunker Oil Convention, and Article 12 of the 2010 HNS Convention.

[9] Article 7(8) of the 1992 CLC; article 7(10) of the 2001 Bunker Oil Convention; and article 12(8) of the 2010 HNS Convention.

[10] Ling Zhu, *Compulsory Insurance and Compensation for Bunker Oil Pollution Damage* (Springer 2006), 211–212.

[11] Erik Røsæg, 'Compulsory Maritime Insurance' (2000) Marlus 258 SIMPLY 9.

explanatory report to the 1993 Lugano Convention comments, 'in order to make this system of strict liability fully effective it is reinforced by an obligation of Parties to provide for a system of compulsory financial security wherever appropriate'.[12] Another opinion considers compulsory insurance or other financial security as a necessary guarantee or a condition for gaining permission to carry out activities which are of a hazardous nature but are beneficial to society as a whole. As is explained by the ILC,

> When it is decided to permit the performance of certain activities, with the knowledge that they may cause injuries, it has generally been considered necessary to provide, in advance, for guarantees for payment of damages. This means that the operator of certain activities must either take out an insurance policy or provide financial security. Such requirements are similar to those stipulated in the domestic laws of a number of States in connection with the operation of complex industries, as well as with more routine activities such as driving a car.[13]

Yet another opinion provides an answer based on the interests of innocent victims. For instance, the concerns for accessibility and obtainability of compensation of the claimant are the first two rationales given by Røsæg for a requirement of compulsory insurance or financial security in the maritime practice.[14]

Thus, the need for compulsory insurance or financial security seems justified on various grounds. However, imposing compulsory insurance for environmental liability in the context of DSM might encounter enormous difficulties. To begin with, it would raise the doubt of whether the international liability of the contractor for damage to the marine environment *per se* is considered as insurable. This doubt has both theoretical and practical dimensions. Theoretically, first of all, international environmental liability insurance, like any other type of insurance, has to conform to the predictability principle. The predictability principle refers to risk. In the case of liability insurance, risk is the

[12] General introduction, paragraph 10, explanatory report to the 1993 Lugano Convention.

[13] Secretariat of the ILC, Survey of liability regimes relevant to the topic of international liability for injurious consequences arising out of acts not prohibited by international law (international liability in case of loss from transboundary harm arising out of hazardous activities), A/CN.4/543, para. 684.

[14] Erik Røsæg, 'Compulsory Maritime Insurance' (2000) Marlus 258 SIMPLY 1. The other three rationales he gives are: third-party providers of financial security generally will contribute to higher standards on board; uniformity of financial responsibility in maritime law; and the avoidance of distortion of international competition.

consequence of assuming liability. It means that the risk of assuming liability has to be statistically predictable. More specifically, the predictability of risk embodies two crucial parts: one is the likelihood that the event will occur; the other is the possible magnitude of the loss if the event occurs. Accurate information on both of these parts is crucial for the insurer to calculate the premium. 'If the insurer ideally has *ex ante* perfect information on the predictability of the probability and the magnitude of the damage, we call the particular risk insurable.'[15]

With reference to international environmental liability of the contractor in the context of DSM, as is demonstrated in Chapter 5, both identification and assessment of damage to the marine environment are problematic. Owing to the fact that there is still a significant knowledge gap about deep-sea ecosystems, and that mining in the deep seabed is a pioneering adventure, the accurate detrimental impacts of DSM activities on the marine environment remain to be observed. On the other hand, largely due to difficulties in monetizing loss to the marine environment, actual damage to the marine environment is far from clear. Thus, both the probability of the occurrence of damage to the marine environment and the exact environmental damage in economic terms are hard to predict. That is, the scope of environmental liability suffers from a low level of certainty. This may cast a reasonable doubt on the insurability of the international environmental liability of the contractor,[16] albeit not necessarily leading to the conclusion that it is uninsurable.[17]

Second, there might also be an argument against the insurability of the international environmental liability of the contractor because of the lack of limitation on liability. Faure, however, does not think limitation on liability is related to the issue of insurability, as he asserts,

> In any case the legislator should not introduce financial caps on liability with the argument that these would be necessary to increase insurability. Caps are not necessary to increase insurability, since insurers could put themselves a financial limit on liability; caps may lead to underdeterrence, undercompensation and violate the polluter pays principle. Hence they should in principle be avoided in a future environmental liability regime.[18]

[15] Michael Faure (ed.), *Deterrence, Insurability, and Compensation in Environmental Liability: Future Development in the European Union* (Springer 2003) 126.

[16] Ibid.

[17] Ibid., 127.

[18] Michaek Faure and David Grimeaud, *Financial Assurance Issues of Environmental Liability* (European Center for Tort and Insurance Law (ECTIL) 2000), iv.

Zhu is of the same opinion. Furthermore, she contends that unlimited liability can be insured when the insurance coverage is limited itself. As she states,

> Although the capping of the insurer's exposure can provide a considerable degree of comfort to the insurance industry and also speed up the settlement of claims, the limitation of the owner's liability should not necessarily be tied up with the insurance obligation; therefore, it is suggested in the thesis that the insurance coverage could be limited while the whole liability is left unlimited.[19]

Thus, the lack of limitation on the international environmental liability of the contractor should not as such be an obstacle to insurability.

In practical terms, two necessary conditions must be met with in order to make the insurance possible. Firstly, the group of participants must be large. This is the natural requirement in accordance with the law of large numbers – the basic tenet underlying the insurance industry. According to the law of large numbers, the insurer must aggregate similar risks in risk groups and spread it,[20] and risk spreading among its insured becomes possible only if the pool is large. Therefore, a large number of participants are necessary. Secondly and more importantly, there must be an available insurance market or at least a prospect of its existence. Faure considers that 'insurability is ultimately the "willingness to insure" of the financial and insurance market'.[21] Truly, to fulfil the requirement of compulsory insurance would not be possible without the participation of insurers in reality.

Turning to the environmental liability of the contractor in the context of DSM, with only twenty-two contractors in DSM, the number of participants in a potential insurance scheme is very small. However, this might not pose an insurmountable problem as such since the contractors can choose to join some existing insurance schemes for similar risk in the international maritime insurance market. This leads to the next point, the availability and the capacity of the insurance market. In its response to the survey conducted by the International Seabed Authority (ISA) for

[19] Ling Zhu, Compulsory Insurance and Compensation for Bunker Oil Pollution Damage (Springer 2006) 213–214.

[20] Michael Faure (ed.), *Deterrence, Insurability, and Compensation in Environmental Liability: Future Development in the European Union* (Springer 2003) 126.

[21] Faure and Grimeaud (ECTIL 2000), 5; Faure (Springer 2003), 186. 'The practical possibilities of an effective enforcement of a duty to insure will obviously to a large extent depend upon the willingness to insure on that particular market.'

the Draft Exploitation Framework in March 2015, the German Insurance Association (GDV) made a general observation:

> Any insurance-related rules the Authority should take into account, inter alia, the scope of cover and the capacities that national and international insurance and reinsurance markets are able to provide so these rules can be compiled with by prospective contract partners. Insurance required by contract partners should be economically viable while providing a high level of protection for the environment and third parties' interests.[22]

In effect, from the wording that 'the contractor shall maintain appropriate insurance policies [. . .] in accordance with generally accepted international maritime practice', it is evident that the international maritime insurance market has been chosen for facilitating the contractor in fulfilling its obligation of compulsory insurance in the context of DSM. With respect to the international maritime insurance market, Røsæg adds:

> The marine liability [insurance] market is dominated by the protection and indemnity (P&I) clubs, and in particular the clubs that participate in the pooling arrangements of the International Group of P&I Clubs.[23]

The P&I Clubs are mutual, non-profit associations. All P&I Clubs have Club Rulebooks that include a list of risks and specify the liabilities, costs and expenses which a member may incur in a maritime adventure.[24] Among the list, the insurance cover for pollution and the omnibus cover are of particular relevance to international environmental liability of the contractor in the context of DSM. In addition, it is generally acknowledged that the capacity of the International Group of P&I Clubs is more than adequate to obtain reinsurance and absorb catastrophic losses in the shipping industry.[25] It is probably reasonable to deduce that the capacity

[22] Available at: www.isa.org.jm/sites/default/files/german_insurance_association.pdf. The other two considerations of the ISA may be (1) defining minimum requirements of cover clearly and unambiguously so as to provide a level playing field for all prospective contract partners irrespective of their home jurisdiction, (2) in compliance with regulatory requirements in insurers' home jurisdictions.

[23] Erik Røsæg, 'Compulsory Maritime Insurance' (2000) Marlus 258 SIMPLY, 4.

[24] Ling Zhu, *Compulsory Insurance and Compensation for Bunker Oil Pollution Damage* (Springer 2006) 59–73.

[25] The thirteen principal underwriting member clubs of the Group between them provide liability cover for approximately 90 per cent of the world's ocean-going tonnage (International Group of P&I Clubs website, available at: www.igpandi.org/). The International Group of P&I Clubs currently purchases reinsurance amounting to more than USD 2 billion per claim. The capacity of the International Group of P&I Clubs to

of the marine liability insurance market will not be a problem for indemnifying international environmental liability of the contractor in the context of DSM. Therefore, as to the question of the insurability of international environmental liability of the contractor, although at a theoretical level the doubt cannot be eliminated completely, at a practical level, it is less problematic. There is an established insurance practice in the international maritime area which the contractor can choose to follow.

However, considering that there is a dual-track regulatory system in the DSM legal regime (the ISA as the centralized international regulator and the sponsoring State as the regulator at a national level), and considering that the Area belongs to the global commons and also that damage to the marine environment *per se* is a 'victimless' situation in the sense that no person is economically and directly affected, there are further open questions. Such as, who will issue the insurance certificate, the ISA or the sponsoring State? Who is entitled to take direct action against the insurer? What is the relationship between commercial insurance and environmental bonds and performance guarantees[26] if the bonds and guarantees are established in the future? In addition, there might be a minor problem: pursuant to maritime practice, it is the registered shipowner who is obligated to purchase the insurance; while under the DSM legal regime, it is the contractor who is obligated to take out the insurance. Thus, problems will arise when the contractor is not at the same time the registered shipowner.

7.3 Compensation Fund for Environmental Damage

In its 2011 Advisory Opinion, the Seabed Disputes Chamber (SDC) suggested that the ISA set up a certain trust fund to fill in the gap left by liability regimes in the context of DSM. This suggestion was formulated as follows:

obtain reinsurance and absorb catastrophic losses is huge, but they also prescribe limits to some types of risk. In particular, there is a limit of insurance cover for oil pollution liability (Zhu, Springer 2007, 59–73). The pooling agreement of the International Group provides insurance cover up to approximately USD 4.25 billion. This certainly appears to reflect adequate insurance capacity for most purposes (Røsæg, 2000, 4–5).

26 It is indicated in *Developing a Regulatory Framework for Mineral Exploitation in the Area* (July 2015) that 'the interaction between commercial insurance and bond mechanisms needs to be investigated together with the terms and conditions, including appropriate quantum of any bond'.

> Taking into account that, as shown above in paragraph 203, situations may arise where a Contractor does not meet its liability in full while the sponsoring State is not liable under article 139, paragraph 2, of the Convention, the Authority may wish to consider the establishment of a trust fund to compensate for the damage not covered. The Chamber draws attention to article 235, paragraph 3, of the Convention which refers to such possibility.[27]

As a response, in the preparatory work of 'Developing a Regulatory Framework for Mineral Exploitation in the Area', there was a proposal that a 'seabed sustainability fund' or 'environmental trust fund' should be set up.[28] Later on, the draft of Exploitation Regulations suggests the establishment of an Environmental Compensation Fund (ECF).[29] This section identifies key factors for establishing a compensation fund for environmental damage in the context of DSM. Yet, prior to taking such a task, the relationship between the concepts of compensation fund and liability is clarified.

7.3.1 *Conceptual Clarification: Relationship between Compensation Fund and Liability Regimes*

The meaning of 'fund' differs according to context. It would be misleading to use the term fund without clearly defining it, as Faure indicated. He classified compensation funds into four categories on the basis of the different goals they are intended to achieve: limitation fund, advancement fund, guarantee fund and general environmental fund.[30] According to Faure, when the liable person limits its liability to the amount brought into the fund, that fund is known as a limitation fund. Within international civil liability regimes, Article 6(5) of the 1977 Convention on Civil Liability for Oil Pollution Damage Resulting from Exploration for and Exploitation of Seabed Mineral Resources[31] and Article 5(3) of the

27 ITLOS, Advisory Opinion of 1 February 2011 (case No. 17), para. 205.

28 Available at: www.isa.org.jm/files/documents/EN/Survey/Report-2015.pdf, the document was discussed within the LTC during the meeting held in July 2015 (Item 12 of provisional agenda of the Legal and Technical Commission, ISBA/21/LTC/L.1, July 2015).

29 See Section 5, Part IV, the 2019 draft Exploitation Regulations, ISBA/25/C/WP.1.

30 Michael Faure and Ton Hartlief, 'Compensation Funds versus Liability and Insurance for Remedying Environmental Damage' (1996) 5(4) *RECIEL* 321–327.

31 Adopted on 1 May 1977, not in force (the 1977 Exploration and Exploitation Convention).

1992 CLC are two pertinent examples of a limitation fund. In almost the same wording, these two articles depict that

> [f]or the purpose of availing himself of the benefit of limitation to which he may be entitled [. . .], the operator shall constitute a fund for the total sum representing the limit of his liability [. . .]. The fund can be constituted either by depositing the sum or by producing a bank guarantee or other guarantee [. . .].

The second and third categories of fund are not included in the existing international civil liability regimes. In Faure's opinion, the term compensation fund is usually used in the sense of the fourth category of fund, namely general environmental fund. Indeed, most existing compensation funds would be classified under the category as general environmental fund Yet, as will be demonstrated below, even within this same category, differences among them can still be easily detected. Nonetheless, they share a common goal which constitutes the reason why such a category of compensation fund is needed.

The rationale of general environmental funds is found in the functions and deficiencies of the liability regime (including the insurance schemes). Liability has been acknowledged to have preventive and reparative functions with respect to environmental damage.[32] Concerning reparative function, the primary purpose of liability regimes is to compensate the victim of the environmental damage or, in the case of damage to the environment *per se*, to restore the damaged environment. However, with respect to the liability of the operator, there are at least five situations in which this purpose cannot be achieved. First, with respect to fault-based liability, when no wrongful acts or omissions can be attributed to the injurer, liability cannot be established. Secondly, with respect to strict liability, when the damage has occurred but the injurer is exempt from liability, there is no liable person. Thirdly, when liability is limited, if damage exceeds the limitation on liability, there is damage left uncompensated. Fourthly, even when the injurer is held liable, there might arise a situation in which he, including the insurer if liability is insured, goes into insolvency or dissolution. In such a situation, assuming liability is de facto impossible. Finally, there might also arise a situation in which no

[32] While a fault-based liability may have a deterrent or corrective function, a strict liability regime does not. For the three functions of liability see Rene Lefeber, *Transboundary Environmental Interference and the Origin of State Liability* (Kluwer 1996).

liable person can be identified.[33] Thus, there are potential gaps in liability regimes. It is exactly because of this limitation in the liability regime that the fund is needed. The purpose of the fund is thus to supplement the liability regimes in order to achieve adequate compensation for the victim and/or restoration of the environment.

The fund is supplementary to liability because the fund is on top of liability and together they attempt to achieve the goal of adequate compensation or restoration. The fund is activated only if liability is exhausted and has proven inefficient. For instance, the International Convention on the Establishment of an International Fund for Compensation for Oil Pollution Damage (the 1992 IOPC Fund Convention) was established 'to provide compensation for pollution damage to the extent that the protection afforded by the 1992 Civil Liability Convention is inadequate'.[34] In turn, 'the 2003 Supplementary Fund shall pay compensation to any person suffering pollution damage if such person has been unable to obtain full and adequate compensation for an established claim for such damage under the terms of the 1992 Fund Convention [. . .]'.[35] To provide another example, the 2010 HNS Fund was meant 'to provide compensation for damage to the extent that the protection by chapter II [liability] is inadequate or not available'.[36] As is explained, the 2010 HNS Fund will pay compensation when the total admissible claims exceed the shipowner's liability, that is, the Fund pays 'top-up' compensation when the shipowner, or his insurer, cannot meet in full the loss or damage arising from an incident.[37] Also, with respect to bunker oil pollution, it is considered that 'complementary measures are necessary to ensure the payment of adequate, prompt and effective compensation for damage caused by pollution resulting from the escape or discharge of bunker oil from ships'.[38] For nuclear damage, the 1963 Brussels Complementary Convention depicts three-layer compensation: with two new layers made up of public funds on top of the first one, which is established in accordance with the liability regime

33 Instances can be found in Article 4(1) of the 1992 Fund Convention; Article 14(1) of the 2010 HNS Convention.

34 Article 2(1) of the 1992 Fund Convention.

35 Article 4(1) of the 2003 Supplementary Fund Convention.

36 Article 13 (1)(a) of the 2010 HNS Convention.

37 An Overview of the 2010 HNS Convention, para. 27. Available at: http://hnsconvention.org/Documents/HNS%20Convention%20Overview_e.pdf.

38 Preamble, paragraph 6 of the 2001 Bunker Oil Convention.

under the 1960 Paris Convention.[39] The 1963 Vienna Convention also envisages compensation funds to complement liability.[40]

It should be noted that the notion of fund differs fundamentally from that of liability. Unlike liability, which has to be channelled to a specific person or persons, a fund is a collective compensation mechanism. A fund attempts to bring in more players whose participation is not based on their blameworthiness for causing the harm but on compensation as such. This is perhaps the reason why Nicolas de Sadeleer thought 'the notion of liability is totally absent from such compensation funds, which is based on solidarity rather than liability'.[41] In this sense, it can be said that the notion of fund is a new way of thinking; it operates as a substitute for liability (including insurance). In sum, fund and liability regimes share the same purpose – to compensate victims and/or restore environmental damage. Functionally, funds are complementary to liability regimes. Yet considering that a fund is based on the notion of solidarity which is fundamentally distinct from liability regimes, funds constitute a new approach which operates as a substitute for the liability regimes.

7.3.2 Environmental Compensation Fund in the Context of DSM

As the SDC suggested, the purpose for the establishment of an environmental compensation fund in the context of DSM is to fill in the gap left by international environmental liabilities. That is, the proposed fund is to top-up the first tier of liabilities. This feature shares a similarity with the existing environmental compensation funds in the fields of, such as, oil shipping and carriage of hazardous and noxious substances by sea. Article 4(1) of the 1992 IOPC Fund Convention stipulates that

> [t]he Fund shall pay compensation to any person suffering pollution damage if such person has been unable to obtain full and adequate compensation for damage under the terms of the 1992 Liability Convention.

39 Article 3(b) of the 1963 Brussels Complementary Convention as amended by the additional protocols of 1964, 1982 and 2004. The 2004 Protocol to amend the 1963 Brussels Supplementary Convention maintains the basic three-tier compensation system but with significantly increased amounts. The amount in article 3(b)(i) is increased to EUR 700 million minimum; in article 3(b)(ii) to EUR 500 million; and in article 3(b)(iii) to EUR 300 million.

40 Article 7(1) of the 1963 Vienna Convention.

41 Nicolas de Sadeleer, *Environmental Principles: From Political Slogans to Legal Rules* (OUP 2002), 59.

Likewise, Article 13(1) of the International Convention on Liability and Compensation for Damage in Connection with the Carriage of Hazardous and Noxious Substances by Sea (the 2010 HNS Convention) prescribes that

> [t]he International Hazardous and Noxious Substances Fund (HNS Fund) is hereby established with the following aims: (a) to provide compensation for damage in connection with the carriage of hazardous and noxious substances by sea, to the extent that the protection afforded by Chapter II is inadequate or not available [. . .].

Indeed, the IOPC Funds and HNS Fund are exemplars of 'top-up' compensation regime complementary to the liability regimes of operators. Although the ECF is similar to the IOPC Funds and HNS Fund in that sense, there are two significant differences between them. First and most importantly, operators in oil and HNS shipping assume strict liability that is subject to exemptions and limitations (liability *sine delicto*),[42] while the contractors in DSM assume liability only for their wrongful act (liability *ex delicto*). This difference is especially worth noting in practice: it would mean that, for the IOPC Funds and HNS Fund, it is relatively easy to determine on what condition and when the Funds should get involved, while for the ECF in DSM, this is not the case. Because the establishment of liability *ex delicto* of the contractor requires a proof of wrongful act, but that of liability *sine delicto* of oil and HNS shipping operators does not. Also, because the limitations to liability make determination of the amount of money that should be liable by oil and HNS shipping operators much easier than that by the contractors of DSM where actual damage must be proved and monetized. Hence, in comparison with the IOPC Funds and HNS Fund, the much larger room of ambiguity and controversy concerning its triggering conditions would make the operation of ECF more difficult in practice. Secondly, the IOPC Funds and HNS Fund are only complementary to liability of the operators, but the ECF is complementary to the liabilities of the contractor, the sponsoring State and the ISA. Considering the establishment and quantification of liability of the sponsoring State and the ISA would be as difficult as, if not more difficult than, that of the contractor, the exhaustion of remedies under liability regimes as the triggering condition of

[42] Article 4, paragraphs 2(a) and 3 of the 1992 IOPC Fund Convention prescribe the exemptions, and paragraph 4 the limitation on payment.

ECF is simply to make it even more difficult to determine when and to what extent the ECF may get involved.

It is noted that since the suggestion of a fund for environmental damage was first made by the SDC in 2011, there has been research and discussion over this topic the cumulative result of which is reflected in Technical Study No. 27 of the ISA published in 2021 (TS 27).[43] As compensation mechanisms are complementary to liabilities, the characteristics of funds are affected by the features of liability regimes. The fact that DSM legal regime depicts liability *ex delicto* rather than liability *sine delicto* and that bearers of liability are of a mixed nature are two marked features that differentiate liability regimes in DSM significantly from most international civil liability regimes, including those in the fields of oil and HNS shipping. Then, could one argue that the existing compensation funds have little precedential value to the establishment and operation of ECF in DSM?

Below it is to consider only one crucial issue relating to compensation funds – the contributing entity/entities – to illustrate whether and if so to what extent ECF may draw on the existing compensation funds. Two distinct funds for the oil pollution compensation and nuclear damage compensation are selected and examined here. With respect to oil pollution compensation, in a sense the 1992 Fund Convention can be seen as a continuation of the 1992 Civil Liability Convention (the 1992 CLC) as both depict strict liability of operators that is subject to exemptions and limitations. However, the question is: if the 1992 Fund Convention follows exactly the same route as the 1992 CLC, why is a new mechanism needed? Cannot the purpose of ensuring full and adequate compensation be achieved by simply raising the limitation on liability under the 1992 CLC? The point is that the 1992 Fund Convention introduces new player to share the onus of compensation for oil pollution. While under the 1992 CLC the parties held liable for compensation are the shipowner and its insurer, the 1992 Fund is financed by contributions levied on any person who has received in a calendar year more than 150,000 tons of crude oil or heavy fuel oil after sea transport in a 1992 Fund Member State.[44] Taking these two tiers of compensation together, it can be seen

[43] ISA, *TS 27: Study on an Environmental Compensation Fund for Activities in the Area*, 2021. TS 27 identifies twelve key issues about that topic and offers suggestions. Professor Lorenzo Schiano di Pepe served as the external consultant with the ISA concerning this topic, he was primarily responsible for the production of this document.

[44] Article 10 of the 1992 Fund Convention.

that the IOPC systems pay special consideration to the balance of interests between the shipping (onus of compensation on the shipowner and its insurer under the 1992 CLC) and the oil industry (onus of compensation on the cargo owner under the 1992 Fund Convention).[45]

If drawing on the 1992 IOPC Fund, one may suggest that metallurgic companies that receive ores extracted from the Area should contribute to the ECF. In this way, the processing and extractive sectors will share the onus for compensating environmental damage caused by DSM activities. The idea of metallurgic companies as contributing entities to ECF appears in TS 27.[46] Yet, at the same time, TS 27 indicates that this is not the practice in the context of land-based mining and the operation of such a system may prove challenging to the DSM regime. Indeed, including metallurgic companies into the compensation system in DSM is an innovative suggestion that does not fit to the practice in terrestrial mining sector. Also, it falls outside of the international DSM legal framework. Since the ISA cannot extend its competence to metallurgic companies which are non-participants in DSM, if metallurgic companies serve as contributing entities, then the ECF must have an independent legal status *vis-à-vis* the ISA, just like the IOPC Funds' being independent from the IMO. Additionally, suppose the idea of metallurgic companies as contributing entities to ECF is accepted, the balance of interests between mining and processing sectors with respect to DSM will be distinct from the balance of interests between shipping and oil sectors with respect to oil pollution compensation. For the latter, the balancing point lies on the cap on liability, while for the former, the distribution of the ECF (the interest of processing sector) depends on the financial capacities of the persons liable (the interest of mining sector).

On the other hand, compensation for nuclear damage shows a certain similarity with compensation for environmental damage caused by DSM

[45] For that reason, when the third tier of compensation which is financed by the cargo owner was introduced in 2005 with the entry into force of the 2003 Supplementary Fund Protocol, it caused an imbalance. To re-establish the balance, new insurance arrangements of the shipowner were made: the International Group of P&I Clubs introduced the Small Tanker Oil Pollution Indemnification Agreement (STOPIA 2006) and the Tanker Oil Pollution Indemnification Agreement (TOPIA 2006). IOPC Funds, The International Regime for Compensation for Oil Pollution Damage, explanatory note, October 2015, available at:
www.iopcfunds.org/fileadmin/IOPC_Upload/Downloads/English/OCT15E.pdf.

[46] ISA, *TS 27: Study on an Environmental Compensation Fund for Activities in the Area*, 2021.

activities insofar as the mixed nature of participants is concerned. It is noted by the ILC,

> The regimes of liability for nuclear damage have been more diverse than in the case of oil damage. These regimes seem to allow for greater accountability for States, a variation that may be explained by the ultra-hazardous nature of nuclear activity and its possible widespread and long-lasting damage.[47]

In stark contrast to the 1992 IOPC Fund where contributions are made by private entities, the additional layers of compensation for nuclear damage beyond liability are made up of public funds provided by states.[48] Alan Boyle observed that 'the liability of the operator is reinforced by state-funded compensation schemes'.[49] He went to explain that

> [t]his is a unique feature of the nuclear conventions; it acknowledges the residual responsibility of states to compensate for damage caused by nuclear activities where the operator is unable to do so or is itself a state.[50]

Indeed, the involvement of States is a salient feature of the compensation mechanism for nuclear damage. In particular, not only the Installation States, but also in some cases States Parties other than Installation States are required to make contributions to the funds. Article 3(b) of the 1963 Brussels Complementary Convention and Article 3(1) of the 1997 Convention on Supplementary Compensation for Nuclear Damage are two key examples. These conventions are based on a strong bond of financial solidarity between its parties.

[47] Secretariat of the ILC, Survey of liability regimes relevant to the topic of international liability for injurious consequences arising out of acts not prohibited by international law (international liability in case of loss from transboundary harm arising out of hazardous activities), A/CN.4/543, para. 157.

[48] In accordance with article 3(b) of the 1963 Brussel Convention Supplementary to the Paris Convention of 29 July 1960, the second and third layers of compensation for nuclear damage are provided by the Installation States and the States Parties, respectively. Article 7(1) of the 1963 Vienna Convention on Civil Liability for Nuclear Damage requires the Installation State to ensure the payment of claims for compensation for nuclear damage by providing the necessary funds. In the same vein, according to article 3 (2) of the 1962 Convention on the Liability of Operators of Nuclear ships, 'the licensing State shall ensure the payment of claims for compensation for nuclear damage established against the operator by providing the necessary funds up to the limit laid down in paragraph 1 of this Article to the extent that the yield of the insurance or the financial security is inadequate to satisfy such claims'.

[49] Patricia Birnie, Alan Boyle and Catherine Redgwell, *International Law and the Environment*, 3rd edn. (OUP 2009) 527.

[50] Ibid.

Interestingly, it seems that the IOPC compensation system also embraced the notion of solidarity. Article 12 of the 2003 Supplementary Fund Protocol stipulates that 'a Contracting State itself may assume the obligation to pay contributions to the Supplementary Fund [. . .]'. According to Article 14 of the 2003 Supplementary Fund Protocol, those Contracting States receiving less than 1 million tons of contributing oil shall themselves step in to make contribution to the 2003 Supplementary Fund. Thus, there is a minimum contribution obligation of all Contracting States, fulfilled either by private entities or by States themselves. This reflects the idea of solidarity.

Drawing on the compensation funds for nuclear damage and the 2003 IOPC Supplementary Fund, one may suggest that the sponsoring States should be contributors of the ECF in DSM. This idea is embraced in TS 27 too. As it is suggested,

> One possible scenario could be that sponsoring States could be required to make contributions to the ECF, potentially in the form of advances. Once the ECF reaches a certain threshold, the requirement for sponsoring State to contribute would cease. As the ECF increases above the threshold, ISA could return the advances made by these States on a proportionate basis.[51]

The suggestion in TS 27 identifies the role of sponsoring State more as helping the ECF to initiate than as a major source of contribution. In the meanwhile, it considers the contractor as the major but not the only contributor. Such a position is natural considering that the 'polluter-pays principle' is taken as the fundamental principle for the establishment of ECF in TS 27. However, it is my view that, while liability of the contractor is built upon the polluter-pays principle, ECF should be built on the idea of 'sharing of onus' and player(s) other than the contractor, in particular the sponsoring State, should be introduced. It is recalled that the SDC was of the opinion that 'the liability regime established by Article 139 of the Convention and in related instruments leaves no room for residual liability'.[52] However, this should not be interpreted as an exclusion of the involvement of the sponsoring State in the ECF. It is worth noting that a sponsoring State's image would be very different between its involvement in a liability regime and that in a compensation fund: being held liable may be associated with the stigma of

[51] TS 27.

[52] ITLOS, Advisory Opinion of 1 February 2011 (case No. 17), para. 204.

'wrongfulness' and 'blameworthiness', but contributing to the ECF is done in the name of solidarity.

Nevertheless, it seems that the current draft of Exploitation Regulations draws neither on the IOPC Funds nor on the compensation funds for nuclear damages. Regulation 56 of the 2019 draft Exploitation Regulations shows that the ECF is funded mainly with fees and penalties paid by the contractor to the ISA.[53] 'The ISA as the primary contributor to the ECF based on monies received from contractors' is also endorsed by TS 27.[54] TS 27 further indicates that, upon the initial threshold of the ECF having been met, it may be preferable for the ECF to rely on an annual levy imposed on the contractor based on the value of extracted minerals as the sole contribution.[55] One may just wonder whether this contractor-centred ECF would be adequate and whether excluding the sponsoring State and the processing sector would be a disadvantage when it comes to compensation for environmental damage caused by DSM activities.

Besides contributing entities, there are other issues relating to the establishment and operation of an ECF that need to be considered. For instance, what is the size of the ECF and how to calculate the contributions? How to determine the amount of the compensation and should there be a compensation cap for an incident or a serial of incidents? What is the legal status of the ECF and who is to administer it? Who are eligible to seek compensation from the ECF and what are the evidential and procedural requirements for the claims? TS 27 covered all these issues, yet, the draft Exploitation Regulations did not. It seems that the willingness of contractors and/or (sponsoring) States to participate in the ECF is still to be manifest. However, irrespective of the direction to be taken in the future, it is argued that, first, compensation fund should not be mixed up with liability regimes, and second, the uniqueness of DSM legal regime should be fully taken into account.

7.4 Administrative Approach to International Environmental Liability of the Contractor

Chapter 6 analysed international liability of the contractor for environmental damages arising out of wrongful acts in DSM activities. That

[53] The 2019 draft Exploitation Regulations, ISBA/25/C/WP.1.
[54] TS 27.
[55] Ibid.

approach bears much similarity with the civil liability approach adopted in existing civil liability treaties, albeit there is a difference in that international liability of the contractor is (mainly) implemented at the international level while liability in those civil liability treaties is implemented at the national level. Following the civil liability approach, to implement liability, normally there should be a litigant who initiates proceedings before a court in order to gain remedies. In the case of DSM, the litigant could be the ISA, the judicial institution the SDC, and the remediation includes restoration and compensation. In this section, I explore an administrative approach to international environmental liability of the contractor – the regulatory liability of the contractor. In contrast to 'the civil liability approach', 'the administrative approach' implies that there is 'a competent authority to deal with the matter (e.g. environmental damage) administratively, without initial recourse to courts'.[56] In this section, the reasons for a shift to an administrative approach and its features (Section 7.4.1) and how that approach would work in the DSM context with respect to the international environmental liability of the contractor will be explained (Section 7.4.2).

7.4.1 Turning to an Administrative Approach to Environmental Liability

The first international instrument which explicitly adopts the administrative approach to environmental liability (the 'regulatory liability') is the 2010 Nagoya-Kuala Lumpur Supplementary Protocol on Liability and Redress to the Cartagena Protocol on Biosafety (the 2010 Supplementary Protocol).[57] Article 5 of the 2010 Supplementary

[56] The use of a 'civil liability approach' and 'administrative approach to environmental liability' follows the line of Nijar's thought as follows: 'it delineates two pathways to dealing with such damage: the administrative approach that empowers a competent authority to deal with the matter administratively, without initial recourse to courts; and a civil liability approach that requires litigants to seek private law remedies through national legal systems'. See Gurdial Singh Nijar, 'The Nagoya-Kuala Lumper Supplementary Protocol on Liability and Redress to the Cartagena Protocol on Biosafety: An analysis and implementation challenges' (2013) 13 *INEA* 271–290.

[57] Lefeber commented that 'the Supplementary Protocol is the first global and comprehensive agreement providing for regulatory liability and a definition of damage to biological diversity'. See René Lefeber, 'The Legal Significance of the Supplementary Protocol: The Result of a Paradigm Evolution', in Akiko Shibata (ed.), *International Liability Regime for Biodiversity Damage: The Nagoya-Kuala Lumpur Supplementary Protocol* (Routledge 2014) 89.

Protocol is the core article reflecting such an approach. Through analysing Article 5, three main features of the regulatory liability of the operator are identified. Firstly, it is strict liability, that is, the operator is obliged to take response measures when environmental emergency occurs. Secondly, it covers exclusively damage to the environment *per se*, excluding traditional damage through impairment of the environment. Thirdly, the regulator plays a central role in (engaging the operator in) dealing with damage or threat of damage to the environment. With these features, regulatory liability demonstrates, in Lefeber's words, 'a paradigm evolution in international liability law'.[58]

To a certain extent, Principle 5 of the 2006 Draft Principles could be considered as a prelude to a paradigm evolution in international liability law which eventually happened in the 2010 Supplementary Protocol. It should be recalled that the ILC had progressively developed the concept of international liability. Its final result, the ILC's 2006 Draft Principles are composed of two parallel liability mechanisms to achieve two parallel purposes: the prompt and adequate compensation mechanism in Principle 4 is designed to achieve the purpose depicted in Principle 3 (a), namely compensation for victims of traditional damage such as personal injuries, damage to property and economic loss. While the response measures mechanism in Principle 5 is for the purpose expressed in Principle 3(b), that is, the restoration of the damaged environment *per se*. Principle 5, titled 'response measures', addresses the concerned State on its obligation in the situation of 'the occurrence of an incident involving a hazardous activity which results or is likely to result in transboundary damage'. The core message of this provision includes two aspects: on the one hand, 'the Principle recognizes the important role that the State plays and should play in taking necessary measures as soon as the emergency arises, given its role in securing at all times the public welfare and protecting the public interest'.[59] On the other hand, 'the operator has a primary responsibility to maintain emergency preparedness and operationalize any such measures as soon as an incident occurs'.[60] Thus, although Principle 5 of the 2006 Draft Principles did not

[58] Rene Lefeber, 'The Legal Significance of the Supplementary Protocol: The Result of a Paradigm Evolution', in Akiko Shibata (ed.), *International Liability Regime for Biodiversity Damage: The Nagoya-Kuala Lumpur Supplementary Protocol* (Routledge 2014) 91.

[59] Commentary to Principle 5 of the 2006 ILC Draft Principles, para. (7).

[60] Ibid., para. (8).

endorse expressly an administrative approach to environmental liability, it did address damage to the environment *per se* separately from traditional damage. And this is an innovative feature. Akiko Shibata has keenly observed that

> [a]fter 30 years of work on international liability with the aim to progressively develop or to codify international law, the ILC has come to recognize a distinct need to address the case of damage to the environment *per se* and a new idea of addressing such damage by effective response measures in addition to monetary compensation. This recognition by the ILC came after several turnarounds in the approaches to the concept of international liability and was based on a conceptual redirection of liability into a regime of 'allocation of loss'.[61]

The fundamental reason for this paradigm evolution from civil liability to regulatory liability is, in my opinion, that the character of the environment as public goods calls for a public-oriented approach.[62] One of the keystones upon which the US environmental law is built is the public trust doctrine. As Sax contended in 1970 that

> [p]ublic trust problems are found whenever governmental regulation comes into question, and they occur in a wide range of situations in which diffuse public interests need protection against tightly organized groups with clear and immediate goals.[63]

Specifically, Section 107(f) of the 1980 Comprehensive Environmental Response, Compensation, and Liability Act (CERCLA) and Section 1006 of the 1990 Oil Pollution Act (OPA) require the designation of trustees and stipulate the responsibilities of trustees for natural resources. With the adoption of these two statutes, the public trust doctrine secured its position as the theoretical basis for an administrative approach to environmental damage in the United States. When the US legal model was transplanted to Europe, the administrative approach as well as its theoretical basis – the public trust doctrine – were accepted without

[61] Akiko Shibata, 'A New Dimension in International Environmental Liability Regimes: A Prelude to the Supplementary Protocol', in Akiko Shibata (ed.), *International Liability Regime for Biodiversity Damage: The Nagoya-Kuala Lumpur Supplementary Protocol* (Routledge 2014) 41.

[62] Emanuela Orlando, 'Public and Private in the International Law of Environmental Liability', in Federico Lenzerini and Ana Vrdoljak (eds.), *International Law for Common Goods* (Hart 2014) 395.

[63] Joseph Sax, 'The Public Trust Doctrine in Natural Resource Law: Effective Judicial Intervention' (1970) 68(3) *Michigan Law Review* 475–566, 556.

questioning. When the time came to negotiate the 2010 Supplementary Protocol to which the European Union (EU) exerted a big influence, the ripple effect arrived at the international level. As a consequence of this turning to administrative approach, judicial interventions regarding environmental damage would be, from the perspective of the courts, judicial reviews of administrative decisions, and, from the perspective of the applicants, administrative litigation.

The administrative approach which places the regulator at the centre of the environmental liability regime has practical advantages in comparison with the court-centred civil liability approach. Firstly, a regulator could be the most suitable guardian of diffused public interests, such as being the trustee of the environment. Secondly, a regulator can monitor the implementation of environmental obligations by the operator much more effectively than a court. This, if achieved, could reinforce the preventive effect on environmental damage. Finally, the flexibility with administrative procedure could also contribute to the effectiveness of the implementation of liability. However, perceiving from a different angle, these advantages could also be considered as disadvantages. Firstly, this method 'requires substantial resources and capacity of the competent authority to be effective'.[64] Secondly, 'the process is left to the discretion of the competent public authority. This could lead to some arbitrary interpretation or uneven implementation'.[65]

7.4.2 International Regulatory Environmental Liability of the Contractor

Turning to the context of DSM, the questions are: does the DSM legal regime embody regulatory environmental liability of the contractor? If so, is it similar to or different from regulatory liability of the operator under the 2010 Supplementary Protocol? And what are the advantages and disadvantages of an administrative approach compared with a civil liability approach when it comes to the environmental liability of the contractor? An examination of national laws on DSM shows that regulatory environmental liability is predominately the primary, if not the only,

[64] Stefan Jungcurt and Nicole Schabus, 'Liability and Redress in the Context of the Cartagena Protocol on Biosafety' (2010) 19(2) *RECIEL* 197–206, 202.

[65] Alejandro Lago Candeira, 'Administrative Approach to Liability: Its Origin, Negotiation and Outcome', in Akiko Shibata (ed.), *International Liability Regime for Biodiversity Damage: The Nagoya-Kuala Lumpur Supplementary Protocol* (Routledge 2014) 99.

type of liability of the contractor.[66] This section, however, seeks answers to the above questions within the international DSM legal regime. Investigation will be conducted in two scenarios: the ISA's invocation of regulatory environmental liability of the contractor in the event of an environmental emergency and that in the event of environmental risk or damage during daily DSM management.

Although Article 162, paragraph 2(w) of the United Nations Convention on the Law of the Sea (UNCLOS) implies regulatory liability of the contractor, it is the Exploration Regulations that expressly prescribe regulatory liability of the contractor. Specifically, the legal bases are Regulation 33 of the Exploration Regulations on Nodules, Regulation 35 of the Exploration Regulations on Sulphides and Crust (Regulation 33/35) and Section 6, Annex IV to the Exploration Regulations. Regulation 33/35 elaborates on the substantive and procedural rules of taking response measures in the event of an environmental emergency. The ISA determines whether an environmental emergency exists, whether to issue an emergency order, what measures must be taken by the contractor; it also oversees the implementation of the emergency order.[67] The first three paragraphs of Section 6 of Annex IV reiterate the obligations of the contractor prescribed under Regulation 33/35. As analysed in Section 4.3.2, one of the main obligations of the contractor is to implement emergency order and to take response measures to prevent, minimize or repair serious harm or the threat of serious harm to the marine environment. It is seen that the contents of these provisions are very similar to Article 5 of the 2010 Supplementary Protocol.

Yet, is the contractor's obligation to take response measures strict liability? Following the line of logic of the 2010 Supplementary Protocol, the answer is affirmative. However, in accordance with Article 22, Annex III to the UNCLOS, liability of the contractor arises only if the condition of wrongful acts of the contractor is satisfied. In other words, there is no strict liability of the contractor in the context of DSM. Thus, the obligation of the contractor to take response measures should be interpreted as obligation, but not liability. However, if one employs the analytical tool used by the ILC in its work on State responsibility – the distinction between primary and secondary rules, and sees

[66] This finding is based on an analysis of database on national legislation with respect to activities in the Area: https://isa.org.jm/national-legislation-database.

[67] Concerning the regulatory powers of the ISA with respect to environmental emergency, see Section 3.4.4 of this book.

that strict liability and obligation in fact are both the primary rule, the different interpretations of the requirement of 'taking response measures' matter very little. In fact, the confusion is caused by the different usages of the same term of 'liability'. Namely, liability could refer to liability *sine delicto* as the secondary rule and strict liability as the primary rule at the same time. In this book, in order to maintain conceptual consistency within the context of DSM, the requirement of the contractor to take response measures is regarded as obligation as discussed in Chapter 4, while the legal consequences of a breach of the obligation to comply with emergency order are regarded as liability discussed in this section.

Therefore, liability of the contractor in the event of an environmental emergency is the legal consequence of non-compliance with an emergency order issued by the ISA. Regulation 33(7) of the Exploration Regulations on Nodules stipulates as follows:

> If a Contractor does not promptly comply with an emergency order to prevent, contain and minimize serious harm or the threat of serious harm to the marine environment arising out of its activities in the area, the Council shall take by itself or through arrangements with others on its behalf, such practical measures as are necessary to prevent, contain and minimize any such serious harm or threat of serious harm to the marine environment.

While Section 6.4, Annex IV to Exploration Regulations promulgates that

> [i]f the Contractor does not promptly comply with such emergency orders or immediate measures of a temporary nature, the Council may take such reasonable measures as are necessary to prevent, contain, minimize or repair any such serious harm or the threat of serious harm to the marine environment at the Contractor's expense. The Contractor shall promptly reimburse the Authority the amount of such expenses. Such expenses shall be in addition to any monetary penalties which may be imposed on the Contractor pursuant to the terms of this contract or the Regulations.

There are important differences between Section 6.4, Annex IV to Exploration Regulations and Regulation 33(7) of the Exploration Regulations on Nodules. First, it is a compulsory obligation for the Council to take response measures, either by itself or through arrangements, in case of non-compliance of the contractor under Regulation 33 (7) but not under Section 6.4, Annex IV. Moreover, the legal consequences of the non-compliance of the contractor are newly added in the standard clauses for an exploration contract. In light of Section 6.4,

Annex IV, not only must the contractor reimburse the costs incurred by the ISA in taking measures but the contractor may also be fined. In accordance with this provision, there could be three scenarios about the legal consequences of non-compliance by the contractor with an emergency order. Namely, the contractor has to pay reimbursement but not monetary penalties or monetary penalties but not reimbursement or both reimbursement and monetary penalties.

They are two forms of liability, reimbursement of the costs and monetary penalties. As to the reimbursement of the costs, Article 5(5) of the 2010 Supplementary Protocol states that

> the competent authority has the right to recover from the operator the costs and expenses of, and incidental to, the evaluation of the damage and the implementation of any such appropriate response measures.

Article 6(1) of the 2005 Antarctic Liability Annex stipulates,

> An operator that fails to take prompt and effective response action to environmental emergencies arising from its activities shall be liable to pay the costs of response action taken by parties pursuant to Article 5(2) to such Parties.

And Article 8(2) of the 2004 EU Environmental Liability Directive (ELD) promulgates,

> [S]ubject to paragraphs 3 and 4, the competent authority shall recover, *inter alia*, via security over property or other appropriate guarantees from the operator who has caused the damage or the imminent threat of damage, the costs it has incurred in relation to the preventive or remedial actions taken under this Directive.

It can be seen that it is a common requirement for the operator to reimburse the costs caused by response or remedial measures taken by others. Yet, again opinions about the nature of the obligation to reimburse costs differ in various contexts. Article 6(3) of the 2005 Antarctic Liability Annex states that it is strict liability of the operator. While Article 8(1) of the 2004 EU ELD implies that this requirement is based on the polluter-pays principle: 'the operator shall bear the costs for the preventive and remedial actions taken pursuant to this Directive'. In the context of DSM, the obligation to reimburse costs as one of the legal consequences of the failure to fulfil its primary obligation to take response measures should be considered as liability for wrongful acts. A further question is who determines the amount of reimbursement of costs, including, *inter alia*, the reasonableness of the costs and payment.

Pursuant to Article 12 of the 2005 Antarctic Liability Annex, request for reimbursement of costs from a party or parties has to be approved by the Antarctic Treaty Consultative Meeting (ATCM) in the form of decision. While in the 2004 EU ELD and the 2010 Supplementary Protocol, the issue of reimbursement of costs is formulated from the angle of the competent authority. It is phrased either as an obligation of the competent authority ('shall recover the cost') or as a right of the competent authority ('has the right to recover'). In the context of DSM, it is stated that 'the Contractor shall promptly reimburse the Authority the amount of such expenses'. It seems that the ISA could unilaterally determine the reimbursement of the costs.

Monetary penalties are another form of regulatory environmental liability of the contractor that is of a punitive nature. It should be noted that general international law does not embody punitive liability, nor do the many existing civil liability conventions and protocols, nor does the 2010 Supplementary Protocol that adopts regulatory liability. It is unique to the special international law of DSM.[68] It seems that the ISA could unilaterally decide whether to impose punitive liability on the contractor and if so how much. In a word, the ISA may exert a high degree of discretion in determining both the amount of reimbursement of costs and that of penalties.

Except in the situation of environmental emergency, the ISA could also invoke regulatory liability of the contractor during its daily management. And regulatory liability in situations other than environmental emergency takes forms of penalty and reimbursement of costs too. Under Regulation 80 of the 2019 draft Exploitation Regulations, the ISA may impose a monetary penalty on a contractor if the former ascertains a violation of the latter to the financial provisions of the exploitation contract. According to Regulations 103 and 104, the Secretary-General of the ISA may issue 'compliance notice' to a contractor at any time should he or she found a breach of the terms and conditions of its exploitation contract on the part of the contractor; if the contractor fails to take actions required under the compliance notice, the ISA may take

[68] It is, however, quite common at the national level. For instance, Canada adopted Environmental Violations in Administrative Monetary Penalties Act (S.C. 2009, c. 14, s. 126). Available at: http://laws-lois.justice.gc.ca/eng/acts/E-12.5/page-1.html. For some other instances, most national laws on DSM embody penalty as a form of environmental liability on sponsored contractors.

remedial actions or measures, then, the contractor is liable for reimbursing the actual and reasonable costs caused by the remedial actions or measures taken by the ISA. In a similar vein, in a situation of a risk of serious environmental damage, the Council may suspend or terminate the exploitation contract, if the contractor failed to comply, the ISA may take remedial actions or measures, then, the contractor is liable for reimbursing the actual and reasonable costs caused by the remedial actions or measures taken by the ISA. The Council may also impose monetary penalties on the contractor in situations of serious violation of contract. And as already pointed out above, the ISA has a high degree of discretion with respect to the establishment and implementation of regulatory liability of the contractor.

But is the discretion of the ISA subject to some sort of control, for instance, judicial review by the SDC? Regulation 103 of the 2019 draft Exploitation Regulations states that decisions on suspension or termination of contracts or on monetary penalties in situations other than environmental emergencies can be enforceable only if effective judicial remedies are exhausted.[69] The first sentence of Article 189 of the UNCLOS prescribes that the SDC shall have no jurisdiction with regard to the exercise of the ISA of its discretionary powers. Yet, the second sentence of the same article states that the SDC shall have jurisdiction over 'claims for damages to be paid or other remedy'. Should the contractor challenge the ISA's decision about reimbursement of costs or monetary penalties, a dispute which falls within the scope of the SDC's jurisdiction under Article 187(c) of the UNCLOS would arise.[70] Additionally, it is noted that Article 5(6) of the 2010 Supplementary Protocol prescribes judicial review of administrative decisions of regulators and Sax expressed similar position in *The Public Trust Doctrine in Natural Resource Law: Effective Judicial Intervention*.[71] Thus, relying on Articles 189 and 187 of the UNCLOS, as well as drawing on experience in other contexts and theoretical account, it concludes that the ISA's discretionary power in determining the regulatory environmental liability of the contractor – the imposition of reimbursement of costs and monetary penalties – will not go unchecked.

[69] Regulation 103 of the 2019 draft Exploitation Regulations, ISBA/25/C/WP.1.

[70] The relationship between the contractor and the ISA is as parties to a contract and at the same time as the regulated and the regulator.

[71] Joseph Sax, 'The Public Trust Doctrine in Natural Resource Law: Effective Judicial Intervention' (1970) 68(3) *Michigan Law Review* 475–566.

To conclude, reimbursement of the costs to the ISA and monetary penalties imposed by the ISA are both of an administrative nature; they belong to the secondary rules. The establishment of this regulatory liability depends on (a) the requirements of the 'emergency order', 'compliance notice' or other administrative orders or notices, and (b) the judgment on whether the contractor has complied with those requirements. The content of the liability is decided unilaterally by the ISA but such decision may be reviewed by the SDC should the contractor challenge it before the SDC. This kind of regulatory liability is different from that in the 2010 Supplementary Protocol, since the former is governed by secondary rules, while the latter by primary rules.

7.5 Conclusions and Potential Ways Forward

After analysing the establishment of international civil liability of the contractor, in particular demonstrating the practical difficulties in establishing liability, two alternative ways have been explored. They are: the concept of 'allocation of loss' in dealing with environmental damage and the regulatory environmental liability of the contractor. The scheme of allocation of loss includes the requirement of compulsory insurance and the establishment of an environmental compensation fund, which focuses on reinforcing and filling the gap left by the liability regimes. The regulatory liability of the contractor, on the other hand, tries to lessen the rigidness in evidential requirements of the traditional civil liability approach. Indeed, by placing the regulatory organ at the centre of the liability regime, the difficulties in satisfying the conditions for the establishment of liability are alleviated to a large extent. It is noted, however, that the regulatory liability of the contractor under discussion in the context of DSM is different from that in the context of, for instance, biological diversity. Yet, they share some core features of an administrative approach towards liability of operators.

How do these alternative regimes overcome the limitation of the international civil liability regime? For regulatory liability, it does so by lowering the evidential standard with the proof of the existence of an environment emergency/environmental risk/environmental damage and the causal-effect link between activities and environmental damage, and by avoiding the difficult task of measuring environmental damages. This does not mean, however, that 'the (threat of) environmental damage' is not a required element for the establishment of regulatory liability. On the contrary, as Edward Brans and Dorith Dongelmans correctly pointed out:

> Eventually, almost the same legal issues are to be addressed under both approaches: has damage been caused by the incident or is it likely to occur, and if so, is it of such an extent that it can be considered significant; who caused the damage; and what response measures can reasonably be required? Thus, in our opinion, the 'administrative approach' does not imply that difficult legal discussions can be prevented.[72]

Nonetheless, there are important differences that Brans and Dongelmans failed to raise. Under the civil liability approach, during a formal judicial proceeding, the applicant must prove the existence of environmental damage and the causation between damage and the activities/incident to the extent that it meets a high evidential standard. Also, the applicant must measure that damage with a degree of accuracy that satisfies the judicial institutions. These are very difficult tasks. As one can see from the UNCC practice, a major reason for the low rate of approval of an application was exactly the failure of the applicant to prove the existence of environmental damage, the causation between damage and the activities and to measure that damage to the extent that satisfied the panel. In contrast, under the administrative approach, first of all, it is the regulator which decides unilaterally whether an environmental emergency exists which has caused or is likely to cause environmental damage. Here no rigid evidential standard is to be met; no-one is entitled to challenge the decision by the competent authority concerning this matter. Furthermore, there is no need to measure the damage since the remediation does not target compensation but simply asks the operator to respond to the environmental emergency in a timely and effective manner. In particular, in the context of DSM, there is no requirement that the ISA must base its decision on the measure of the environmental damage when imposing monetary penalties on the contractor for its non-compliance with the emergency order.[73] Nonetheless, although overcoming the drawback of traditional civil liability from a certain angle, the administrative approach has its own limits: it relies heavily

[72] Edward Brans and Dorith Dongelmans, 'The Supplementary Protocol and the EU Environmental Liability Directive: Similarities and Differences', in Akiko Shibata (ed.), *International Liability Regime for Biodiversity Damage: The Nagoya-Kuala Lumpur Supplementary Protocol* (Routledge 2014) 190.

[73] Although the legitimacy of such a decision would be higher if it is accompanied with an explanation of how that amount of monetary penalties was arrived at.

on the capacity of the regulator to deal with (the threat of) environmental damage.

As to the compulsory insurance mechanism and the environmental compensation fund, both are intended to tackle the problem of inadequacy of compensation of the existing liability regimes. They overcome the limitation of liability regimes by introducing additional sources for compensation which find their basis not in the notion of liability but in 'allocation of loss'. Specifically, the compulsory insurance mechanism adds a new player – the insurer or financial security provider – to reinforce the compensation capacity of the operator. The compensation fund functions as a supplementary or substitute compensation mechanism to fill the gap left by the liability regimes. The salient feature of this idea of allocation of loss is to refocus on compensation for victims and/or restoration of the environment itself. Yet, the viability of this idea completely depends on the willingness of related players to participate in the absence of blameworthiness for causing environmental damage.

It seems that neither the regulatory liability (Section 7.4) nor the idea of allocation of loss as implemented through compulsory insurance (Section 7.2) and the fund mechanisms (Section 7.3) is a perfect substitute for liability of the contractor as analysed in Chapter 6. Yet, by and large, these two alternative ways do have their strengths in dealing with the subject matter – the remediation of marine environmental damage *per se* caused by DSM activities, although their practical effects remain to be tested.

To summarize, Chapters 6 and 7 analyse the conditions, features and contents of international environmental liability of the contractor and two alternative regimes. The analysis shows that each regime has its strengths and limits. Which regime to take in the future is a matter of choice of policy. At this time, the LTC is undertaking the task of drafting the Exploitation Regulations, which includes the issue of marine environmental protection. At the twenty-first session in 2015, the delegation of the Netherlands submitted to the Council a proposal on 'addressing serious harm to the marine environment in the regulations for the exploitation of mineral resources in the Area'.[74] In the submission it is recommended that

[t]he Council is also invited to request the Legal and Technical Commission to consider recommending that

[74] ISBA/21/C/13, 2015.

(a) [t]he Exploitation Regulations be based on the provisions on emergency orders in the exploration regulations in order to address threats of serious harm to the marine environment following an incident resulting from or caused by a Contractor's activities in the Area;
(b) The Exploitation Regulations include an obligation requiring Contractors to address serious harm to the marine environment by: (i) assessing the technical and economic feasibility of implementing restoration measures and; (ii) providing for restoration by equivalent, compensatory measures and/or the payment of monetary compensation if no adequate restoration measures have been or can be implemented;
(c) Private sector initiatives to address harm to the marine environment be supported and encouraged.[75]

Apparently, this submission does not adopt the models of traditional international civil liability treaties. On the contrary, it follows the line of the current Exploration Regulations, and takes account of the latest developments in the environmental liability regimes, including in particular the 2010 Supplementary Protocol, the 2004 EU ELD, the 2005 Antarctic Liability Annex and the 2006 ILC Draft Principles. With respect to subparagraph (a), it recommends that the Exploitation Regulations should put the ISA at the centre in dealing with the (threat of) marine environmental damage. Essentially, this is tantamount to suggesting an administrative approach to international environmental liability of the contractor. As to subparagraph (b), notably, it recommends a comprehensive remediation framework concerning environmental damage. Here, the strong influence of the 2004 EU ELD is obvious, specifically, the common framework of measures to ensure the remedying of environmental damage in Annex II. By contrast, it is considered that the 2005 Antarctic Liability Annex should adopt a narrow approach since it includes the response action to environmental emergencies only:

> The Annex as adopted reflects that 'step-be-step' approach. Liability under the Annex is built around the key concepts of 'environmental emergency' and 'response action' rather than 'damage to the environment' *per se*.[76]

[75] ISBA/21/C/13, 2015, para. 12.

[76] Elana Geddis, 'Liability for Environmental Emergencies in Antarctica' (2006) 3 *NZYIL* 201–206, 202–203.

The consequence of this narrow approach is that liability of the operator is limited to either taking response action or paying the costs incurred by others taking such response action; while the difficult task of measuring environmental damage is avoided. Yet, if the broad approach as recommended by the delegation of the Netherlands is to be adopted, remediation of environmental damage is a very complicated system many aspects of which, including the measure of environmental damage, will encounter difficulties when put into practice. With regard to subparagraph (c), the inspiration might come from the experience of the 2010 Supplementary Protocol.[77]

Whether the LTC will follow the recommendations in this submission remains to be seen. However, a comprehensive remediation system similar to the 2004 EU ELD will very likely be needed in the exploitation phase. Furthermore, considering the practical difficulties in the establishment of international environmental liability of the contractor as prescribed under the UNCLOS, the idea of allocation of loss and the administrative approach to liability of the contractor will very likely be taken into consideration in the exploitation phase.

[77] J. Thomas Carrato, John Barkett and Phil Goldberg, 'The Industry's Compact and Its Implications for the Supplementary Protocol', in Akiko Shibata (ed.), *International Liability Regime for Biodiversity Damage: The Nagoya-Kuala Lumpur Supplementary Protocol* (Routledge 2014).

8

International Environmental Liabilities of the Sponsoring State and the International Seabed Authority

8.1 Introduction

Chapter 6 examined the issue of international environmental liability of the contractor, including the establishment, forms and content, and implementation of that liability. As will be shown below, the international environmental liability of the sponsoring State and of the International Seabed Authority (ISA) share many similarities with that of the contractor. For the sake of being concise, lengthy parallel discussions will be avoided in this chapter; instead, analogies can be drawn from previous discussions whenever appropriate. The emphasis in this chapter is on the special issues attached to the sponsoring State and to the ISA. Section 8.2 discusses the international environmental liability of the sponsoring State. Considering that the Seabed Disputes Chamber's (SDC's) clarification of this issue in the 2011 Advisory Opinion is deemed as an authoritative interpretation, the main task in this section is to comment on the SDC's 2011 Advisory Opinion, in particular, the SDC's response to the second question posed by the ISA.[1] Section 8.3 examines the international environmental liability of the ISA. The emphasis is on the special issue of liability of (member) States for acts of international organizations, on the basis of an examination of existing instruments.

[1] The second question posed before the SDC is as follows: '[w]hat is the extent of liability of a State Party for any failure to comply with the provisions of the Convention in particular Part XI, and the 1994 Agreement, by an entity whom it has sponsored under Article 153, paragraph 2(b), of the Convention?'

8.2 International Environmental Liability of the Sponsoring State: Commentary Notes on the Seabed Disputes Chamber's 2011 Advisory Opinion

8.2.1 Establishment of International Environmental Liability of the Sponsoring State

8.2.1.1 Related Provisions

Article 139(2) prescribes the liability of the sponsoring State in both positive and negative ways. In a positive way, the first sentence of the provision lays down the conditions for the establishment of liability as follows:

> Without prejudice to the rules of international law and Annex III, article 22, damage caused by the failure of a State Party or international organization to carry out its responsibilities under this Part shall entail liability

In a negative way, the ensuing second sentence describes those circumstances where a State is exempted from liability:

> A State Party shall not however be liable for damage caused by any failure to comply with this Part by a person whom it has sponsored under article 153, paragraph 2(b), if the State Party has taken all necessary and appropriate measures to secure effective compliance under article 153, paragraph 4, and Annex III, article 4, paragraph 4.

A more specific construction on the key phrase 'necessary and appropriate measures' can be found in Article 4(4), Annex III to United Nations Convention on the Law of the Sea (UNCLOS), which reads that

> [a] sponsoring State shall not, however, be liable for damage caused by any failure of a contractor sponsored by it to comply with its obligations if that State Party has adopted laws and regulations and taken administrative measures which are, within the framework of its legal system, reasonably appropriate for securing compliance by persons under its jurisdiction.

From these provisions, it is seen that a sponsoring State cannot be exempt from liability by simply contending that it is not the operator; on the other side, a sponsoring State cannot be held liable simply because of the sponsorship or based on the mere fact that damage has occurred either. Instead, three conditions for establishing its liability can be identified from Article 139(2): (i) internationally wrongful act of the sponsoring State, (ii) environmental damage and (iii) the causal link between the act and the damage.[2]

8.2.1.2 Internationally Wrongful Act of the Sponsoring State

Article 2 of the 2001 Articles on State Responsibility (ASR) prescribes two constituent elements of 'an internationally wrongful act' as follows:

> There is an internationally wrongful act of a State when conduct consisting of an action or omission: (a) is attributable to the State under international law; and (b) constitutes a breach of an international obligation of the State.[3]

This general rule can also apply to the sponsoring State in the context of deep seabed mining (DSM). Thus, for ascertaining the internationally wrongful act of the sponsoring State, the first constituent element is that there is 'a breach of an international obligation of the sponsoring State' and the second one is that 'the act is attributed to the sponsoring State'. Here, the SDC emphasized that the sponsoring State is liable for the failure to carry out its own obligations rather than 'the failure of the sponsored contractor to meet its obligations'.[4] In a word, the sponsoring State is responsible for its own internationally wrongful act. Brownlie observed that

> [i]n some cases, however, the conduct of private persons or groups, although not directly attributable, may indicate a failure by the State to perform adequately its own obligations of regulation, protection, or control. Here responsibility arises because of the State's own actions or omissions.[5]

[2] The SDC stated that '[t]he wording of article 139, paragraph 2, of the Convention clearly establishes two conditions for liability to arise: the failure of the sponsoring State to carry out its responsibilities; and the occurrence of damage'. (ITLOS, Advisory Opinion of 1 February 2011 (case No. 17), para. 176). This statement failed to capture the third condition: the causal link between environmental damage and the internationally wrongful acts of the sponsoring State.

[3] Article 2, the 2001 ASR.

[4] ITLOS, Advisory Opinion of 1 February 2011 (case No. 17), para. 172. The reason why the SDC made such an emphasis is because the failure to fulfil the international obligations of the sponsoring State is closely connected with the failure to fulfil the international obligations of the sponsored contractor. Thus, the liabilities of the sponsoring State and the sponsored contractor are easily mixed.

[5] Ian Brownie, *System of Law of Nations (Part I): State Responsibility* (OUP 1983), Chapter 8.

As an illustrative example consider the responsibility of host States in the context of the protection of aliens and their properties. When aliens or their properties are injured by private persons, the conduct of private persons cannot be attributed to the host State, it may however indicate that the host State fails to provide adequate police protection or indiscriminate access to its judicial system to protect aliens and their properties. If the host State can prove that it has taken adequate measures to protect aliens and their properties, then the host State is not responsible, otherwise State responsibility arises. There the host State is responsible for its own failure to provide protection or remedies but not for the conduct of private persons. From the statement of Ian Browlie and this illustrative example, it is seen that, materially speaking, the acts (actions or omissions) of State and private persons are joint contributing factors to the injury, yet, legally speaking, State responsibility is independent from liability of private actors. The State responsibility is a legal fiction that should be distinguished from the material element of proof of causal effect. Similarly, in the case of DSM, the sponsoring State is liable only if it fails to fulfil its own international environmental obligations as the regulator, this liability is independent from liability of the contractor, although acts of the sponsoring State and the conduct of the sponsored contractor jointly contribute to the same consequence of environmental damage.

To determine whether there is a breach of obligations, clarification of the content of the primary obligations of the sponsoring State becomes the key question. As the SDC commented, 'whether a sponsoring State has carried out its responsibilities depends primarily on the requirements of the obligation which the sponsoring State is said to have breached'.[6] Thus, although in principle the responsibility or liability (as the secondary rule) can be examined independently from the obligations (as the primary rule), in practice, it is not possible to establish the responsibility or liability without investigating the obligations. In this respect, the SDC categorized the primary obligations of the sponsoring State into two groups: the obligations to ensure compliance of its sponsored contractor and direct obligations. As to the former category, they are obligations of conduct; the criterion for the determination of their fulfillment is 'due diligence', namely, the sponsoring State needs to take 'all necessary and appropriate measures to secure effective compliance of the contractor'. If

[6] ITLOS, Advisory Opinion of 1 February 2011 (case No. 17), para. 177.

the sponsoring State meets this criterion, it would be exempt from liability. The latter category, however, are obligations of result. For obligations of result, once established, there is no exemption from liability. Also, Chapter 4 of this book elaborated the main international environmental obligations of the sponsoring State in more detail.

In sum, liability of the sponsoring State does not arise if a wrongful act of the sponsoring State cannot be identified under international law. Determination of an internationally wrongful act requires two elements: one is attribution of acts to the sponsoring State and the other is breach of primary obligations. And the answer to the question of whether there is a breach of obligations depends on the requirement of the primary obligations. This shows the connection between the primary rule of obligation and the secondary rule of responsibility or liability. It should be noted that, when ascertaining if an internationally wrongful act of the sponsoring State exists, the occurrence of damage is not related. Damage is a separate condition for establishing liability of the sponsoring State.

8.2.1.3 Environmental Damage and the Causal Link

Environmental damage is the prerequisite condition and triggering element for the establishment of international environmental liabilities of any participants in DSM, including the sponsoring State. Just as the SDC observed, 'the failure of a sponsoring State to carry out its responsibilities entails liability only if there is damage'.[7] In addition, the condition of the causal link between the environmental damage and the internationally wrongful act of the sponsoring State can also be inferred from the phrase 'caused by' in Article 139(2) UNCLOS. Moreover, this causal link cannot be presumed but must be proven.[8]

As has been shown in Chapters 5 and 6, both the identification and the measure of the environmental damage and the proof of the causal link between the environmental damage and the wrongful act are difficult tasks. The analysis of these two conditions concerning the contractor in Chapter 6 applies equally to the sponsoring State. Yet, one more point should be made. In Section 6.4.3, the causal link to be proven is between the environmental damage and the wrongful act of the contractor, while in this chapter, it is the causal link between the environmental damage and the wrongful act of the sponsoring State. However, unlike the contractor who is in direct control of the operation of DSM activities,

[7] Ibid., para. 178.
[8] Ibid., para. 182.

the relationship between the sponsoring State as the regulator and the environmental damage arising out of DSM activities is indirect. From both theoretical and practical perspectives, it is difficult to ascertain how much the failure to regulate on the part of the sponsoring State contributes to the occurrence of environmental damage caused by the DSM activity operated by the contractor. This difficulty together with the problem regarding the measure of environmental damage makes the establishment of international environmental liability of the sponsoring State a very difficult, if not impossible, task.

In effect, the requirement of environmental damage not only makes the establishment of international environmental liability of the sponsoring State difficult, but also makes it different from the notion of State responsibility under the 2001 ASR. The fundamental principle of State responsibility is that 'every internationally wrongful act of the State entails its international responsibility of that State'.[9] Since liability of the sponsoring State in DSM requires the occurrence of environmental damage, it departs here from the fundamental principle of State responsibility.

8.2.2 *Differentiation of State Liability* Ex Delicto *from State Responsibility*

When examining the element of damage, the SDC noted the difference between the liability of the sponsoring State in the context of DSM and the general rule of State responsibility as codified in the 2001 ASR. It observed that

> [. . .] the provision covers neither the situation in which the sponsoring State has failed to carry out its responsibilities but there has been no damage, nor the situation in which there has been damage but the sponsoring State has met its obligations. This constitutes an exception to the customary law on liability since, as stated in the Rainbow Warrior Arbitration, and in paragraph 9 of the Commentary to article 2 of the ILC Articles on State Responsibility, a State may be held liable under customary international law even if no material damage results from its failure to meet its international obligations.[10]

[9] Article 1 of the 2001 ILC ASR stipulates this principle which is regarded as reflecting customary international law.

[10] ITLOS, Advisory Opinion of 1 February 2011 (case No. 17), para. 178.

It is noted that Crawford made it clear that

> [t]here seems to be general acceptance of the proposition that damage is not a necessary constituent of every breach of international law, and that articles 1 and 2 should not therefore include any specific reference to 'damage'. It will be a matter for the primary rule in question to determine what is the threshold for a violation.[11]

Why then is an additional condition – the occurrence of environmental damage – required for establishing international environmental liabilities in DSM? In effect, a similar question was raised during the period when the International Law Commission (ILC) was working on the topic of international liability, before it turned to civil liability in 1990. This question is related to the debates over the distinction between the two terms of 'state liability *ex delicto*' and 'state responsibility'. Some contended that such a distinction between the two is unnecessary[12] because State liability *ex delicto* has been completely assimilated by State responsibility. Taking Alan Boyle as the representative of the position, he expressed that 'to state in general terms that damage is a necessary element to liability while not to responsibility, although it may be true, misses the point'.[13] In his view, 'what is in issue is the particular obligation', and 'general propositions regarding the absence of harm or injury in the concept of State responsibility may therefore be unhelpful or misleading'.[14] He further used the 'no harm principle' introduced in the seminal case of *Trail Smelter* as the example which, in his opinion, was exactly 'a specific obligation whose content is defined in terms requiring harm and injury'.[15]

It is true that there are various types of international obligation with distinctive characteristics that have an effect on the conditions for determining their breach. In some cases, failure to adopt a certain course of conduct will be tantamount to a breach of the international obligation; while in other cases, it is the failure to achieve a particular result; still

[11] ILC, the fourth report on the topic of State responsibility by the last Special Rapporteur (Crawford), A/CN.4/517, 2001, para. 28.

[12] A representative of this view can be found in Alan Boyle, 'State Responsibility and International Liability for Injurious Consequences of Acts Not Prohibited by International Law: A Necessary Distinction?' (1990) 39 *ICLQ* 1–26. Boyle rejected the distinction between State liability and State responsibility and argued against the conceptual viability of the topic of international liability.

[13] Ibid., 16–17.

[14] Ibid.

[15] Ibid.

others require that the occurrence of a certain event is a necessary condition for constituting a breach of the international obligation.[16] It is also true that whether 'damage' is a condition for meeting the threshold of a breach depends on the specific primary obligation. In effect, the reasoning of Boyle was in line with the ILC's on State responsibility and the SDC's in the 2011 Advisory Opinion. However, Boyle's interpretation of the 'no harm principle' in the area of International Environmental Law (IEL) was contestable. Pursuant to his interpretation, 'damage' is a condition for meeting the threshold of the breach of obligation under the 'no harm rule'. In other words, the occurrence of damage is a condition to establishing a wrongful act: no damage, no wrongful act. Akehurst was of a similar opinion with respect to the interpretation of the no harm rule. According to Akehurst, 'attaching liability *sine delicto* to the environment is a misunderstanding on the part of the Commission, since rules of international law concerning the environment are phrased in terms of duty not damage to the environment, from which it follows that any resulting liability for damage to the environment is liability *ex delicto* not *sine delicto*'.[17]

By implanting damage into the element of internationally wrongful act, both Boyle and Akehurst had the underlying understanding that obligations under the no harm principle are, by their nature, 'obligations of result'. The problem is, however, that that understanding is contrary to the established opinion of international judicial institutions, State practice subsequent to the *Trail Smelter* arbitral case and the prevailing position in the scholarly literature. To date, the established understanding of the no harm principle can be exemplified by the statement below:

> [. . .] a State can only breach the no harm principle if it fails to act with due diligence. This is the reason why some scholars refer to this principle as the principle of due diligence. [. . .] Due diligence obligations can well be categorized as obligations of conduct, i.e. those primary

[16] The ILC once made an effort to categorize international primary obligations. For more information see the reports of the second Special Rapporteur on the topic of State responsibility (Ago): Article 20 (breach of an international obligation calling for the State to adopt a specific course of conduct) and Article 21 (breach of an international obligation requiring the State to achieve a particular result) in the sixth report, 1977. UN Doc. A/CN.4/302 and Add. 1, 2 & 3. Article 23 (breach of an international obligation to prevent a given event) in the seventh report, 1978. UN Document A/CN.4/307 and Add. 1 & 2 and Corr. 1 & 2.

[17] Michael Akehurst, 'International Liability for Injurious Consequences Arising out of Acts Not Prohibited by International Law' (1985) 16 *NYIL* 3–16, 3.

> obligations that require States to endeavor to reach the result set out in the obligation.[18]

The SDC took the same position in its 2011 Advisory Opinion.[19] Also, as can be seen from the analysis in Chapter 4, the obligations of States emanating from the no harm principle and the principle of prevention are obligations of conduct. In short, the no harm principle only indicates the obligation to prevent the occurrence of damage, a breach of that obligation is not necessarily connected with the occurrence of damage. Occasions do exist where breach of the obligation can be identified but environmental liability of the State does not arise for the reason that the trigger element – occurrence of environmental damage – is absent. In other words, environmental damage is always the required, more precisely the prerequisite, element of liability but not of responsibility. To sum up, the importance of 'environmental damage' in the international environmental liability regime must not be underestimated. State liability *ex delicto* constitutes a departure from the fundamental principle of State responsibility: While every internationally wrongful act entails State responsibility, not every internationally wrongful act entails State liability *ex delicto*. In this sense, State liability *ex delicto* cannot be completely assimilated by the general rule of State responsibility.

The ILC provided a new view on the nature of State liability *ex delicto* and its relationship with State responsibility in the study of the topic of international liability.[20] In the analysis of Article 8(3) of the Convention on the Regulation of Antarctic Mineral Resource Activities (the 1988 CRAMRA),[21] the ILC wrote:

> This is a unique form of accountability of the sponsoring State, even though, theoretically, it arises from the failure to perform obligations. The difference between this form of accountability and 'responsibility' derives from the triggering element of accountability, and the consequences of accountability, both of which resemble 'liability' and not classical

[18] Timo Koivurova, 'Due Diligence', MPEPIL (last updated in February 2010), para. 15.

[19] ITLOS, Advisory Opinion of 1 February 2011 (case No. 17), para. 111.

[20] Secretariat of the ILC, Survey of liability regimes relevant to the topic of international liability for injurious consequences arising out of acts not prohibited by international law, 1995, UN Doc. A/CN.4/471.

[21] The text of Article 8(3): damage of the kind referred to in paragraph 2 above which would not have occurred or continued if the Sponsoring State had carried out its obligations under this Convention with respect to its Operator shall, in accordance with international law, entail liability of that Sponsoring State. Such liability shall be limited to that portion of liability not satisfied by the Operator or otherwise.

> 'responsibility' doctrine. As for the triggering element, contrary to State responsibility, the failure to perform an obligation is insufficient, by itself, to entail responsibility. There should always be damage or injury, the *sine qua non* of a liability doctrine. As regards remedies, the normal ones of State responsibility, namely, cessation, restitution, satisfaction, do not arise in this case.[22]

It further indicated explicitly in the same document that 'this type of State accountability is a hybrid between State responsibility and liability'.[23] This observation captured the nature of State liability *ex delicto.*

The ILC opined that the application of the general rules of State responsibility as codified in the 2001 ASR can be excluded partially or entirely by special legal regimes; the 2001 ASR operates in a residual way.[24] This is the endorsement of the principle of *lex specialis*, an approach to deal with 'conflict of rules'. Insofar as the international environmental liability of the sponsoring State in the context of DSM is concerned, being identified above as the State liability *ex delicto*, it departs from the fundamental principle of State responsibility. There exist 'conflict of rules'. According to Article 55 of the 2001 ASR and the principle of *lex specialis*, the State liability *ex delicto* as prescribed in UNCLOS is a *lex specialis* to State responsibility, the application of State liability *ex delicto* excludes that of State responsibility where and to the extent the former departs from the latter. Yet, on issues about which UNCLOS is silent, such as invocation of State liability *ex delicto*, the 2001 ASR could still be applicable. Thus, it is argued here that State liability *ex delicto*, in nature, is a hybrid between State responsibility and liability, while from a structural perspective should be seen as *lex specialis* to State responsibility.

In brief, although both in the sphere of secondary rules, State liability *ex delicto* still needs to be differentiated from State responsibility. First, State responsibility and State liability differ in the governing element. While 'internationally wrongful act' is the governing element for State responsibility, the governing element for State liability is 'the objective fact of harm having occurred'.[25] Second, State responsibility and liability have distinct concerns. Indeed, 'wrongful acts are the focus of State

[22] The 1995 Survey of the ILC, UN Doc. A/CN.4/471, para. 81.
[23] Ibid., para. 161.
[24] Commentary to Article 55 of the 2001 ASR, para. 2.
[25] Francisco Orrego Vicuna, 'Responsibility and Liability for Environmental Damage under International Law: Issues and Trends', final report prepared for the Eighth Committee of the Institut De Droit International, 285.

responsibility, whereas compensation for damage became the focus of international liability'.[26] For these reasons, this chapter employs the term 'State liability' rather than 'State responsibility' when referring to the legal consequences for breach of the international environmental obligations of the sponsoring State. Moreover, as the reflection on the ILC's work on international liability in the first chapter of this book has shown, it was precisely because of the poor adaptability of State responsibility to the subject matter of environmental protection that the new topic of international liability was initiated. The liability regimes involve not only States but also operators, and there are close connections between State liability and the liability of the operator when it comes to prevention and remediation of environmental damage.

8.2.3 *Connection between International Environmental Liabilities of the Sponsoring State and of the Contractor*

The international DSM regime does not touch upon the relationship between liabilities of the sponsoring State and of its sponsored operator. Yet, the SDC explored this issue. The SDC's basic position was that 'both forms of liability exist in parallel'.[27] As to the question of whether the liability of the sponsoring State is residual or complementary to that of the operator, the SDC's answers can be found in several paragraphs. In paragraph 200, in a reference to Article 22, Annex III to the UNCLOS, the SDC observed:

> No reference is made in this provision to the liability of sponsoring States. It may therefore be deducted that the main liability for a wrongful act committed in the conduct of the contractor's operations or in the exercise of the Authority's powers and functions rests with the contractor and the Authority, respectively, rather than with the sponsoring State.

After assigning the primary places to the contractor and the ISA in the DSM liability regime, the SDC went deeper into two different scenarios. In paragraph 202, it opined: 'if the contractor has paid the actual amount of damage, there is no room for reparation by the sponsoring State'. In paragraphs 203 and 204, it expressed that

[26] ILC, Third report on subtopic prevention of transboundary damage from hazardous activities, 2000. UN Doc. A/CN.4/510, para. 27.

[27] ITLOS, Advisory Opinion of 1 February 2011, paras. 201 and 204.

> [t]he situation becomes more complex if the contractor has not covered the damage fully. In the view of the Chamber, the liability regime established by article 139 of the Convention and in related instruments leaves no room for residual liability.

In short, the SDC pointed out correctly that, as far as the issue of establishment of liabilities is concerned, liability of the sponsoring State and liability of the contractor are independent from each other, they run in parallel. However, the SDC failed to elaborate fully on their connection. As has been examined carefully in Chapters 1 and 6, civil liability (that is, liability imposed on the operator) and State liability are a two-track system deliberately designed for better compensation for the damaged environment. In some cases, a third track, such as the compensation fund, might be designed to fill in the gap left by the two tracks. Be it a two-track system or three-layer or multilayer system, all forms of liability are triggered by the same environmental damage, and have the common goal to provide remedies to the same damaged environment which include primarily restoration and secondarily complementary or compensatory remediation.[28] Therefore, in my view, if both are established, liability of the sponsoring State and of the sponsored operator will be closely linked to each other. Putting it concretely, when it comes to distribution of the amount of payment, if the sponsoring State is obliged to pay, it will only pay the portion of damage which the contractor is unable to make whole. This idea was perfectly reflected in the second sentence of Article 8(3) of the CRAMRA: 'Such liability [i.e., liability of the sponsoring State] shall be limited to that portion of liability not satisfied by the Operator or otherwise.' The SDC touched upon that idea partially in paragraph 202; yet it stopped short of embracing it explicitly.

Another aspect of the connection between the international environmental liability of the sponsoring State and that of the contractor is whether the sponsoring State has residual liability *vis-à-vis* the primary liability of the contractor. In this respect, I agree with the SDC that under

[28] While acknowledging that damage is a point of connection between both forms of liability, the SDC did not see it as a critical factor which had effect on the relationship between liability of the sponsoring State and liability of the contractor. See the two sentences in para. 201, which states: 'there is only one point of connection, namely, that the liability of the sponsoring State depends upon the damage resulting from activities or omissions of the sponsored contractor. But, in the view of the Chamber, this is merely a trigger mechanism'. Apparently, the Chamber did not consider damage as the most fundamental basis for the liability regime. Nor did it consider the liability regime (including liabilities of the sponsoring State and the contractor) as a whole.

the current DSM legal regime there is no room for such residual liability. Here, a legal loophole on reparation of the damaged environment was discovered. As already pointed out by the SDC, 'situations may arise where a contractor does not meet its liability in full while the sponsoring State is not liable under article 139, paragraph 2, of the Convention'.[29] It continued, 'the Authority may wish to consider the establishment of a trust fund to compensate for the damage not covered'.[30] This subject has already been discussed in Section 7.3.

8.2.4 Forms and Contents of Liability: The Full Reparation Principle for Environmental Damage

As to the forms and content of international environmental liability of the sponsoring State, again, the discussions of the same issues concerning the contractor in Section 6.5 apply by analogy. The main ideas in Section 6.5 were: (a) restoration should be the primary form of reparation; (b) the criterion for reparation is 'the actual amount of damage'; and (c) reparation is substantially dependent on the definition and measure of environmental damage discussed in Chapter 5. These same ideas are also valid for international environmental liability of the sponsoring State. Additionally, this section further considers: whether, and if so to what extent, the full reparation principle is applicable to the sponsoring State in the context of DSM?

The Permanent Court of International Justice (PCIJ) elaborated on the meaning of the full reparation principle (*restituto in integrum*) in the *Factory at Chorzow* case as follows:

> The essential principle contained in the actual notion of an illegal act is that reparation must, as far as possible, wipe out all the consequences of the illegal act and reestablish the situation which would, in all probability, have existed if that act had not been committed. Restitution in kind, or, if this is not possible, payment of a sum corresponding to the value which a restitution in kind would bear; the award, if need be, of damages for loss sustained which would not be covered by restitution in kind or payment in place of it – such are the principles which should serve to determine the amount of compensation due for an act contrary to international law.[31]

[29] ITLOS, Advisory Opinion of 1 February 2011, para. 205.
[30] Ibid.
[31] PCIJ, *Factory at Chorzow case (merits)(Germany/Poland)*, Judgment of 26 July 1927, Series A, No. 13, 1928, 47.

The full reparation principle is one of the fundamental tenets in the general rule of State responsibility. It is described in Article 31 of the 2001 ASR as follows:

1. The responsible State is under an obligation to make full reparation for the injury caused by the internationally wrongful act.
2. Injury includes any damage, whether material or moral, caused by the internationally wrongful act of a State.

The full reparation principle was also endorsed by the International Law Institute (IDI)[32] and the United Nations Compensation Commission (UNCC)[33] as well as the SDC in the 2011 Advisory Opinion. When commenting on the amount of compensation of the sponsoring State, the SDC enunciated that

> [t]he obligation for a State to provide for a full compensation or *restituto in integrum* is currently part of customary international law[34] and that the provisions concerning liability of the contractor for the actual amount of damage [...] equally valid with regard to the liability of the sponsoring State.[35]

Apparently, the full reparation principle is widely accepted as the criterion for environmental compensation. The SDC considered the full reparation principle also applicable to international environmental liability of the sponsoring State.

However, the practical difficulties in applying the full reparation principle with regard to environmental damage[36] mark the limitations of the principle in the field of IEL and that the full reparation principle is not well adaptable to environmental liability regimes, in particular, the international environmental liabilities of the sponsoring State and of the ISA under discussion in this chapter. This same argument was made and

[32] International Law Institute, Responsibility and Liability under International Law for Environmental Damage, Session of Strasbourg, 1997, Article 25: 'full reparation of environmental damage should not result in the assessment of excessive, exemplary or punitive damages'.

[33] The fifth 'F4' report, 2005, para. 80. 'The overall criterion is always that of effective reparation for the wrongful act'. '[...]particular the principle that reparation must, as far as possible, wipe out all the consequences of the illegal act'.

[34] ITLOS, Advisory Opinion of 1 February 2011, para. 193.

[35] Ibid., para. 195.

[36] Again, attention should be drawn to the fact that I discuss in this book only the reparation of 'damage to the environment *per se*', while reparation of 'damage relating to death, personal injury or loss of property or economic value' is excluded.

systematically explained by Hardman Reis.[37] After an overview of compensation standards in international law, Hardman Reis closed a chapter by stating that

> [a]ll the reports analysed seems to have difficulties in applying the existing criteria [full compensation and adequate compensation] with regard to environmental damages. It seems that none of these standards are capable of remediating environmental damages.[38]

Gray and Greafrath emphasized that the full reparation principle is an abstract norm of a high level of generality the specific contents of which are left to be determined by more concrete rules. As Gray stated,

> The basic principle of full reparation cannot be a practical guide to the assessment of damages, as can be seen from the fact that although all legal systems share this aim, their methods of assessment and the results arrived at vary considerably and also that full compensation must be given content by particular detailed rules: it has no single, logically determined, fixed meaning.[39]

Similarly, Greafrath stated that

> [i]n general it is recognized that the purpose of reparation is 'to wipe out all consequences of the wrongful act'. Scholars, however, agree that only a broad orientation is given by this formula. On the one hand, it would very rarely be possible to wipe out all consequences of a wrongful act – if simply for the reason that dead persons cannot be revived. On the other hand, however, it is not so easy to determine all the consequences that have to be covered by the duty to reparation.[40]

It is not problematic that the content of the full reparation principle is not yet determined. Yet, it would be problematic if the concrete rules with respect to the measure of damage were lacking. Unfortunately, that is the case for environmental liability regimes. The largest problem in environmental cases is that methods for assessing environmental damage are controversial and environmental damage cannot be measured with accuracy. How can the full reparation principle be implemented if one

[37] Tarcisio Hardman Reis, *Compensation for Environmental Damages under International Law – The Role of the International Judge* (Wolters Kluwer 2011).

[38] Ibid., 114.

[39] Christine Gray, *Judicial Remedies in International Law* (Clarendon 1987) 7.

[40] Bernard Graefrath, 'Responsibility and Damages Caused: Relationship between Responsibility and Damages' (1984-II) 185 RdC 94.

does not even know what precisely the environmental damage is? Indeed, a failure to give a satisfactory answer to this question will reasonably lead to doubt about the adaptability of the full reparation principle to the environmental liability regime.

Considering that the SDC did not go into detailed discussion on the questions of how to define and assess environmental damage, it is not surprising that it failed to point out the mutual influences between the measure of environmental damage and the reparation. Suppose that the impracticality of the full reparation principle is agreed, what would be the alternative? An answer is by no means easy to give. For Hardman Reis who conducted in-depth research into this specific topic, he turned to analyse the relevance of equity elements in the establishment of fair compensation which in his opinion was more adaptable to environmental liability than the standard of full compensation. From there, he moved further to work out a framework of four elements for compensation for environmental damages.[41] In the end, he advocated for a case-by-case approach[42] and correspondingly appealed to subjectivity as a result of accepting the role played by international judges.[43] Taking into account the inherent difficulty in measuring environmental damage, Hardman Reis' proposal might be more realistic.

As to the forms of the reparation, Article 34 of the 2001 ILC ASR lists restitution, compensation and satisfaction. In the area of environment law, restoration of the damaged environment is the primary purpose of the reparation. Therefore, restitution is the preferred form of reparation, while compensation as a form might also be resorted to because restoration is not always feasible, as has been commented, 'it is the view of the Chamber that the form of reparation will depend on both the actual damage and the technical feasibility of restoring the situation to the *status quo ante*'.[44]

[41] In the last part of the book, Hardman Reis makes once again clear: 'in the present study, it was defended that the criteria of full restitution commonly adopted in international law, is not properly adapted to environmental damages'. Tarcisio Hardman Reis, *Compensation for Environmental Damages under International Law – The Role of the International Judge* (Wolters Kluwer 2011) 157.

[42] Tarcisio Hardman Reis, *Compensation for Environmental Damages under International Law – The Role of the International Judge* (Wolters Kluwer 2011) 158.

[43] Please note the subtitle of the book: 'the role of the international judge'.

[44] ITLOS, Advisory Opinion of 1 February 2011, para. 197.

8.2.5 *Invocation of Liability of the Sponsoring State:* Locus Standi

8.2.5.1 The Issue of Invocation under the ILC's 2001 Articles on State Responsibility

Concerning the issue of invocation, there is no distinction made between the two concepts of State liability *ex delicto* and State responsibility. Thus, this section first draws on the ILC's 2001 ASR. The core question concerning the invocation of State responsibility is, from a substantive perspective, who has the right or legal interest and therefore is entitled to invoke State responsibility; this is, from a procedural perspective, the issue of *locus standi*.[45] The ILC's 2001 ASR presents two categories of subject who are entitled and have the *locus standi* to invoke State responsibility: the injured State and the State other than the injured State (also referred to as 'the non-injured state' or 'the third party'). Then how to define the scope of 'the injured State' and 'the State other than the injured State' on whom is conferred the right to invoke State responsibility?

The ILC prescribes three different situations under which a State can be regarded as the injured State in Article 42 as follows:

> A State is entitled as an injured State to invoke the responsibility of another State if the obligation breached is owed to:
>
> (a) that State individually; or
> (b) a group of States including that State, or the international community as a whole, and the breach of the obligation:
>
> (i) specifically affects that State; or
> (ii) is of such a character as radically to change the position of all the other States to which the obligation is owed with respect to the further performance of the obligation.

The first situation is stipulated in Article 42(a). It should be indicated here, however, that by the phrase 'the obligation breached is owed to a State individually' is meant the primary obligation is of a bilateral character, while the legal sources from which the obligation derives are not necessarily in bilateral forms. For that reason, a State party to a multilateral treaty can claim against another party as long as a bilateral legal relation exists between the party who makes the claim and the party who is alleged to breach the obligation. To illustrate this point: for

[45] Under the 2001 ASR, invocation of State responsibility means 'taking measures of a relatively formal character'. Commentary to Article 42 of the ILC's 2001 ASR, para. 2.

instance, the Vienna Convention on Diplomatic Relations is a multilateral treaty. Yet, the obligation under Article 22 to protect the premises of a mission is owed to the sending State individually, this obligation is thus of a bilateral character.[46] This kind of multilateral treaties is considered as 'giving rise to bundles of bilateral relations'[47] or 'containing dyads of bilateral relationships'.[48] In the same vein, bilateral obligations can also be created in other legal forms, such as, unilateral commitment, judicial decisions and general or customary international law. Simply put, the key requirement to make use of Article 42(a) is that the primary obligation, whatever its sources, can be differentiated or individualized.[49]

By contrast, the two other situations as stipulated in Article 42(b)(i) and (ii) are totally different. Because under these two situations the legal relation under primary rules is between the State which has allegedly breached the obligation and a group of States or the international community as a whole. The primary obligation is not bilateral in its nature since it cannot be differentiated or individualized. In this sense, they are closer to the situations depicted in Article 48(1) as follows:

> Any State other than an injured State is entitled to invoke the responsibility of another State in accordance with paragraph 2 if:
>
> the obligation breached is owed to a group of States including that State, and is established for the protection of a collective interest of the group; or
>
> the obligation breached is owed to the international community as a whole.

If the primary obligations described in Article 42(b) and Article 48(1) are not different – both are bilateral in their nature, then the question is why a State is regarded as the injured State in Article 42(b) but a third party in Article 48(1). In comparison with Article 48(1), Article 42(b) contains additional conditions, namely the State is 'specifically affected' by the breach of the obligation. This condition promotes a State as a third party to an injured State. However, Article 42 (b)(i) 'does not define the nature or extent of the special impact that a State must have sustained in order

46 Commentary to Article 42 of the 2001 ASR, para. 8.
47 Ibid.
48 Jan Klabbers, 'The Community Interest in the Law of Treaties: Ambivalent Conceptions', in Ulrich Fastenrath et al. (eds.), *From Bilateralism to Community Interest: Essays in Honour of Bruno Simma* (OUP 2011).
49 Ibid.

to be considered "injured". This will have to be assessed on a case-by-case basis, having regard to the object and purpose of the primary obligation breached and the facts of each case'.[50] One condition in Article 42(b)(ii) is that 'the breach of the obligation is of such a character as it radically changes the position of all other States to which the obligation is owed with respect to the further performance of the obligation'. The subparagraph deals with a special category of obligations, the 'integral' or 'interdependent' obligations, the breach of which must be considered as affecting *per se* every other State to which the obligation is owed.[51] According to the ILC, interdependent obligations covered by Article 42(b)(ii) will usually arise under treaties establishing particular regimes.[52] In this case, every party to this type of the treaty is qualified as the injured State if the breach places the very existence of the regime under peril. Therefore, although the nature of the primary obligation does not differ between Articles 42(b) and 48(1), the effects of the breach of the primary obligations differ. It is this difference in the effect of the breach, namely the different new legal relation under the secondary rule, that distinguishes these two articles.

It is revealed from the analysis above that there are actually two criteria underlying the categorization of the situations stipulated in Articles 42 and 48. One criterion is the nature of the primary obligation, based on which the bilateral obligation involving individual interests (Article 42 (a)) is distinguished from the multilateral obligation seeking to safeguard the collective interests (Article 42(b) and 48(1)). The other criterion is the nature of the legal relation under the secondary rule, based on which the situations where a State can be singled out as the injured State (Article 42) are separated from the situations where singling out a State with a special interest of its own is not possible (Article 48(1)). The first criterion plays a fundamental role in shaping the conceptualization process through which the invocation system is designed. Yet, with respect to the provisions, it seems the ILC employs only the second criterion which results in the usage of such a pair of binary notions as 'the injured State' (Article 42) and 'the State other than the injured State' (Article 48). As to the relationship between the two articles, the ILC states clearly that Article 48 complements the rule contained in Article 42.[53] Implicitly, the invocation by the injured State under Article 42 would prevail over

[50] Commentary to Article 42 of the ILC's 2001 ASR, para. 12.
[51] Ibid., para. 13.
[52] Ibid., para. 15.
[53] Commentary to Article 48 of the ILC's 2001 ASR, para. 1.

that by the State other than the injured State under Article 48 if invocations under both articles were to occur simultaneously.

Indeed, it is generally acknowledged that the well-known obiter dictum of the 1970 *Barcelona Traction* case[54] ushered in a new era with respect to understanding the nature of obligations as well as invocation of State responsibility. Following this line, there is enormous amount of scholarly discussion about the concepts of '*obligations erga omnes*', 'multilateral obligations', 'international community', '*Jus Cogens*' and others which reflect community interests, as has been shown in Chapter 2. There are also cases before the International Court of Justice (ICJ) where the 1970 *Barcelona Traction* case's *obiter dictum* was reaffirmed.[55] Within the ILC, there had been decades of fierce debates over the inclusion of invocation by a third party.[56] Ultimately, Articles 42 and 48 were included in the 2001 ASR. 'The recognition that States may have a range of legal interests in the performance of obligations where they are not the primary beneficiaries of those obligations is an important step forward.'[57]

Being aware that traditionally the entitlement to invoke State responsibility was vested only in the injured State,[58] it is not surprising that Article 48 appeared innovative. Admittedly, even though the key notions within Article 48 have already been discussed for decades, their conceptual meaning is still not entirely settled.[59] Moreover, when Article 48 is implemented, it will encounter many theoretical as well as practical problems. First, are there accompanied procedures through which claims for the protection of common interests can be made? If not, should

[54] ICJ, *Case concerning The Barcelona Traction, Light and Power Co., Ltd (Second Phase) (Belgium v. Spain)*, Judgment of 5 February 1970, para. 33.

[55] For instance: *East Timor (Portugal v. Australia)*, Judgment of 30 June 1995, para. 29; *Application of the Convention on the Prevention and Punishment of the Crime of Genocide (Bosnia and Herzegovina v. Yugoslavia)*, Judgment of 11 July 1996 (preliminary objection), para. 31; *Legal Consequences of the Construction of a Wall in the Occupied Palestinian Territory*, the advisory opinion of 9 July 2004, para. 88; and *Application of Convention on the Prevention and Punishment of Crime of Genocide (The Gambia v. Myanmar)*, Judgment of 22 July 2022 (preliminary objection), para. 107.

[56] Article 40 of the Draft Articles on State Responsibility (first reading), 1998.

[57] James Crawford, 'Responsibility to the International Community as a Whole' (2001) 8(2) *Ind. J. Global Legal Stud* 319.

[58] Jonathan Charney, 'Third State Remedies in International Law' (1989) 10 *Mich. J. Int'l L.* 57–101.

[59] For instance, who will and how to identify obligations *erga omnes*? To whom exactly are obligations *erga omnes* owed to? In Crawford's words, that is, what is lurking behind the Latin phrase '*erga omnes*'?

procedures be designed, and if so, how?[60] Secondly, what to do if there are concurrent invocations? Thirdly, what are the limitations of Article 48? Is obligation *erga omnes* owed to the international community as a whole, including not only all States but also all individuals and entities? Are those non-State actors also entitled to invoke State responsibility for breach of obligations *erga omnes*? If so, how to accommodate this into the existing inter-State international law system? Or to think reversely, should international law be developed in order to catch up with the new international reality/ideal? There are still continuing discussions over these questions. In the following section, however, I will not join these discussions in a general sense, but will try to raise the problems and the attempted answers with regard to application of Article 42 and particularly Article 48 in the context of DSM.

8.2.5.2 Invocation of Liability of the Sponsoring State in the Context of Deep Seabed Mining

The core question in this subsection is that of *locus standi*, namely who has the legal standing to appear before a judicial body to invoke liability of the sponsoring State. This question constitutes a procedural barrier which needs to be overcome before a case can go into the merits phase if invocation of liability is made before a judicial body. In the absence of an answer in the UNCLOS, it is suggested that States Parties to the UNCLOS and the ISA have standing, with the ISA being the better choice.

Scenario A: Invocation by States Following the approach adopted by the ILC's 2001 ASR, the liability of the sponsoring State could be invoked by an injured State or a State other than an injured State. The application of Article 42 of the 2001 ILC ASR in the context of DSM is relatively easy: any State the rights and legitimate interests of which are specifically affected by the internationally wrongful acts of the sponsoring State is certainly entitled to invoke liability of the sponsoring State. Since the Area and its resources are declared as the common heritage of mankind (CHM),[61] and States are considered as having common interests in the

[60] The backwardness of the procedural aspect with respect to obligations *erga omnes* is highlighted by Shabtai Rosenne, 'Some Reflections *Erga Omnes*', in Antony Anghie, and Garry Sturgess (eds.), *Legal Visions of the 21st Century: Essays in Honour of Judge Christopher Weeramantry* (Kluwer 1998), 512, 518 and 520.

[61] Article 136, UNCLOS.

use of resources in the Area and the protection of the marine environment, a non-injured State could also invoke liability of the sponsoring State via application of Article 48 of the 2001 ILC ASR. Under this article, a State Party to a treaty can invoke liability of another State Party for protecting the common interests under the convention, and any States (including non-States Parties) can invoke liability of a State Party if it is for the protection of the common interests of the international community as a whole. Both means of invocation are possible in the context of the DSM regime.

However, invocation by a State Party to the UNCLOS is more practical because the dispute settlement mechanism under the UNCLOS is available for States Parties only. Article 187(a) of the UNCLOS prescribes that the SDC has jurisdiction over 'disputes between States Parties concerning the interpretation or application of this Part and the Annexes relating thereto'. Moreover, Article 188(1) states that

> [d]isputes between States Parties referred to in Article 187, subparagraph (a), may be submitted:
>
> (a) at the request of the parties to the dispute, to a special chamber of the International Tribunal for the Law of the Sea to be formed in accordance with Annex VI, articles 15 and 17; or
> (b) at the request of any party to the dispute, to an ad hoc chamber of the Seabed Disputes Chamber to be formed in accordance with Annex VI, article 36.

Invocation by a non-State Party will encounter a practical problem, namely the lack of a compulsory judicial mechanism. The ICJ could have jurisdiction under Article 36(2) of the Statute of the International Court of Justice. However, such a mechanism is still preconditioned on the consent of the States.

Despite the availability of judicial dispute settlement mechanisms, there are other potential problems with the invocation of liability of the sponsoring State by States Parties. Following Article 48(a) of the 2001 ILC ASR, each individual State Party is entitled to invoke liability of the sponsoring State. Since each State is entitled to invoke liability, theoretically, there might be a situation where two or more States invoke liability of the sponsoring State simultaneously. This is the first potential problem of concurrent invocation. The UNCLOS embodies a procedure for coordinating claims. Article 32 of the International Tribunal for the Law of the Sea (ITLOS) Statute prescribes the right to intervene in cases of interpretation or application as follows:

1. Whenever the interpretation or application of this Convention is in question, the Registrar shall notify all States Parties forthwith. [. . .]
3. Every party referred to in paragraphs 1 and 2 has the right to intervene in the proceedings; if it uses this right, the interpretation given by the judgment will be equally binding upon it.

Through the procedural mechanism of intervention, the problem of concurrent invocation is solved. Second, even though concurrent invocation is not problematic, some might worry that recognition of the entitlement of each individual State to invoke liability of the sponsoring State might open the floodgates of international litigation against the sponsoring State, thereby significantly increasing the legal risk of sponsoring DSM activities. Third, and conversely, others might argue that empowerment of everyone is tantamount to empowerment of no-one because of the classic free rider problem. To illustrate, a key example can be found in the area of international human rights protection. Although established as an enforcement mechanism in almost all human rights treaties, the interstate complaint mechanisms are rarely used in reality. One might argue that what makes States reluctant to accuse other States of breaching their human right obligations will also make States reluctant to invoke liability of the sponsoring State for breaching its international obligations in the context of DSM. Finally, one may also contend that invocation of liability of the sponsoring State by a State Party carries the risk of being politicized. For instance, a non-sponsoring State Party might use the entitlement to invoke liability of the sponsoring State as a weapon to check the right of the latter for the sake of its own economic interests rather than the common interest of mankind. Although only hypothetical, the potential problems outlined above cannot be ruled out. It thus seems that invocation of liability by States Parties is far from ideal. Accordingly, the ISA's role as a guardian of the common heritage of mankind is examined next.

Scenario B: Invocation by the International Seabed Authority The ISA is also entitled to invoke liability of the sponsoring State. There are two channels through which it can do so. On the one hand, the ISA can invoke liability of the sponsoring State through political channels. Article 162(2)(a) of the UNCLOS states that the Council is empowered to 'supervise and coordinate the implementation of the provisions of this Part on all questions and matters within the competence of the Authority and invite the attention of the Assembly to cases of non-compliance'. On the other hand, the ISA can invoke liability of the sponsoring State through the judicial channel. Article 162(2)(u) of the UNCLOS states that the Council shall 'institute proceedings on behalf of the Authority before the SDC in cases of non-compliance'. Moreover, a judicial dispute settlement mechanism is available. Pursuant to Article 187(b)(i) of the UNCLOS, the SDC has jurisdiction over 'disputes between a State Party and the Authority concerning acts or omissions of a State Party alleged to be in violation of this Part or the Annexes relating thereto or of rules, regulations and procedures of the Authority adopted in accordance therewith'. It is therefore undoubtable that, under the DSM legal regime, the ISA is entitled to invoke liability of the sponsoring State either through the political or judicial channel, and there is a judicial dispute settlement mechanism available.

In comparison to invocation of liability by States Parties to the UNCLOS, the advantages of the invocation by the ISA are obvious. Namely, all of the potential problems analysed above concerning invocation by individual States can be avoided. First, there will be no concurrent invocations. Secondly, the invocation cannot be omitted or deliberately avoided, that is, the ISA has to invoke the liability of the sponsoring State when non-compliance occurs, otherwise the liability of the ISA itself would arise. Thirdly, the invocation of liability would be less likely to be used as a weapon against the sponsoring States to further the economic interests of non-sponsoring States since the decision is made by the ISA as an organization.

However, there is one drawback to the invocation of liability by the ISA. This drawback is related to the composition and decision-making procedure of the Council. According to section 3 of the annex to the 1994 Agreement, decisions of the Council are normally made on the consent of its members. Considering that most sponsoring States are members of the Council, this means that if the Council intends to invoke liability of a sponsoring State which is a member of the Council, the Council must obtain the consent of the sponsoring State itself. This procedural arrangement paralyses the functioning of the Council. The problem could be resolved by amending or interpreting the decision-making procedure, for instance, by requiring the State whose liability is at issue not to participate in the decision-making procedure. Upon comparison, it seems that the advantages of invocation by the ISA prevail.

8.2.6 Conclusions

This section examines the establishment, forms and content and invocation of international environmental liability of the sponsoring State.

International environmental liability of the sponsoring State is identified as State liability *ex delicto* distinct from the notion of State responsibility. Also, it is found that the connection between the international environmental liabilities of the sponsoring State and of the contractor lies in the fact that they face the same environmental damage and share the same aim of reparation for that damage.[62] The overall position of this section is that the ILC's 2001 ASR is not well adapted to the field of environmental protection; the notion of liability is preferable because it has environmental damage and compensation rather than internationally wrongful acts at its core. It is necessary to take note of the subtle differences between these two notions and to consider which parts of the ILC's 2001 ASR apply to the liability regime and which do not. However, in giving its 2011 Advisory Opinion, the SDC completely followed the line of State responsibility as described in the 2001 ILC ASR; it failed to pay attention to the particularity of the liability regime in the field of environmental protection. This constitutes the main defect of the 2011 Advisory Opinion of the SDC. Such defect includes three aspects. With regard to the establishment of liability of the sponsoring State, the SDC did not explain the departure of the liability regimes in the context of DSM from the fundamental principle of State responsibility, namely 'every internationally wrongful act of State entails State responsibility'. With regard to reparation, the SDC did not give due attention to the practical difficulties in applying the full reparation principle with respect to environmental damage. This is related to the greatest flaw, which is the SDC did not take up the difficult task of defining and measuring damage to the marine environment which, however, constitutes the core of both establishing international environmental liability and reparation.[63]

[62] A similar statement can be made with regard to the connection between environmental liabilities of the contractor and the ISA. Plakokefalos regards these liabilities as 'shared responsibility' which 'refers to the instances where a multiplicity of actors contributes to a single harmful outcome'. See Ilias Plakokokefalos, 'The Practice of Shared Responsibility in relation to Environmental Protection of the Deep Seabed' SHARES Research Paper 94 (2016). The conceptual clarification of the term 'shared responsibility' can be found in Andre Nollkaemper and Dov Jacobs, 'Shared Responsibility in International Law: A Conceptual Framework' (2013) 34(2) *MIJIL* 359–438. This research follows the conceptual frameworks concerning 'state responsibility' and 'international liability' of the ILC in general.

[63] As it is expressed in the context of the CBD: 'establishing the damage to biodiversity as a result of an incident is a fundamental step in applying liability and redress rules. The determination would provide the basis to establish the extent of actual restoration

With respect to the invocation of liability of the sponsoring State, it is argued that owing to the silence of the UNCLOS, the related part of the 2001 ILC ASR is applicable. Following the ILC's approach, international environmental liability of the sponsoring State could be invoked by injured States or third parties. However, in the specific context of DSM, apart from States, the ISA serves as the guardian of the marine environment and is thus entitled to invoke international environmental liability of the sponsoring State. Moreover, the invocation of the ISA is a preferable choice because, as a centralized international administrator, the ISA is not motivated by individual interests and thus can better safeguard the community interests through the implementation of liability of the sponsoring State.

8.3 International Environmental Liability of the International Seabed Authority

8.3.1 Establishment and Contents of International Environmental Liability of the ISA

Article 22, Annex III to the UNCLOS prescribes that

> [t]he Authority shall have responsibility or liability for any damage arising out of wrongful acts in the exercise of its powers and functions, including violations under article 168, paragraph 2, account being taken of contributory acts or omissions by the contractor. Liability in every case shall be for the actual amount of damage.

Thus, three constituent elements need to be met to establish international environmental liability of the ISA: internationally wrongful acts of the ISA, environmental damage and the causal link between the two. This is the same as establishing international environmental liability of the contractor and sponsoring State. As to the forms and content of liability, again it is the same as for the contractor and sponsoring State. The primary form is restoration, namely to restore the overall functioning

needed, any additional complementary and compensatory measures, then, their cost and, ultimately, who will be liable for them'. (para. 5) 'A clear definition of damage to biodiversity would be central to the application of any liability and redress rules.' (para. 7) See 'liability and redress in the context of paragraph 2 of article 14 of the convention on biological diversity: synthesis report on technical information relating to damage to biological diversity and approaches to valuation and restoration of damage to biological diversity, as well as information on national/domestic measures and experiences', UNEP/CBD/COP/9/20/Add.1, 20 March 2008.

of marine ecosystems. If restoration is not possible or if there is interim loss, then compensation is required. The content for liability is 'the actual amount of damage'. Thus, any discussions concerning the conditions for the establishment, forms and content of international environmental liabilities of the contractor and the sponsoring State would apply *mutatis mutandis* to the ISA. However, the issue of liability of the ISA as an international organization raises a special question: whether and, if so, in what situations are member States held liable for the ISA?

8.3.2 *Liability of Member States for Acts of International Organizations*

8.3.2.1 Account of the General Rule

Since the DSM legal regime is silent on the issue of liability of member States for the acts of the ISA,[64] to answer the question raised above, reference must be made to other relevant instruments. The following three instruments are examined below: the 1995 resolution on 'the legal consequences for member states of the non-fulfilment by international organizations of their obligations toward third parties' by the Institute of International Law (the 1995 IDI Resolution), the 2004 resolution on the 'accountability of international organizations' by the International Law Association (the 2004 ILA Resolution) and the 2011 Articles on the Responsibility of International Organizations of the ILC (the 2011 ILC ARIO).[65] Upon examination, it is shown that there is a 'no liability of member States' rule which is subject to certain exceptions.

[64] However, it is written in Article 3, Annex IV to the UNCLOS that 'without prejudice to article 11, paragraph 3, of this Annex, no member of the Authority shall be liable by reason only of its membership for the acts or obligations of the Enterprise'. From this article, it might infer that the drafter of the UNCLOS would take the same position that members of the ISA shall not be liable by reason only of its membership for the acts of the ISA as an international regulator.

[65] The ILC's work on the codification and progressive development of the general rule of the responsibility of international organizations had lasted for about a decade (2002–2011). Subsequent to the close of the project on State responsibility in 2001, the ILC launched the project on responsibility of international organizations. Gaja was appointed as the Special Rapporteur in 2002. From 2003 to 2009, for a consecutive seven years, Gaja submitted seven reports, one each year. In 2009, the first reading of the draft articles was completed. Following the consideration of the comments and observations received from governments and international organizations, the second reading of the draft articles was finished in 2011. In the same year, the final draft article was adopted by the General Assembly of the UN by Resolution 100. See: ILC, Draft Articles on the Responsibility of International Organizations, with Commentaries, Yearbook of the International Law

There is a consensus that an international organization possessing international legal personality is responsible for breach of its obligations.[66] However, the answer to the question of whether member States of an international organization are liable for the acts of the organization is not consistent.[67] In Amerasinghe's opinion, different answers to the question can derive from the different interpretations of the implication of the international legal personality of the organization. As he observed when commenting on the *International Tin Council* cases before English courts:

> From a conceptual standpoint, it becomes important to establish what the nature of the juridical personality of an international organization basically involves in regard to liability; that is, whether, in the absence of any positive indications in the constituent instrument, there is a presumption flowing from the concept of international judicial personality that members of an organization assume concurrent or secondary liability for its obligations, or whether their liability in this respect is limited.[68]

Nonetheless, a prevailing opinion can be identified: member State shall not be liable for acts of the international organization by reason only of their membership to that organization. Such an opinion is reflected in Article 6 of the 1995 IDI Resolution:

> Save as specified in Article 5, there is no general rule of international law whereby states members are, due solely to their membership, liable concurrently or subsidiarily for the obligations of an international organization of which they are members.

Commission, 2011, Vol. II, Part Two; And UN General Assembly Resolution, UN Doc. A/RES/66/100. Despite challenges to the desirability or feasibility and the approach adopted by the ILC, discussions on the topic of responsibility or liability of international organizations among researchers have been very much revolving around the work of the ILC.

66 ICJ, *interpretation of the Agreement of 25 March 1951 between the WHO and Egypt (advisory opinion), 1980*, para. 37; Article 3 of the 1995 IDI Resolution; Alain Pellet, 'International Organizations Are Definitely Not States: Cursory Remarks on the ILC Articles on the Responsibility of International Organizations', in Maurizio Ragazzi (ed.), *Responsibility of International Organizations: Essays in Memory of Sir Ian Brownlie* (Martinus Nijhoff 2013) 42; and Matthias Hartwig, 'Responsibility and Liability of International Organizations or Institutions', MPEPIL (last updated in May 2011), para. 11.

67 Amerasinghe examined the opinions of Adam, Seidl-Hohenveldern, Schermers, Mann and Shihata on the topic of responsibility of member states for the acts of the organization and concluded that there was 'evidently serious disagreement' among them. See C. F. Amerasinghe, 'Liability to Third Parties of Member States of International Organizations: Practice, Principle and Judicial Precedent' (1991) 85(2) *AJIL* 259–280.

68 Ibid., 276.

The same opinion is expressed in the 2011 ILC Articles on the Responsibility of International Organizations (ARIO): 'membership does not as such entail for member States international responsibility when the organization commits an internationally wrongful act'.[69] It is also the mainstream opinion as demonstrated in literature. For instance, Hartwig contended,

> Responsibility of the member States for the acts of the international organization based on their membership cannot be established under international law. The introduction of such a responsibility for membership, be it joint and several, concurrent, subsidiary, or whatever, would run counter to the idea of inter-State co-operation through independent international organizations, because to the extent to which the member States will be held liable for the actions of the international organization they will try to keep them under control.[70]

For Hartwig, the purpose of preserving the autonomy of the organization serves as the reason to argue against the responsibility of member States for the acts of the organization. That very same reason also underpinned the statement of Niels Blokker who took a clear position that 'denying or restricting *responsabilité distincte* can in the end sacrifice the *volonté distincte* which is sought'.[71]

Apparently, a high value is placed on the autonomy of the international organization: international legal personality of the organization

[69] Commentary to Article 62, the 2011 ILC ARIO. Gaja explained briefly that 'Article 62 is based on the idea that, given the separate legal personality of the organization, responsibility does not as a rule fall on its members. There are two exceptions which do not contradict this principle.' (Giorgio Gaja, 'Articles on Responsibility of International Organizations' UN Audiovisual Library of International Law, New York, 9 December 2011, para. 12. Available at: http://legal.un.org/avl/ha/ario/ario.html). The text of article 62 is dedicated to the two situations where member States are responsible for the acts of international organizations; the commentary to the article, however, mainly elaborates the rule that member States are in principle not responsible for the acts of international organizations. This book does not subscribe to the approach of the ILC but agrees with Amerasinghe that 'article 62 should be framed differently. It should be made clear initially that in general the rule is that member States are not *per se* responsible for the unlawful acts of an organization which has international personality. Exceptionally, responsibility may arise, as stated in Article 62 (1) (a) and (b)'. (C. F. Amerasinghe, 'Comments on the ILC's Draft Articles on the Responsibility of International Organizations' (2012) 9 *IOLR* 29–31, 30).

[70] Matthias Hartwig, 'Responsibility and Liability of International Organizations or Institutions', MPEPIL (last updated in May 2011), para. 32.

[71] Niels Blokker, 'International Organizations and Their Members: "International Organizations Belongs to All Members and to None" – Variations on a Theme' (2004) 1 *IOLR* 139–161, 161.

serves as a firewall which excludes member States from assuming responsibility of the organization. With this understanding, a prevailing opinion arises that member States are not in principle liable for acts of international organizations.[72] This prevailing opinion is dubbed as the 'no liability of member states' rule in this section.

However, the 'no liability of member states' rule is not absolute; there are situations in which responsibility or liability is attributed, jointly or subsidiarily, to member States, albeit the conduct in itself is attributed to the organization.[73] In this respect, reference can, in the first place, be made to Part V (Articles 58 to 63) of the 2011 ILC ARIO. Articles 58, 59 and 60 are modelled on the 2001 ILC ASR, describing those respective situations where a State aids or assists, directs or controls and coerces an international organization in the latter's commission of an internationally wrongful act.[74] In these situations, responsibility is attributed to the State provided that certain conditions are met. Here, the State involved is not restricted only to the member State of the organization. In contrast, Articles 61 and 62 deal only with member States.[75] Article 62 stipulates two general exceptions to the 'no liability of member states' rule. In accordance with paragraph 1(a), a State may be held directly responsible

[72] There is an opposite view. For instance, Yee strongly argued for a concurrent or joint and several responsibility regime; his opinion remained unchanged before and after the adoption of the 2011 ILC ARIO. Sienho Yee, 'The Responsibility of States Members of an International Organization for its Conduct as a Result of Membership or Their Normal Conduct Associated with Membership', in Maurizio Ragazzi (ed.), *International Responsibility Today – Essays in Memory of Oscar Schachter* (Martinus Nijhoff 2005); Sienho Yee, 'Member Responsibility and the ILC Articles on the Responsibility of International Organizations: Some Observations', in Maurizio Ragazzi (ed.), *Responsibility of International Organizations: Essays in Memory of Sir Ian Brownlie* (Martinus Nijhoff 2013).

[73] Please note the distinction between 'attribution of act' and 'attribution of responsibility' in this section. 'Attribution of act' is used in similar manner as Part II of the 2001 ILC ARS; it means 'the process by which international law establishes whether the conduct of a natural person or other intermediary can be considered as an "act of the organization"' (James Crawford, *State Responsibility* (CUP 2013) 113). While 'attribution of responsibility' is used for the purpose of accommodating the situations where ancillary and secondary responsibility are involved. See Yifeng Chen, 'Attribution, Causation and Responsibility of International Organization', in Dan Sarooshi (ed.), *Remedies and Responsibility for the Actions of International Organizations* (Martinus Nijhoff 2014); See also Jean D'Aspremont, 'Abuse of the Legal Personality of International Organizations and the Responsibility of Member States' (2007) 4 *IOLR* 91–119.

[74] Articles 58, 59 and 60 of the 2011 ILC ARIO correspond respectively to Articles 16, 17 and 18 of the 2001 ILC ARS.

[75] Commentary to Part V of the 2011 ILC ARIO, para. 4.

for the conduct of the organization if 'it has accepted the responsibility towards the injured party'. This situation of the responsibility of member States is, as the ILC put it, the least controversial. In a similar vein, to protect the reasonable interests of reliance on the third party, paragraph 1(b) prescribes that a member State shall be responsible if 'it has led the injured party to rely on its responsibility'. Article 61, however, prescribes a situation strikingly different from those in Articles 58, 59, 60 and 62. It stipulates,

1. A State member of an international organization incurs international responsibility if, by taking advantage of the fact that the organization has competence in relation to the subject matter of one of the State's international obligations, it circumvents that obligation by causing the organization to commit an act that, if committed by the State, would have constituted a breach of the obligation.
2. Paragraph 1 applies whether or not the act in question is internationally wrongful for the international organization.

This is a novel provision which cannot find a parallel in the 2001 ILC ASR. It is analogous to the 'piercing the corporate veil' rule in company laws of most domestic legal systems; for this reason, Article 61 is regarded as the 'piercing the organizational veil' provision. How, then, does the 'piercing the organizational veil' situation differ from the situations described in the other four articles? In the first place, under Articles 58, 59, 60 and 62, States are held responsible for the organization only if the act of the organization is internationally wrongful. That is, internationally wrongful act on the part of the organization is the precondition for the attribution of responsibility to States. In such situations, State responsibility is always concurrent with the responsibility of the organization. However, under Article 61, the act is not necessarily an internationally wrongful act for the organization. The responsibility of the State can occur without the responsibility or liability on the part of the organization. In fact, it is more likely that the act is not internationally wrongful for the organization but would be wrongful if it is committed by the State. In other words, the State deliberately seeks acts of the organization with an intention to avoid potential State responsibility; 'the existence of an intention to avoid compliance is implied in the use of the term "circumvention"'.[76] This reveals the second difference between Article 61 and the other articles.

[76] Commentary to Article 61 of the 2011 ILC ARIO, para. 2.

A subjective element is required in the establishment of responsibility of the member State under Article 61. This is not only in contrast to Articles 58, 59, 60 and 62, but also departs from the overall attempt to build an objective system of secondary rules in the 2011 ILC ARIO. Thirdly, under Articles 58, 59, 60 and 62, international legal personality of the organization is respected. However, under Article 61, the independent legal personality of the organization is denied.

In sum, Part V of the 2011 ILC ARIO constitutes an important attempt to codify or progressively develop comprehensive rules with regard to responsibility of a State in connection with the acts of an international organization. The situations described in Articles 58, 59 and 60 are those where injuries are caused concomitantly by the international organization and the State; the nature of the responsibility of the State can be either concurrent or subsidiary. The situations in Article 62 are prescribed in light of the general principle of international law; the nature of the responsibility of member States is subsidiary.[77] And the situation in Article 61 concerns the responsibility of the member State, irrespective of the responsibility on the part of the organization. Yet, it generates new issue of the extent to which the international legal personality of the organization should be denied.[78]

In the second place, Article 5 of the 1995 IDI Resolution is also relevant. First, it prescribes that the rules adopted by the organization provide the legal basis for the liability of the member States and, in particular circumstances, a relevant general principle of international law can also be the legal basis.[79] Secondly, it also endorses the situation of the acceptance of liability by member States as depicted in Article 62, paragraph 1(a), of the 2011 ILC ARIO as an exception to the 'no liability of member states' rule.[80] Finally, it includes the situation that 'the international organization has acted as the agent of the State, in law or

[77] Article 62(2), the 2011ARIO.

[78] Criticism of an earlier draft of Article 61 can be found, for instance, in D'Aspremont's comment. He contends that 'draft article 28 is unsatisfactory' because it 'only embodies situations of the *provision of competence* to the organization with the aim of circumventing international obligations binding the member states' but 'fails to embody cases where member states abuse the legal personality of the international organization *at the decision-making level* when exerting overwhelming control over the decision-making process of the organization'. Jean D'Aspremont, 'Abuse of the Legal Personality of International Organizations and the Responsibility of Member States' (2007) 4 *IOLR* 91–119.

[79] Article 5, paragraphs (a) and (b) of the 1995 IDI Resolution.

[80] Article 5, paragraph (c) (i) of the 1995 IDI Resolution.

in act' as another exception for a member State's liability to third parties.[81] The inclusion of the last situation mentioned above raises a question of how the different power-conferring relationship between member States and the organization and its exercise in practice affect the distribution of responsibility between member States and the organization. In this respect, Sarooshi pointed out that

> [s]tates confer powers on international organizations to allow them to achieve specified objectives. However when considering issues of responsibility, there needs to be careful consideration given to the nature of the specific relationship between a state and an international organization since they vary greatly in practice.[82]

It is therefore appropriate to indicate that it might not be sufficient to argue for an exclusive responsibility of the organization based solely on the concept of international legal personality of the organization; specific circumstances like the power-conferring relationship and its exercise in practice in each case should be taken into account in the analysis of the responsibility of the organization and its member States.

In the third place, apart from Part V of the 2011 ILC ARIO and Article 5 of the 1995 IDI Resolution which depict exceptions to the 'no liability of member states' rule, there is still another situation in which a member State is held liable for the acts of the organization. This opinion is based on the practical reason of, in particular, the limited capacities of organizations to make reparation. For instance, Pellet observed that 'for practical reasons, it seems indispensable to pierce through the "organizational veil", if the principle of full reparation is to be respected'.[83] Looking through the same lens, Martín argues that 'the eventual subsidiary responsibility of member States would exclusively arise under its membership condition'.[84] This opinion, however, is inconsistent with the

[81] Article 5, paragraph (c) (ii) of the 1995 IDI Resolution.

[82] Dan Sarooshi, 'International Organizations: Personality, Immunities and Responsibility', in Dan Sarooshi (ed.), *Remedies and Responsibility for the Actions of International Organizations* (Martinus Nijhoff 2014) 20. He subdivided the power-conferring relationship into 'agency relationship', 'delegation of powers' and 'transfer of powers' and analysed the distribution of responsibility in each scenario.

[83] Alain Pellet, 'International Organizations Are Definitely Not States: Cursory Remarks on the ILC Articles on the Responsibility of International Organizations', in Maurizio Ragazzi (ed.), *Responsibility of International Organizations: Essays in Memory of Sir Ian Brownlie* (Martinus Nijhoff 2013) 50.

[84] José Manuel Cortés Martin, 'The Responsibility of Members due to Wrongful Acts of International Organizations' (2013) 12 *CJIL* 679–721.

position of the ILC. Being fully aware of the limited capacities of international organizations to make reparation,[85] Article 40 of the 2011 ILC ARIO imposes a duty on member States to ensure the fulfillment of the obligation to make reparation by the organization, which states:

1. The responsible international organization shall take all appropriate measures in accordance with its rules to ensure that its members provide it with the means for effectively fulfilling its obligations under this chapter.
2. The members of a responsible international organization shall take all the appropriate measures that may be required by the rules of the organization in order to enable the organization to fulfil its obligations under this chapter.

As to the nature of the obligation of member States under Article 40, the ILC explains that '[Article 40] does not envisage any further instance in which states [. . .] would be held internationally responsible for the act of the organization of which they are members.'[86] It further clarifies that 'member States only bind themselves towards the organization or agree to provide the necessary financial resources as an internal matter'.[87] Therefore, although taking notice of the same problem (the inadequacy in the financial capacity of the organization to make reparation), the ILC resorts to a different solution. While Pellet and Martín proposed to hold member States responsible towards the third parties directly, the ILC imposes an obligation on members to finance the organization which as an internal matter is opposable only to the organization, but not the third parties. This obligation of member States, in the view of the ILC, finds its legal basis in the rules adopted by the organization. And if the organization does not adopt such rules as found in Article 40 of the 2011 ILC ARIO, the obligation of member States to finance the organization can derive from the general principle of cooperation.[88]

There might be criticism of the approach adopted by the ILC in Article 40. Prominently, the ILC's approach fails to take adequate consideration of the effective remedies of third parties. Following the approach of the ILC, the remedies of third parties depend solely on the fulfillment of the

[85] Commentary to Article 31 of the 2011 ILC ARIO, para. 4.
[86] Commentary to Article 40 of the 2011 ILC ARIO, para. 1.
[87] Commentary to Article 62 of the 2011 ILC ARIO, para. 7.
[88] Commentary to Article 40 of the 2011 ILC ARIO, para. 5.

obligation of reparation by the organization,[89] while the latter in turn must rely on the fulfillment of the financial obligation by its member States. Here, the problem consists in the fact that 'the organizations lack effective means for ensuring the enforcement of the obligation of members to contribute to the expenses, including the expenses arising from its responsibility *vis-à-vis* an injured state'.[90] It therefore puts the remedies of third parties in an uncertain situation. In addition, if one takes into account the lack of remedy mechanisms towards international organization at both international and national levels, that uncertainty would increase. Taken together, it seems that the third parties would be left with little chance of effective remedies if claims cannot be made directly against member States. Certainly, it is the concern about the remedies of the third parties that gives rise to questioning not only the nature of the financial obligations of members, but more fundamentally, the overall approach of the ILC in dealing with the issue of distribution of liability between the organization and its member States.

Consideration of the remedies of the third parties is now confronted with that of the autonomy of the organization. While the latter points to an exclusive responsibility of the organization, the former is drawn in the direction of the responsibility of member States. Indeed, these two opposite considerations generate the tensions which are at the core of the issue of responsibility of international organizations, in particular, the distribution of responsibility between the organization and its member States. A balance between the two considerations needs to be struck. The IDI pointed out such tensions in its 1995 Resolution.[91] Likewise, the ILA reported that 'the Committee considers it crucial that its proposals should maintain the delicate balance between preserving the necessary autonomy in decision-making for the international organizations and treaty-organs and responding to the need, both in the sphere of international law and international relations, to have these actors accountable for their acts and omissions'.[92] With such an understanding, it is suggested in this chapter that on the one hand, the 'no liability of member states' rule should be accepted as a general assumption which constitutes

[89] Commentary to Article 40 of the 2011 ILC ARIO, para. 3.

[90] Paolo Palchetti, 'Exploring Alternative Routes: The Obligation of Members to Enable the Organization to Make Reparation', in Maurizio Ragazzi (ed.), *Responsibility of International Organizations: Essays in Memory of Sir Ian Brownlie* (Martinus Nijhoff 2013) 310.

[91] Preamble, the 1995 IDI Resolution.

[92] 2004 ILA Resolution, 6.

only the first step of a complex process of the enquiry into the responsibility or liability of the international organization. On the other hand, rebuttal of the assumption can be made based on various reasons and the interpretation of the exceptions to the rule should not be too strict.

8.3.2.2 Liability of Members of the ISA for the Acts of the ISA

Turning to the issue of the liability of members for the acts of the ISA in the context of DSM, nothing more can be added to the general rule identified above, nor is there any reason that calls for a departure from the general rule. This is because, first, the DSM legal regime is silent on this issue and second, no practice can be referred to. Indeed, the lack of practice poses an inherent limit to the interpretation of liability of the ISA in the context of DSM. In a broader context, the lack of practice is regarded by the ILC as a significant obstacle for codification and progressive development of a general rule with regard to the responsibility of international organizations, as it is said: 'one of the main difficulties in elaborating rules concerning the responsibility of international organizations is due to the limited availability of pertinent practice'.[93] Nonetheless, since 1985 when the dissolution of the International Tin Council triggered several claims before English courts, the topic of the liability of international organizations has been increasingly familiarized. Until now, it can be said that 'the international organization shall be held liable for its wrongful acts' has become a widely accepted general rule. As a corollary, clarification or further development of the liability regime in a general or specific context is still needed. The question, however, is how that task can be carried out against the background of a scarcity of pertinent practice. Eagleton chose to compose hypothetical cases.[94] The ILC on the other hand resorted to an analogy strategy.[95] Certainly, both approaches can easily be subject to criticism.[96] However, if the lack of

[93] Commentary to 2011 ARIO, general commentary, para. 5.

[94] Clyde Eagleton, 'International Organizations and the Law of Responsibility' (1950) 76 *RdC* 323–423, 386.

[95] The reason for adopting an analogy approach was explained by the Special Rapporteur Gaja in his first report in 2002 (UN Doc. A/CN.4/532, para. 11) and second report in 2003 (UN Doc. A/CN.4/541, para. 5).

[96] For Eagleton's approach, criticism might be that, in the first place, he was drawing the picture out of the blue. Besides, the defect of this approach also lies in the fact that one cannot anticipate all the possible scenarios for the incurrence of liability, therefore, the value of the exploration, if any, would be limited. For the ILC's approach, criticism is prevalent. For instance, Wouters and Odermatt argued that 'the flaw lies in the way the ILC used the ASR as its logical starting point'. (Jan Wouters and Jed Odermatt, 'Are all

practice is the undeniable fact and if the liability regime is deemed as desirable, how can the liability regime be developed in other ways except by using one's imagination or drawing an analogy to the well-established general rules on the responsibility of States?[97] In spite of the criticisms of the work of the ILC, the analysis of liability of the ISA in this chapter resorts to both its work approach and the product in dealing with the establishment of liability of the ISA. It is also proposed that the analysis of liability of the sponsoring State be applied to the ISA by analogy. In dealing with liability of member states for the acts of the ISA, it relies heavily on the content of Part V of the 2011 ILC ARIO.

Finally, it should be emphasized that when discussing liability of the ISA, the issue of liability of its member States for the acts of the ISA is inescapable. This is because, theoretically, the ISA is by nature a creature of States, albeit it operates independently; and realistically, the ISA is, after all, only a small, specialist international organization with limited human and budgetary resources, but which, on the other hand, is entrusted with broad powers with regard to environmental protection. For these reasons, the relationship between the ISA and its member States should be checked in every specific case whenever the issue of liability arises.

8.3.3 *Invocation of Liability of the ISA*

Article 187(e) of the UNCLOS expressly states that the SDC has jurisdiction over disputes concerning liability of the ISA. Moreover, contractors and any State Party to the UNCLOS are entitled to invoke liability of the ISA before the SDC. Yet, claims by States Parties and contractors have different legal bases. For the contractor, the legal basis is the contract; while for States Parties, it is the UNCLOS, the 1994 Agreement or the

International Organizations Created Equal?' (2012) 9 *IOLR* 7–14.) In Aspremont's observation, the conceptual impairment inherited from the ASR has swollen in ARIO. (Jean D'Aspremont, 'The Articles on the Responsibility of International Organizations: Magnifying the Fissures in the Law of International Responsibility' (2012) 9 *IOLR* 15–28.)

97 It should be noted, however, there is a fundamental challenge to the desirability or feasibility of the work of the ILC on the topic of international responsibility of the international organizations. See Gerhard Hafner, 'Is the Topic of Responsibility of International Organizations Ripe for Codification? Some Critical Remarks', in Ulrich Fastenrath et al. (eds.), *From Bilateralism to Community Interest: Essays in Honour of Judge Bruno Simma* (OUP 2011). See also Jan Wouters and Jed Odermatt, 'Are All International Organizations Created Equal?' (2012) 9 *IOLR* 7–14.

Regulations issued by the ISA. Moreover, owing to the different legal relationships between the parties to a dispute, the content of the claims by a contractor or a State Party could also be different. A contractor is likely to invoke liability of the ISA for the reason that the ISA infringes its contractual rights under the contract. A State Party, on the other hand, might invoke liability of the ISA because it believes the ISA has failed to fulfil its regulatory powers or obligations. However, since the SDC must refrain from reviewing the regulatory acts and the exercise of the discretionary powers of the ISA,[98] the judicial mechanism as depicted in Article 187 of the UNCLOS may be of limited practical value. Alternatively, States Parties might also invoke liability of the ISA through its internal procedures. They might, for example, question the ISA during the annual sessions of the Assembly or Council of the ISA. This is a political way of addressing and perhaps settling disputes.

8.3.4 *Conclusions*

It is argued that the discussions concerning the conditions for the establishment, forms and content of the international environmental liabilities of the contractor and the sponsoring State can apply *mutatis mutandis* to the ISA. This section focuses on a special issue of the liability of the international organization – liability of member States for the acts of international organizations. Through the analysis of the work of international law forums such as the IDI, the ILC and the ILA, it is shown that there exists a 'no liability of member states' rule which allows for exceptions in certain circumstances. It contends that the findings of the analysis can be applicable to the ISA in the context of DSM. One problem concerning the topic of responsibility or liability of the international organization in both general international law and the specific context of DSM is a paucity of practice. As to the procedural aspect of the issue of liability, it is found that the contractor and the States Parties to UNCLOS have the *locus standi* to invoke liability of the ISA before the SDC. Yet, it should be noted that the compulsory jurisdiction of the SDC is compromised by the consideration of the independent functioning of the ISA. Additionally, the liability of the ISA could also be addressed through a political way within the organization.

[98] Article 189, UNCLOS.

9

Conclusions

The principle of common heritage of mankind (CHM) is the basic tenet of the deep seabed mining (DSM) legal regime which requires that DSM activities serve community interests. It is argued that the principle of CHM is not and will not become outdated not only because of Article 311(6) of the United Nations Convention on the Law of the Sea (UNCLOS), but more importantly because of the discernible trend of community interests in international law. The marine environmental protection in DSM as a restrictive element of CHM is one specific manifestation of community interests (Chapter 2). The overall objective of this book is to ascertain how the participants in DSM operationalize the principle of CHM by exercising environmental powers and rights, complying with environmental obligations and assuming environmental liabilities at the international level. It argues that political as well as legal discourses over the future development of the DSM legal regime must be subject to the community interests test.

9.1 The Roles of Participants in DSM

The International Seabed Authority (ISA) is a small specialized international organization for operationalizing the principle of CHM; it is assigned with the primary duty to protect the marine environment and entrusted with broad environmental mandates. The analysis in Chapter 3 demonstrated that the ISA is empowered to adopt regulations, grant licences (approve plans of work and sign contract), review the implementation of plans of work, issue orders in the event of an environmental emergency, conduct inspections, impose penalties on the contractor and institute legal proceedings before the Seabed Disputes Chamber (SDC), etc. The Legal and Technical Commission (LTC), Council and Secretariat are the three most important organs of the ISA. Specifically, the LTC as the subsidiary expert body is entitled to draft regulations, issue administrative and technical guidance to the contractor and review reports from the contractor, etc.; the Council as the core decision-making political organ decides on questions of whether to adopt regulations or standards, whether to issue environmental emergency orders or to suspend or terminate a contract, whether to institute a legal proceeding or request for an advisory opinion from the SDC, etc.; while the Secretariat as the only permanent administrative organ provides technical assistance and administrative services to other organs, in particular to the LTC, promotes and encourages marine scientific research and manages data and contracts, etc. On the basis of these findings, it is seen that the ISA occupies a central position in the international regulation of DSM. The ISA is endowed with centralized law-making powers which could contribute to the progressive development of international environmental law. Moreover, considering that the ISA exercises its regulatory powers not through member States but directly *vis-à-vis* the contractor at the international level, it argues that the ISA exercises international public authority, which can be analogous to the exercise of administrative power by executive organs at national level.

Nevertheless, the broad powers conferred on the ISA stand in contrast to the limited resources in terms of personnel, finance, technology and facilities at its disposal. Namely, the ISA is paradoxically a (legally speaking) strong and a (practically speaking) weak international regulator. The DSM legal regime embodies a sponsorship mechanism which obliges the sponsoring State to assist the ISA in regulating the contractor at the international level and establish regulatory system concerning DSM at the national level. The parallel existence of international and national regulation for DSM is called the dual-track regulatory system. To avoid duplicate regulatory burden on the contractor imposed by the two tracks of regulation, it is argued that the international regulation centred on the ISA should be of the primary status while national regulation presided by the sponsoring State subordinate and complementary, and that the sponsoring State should serve as a backup to the ISA in practical realm. Specifically, the sponsoring State as the secondary regulator should focus on monitoring and enforcement in its national legislation for the purpose of assisting the ISA.

The contractor is the operator of DSM activities. It acts *vis-à-vis* the ISA at the international level and the sponsoring State at the national level. The legal relationship between the contractor and the ISA is of a regulatory character in light of DSM legal framework, but it could also be of a contractual character since they are parties to contracts. The legal relationship between the contractor and the sponsoring State is of a regulatory character in light of domestic law concerning DSM, but they could also be co-stakeholders *vis-à-vis* the ISA with respect to, for instance, security of tenure of a contract, or be co-respondents in proceedings for sharing liability for environmental damage. There are three different categories of actors which may serve as the contractor: private or public funded entities, States and the Enterprise (of the ISA). Regardless of a different nature, contractors must comply with the international (environmental) obligations on an equal footing since the DSM legal regime adopts 'the market-oriented approaches' which implies equal treatment among contractors. Specifically, the Enterprise, albeit an organ of the ISA, possesses an independent international and national legal personality, and thus can fulfil obligations and assume liability independently from the ISA as the regulator. States as contractors cannot invoke immunities before international regulatory or judicial institutions.

9.2 The Role of Marine Sciences and Response to Their Limitations

It is argued that marine scientific knowledge provides the factual basis upon which legal norms concerning marine environmental protection in DSM are formulated, interpreted and implemented. The fulfillment of the ISA's function concerning marine environmental protection relies heavily on marine scientific knowledge. And the ISA has to date focused primarily on the scientific and technical work necessary to carry out its functions. It is anticipated that when DSM enters into the exploitation stage, marine scientific knowledge will play an even larger role. Correspondingly, the LTC of the ISA will need to assess marine scientific knowledge on a continual basis and the Secretariat of the ISA must also improve its scientific and data management abilities. Similar to the ISA, the sponsoring State must also rely on marine scientific knowledge to implement its international environmental obligations and to establish its national regulatory system. For the contractor, marine scientific knowledge as well as mining technologies and facilities are the keys to fulfilling its environmental obligations in DSM.

Also, both the establishment of international environmental liabilities in DSM and remediation rely on marine scientific knowledge. First, there is a scientific definition for the concept of 'marine environment'. Second, the establishment of a marine environmental baseline and the assessment of the natural or human-made variations of the environment which are critical steps for identifying marine environmental damage are matters of scientific work. Third, the proof of causal links between DSM activities of the contractor and marine environmental damage, and between regulatory acts of the ISA and the sponsoring State and marine environmental damage all rely on scientific evidence. Fourth, remediation such as the availability and feasibility of restoration measures has to be determined on the basis of scientific knowledge. In short, environmental obligations and liabilities are not only legal issues but also very much scientific issues.

Thus, it is evident that marine scientific knowledge plays a prominent role in both the obligation and liability parts of this book. If marine sciences fail or are inadequate, then the substantive content of most of the environmental obligations would become vague and the environmental liability regimes would be difficult to apply. Nevertheless, the current situation is that marine sciences are at the nascent stage of development and there are still great gaps in marine scientific knowledge.

This raises the question of how to respond to the limitations of marine sciences. Both the obligation and liability parts of this book include rules (potentially) applicable or suggestions to deal with the problems caused by gaps in marine scientific knowledge. In the obligation part, it was seen that the precautionary principle/approach applies in the situation of 'scientific uncertainty'. The precautionary principle/approach provides general guidance for the policy-maker as well as the operator when science becomes silent or undecided, that is, 'precaution' (Chapter 4). In the liability part, it is demonstrated that an administrative approach to the environmental liability of the contractor was suggested. The administrative approach has a lower level of evidential requirement for the establishment of liability, and thus can overcome to some extent the difficulties in establishing the liability of the contractor under the UNCLOS (Chapter 7). However, neither the precautionary principle/approach nor the administrative approach to environmental liability of the contractor denies the role of marine scientific knowledge. Rather, these two approaches constitute attempts to set rules for participants in DSM in the situation when marine sciences reach their limits. In short, this book has elucidated the legal rules on how the ISA, the sponsoring State and the contractor should act to prevent marine environmental damage and to redress the damaged marine environment with or in the absence of adequate marine scientific knowledge.

9.3 International Environmental Obligations

Although playing different roles and of different nature, the participants in DSM must fulfil some essentially same international environmental obligations. Most prominently, they are all required to apply the principle of prevention, the precautionary approach, environmental impact assessment (EIA), respond to an environmental emergency and take seriously the obligation to cooperate. Above all, participants shall all endorse the overarching principles of sustainable development. These are general international environmental principles and rules but are either incorporated or can be read into the *lex specialis* of DSM. Therefore, they are binding not only on States but on all participants in DSM, albeit may be of different implications for different kind of participants. Only if all participants in DSM diligently observe their international environmental obligations emanating from these principles and rules can the common goal of marine environmental protection in DSM be achieved.

At the international level, the ISA and the contractor are the primary actors, while the sponsoring State secondary. For the ISA, the question is how to discharge its environmental mandate in DSM by exercising six categories of powers and obligations (Chapter 3). The international environmental obligations of the contractor are corresponding to the environmental mandate of the ISA (Section 4.3). While international environmental obligations of the sponsoring State are elucidated in accordance with both *lex specialis* of DSM and general international environmental law, drawing on the SDC of the International Tribunal for the Law of the Sea's (ITLOS's) Advisory Opinion of 2011(Section 4.2).

The prevention principle is the cornerstone of International Environmental Law (IEL). All participants in DSM shall take preventive measures to protect the marine environment from detrimental effects of DSM activities. The key is what preventive measures each participant can take and how to determine their adequacy. It appears that preventive measures are broad and may be expanding with the passage of time. For the ISA, it shall take preventive measures while administering mineral resources and controlling activities. To begin with, it examines the documents (including EIS) submitted as well as the technical and financial capacities of an applicant for fulfilling its environmental requirements, in order to decide whether to approve a plan of work and subsequently grant a contract. That is, the licensing system is by itself a preventive measure. Then, during the period of contract, the LTC reviews annual reports (including EISs) submitted by the contractor; the Secretariat conducts daily environmental management (including especially, environmental data management), establishes and implements monitoring system in cooperation with the contractor and the sponsoring State. At the exploitation stage, the ISA may conduct inspection (by sending inspector or remote inspection) over the operation, the Secretary-General may issue compliance notes. In a word, all measures taken by the ISA for preventing the occurrence of environmental damage count. For the contractor, taking preventive measures is mainly reflected on the conduct of EIAs, submission of environmental impact statements (EISs), annual reports and periodical reports, as well as maintaining environmental management (including the internal governance and standard management procedure) and monitoring system. The sponsoring State, which plays a similar but complementary role to the ISA as the regulator, shall take all necessary measures to ensure compliance with environmental obligations by the contractor within its own jurisdiction and assist the ISA at the international level. The prevention obligation imposed on the three participants is of the same nature: it is obligation of conduct. A same standard of 'due diligence' can be employed to determine the fulfillment of obligation. Yet, the substantive content of 'due diligence' is distinct among them since they play different roles and are endowed with different capacities. It is anticipated that the substantiation of the standard of 'due diligence' would become the focal point of controversy if a dispute about the fulfillment of obligation of prevention arises in the future.

Likewise, all participants are required to apply precautionary approach in the event of scientific uncertainty about the DSM's impact on the marine environment. Since scientific uncertainty is exactly the case for DSM, the precautionary approach is of particular relevance. Yet, unlike the prevention principle, the exact legal meaning of the precautionary approach is not settled, which makes the implementation more difficult. In general, precautionary measures overlap with preventive measures to a large extent. Beyond that, in practice, the ISA has been exploring ways for the implementation of precautionary approach in practice. For instance, it employs environmental management tools, including environmental management strategy, adaptive environmental management and regional environmental management. It also sets environmental standards and requirements against a background of scientific uncertainty. In effect, to fulfil the obligation to apply precautionary approach necessarily means practical creativity for the ISA for two reasons. First, although EIA and best available technologies (BATs), best environmental practices (BEPs) are generally accepted as precautionary measures, the substantive content of these measures must be determined by the ISA. Second, these measures are not enough since DSM is a pioneer industry in a unique environment. Indeed, the ISA must take all necessary measures for the marine environmental protection. It is thus no surprise that the ISA has turned to a result-oriented approach. With this change, the ISA is exerting larger discretionary powers, and it becomes more difficult to evaluate the fulfillment of obligation to apply the precautionary approach from a normative than a practical perspective. Additionally, the ISA's implementation of the precautionary approach entails procedural, substantive, scientific and institutional implications.

For the contractor, to take precautionary measures include the conduct of EIAs, the establishment of impact and preservation reference zones (IRZ and PRZ), the preparation of various management plans to meet the highest environmental standards. At the moment, the LTC takes up the challenging work of defining environmental standards by issuing (compulsory) Standards and (recommendatory) Guidelines. Yet, in practice twilight zone and ambiguity of the standards may exist. Besides, a certain degree of discretionary rights and self-regulation of contractors are inevitable. These make the application of the highest standards of environmental protection difficult. For the sponsoring State, the book argues for a unifying interpretation of the precautionary approach in DSM via sponsoring States' following the ISA. However, an international consensus about the meaning of the precautionary approach in the field of DSM is still to be achieved. For this reason, it anticipates that allegation of a breach of the obligation to apply the precautionary approach of a sponsoring State would be more difficult than that of the prevention obligation. In a word, with respect to the obligation to apply the precautionary approach, the ISA leads the way, the sponsoring State follows, while the contractor complies.

As the most commonly recognized tool for the implementation of the principle of prevention and the precautionary approach, the necessity of EIA in DSM context is without doubt. The contractor is obliged to conduct different kinds of EIAs during the process of the formulation and implementation of plans of work for DSM, while the ISA and the sponsoring State are obliged to review the EIA reports of the contractor and to establish and maintain monitoring programmes. The key is the effectiveness of EIA. From a scientific point of view, the quality of EIAs could only be enhanced progressively along with the development of marine sciences and technologies. But procedures could also affect the effectiveness of EIAs. Transboundary EIA procedures as exemplified in the 1991 Espoo Convention and the 2001 Draft Articles on Prevention are not suitable in the DSM context. In the context of DSM, the ISA, rather than States, plays the central role. The LTC is authorized to issue guidance concerning EIA to contractors which, although not legally binding, has significant practical effect. In recent years, external expert review and public participation have been introduced into the EIA review process and new practice of EIA with a higher level of transparency appears; this improvement of EIA procedure affects the way an EIA is conducted by the contractor and its quality as well. For the sponsoring State, it suggests that the sponsoring State should endorse the EIA guidance issued by the LTC and cooperate with the ISA.

Also, participants have obligations in the event of environmental emergency: the contractor is obliged to report an accident to the ISA and to take measures in accordance with its own emergency plans or emergency orders issued by the ISA. The ISA is obliged to circulate the information about incidents (the Secretariat), to decide on the responding measures, to issue emergency orders (the Council on basis of recommendation of the LTC) and to take measures when necessary. The ISA could also decide to suspend or terminate a contract for the purpose of avoiding serious environmental damage. While the sponsoring State is obliged to ensure the compliance of the contractor with the ISA's emergency order. In comparison between the Exploration Regulations and the draft Exploitation Regulations, the most notable difference is that, in the former, the 'emergency order' issued by the Council of the ISA plays a central role, while in the latter, it is the 'Emergency Response and Contingency Plan' of the contractor. This signals a shifting of centre from the ISA to the contractor in dealing with environmental emergency.

Additionally, the ISA is entrusted with the power to encourage and promote marine scientific research. Considering the significant role marine sciences play in the protection of marine environment in DSM, this empowerment is important. In practice, the primary focus of the substantive work of the ISA has been the scientific and technical work necessary to carry out its functions, including in particular the environmental function. Now in a transitional period towards exploitation, the need to close the gap in marine scientific knowledge is increasingly felt. It is argued that the ultimate solution to the knowledge gap is to boost marine sciences. The ISA will certainly contribute to it. Although not being able to generate marine scientific knowledge itself, its Secretariat could act as a knowledge centre. Also, it suggests that the LTC will need to undertake the difficult task of assessing the current state of marine scientific knowledge on a continual basis, by either cooperating with other existing scientific bodies in the field of marine sciences or establishing a new mechanism similar to the Intergovernmental Panel for Climate Change (IPCC).

Finally, general obligation to cooperate is essential for implementing the principle of CHM in DSM, including in particular, for marine environmental protection in the Area. The international environmental obligations in DSM are not only obligations 'of all (participants in DSM)' but also obligations 'to all' which are commonly called 'obligations *erga omnes*'. As stated in Chapter 2, it is now generally acknowledged that environmental protection is a common interest of the international community as a whole, that the problem of environmental degradation such as climate change and loss of biodiversity has become a common concern of mankind. Correspondingly, obligations relating to issues of common interests and common concerns are *erga omnes* in nature. Marine environmental protection in DSM is such a case in point. Additionally, the CHM status of the Area and its resources further strengthens this argument. The *erga omnes* nature of the international environmental obligations has implications on the question of who is entitled to invoke liabilities of the contractor, the sponsoring State and/or the ISA. Also, the *erga omnes* nature of these obligations might serve as a basis for an argument of broader public participation in the formulation, implementation and enforcement of these obligations.[1]

9.4 International Environmental Liabilities

The analysis of the international environmental liabilities of the contractor, the sponsoring State and the ISA in Chapters 6 and 8 follows the same pattern: each covers the establishment, the content and forms (remediation) and the implementation of liability. The conditions for establishing the international environmental liabilities of the participants in DSM are similar. To establish these liabilities, one needs to define and measure environmental damage, that is, the common triggering element, determine internationally wrongful acts on the part of the contractor/the sponsoring State/the ISA and prove the causal link between the wrongful acts of participants and the environmental damage. Only if these three conditions are satisfied cumulatively can the liabilities of the participants

[1] This argument can also base itself on the idea of the international community as a whole. However, at this time there are controversies over the existence of an international community and its components. Some acknowledge the existence of an international community, while others deny it; some contend that the international community is composed of States only, while others claim that besides States, it comprises also individuals and entities.

be established. In practice, however, there are formidable difficulties in satisfying each of these three conditions.

The content and forms of the international environmental liabilities of the participants in DSM, that is remediation, are also similar. Article 22, Annex III to UNCLOS states that 'liability in every case shall be for the actual amount of damage'. Thus, the key is the identification and measurement of environmental damage (Chapter 5). Similar to many other contexts, the detrimental impact on the marine environment has to cross a certain threshold in order to be identified as 'marine environmental damage' in the context of DSM. As to the question of how to measure environmental damage, drawing mainly on the practical experience of the International Oil Pollution Compensation (IOPC) and United Nations Compensation Commission (UNCC) compensation regimes, it is suggested that environmental damage should be measured primarily in the form of the costs of taking preventive measures, restoration measures and post-incident studies, etc. In a situation where damage is irreversible and reinstatement impossible, one could refer, for example, to the contingent valuation method to assess pure/interim environmental damage. As to the forms of liability, drawing mainly on the remediation framework in the 2004 EU Environmental Liability Directive (ELD), it suggests that environmental liability should first take the form of restoration of the damaged environment to its baseline condition. If that is not possible, then a substitute or compensation should be provided. These three categories of environmental remediation are called primary remediation, complementary remediation and compensatory remediation, respectively. In addition, it was noted that it is difficult to apply the full reparation principle in environmental liability regimes since it is, on a practical level, difficult to measure environmental damage with preciseness. Finally, as Boyle observed, 'the international law of remedies for breach of obligation has not yet caught up with the expansion of international legal commitments to the protection of the environment'.[2] Indeed, remediation for the damaged environment also faces practical difficulties. In this sense, environmental protection legal regimes should place more emphasis on prevention (of the occurrence of environmental damage in the obligation part) rather than remediation (of the damaged environment in the liability part).

[2] Alan Boyle, 'Reparation for Environmental Damage in International Law: Some Preliminary Problems', in Michael Bowman and Alan Boyle (eds.), *Environmental Damage in International and Comparative Law* (OUP 2002) 25.

As to the implementation of liabilities, the specialized dispute settlement mechanisms stipulated in Section 5, Part XI, UNCLOS are of utmost importance. In particular, Article 187 UNCLOS confers compulsory jurisdiction on the SDC to deal with disputes relating to DSM.[3] The DSM legal regime is unique because of the special geographical scope – the Area as global commons, the internationalization of DSM, the principle of CHM and the special institutional arrangement. These features have impacts on the issue of the implementation of international environmental liabilities in DSM. This book focuses on the question of who is entitled to invoke liability. The answers on the basis of existing international law are: the ISA and the contractor can invoke the liability of each other since they have legal relations under both Exploration Regulations and contracts. Furthermore, States can invoke liability of the sponsoring State on the basis of either Article 42 (as the injured State) or Article 48 (as a State other than the injured State) of the International Law Commission's (ILC's) 2001 Articles on State Responsibility (ASR). At the same time, the ISA is also entitled to invoke liability of the sponsoring State in accordance with the DSM legal regime. And the ISA's invocation of liability was considered a better choice. Moreover, with the development of international law, in particular the broader availability of dispute settlement mechanisms in the future, the possibility of the invocation of liabilities for the purpose of common interests by other actors such as individuals and NGOs cannot be excluded.

International environmental liability in DSM is placed primarily on the contractor as the operator. This is a common feature shared by all existing environment-related liability treaties except the 1972 Space Treaty. This argument has its theoretical basis in the polluter-pays principle which requires that the one who has the control over activities ('the operator') should assume primary liability to compensate the victim and/or to restore the environment when environmental damage occurs. However, international environmental liability of the contractor in the context of DSM differs from liability regimes in existing environment-related liability treaties in two significant aspects. The first aspect is the standard for the establishment of liability. The existing liability treaties adopt the standard of strict liability according to which the operator must

[3] On dispute settlement mechanisms under the UNCLOS in general, see Natalie Klein, *Dispute Settlement in the UN Convention on the Law of the Sea* (CUP 2005); on dispute settlement mechanisms relating to DSM in particular, see Linlin Sun, 'Dispute Settlement relating to Deep Seabed Mining: A Participant's Perspective' (2017) 18(1) *MJIL* 71–94.

be held liable should environmental damage occur. In contrast, the establishment of liability of the contractor in the context of DSM requires an internationally wrongful act of the contractor. The second aspect relates to the procedures for the implementation of liability. Under the existing liability treaties, liability of the operator is normally implemented through a judicial or administrative channel within domestic legal systems. In contrast, owing to the internationalization of DSM and, in particular, the specialized dispute settlement mechanisms relating to DSM as stipulated in Section 5, Part XI, UNCLOS, the implementation of international environmental liability of the contractor can operate at an international level. Furthermore, it disagrees with the SDC which stated that the sponsoring State must, in accordance with Article 235 (2) UNCLOS, make sure that recourse is available within its legal system for prompt and adequate compensation or other relief for environmental damage. It is argued in this book that international environmental liability of the contractor is better implemented at an international level only. A parallel existence of international and national channels for implementation of liability is not desirable since it would erect a hurdle for a unifying application of liability and places an unnecessary burden on the sponsoring State.

International environmental liabilities of the sponsoring State and the ISA as the regulators are independent from the international liability of the contractor. Furthermore, the international liability of the sponsoring State as the regulator is only secondary in comparison with that of the ISA because the international regulatory power is assigned primarily to the ISA. One special issue relating to the international environmental liability of the ISA was examined. That is, whether and in what circumstances should member States of the ISA be liable for acts of the ISA? In answering these questions, general discussions on this issue within international law forums were referred. Upon analysis, it came to the conclusion that a general 'no-liability' rule[4] exists which, however, allows for exceptions in situations where piercing the organizational veil is possible. These general discussions are valid for the ISA in the specific context of DSM.

International environmental liability of the sponsoring State is considered as State liability *ex delicto*. It has a complex relationship with the

[4] The 'no liability' rule means that member States shall not be liable by reason only of their membership for acts of the international organization. See Article 6 of the 1995 IDI Resolution, and Commentary to Article 62, the ILC's 2011 ARIO.

general rules of State responsibility as depicted in the ILC's 2001 ASR. State liability *ex delicto* falls within the scope of State responsibility since they both are secondary rules. Yet, it was argued that the concept of State liability *ex delicto* as employed in this book should be differentiated from State responsibility since they have different starting points and purposes: the concept of State responsibility is centred on 'internationally wrongful act', in contrast, the concept of State liability in the field of IEL revolves around the element of 'environmental damage'. 'Environmental damage' is a common trigger element for the establishment of environmental liabilities and a determinant for the content and forms of liability. International liability of the sponsoring State can be considered as a *lex specialis* which departs partially from the general rules of State responsibility as depicted in the ILC's 2001 ASR: for matters where the DSM legal regime has specific rules, the application of the general rules is excluded; for matters which the DSM legal regime does not cover, one can fall back on the general rules.

On the basis of a thorough conceptual clarification of the international environmental liabilities of the three categories of participants in DSM in Chapters 6 and 8, it arrived at the overall conclusion that the role of the liability regimes for marine environment protection in DSM should not be overestimated because of the formidable practical difficulties in the satisfaction of each of these three conditions for establishing liabilities. Put it more simply, the environmental liability regimes are difficult to establish in practice.[5] This conclusion seems counter-intuitive. Nonetheless, it by no means intends to deny any value to liability regimes. Just as the commentary reads,

> The problems in constructing a viable regime for the protection of the global commons that incorporates a liability component are, as we have seen, formidable. But the consequences of not fashioning such a regime – and doing it soon – may well constitute the most profound common threat to humanity in the twenty-first century.[6]

[5] The same conclusion can be found in Jutta Brunnée, 'Of Sense and Sensibility: Reflections on International Liability Regimes as Tools for Environmental Protection' (2004) 53(2) *ICLQ* 351–367. See also Anne Daniel, 'Civil Liability Regimes as a Complement to Multilateral Environmental Agreements: Sound International Policy or False Comfort?' (2003) 12(3) *RECIEL* 225–241.

[6] Mahnoush Arsanjani and W. Michael Reisman, 'The Quest for an International Liability Regime for the Protection of the Global Commons', in Karel Wellens (ed.), *International Law: Theory and Practice - Essays in Honour of Eric Suy* (Martinus Nijhoff 1998).

One should not forget that the liability regime has preventive, reparative and corrective functions. Even though the latter two functions might not be activated, the very existence of liability regimes could have the function of prevention or deterrence, which is valuable. Therefore, despite its inherent weakness, the liability regimes in DSM are still needed.

Considering the difficulties in the application of liability, alternatively mechanisms for 'allocation of loss', including compulsory insurance and compensation funds, were explored in Chapter 7. There are two salient features of these alternative mechanisms: they allow for the participation of more actors, and have a direct focus on remediation of the damaged marine environment. These alternative mechanisms might be the direction to take for the future development of the DSM legal regime.

To sum up, in dealing with the issue of international environmental liabilities of participants in DSM, the book made use of the structure of the ILC's 2001 ASR. However, it is emphasized that the concept of 'liability' should be distinguished from the concept of State responsibility, and the former concept has been employed throughout the book. DSM is a specific category of 'activities not prohibited by international law', for which the focal point of the legal regime is preventing and redressing the 'injured consequences' rather than detecting and correcting the 'wrongfulness of the act'. Although the ILC discontinued its efforts to formulate general rules of international liability as opposed to those of State responsibility, the different rationales underlying the concepts of liability and State responsibility remain. A major problem with the SDC's 2011 Advisory Opinion was that the SDC completely followed the logic of State responsibility. Although the SDC identified (environmental) damage as a constituent element for establishing (environmental) liability, it did not give centrality to the element.[7] In a sense, the entire book revolves around the concept of environmental damage – prevention of environmental damage in the obligations part and remediation for environmental damage in the liability part.

9.5 Final Observations about the Future Development of the international DSM Legal Regime

Will a moratorium be imposed on the DSM? Will there be a rush towards exploitation? This book approves neither. Instead, it endorses such a

[7] See explanatory notes on the term of 'liability' in the Introduction chapter and Section 8.2.2.

concept of 'conservation science' that integrates human needs and nature conservation; it takes a position that, in a 'risk society', refusing to take any risks is tantamount to rejecting any chances to benefit from risky activities; and it appeals for a dynamic view about environmental problems being tackled in the process of industrial development. In a word, it anticipates a prospect of development of DSM without destruction to the deep sea in the future. With this prospect in mind, three points about the future development of the DSM legal regime are explained below.

First, to discharge its environmental mandate, the ISA will focus less on adopting general environmental principles and rules than on setting and updating specific environmental standards and ensuring the compliance by the contractor. As shown in Chapter 3, the ISA is undertaking the task of developing a set of Exploitation Regulations. The Exploitation Regulations (environmental aspects) would only lay down principles or rules at a highly abstract level which, if applied in practice, would need to be operationalized by technical guidance, guidelines and recommendations. Indeed, the LTC is simultaneously drafting many sets of Standards and Guidelines. It seems that, the further DSM advances, the more intense the need for specific environmental standards will be, and the more the ISA will turn out to be a technical organization as well as a marine scientific knowledge centre.

At the same time, the ISA will increasingly feel the need to justify its authority as a response to questions about the legitimacy of international environmental governance in DSM. As Daniel Bodansky argued, the issue of legitimacy would arise when authority is exercised at the international level by institutions,[8] and the stronger the institution, the greater the concern about its legitimacy.[9] In the specific case of DSM, the ISA will inevitably encounter a problem with legitimacy since the ISA is an international institution empowered to directly control and manage DSM *vis-à-vis* the contractor, and the further DSM advances, the greater international public authority the ISA will exercise. Then the question will be: are there ways to help make the ISA 'resilient to claims of illegitimacy'?[10] Concurring with Bodansky, it is noted that a general consent of States in respect of authorization by means of the UNCLOS will not be sufficient. The ISA would have to resort to public

[8] Daniel Bodansky, 'The Legitimacy of International Governance: A Coming Challenge for International Environmental law?' (1999) 93 *AJIL* 596–624, 605.

[9] Ibid., 623.

[10] Ibid., 624.

participation as well as the expertise of marine scientists as justifications for international environmental governance in DSM.[11] In effect, as demonstrated in Chapter 3, the ISA has already given special attention to the involvement of stakeholders in the drafting process of the Exploitation Regulations. As it was suggested in Chapter 3, the LTC of the ISA should explore new ways to assess marine scientific knowledge on a continual basis. It is noted here that seeking experts' assistance is not only necessary on a practical level for fulfilling the ISA's environmental mandates but will also serve as a relatively objective justification for the ISA's exercise of international public authority. In short, future concerns for international environmental protection in DSM will include not only the substantive content of environmental standards and their compliance but also how environmental standards are made within the ISA and implemented or enforced by the ISA (and others).

Second, the relationship between the ISA and the sponsoring State as regulators of DSM will become an issue of increasing importance. As argued in Chapter 4, the DSM legal regime embodies a dual-track regulatory system. To date, the ISA has played a dominant role in the functioning of the DSM legal regime: it has been the ISA that adopts regulations, issues dozens of exploration contracts and supervises the compliance with the contracts. Although in recent years some sponsoring States have also promulgated national laws on DSM, this has been just a matter of transposing international law at a national level. If DSM further advances, the sponsoring State would play an increasingly important role since the ISA, being a small specialized international organization equipped with limited practical ability, relies on States with respect to the implementation and enforcement of international rules. There, the problem of coordination and division of labour between the ISA and the sponsoring State with respect to regulatory powers at both legal and practical levels will arise. This problem, if not handled well, would almost certainly result in confusion on the part of the contractor and low level of effective regulation on the part of the ISA and the sponsoring State.

[11] Bodansky argued that State consent is not sufficient to justify international environmental institutions with greater rulemaking and enforcement authority. Alternatively, he considered democracy, public participation and expertise as three bases of legitimacy. He further contended that democracy as a basis of legitimacy at the international level is unrealistic at the time; while public participation can provide a kind of democratic legitimacy, and expertise is needed to provide continuing legitimacy once State consent is initially conferred on an international environmental institution. Ibid.

Third, DSM would not be able to move full steam ahead towards the exploitation stage since there exists an inherent restrictive factor, that is, the environmental protection requirement. The reason why the environmental protection requirement will certainly impede the rapid progress of DSM activities is because of the substantial unknowns about the deep sea. Exploiting mineral resources in the Area now is like walking in a vast darkness with a dim torchlight. Considering the fact that on the one hand, deep-sea ecosystems are so fundamental to the survival of all species on Earth, including we human beings, and on the other hand, that great gaps exist in marine scientific knowledge, we have no choice but to conduct DSM activities alongside precautionary measures and to make progress with extreme caution. All in all, as the development of marine sciences is a matter that takes time, patience is what is needed with respect to the development of DSM. This is for the sake of CHM to which DSM is supposed to serve.

BIBLIOGRAPHY

Cases

ICJ and PCIJ

Application of Convention on the Prevention and Punishment of Crime of Genocide (The Gambia v. Myanmar), Judgment (preliminary objection), I.C.J. Reports 2022.

Certain Activities Carried Out by Nicaragua in the Border Area (Costa Rica v. Nicaragua), Compensation, Judgment, I.C.J. Reports 2018.

Certain Activities Carried Out by Nicaragua in the Border Area (Costa Rica v. Nicaragua) and Construction of a Road in Costa Rica along the San Juan River (Nicaragua v. Costa Rica), Judgment, I.C.J. Reports 2015.

Whaling in the Antarctic (Australia v. Japan: New Zealand intervening), Judgment, I.C.J. Reports 2014.

Pulp Mills on the River Uruguay (Argentina v. Uruguay), Judgment, I.C.J. Reports 2010.

Legal Consequences of the Construction of a Wall in the Occupied Palestinian Territory, Advisory Opinion, I.C.J. Reports 2004.

Gabčíkovo-Nagymaros Project (Hungary/Slovakia), Judgment, I.C.J. Reports 1997.

Application of the Convention on the Prevention and Punishment of the Crime of Genocide (Bosnia and Herzegovina v. Yugoslavia), Judgment (preliminary objection), I.C.J. Reports 1996.

Legality of the Threat and Use of Nuclear Weapons, Advisory Opinion, I.C.J. Reports 1996.

East Timor (Portugal v. Australia), Judgment, I.C.J. Reports 1995.

Request for an Examination of the Situation in Accordance with Paragraph 63 of the Court's Judgment of 20 December 1974 in the Nuclear Tests (New Zealand v. France) Case, Order, I.C.J. Reports 1995.

Case concerning The Barcelona Traction, Light and Power Co., Ltd (Belgium v. Spain), Judgment (second phase), I.C.J. Reports 1970.

Factory at Chorzow Case (Merits) (Germany/Poland), Judgment of 26 July 1927, PCIJ documents Series A, No. 13, 1928.

ITLOS

Responsibilities and Obligations of States Sponsoring Persons and Entities with Respect to Activities in the Area (Request for Advisory Opinion submitted to the Seabed Disputes Chamber), Advisory Opinion of 1 February 2011, ITLOS Case No. 17.

Case concerning Land Reclamation by Singapore in and around the Straits of Johor (Malaysia v. Singapore) (Request for Provisional Measures), Order of 8 October 2003, ITLOS Case No. 12.

MOX Plant (Ireland v. United Kingdom) (Request for Provisional Measures), Order of 3 December 2001, ITLOS Case No. 10.

Southern Bluefin Tuna Cases (New Zealand v. Japan; Australia V. Japan) (Request for Provisional Measures), Order of 27 August 1999, ITLOS Cases Nos 3 & 4.

Arbitral Tribunals and National Courts

Iron Rhine Railway Arbitration (Belgium v. the Netherlands), Award of 24 May 2005.

Trail Smelter case (United States v. Canada), Awards of 16 April 1938 and 11 March 1941, UNRIAA, Vol. III, 1905–1982.

Commonwealth of Puerto Rico et al., v. the Ss Zoe Colocotroni, U.S. 628 F.2d 652, 1980.

Ohio v. United States Department of the Interior, U.S. 880 F.2d 432, 1989.

Treaties

United Nations Conventions on the Law of the Sea, adopted on 10 December 1982, entered into force on 14 November 1994.

Agreement relating to the Implementation of Part XI of the United Nations Convention on the Law of the Sea of 10 December 1982, adopted on 28 July 1994, entered into force on 28 July 1996.

Treaty on Principles Governing the Activities of States in the Exploration and Use of Outer Space, including the Moon and Other Celestial Bodies, adopted on 19 December 1966, entered into force on 10 October 1967.

Convention on International Liability for Damage Caused by Space Objects, adopted on 29 November 1971, entered into force on 1 September 1972.

Agreement Governing the Activities of States on the Moon and Other Celestial Bodies, adopted by on 18 December 1979, entered into force on 11 July 1984.

Antarctic Treaty, adopted on 1 December 1959, entered into force on 23 June 1961.

Convention on the Conservation of Antarctic Marine Living Resources, adopted on 20 May 1980, entered into force on 7 April 1982.

Protocol on Environmental Protection to the Antarctic Treaty, adopted on 4 October 1991, entered into force on 14 January 1998. Annex V to the Protocol on Environmental Protection to the Antarctic Treaty – Area Protection and Management, adopted on 17 October 1991, entered into force on 24 May 2002. Annex VI to the Protocol on Environmental Protection to the Antarctic Treaty – Liability Arising from Environmental Emergencies, adopted on 17 June 2005, not yet in force.

Convention on the Regulation of Antarctic Mineral Resource Activities, 25 November 1988, not in force. [It is expected this Convention will not ever enter into force.]

Convention on Environmental Impact Assessment in a Transboundary Context, adopted on 25 February 1991, entered into force on 10 September 1997.

International Convention on Civil Liability for Oil Pollution Damage (adopted on 29 November 1969, entered into force on 19 June 1975) replaced by 1992 Protocol, adopted on 27 November 1992, entered into force on 30 May 1996.

Civil Liability for Bunker Oil Pollution Damage, adopted on 23 March 2001, entered into force on 21 November 2008.

International Convention on Liability and Compensation for Damage in Connection with Carriage of Hazardous and Noxious Substances by Sea (adopted on 3 May1996, not in force) as amended by the Protocol of 2010, adopted on 1 June 2010, not yet entered into force.

Convention on Third Party Liability in the Field of Nuclear Energy, adopted on 29 July 1960, entered into force on 1 April 1968; amended by the 1964 Protocol (entered into force on 1 April 1968), the 1982 Protocol (entered into force on 7 October 1988), and the 2004 Protocol (not yet entered into force).

Convention on the Liability of Operators of Nuclear Ships, adopted on 25 May 1962, not in force.

Convention on Civil Liability for Nuclear Damage, adopted on 21 May 1963, entered into force on 12 November 1977, as amended by the 1997 Protocol (entered into force on 4 October 2003).

Convention on Civil Liability for Damage Resulting from Activities Dangerous to the Environment, adopted on 21 June 1993, not yet in force.

Protocol on Liability and Compensation for Damage Resulting from Transboundary Movements of Hazardous Wastes and Their Disposal, adopted on 10 December 1999, not in force. [It is expected that this Protocol will not ever enter into force.]

Books and Articles

Aguon, J. and J. Hunter, 'Second Wave Due Diligence: The Case for Incorporating Free, Prior, and Informed Consent into the Deep Sea Mining Regulatory Regime' (2018) 38(3) *Stan. Envtl. L. J.* 1–55.

Ahlborn, C., 'The Rules of International Organizations and the Law of International Responsibility' (2011) 8(2) *IOLR* 397–482.

'The Use of Analogies in Drafting the Articles on the Responsibility of International Organizations: An Appraisal of the "Copy-Paste Approach"' (2012) 9 *IOLR* 53–66.

Akehurst, M., 'International Liability for Injurious Consequences Arising out of Acts Not Prohibited by International Law' (1985) 16 *NYIL* 3–16.

'Reprisal by Third States' (1967) 44 *BYIL* 1–18.

Alshdaifat, S. A., 'Who Owns What in Outer Space? Dilemmas Regarding the Common Heritage of Mankind' (2018) 21 *Pecs Journal of International and European Law*.

Ambrus, M., 'The Precautionary Principle and a Fair Allocation of the Burden of Proof in International Environmental Law' (2012) 21(3) *RECIEL* 259–270.

Amerasinghe, C., 'Comments on the ILC's Draft Articles on the Responsibility of International Organizations' (2012) 9 *IOLR* 29–31.

'Liability to Third Parties of Member States of International Organizations: Practice, Principle and Judicial Precedent' (1991) 85(2) *AJIL* 259–280.

Amon, Diva et al., 'Assessment of Scientific Gaps Related to the Effective Environmental Management of Deep-Seabed Mining' (2022) 105006 *Marine Policy* 138.

Anderson, C., 'Damage to Natural Resources and the Costs of Restoration' (1997) 72 *Tul. L. Rev.* 417–491.

Andresen, S. and J. B. Skjaerseth, 'Science and Technology: From Agenda Setting to Implementation', in D. Bodansky, J. Brunnee and E. Hey (eds.), *The Oxford Handbook of International Environmental Law* (OUP 2008).

Annacker, C., 'The Legal Regime of *Erga Omnes* Obligations in International Law' (1994) 46(2) *AJPIL* 131–166.

Ardron, J. et al., 'Incorporating Transparency into the Governance of Deep-Seabed Mining in the Area beyond National Jurisdiction' (2018) 89 *Marine Policy* 58–66.

Arsanjani, M. and W. M. Reisman, 'The Quest for an International Liability Regime for the Protection of the Global Commons', in K. Wellens (ed.), *International Law: Theory and Practice: Essays in Honour of Eric Suy* (Martinus Nijhoff 1998).

Baker, M. et al., 'Restoration Scaling Approaches to Addressing Ecological Injury: The Habitat-Based Resource Equivalency Method' (2020) 65 *Environ. Manage.* 161–177.

Barboza, J., *The Environment, Risk, and Liability in International Law* (Martinus Nijhoff 2011).

Baslar, K., *The Concept of the Common Heritage of Mankind in International Law* (Martinus Nijhoff 1998).

Bastmeijer, K. and T. Koivurova (eds.), *Theory and Practice of Transboundary Environmental Impact Assessment* (Martinus Nijhoff 2008).

Baxter, R., 'Multilateral Treaties as Evidence of Customary International Law' (1965) 41 *BYIL* 275–300.

Beck, U., *Risk Society: Towards a New Modernity*, trans. M. Ritter (Sage 1992).

Bergkamp, L. and B. Goldsmith (eds.), *The EU Environmental Liability Directive: A Commentary* (OUP 2013).

Berwick, T. A., 'Responsibility and Liability for Environmental Damage: A Roadmap for International Environmental Regimes' (1998) 10 *Georgetown IELR* 257–267.

Beyerlin, U., 'State Community Interests and Institution-Building in International Environmental Law' (1996) 56 *ZaoRV* 602–627.

Birnie, P., A. Boyle and C. Redgwell, *International Law and the Environment*, 3rd ed. (OUP 2009).

Blokker, N., 'International Organizations and Their Members: "International Organizations Belong to All Members and To None": Variations on a Theme' (2004) 1 *IOLR* 139–161.

Blokker, N. and R. Wessel, 'Introduction: First Views at the Articles on the Responsibility of International Organizations' (2012) 9 *IOLR* 1–6.

Bloom, E., 'Introductory Note to Antarctic Treaty Environmental Protocol Liability Annex' (2006) 45 *ILM* 1–4.

Bodansky, D., 'Deconstructing the Precautionary Principle', in D Caron and H Scheiber (eds.), *Bringing New Law to Ocean Waters* (Martinus Nijhoff 2004).

'The Legitimacy of International Governance: A Coming Challenge for International Environmental Law?' (1999) 93 *AJIL* 596–624.

Bodansky, D., J. Brunnee and E. Hey (eds.), *The Oxford Handbook of International Environmental Law* (OUP 2008).

Bonatti, E. and Y. Rammohanroy Nayudu, 'The Origin of Manganese Nodules on the Ocean Floor' (1965) 263(1) *American Journal of Science* 17–39.

Borchard, E., 'Relation between International Law and Municipal Law' (1940) 27 (2) *Va. Law Rev.* 137–148.

Borowy, I., *Defining Sustainable Development for Our Common Future: A History of the World Commission on Environment and Development (Brundtland Commission)* (Routledge 2014).

Boschen, R. et al., 'Mining of Deep-Sea Seafloor Massive Sulfides: A Review of the Deposits, Their Benthic Communities, Impacts from Mining, Regulatory Frameworks and Management Strategies' (2013) 84 *Ocean Coast Management* 54–67.

Boschen, R. E. et al., 'Seafloor Massive Sulfide Deposits Support Unique Megafaunal Assemblages: Implications for Seabed Mining and Conservation' (2016) 115 *Marine Environmental Research* 78–88.

Bowman, M. and B. Alan (eds.), *Environmental Damage in International and Comparative Law* (OUP 2002).

Bowman, M., 'Environmental Protection and the Concept of Common Concern of Mankind', in M. Fitzmaurice, D. M. Ong and P. Merkouris (eds.), *Research Handbook on International Environmental Law* (Edward Elgar 2010).

'The Definition and Valuation of Environmental Harm: An Overview', in M. Bowman and A. Boyle (eds.), *Environmental Damage in International and Comparative Law* (OUP 2002).

Boyle, A., 'Developments in the International Law of Environmental Impact Assessments and Their Relation to the Espoo Convention' (2012) 20(3) *RECIEL* 227–231.

'Globalising Environmental Liability: The Interplay of National and International Law' (2005) 17(1) *JEL* 3–26.

'Making the Polluter Pay? Alternatives to State Responsibility in the Allocation of Transboundary Environmental Cost', in F. Francioni and T. Scovazzi (eds.), *International Responsibility for Environmental Harm* (Graham and Trotman 1991).

'Reparation for Environmental Damage in International Law: Some Preliminary Problems', in M. Bowman and A. Boyle (eds.), *Environmental Damage in International and Comparative Law* (OUP 2002).

'State Responsibility and International Liability for Injurious Consequences of Acts Not Prohibited by International Law: A Necessary Distinction?' (1990) 39 *ICLQ* 1–26.

Brager, S., Q. Gabriela, R. Romero and M. Sandor, 'The Current Status of Environmental Requirements for Deep Seabed Mining Issued by the International Seabed Authority' (2020) 103258 *Marine Policy* 114.

Brans, E., 'Liability and Compensation for Natural Resource Damage under the International Oil Pollution Conventions' (1996) 5(4) *RECIEL* 297–304.

'Liability for Damage to Public Natural Resources under the 2004 EC Environmental Liability Directive: Standing and Assessment of Damages' (2005) 7 *ELR* 90–109.

Liability for Damage to Public Natural Resources: Standing, Damage and Damage Assessment (Kluwer 2001).

Brans, E. and D. Dorith, 'The Supplementary Protocol and the EU Environmental Liability Directive: Similarities and Differences', in S. Akiko (ed.), *International Liability Regime for Biodiversity Damage: The Nagoya-Kuala Lumpur Supplementary Protocol* (Routledge 2014).

Brownlie, I., *System of Law of Nations: State Responsibility* (OUP 1983).

Brunnée, J., 'Of Sense and Sensibility: Reflections on International Liability Regimes as Tools for Environmental Protection' (2004) 53(2) *ICLQ* 351–367.

Burmester, H., 'Liability for Damage from Antarctica Mineral Resource Activities' (1989) 29 *Virginia JIL* 621–660.

Cameron, J. and A. Juli, 'The Precautionary Principle: A Fundamental Principle of Law and Policy for the Protection of the Global Environment' (1991) 14(1) *B.C. Int'l & Comp* 1–27.

'The Status of the Precautionary Principle in International Law', in D. Freestone and E. Hey (eds.), *The Precautionary Principle and International Law: The Challenge of Implementation* (Kluwer 1996).

Cancando Trindade, A., 'International Law for Humankind: Towards a New *Jus Gentium*' (2005) 316 *RdC* 9–439.

Carrato, J., B. John and G. Phil, 'The Industry's Compact and Its Implications for the Supplementary Protocol', in A. Shibata (ed.), *International Liability Regime for Biodiversity Damage: The Nagoya-Kuala Lumpur Supplementary Protocol* (Routledge 2014).

Cassar, A. and B. Carl, 'Transboundary Environmental Impact Assessment in International Watercourse Management' (2003) 12 *NYU ELJ* 169–244.

Castllo-Winckels, N., 'Why "Common Concern of Humankind" Should Return to the Work of the International Law Commission on the Atmosphere' (2016) 29 *Georgetown IELR* 131.

Charles, E., 'The Enterprise under the 1982 United Nations Convention on the Law of the Sea and the Common Heritage of Mankind', in A. Ascencio-Herrera and M. H. Nordquist (eds.), *The United Nations Convention on the Law of the Sea, Part XI Regime and the International Seabed Authority: A Twenty-Five Year Journey* (Brill 2022).

Charney, J., 'Third State Remedies in International Law' (1989) 10 *Michigan JIL* 57–101.

Chen, Y., 'Attribution, Causation and Responsibility of International Organization', in D. Sarooshi (ed.), *Remedies and Responsibility for the Actions of International Organizations* (Martinus Nijhoff 2014).

Christiansen, S., S. Brager and A. Jaeckel, 'Evaluating the Quality of Environmental Baselines for Deep Seabed Mining' (2022) 9 *Front. Mar. Sci.* 898711.

Christiansen, S. et al., 'Towards a Contemporary Vision for the Global Seafloor: Implementing the Common Heritage of Mankind' (2019) *Heinrich Boll Stifung* (Publication Series Ecology Vol. 45).

'Towards an Ecosystem Approach to Management in Areas Beyond National Jurisdiction: REMPs for Deep Seabed Mining and the Proposed BBNJ Instrument' (2022) 9 *Front. Mar. Sci.*.

Clark, M., J. Durden and S. Christiansen, 'Environmental Impact Assessment for Deep-Sea Mining: Can We Improve Their Future Effectiveness?' (2020) 114 *Marine Policy* 1–9.

Cogolati, S. and J. Wouters (eds.), *The Commons and A New Global Governance* (Edward Elgar 2018).

Collins, P. et al., 'A Primer for the Environmental Impact Assessment of Mining at Seafloor Massive Sulfides Deposits' (2013) 42 *Marine Policy* 198–209.

Craik, N., 'Implementing Adaptive Management in Deep Seabed Mining: Legal and Institutional Challenges' (2020) 103256 *Marine Policy* 114.

'The Duty to Cooperate in the Customary Law of Environmental Impact Assessment' (2020) 69(1) *ICLQ* 239–259.

Crawford, J. 'Responsibility to the International Community as a Whole' (2001) 8 (2) *Ind. J. Global Legal Stud* 303–322.

'Multilateral Rights and Obligations in International Law' (2006) 319 *RdC* 335.

State Responsibility: The General Part (CUP 2013).

Cross, F., 'Natural Resource Damage Valuation' (1989) 42(2) *Vand. L. Rev.* 269.

Crutzen, P., 'Geology of Mankind' (2002) 415(6867) *Nature* 23.

D'Aspremont, J., 'Abuse of the Legal Personality of International Organizations and the Responsibility of Member States' (2007) 4 *IOLR* 91–119.

'The Articles on the Responsibility of International Organizations: Magnifying the Fissures in the Law of International Responsibility' (2012) 9 *IOLR* 15–28.

Daniel, A., 'Civil Liability Regimes as a Complement to Multilateral Environmental Agreements: Sound International Policy or False Comfort?' (2003) 12(3) *RECIEL* 225–241.

Danovaro, R. et al., 'An Ecosystem-Based Deep Ocean Strategy' (2017) 355(6324) *Science* 452–454.

Davenport, T., 'Responsibility and Liability for Damage Arising Out of Activities in the Area: Potential Claimants and Possible Fora' CIGI, Liability Issues for Deep Seabed Mining Series Paper No. 5, February 2019.

De la Fayette, L., 'The ILC and International Liability: A Commentary' (1997) 6(3) *RECIEL* 322–333.

De Sadeleer, N., 'Preliminary Reference on Environmental Liability and the Polluter Pays Principle: Case C-534/13, Fipa' (2015) 24(2) *RECIEL* 232–237.

'The Principles of Prevention and Precaution in International Law: Two Heads of the Same Coin?', in M. Fitzmaurice, D. M. Ong and P. Merkouris (eds.), *Research Handbook on International Environmental Law* (Edward Elgar 2010).

Environmental Principles: From Political Slogans to Legal Rules (OUP 2002).

Deacon, M., T. Rice and C. Summerhayes (eds.), *Understanding the Oceans: A Century of Ocean Exploration* (Routledge, 2001).

Dingwall, J., *International Law and Corporate Actors in Deep Seabed Mining* (OUP 2021).

Durant, R., D. Fiorino and R. O'Leary (eds.), *Environmental Governance Reconsidered: Challenges, Choices, and Opportunities* (MIT 2004).

Durden, J. et al., 'A Procedural Framework for Robust Environmental Management of Deep-Sea Mining Projects Using a Conceptual Model' (2017) 84 *Marine Policy* 193–201.

'Environmental Impact Assessment Process for Deep-Sea Mining in "the Area"' (2018) 87 *Marine Policy* 194–202.

Duvic-Paoli, L.-A., *The Prevention Principle in International Environmental Law* (CUP 2018).

Eagleton, C., 'International Organizations and the Law of Responsibility' (1950) 76 *RdC* 319.

Egede, E., *Africa and the Deep Seabed Regime: Politics and International Law* (Springer 2011).

Elias, O., 'Environmental Impact Assessment', in M. Fitzmaurice, D. M. Ong and P. Merkouris (eds.), *Research Handbook on International Environmental Law* (Edward Elgar 2010).

'The UN Compensation Commission and Liability for the Costs of Monitoring and Assessment of Environmental Damage', in M. Fitzmaurice and D. Sarooshi (eds.), *Issues of State Responsibility before International Judicial Institutions* (Hart 2004).

Fastenrath, U. et al., (eds.), *From Bilateralism to Community Interest: Essays in Honour of Bruno Simma* (OUP 2011).

'Relative Normativity in International Law' (1993) 4 *EJIL* 305–340.

Faure, M. (ed.), *Deterrence, Insurability, and Compensation in Environmental Liability: Future Development in the European Union* (Springer 2003).

(ed.), *Elgar Encyclopedia of Environmental Law* (Edward Elgar 2016).

Faure, M. and A. Verheij (eds.), *Shifts in Compensation for Environmental Damage* (Springer 2007).

Faure, M. and Ton Hartlief, 'Compensation Funds versus Liability and Insurance for Remedying Environmental Damage' (1996) 5(4) *RECIEL* 321–327.

'Alternative Compensation Mechanisms as Remedies for Uninsurability of Liability' (2004) 29(3) *GRIR* 455–489.

Feichtner, I., 'Community Interest', MPEPIL (last updated February 2007).

Fellmeth, A. and M. Horwitz, *Guide to Latin in International Law* (OUP 2009).

Fiorino, D., 'Rethinking Environmental Regulation: Perspectives on Law and Governance' (1999) 23(2) *HELR* 441–469.

Fisher, E., 'Precaution, Precaution Everywhere: Developing a "Common Understanding" of the Precautionary Principle in the European Community' (2002) 9 *MJECL* 7–28.

Fitzmaurice, M., 'International Protection of the Environment' (2001) 293 *RdC*.

Fitzmaurice, M., D. M. Ong and P. Merkouris (eds.), *Research Handbook on International Environmental Law* (Edward Elgar 2010).

Francioni, F. and T. Scovazzi (eds.), *International Responsibility for Environmental Harm* (Graham and Trotman 1991).

Freestone, D. and E. Hey (eds.), *The Precautionary Principle and International Law: The Challenge of Implementation* (Kluwer 1996).

French, D., 'From the Depths: Rich Pickings of Principles of Sustainable Development and General International Law on the Ocean Floor: The Seabed Disputes Chamber's 2011 Advisory Opinion' (2011) 26(4) *IJMCL* 525–568.

French, D. and B. Pontin, '*The Science of Climate Change: A Legal Perspective on the IPCC*', in D. Farber and M. Peeters (eds.), *Climate Change Law* (Edward Elgar 2016).

Friedmann, W., General Course at The Hague Academy (1969) 127 *RdC*.

Frowein, J., 'Reaction by Not Directly Affected States to Breaches of Public International Law' (1994-IV) 248 *RdC* 345.

Gaines, S., 'The Polluter-Pays Principle: From Economic Equity to Environmental Ethos' (1991) 26(3) *TILJ* 463–495.

Gaja, G., 'Articles on Responsibility of International Organizations', UN Audiovisual Library of International Law, New York, 9 December 2011. Available at: http://legal.un.org/avl/ha/ario/ario.html.

Gerber, L. and R. Grogan, 'Challenges of Operationalising Good Industry Practice and Best Environmental Practice in Deep Seabed Mining Regulation' (2020) 114 *Marine Policy* 1–6.

Ginzky, H., S. Pradeep and T. Markus, 'Strengthening the ISA's Knowledge-Base: Addressing Uncertainties to Enhance Decision-Making' (2020) 114 *Marine Policy* 103823.

Godet, L. et al., 'Scientists as Stakeholders in Conservation of Hydrothermal Vents' (2011) 25(2) *Conservation Biology* 1–9.

Grady, K., 'Commonwealth of Puerto Rico v. SS Zoe Colocotroni: State Action for Damage to Non-Commercial Living Natural Resources' (1980) 9(2) *B.C. Envtl. Aff. L. Rev*. 397–429.

Graefrath, B., 'Responsibility and Damages Caused: Relationship between Responsibility and Damages' (1984-II) 185 *RdC* 9.

Gundling, L., 'The Status in International Law of the Principle of Precautionary Action', in D. Freestone and T. Ijlstra (eds.), *The North Sea: Perspectives on Regional Environmental Co-operation* (Graham & Trotman 1990).

Hafner, G., 'Is the Topic of Responsibility of International Organizations Ripe for Codification? Some Critical Remarks', in U. Fastenrath et al. (eds.), *From Bilateralism to Community Interest: Essays in Honour of Bruno Simma* (OUP 2011).

Hanley, N., 'The Economic Value of Environmental Damage', in M. Bowman and A. Boyle (eds.), *Environmental Damage in International and Comparative Law* (OUP 2002).

Hardin, G., 'The Tragedy of the Commons' (1968) 162(3859) *Science* 1243–1248.

Hardman Reis, T., *Compensation for Environmental Damages under International Law: The Role of the International Judge* (Kluwer 2011).

Hart, H. L. A., *The Concept of Law* (OUP 1961) 79–88.

Essays on Bentham: Jurisprudence and Political Philosophy (OUP 1982) 127.

Hartwig, M., 'Responsibility and Liability of International Organizations or Institutions', MPEPIL (last updated in May 2011).

Horbach, N., *Liability versus Responsibility under International Law, Defending Strict State Responsibility for Transboundary Damage* (S.l.: s.n. 1996) [Proefschrift Rijksuniversiteit te Leiden].

Huguenin, M., M. Donlan, A. Van Geel and R. Paterson, 'Assessment and Valuation of Damage to the Environment', in P. Cymie and P. Sand (eds.), *Gulf War Reparations and the UN Compensation Commission: Environmental Liability* (OUP 2011).

Jacobsson, M. and N. Trotz, 'The Definition of Pollution Damage in the 1984 Protocols to the 1969 Civil Liability Convention and the 1971 Fund Convention' (1986) 17(4) *JMLC* 467–491.

Jaeckel, A., G. Kristina and J. Ardron, 'Conserving the Common Heritage of Humankind: Options for the Deep Seabed Mining Regime' (2017) 78 *Marine Policy* 150–157.

Jaeckel, A., 'An Environmental Management Strategy for the International Seabed Authority? The Legal Basis' (2015) 30 *IJMCL* 93–119.

'Deep Seabed Mining and Adaptive Management: The Procedural Challenges for the International Seabed Authority' (2016) 70 *Marine Policy* 205–211.

'Strategic Environmental Planning for Deep Seabed Mining in the Area' (2020) 114 *Marine Policy* 103423.

The International Seabed Authority and the Precautionary Principle: Balancing Deep Seabed Mineral Mining and Marine Environmental Protection (Brill 2017).

Jenks, C. W., 'Liability for Ultra-Hazardous Activities in International Law' (1966-I) 117 *RdC* 99.

Jessup, P., *A Modern Law of Nations: An Introduction* (Macmillan 1948).

Johnson, D. and M. A. Ferreira, 'ISA Areas of Particular Environmental Interest in the Clarion-Clipperton Fracture Zone' (2015) 30(3) *IJMCL* 559–574.

Johnston, J., 'Is the Polluter-Pays Principle Really Fundamental? An Economic Explanation of the Relative Unimportance of Environmental Liability and Taxes in the US Environmental Law', in M. Faure, L. Han and H. Shan (eds.), *Maritime Pollution Liability and Policy: China, Europe and the US* (Kluwer 2010).

Jones, D. et al., 'Environmental Considerations for Impact and Preservation Reference Zones for Deep-Sea Polymetallic Nodule Mining' (2020) 118 *Marine Policy* 103312.

et al., 'Existing Environmental Management Approaches Relevant to Deep-Sea Mining' (2019) 103 *Marine Policy* 172–181.

Jungcurt, S. and N. Schabus, 'Liability and Redress in the Context of the Cartagena Protocol on Biosafety' (2010) 19(2) *RECIEL* 197–206.

Kareiva, P. and M. Marvier, 'What Is Conservation Science?' (2012) 62(11) *BioScience* 962–969.

Kazazi, M., 'Environmental Damage in the Practice of the UN Compensation Commission', in M. Bowman and A. Boyle (eds.), *Environmental Damage in International and Comparative Law* (OUP 2002).

Kennett, J., *Marine Geology* (Prentice-Hall 1982).

Kim, R., 'Should Deep Seabed Mining Be Allowed?' (2017) 82 *Marine Policy* 134–137.

Kini, E., *The Precautionary Principle, Multilateral Treaties and the Formation of Customary International Law* (Editions interuniversitaires suisses-Edis 2008).

Klein, N., *Dispute Settlement in the UN Convention on the Law of the Sea* (CUP 2005).

Knox, J., 'Assessing the Candidates for A Global Treaty on Transboundary Environmental Impact Assessment' (2003) 12 *N.Y.U. Envtl. L. J.* 153–168.

'The Myth and Reality of Transboundary Environmental Impact Assessment' (2002) 96(2) *AJIL* 291–319.

Koivurova, T., 'Due Diligence', MPEPIL (2010).

'The Transnational EIA Procedure of the Espoo Convention' (1997) 8 *FinnishYBIL* 161–199.

Kojima, C., 'Compensation Fund', MPEPIL (last updated November 2009).

Kong, L., 'Environmental Impact Assessment under the United Nations Convention on the Law of the Sea' (2011) 10 *Chinese JIL* 651–669.

La Fayette, L., 'The Concept of Environmental Damage in International Liability Regimes', in M. Bowman and A. Boyle (eds.), *Environmental Damage in International and Comparative Law* (OUP 2002).

Lallier, L. and F. Maes, 'Environmental Impact Assessment Procedure for Deep Seabed Mining in the Area: Independent Expert Review and Public Participation' (2016) 70 *Marine Policy* 212–219.

Le Gurun, G., 'Environmental Impact Assessment and the International Seabed Authority', in K. Bastmeijer and T. Koivurova (eds.), *Theory and Practice of Transboundary Environmental Impact Assessment* (Martinus Nijhoff 2008).

Lefeber, R., *Transboundary Environmental Interference and the Origin of State Liability* (Kluwer 1996).

Lefeber, R. and J. Nieto Carrasco, 'Negotiating the Supplementary Protocol: The Co-Chairs' Perspective', in A. Shibata (ed.), *International Liability Regime for Biodiversity Damage: The Nagoya-Kuala Lumpur Supplementary Protocol* (Routledge 2014).

Leigh, K., 'Liability for Damage to the Global Commons' (1992) 14 *AustYBIL* 129–156.

Levin, L. et al, 'Defining "Serious Harm" to the Marine Environment in the Context of Deep-Seabed Mining' (2016) 74 *Marine Policy* 245.

Levy, J-P., 'International Seabed Authority: 20 Years', (2014) paper submitted at the special session in memory of the 20th Anniversary of the ISA.

Li, Y., *Transfer of Technology for Deep Sea-Bed Mining: the 1982 Law of the Sea Convention and Beyond* (Martinus Nijhoff 1994).

Lindhout, P. and B. van den Broek, 'The Polluter Pays Principle: Guidelines for Cost Recovery and Burden Sharing in the Case Law of the European Court of Justice' (2004) 10 *Utrecht L. Rev.* 46–59.

Lodge, M. et al., 'Seabed Mining: International Seabed Authority Environmental Management Plan for the Clarion-Clipperton Zone: A Partnership Approach' (2014) 49 *Marine Policy* 66–72.

'Improving International Governance in the Deep Sea' (2004) 19 *IJMCL* 299–316.

'Some Legal and Policy Considerations Relating to the Establishment of a Representative Network of Protected Areas in the Clarion-Clipperton Zone' (2011) 26(3) *IJMCL* 463–480.

'The Common Heritage of Mankind' (2012) 27 *IJMCL* 733–742.

Macdonald, R. and D. Johnston (eds.), *The Structure and Process of International Law: Essays in Legal Philosophy Doctrine and Theory* (Martinus Nijhoff 1983).

Madereira, P. et al., 'Exploration of Polymetallic Nodules in the Area: Reporting Practices, Data Management and Transparency' (2016) 70 *Marine Policy* 101–107.

Makarczyk, J. and K. Krzysztof Skubiszewski (eds.), *Theory of International Law at the Threshold of the 21st Century: Essays in Honour of Krzysztof Skubiszewski* (Kluwer 1996).

Mark V., *Customary International law and Treaties*, 2nd ed. (Brill, 1997).

Marr, S., 'The Southern Bluefin Tuna Cases: The Precautionary Approach and Conservation and Management of Fish Resources' (2000) 11(4) *EJIL* 815–831.

The Precautionary Principle in the Law of the Sea (Martinus Nijhoff 2003).

Martin, J., 'The Responsibility of Members Due to Wrongful Acts of International Organizations' (2013) 12 *Chinese JIL* 679–721.

Mason, M., 'Civil Liability Oil Pollution Damage: Examining the Evolving Scope for Environmental Compensation in the International Regime' (2003) 27 *Marine Policy* 1–12.

McDonald, J. and Megan Stules, 'Legal Strategies for Adaptive Management under Climate Change' (2014) 26 *JEL* 25–53.

Mengerink, K. et al., 'A Call for Deep-Ocean Stewardship' (2014) 344 *Science* 696–698.

Mensah, T., 'The Civil Liability and Compensation for Environmental Damage in the 1982 Convention on the Law of the Sea', in the Hamburg Lectures on Maritime Affairs (2007 and 2008).

Mero, J., 'Ocean Floor Manganese Nodules' (1962) 57 *Economic Geology* 747, 756–758.

The Mineral Resources of the Sea (Elsevier 1965) 235.

Mickelson, K., 'Common Heritage of Mankind as a Limit to Exploitation of the Global Commons' (2019) 30(2) *EJIL* 635–663.

Moldner, M., 'Responsibility of International Organizations: Introducing the ILC's DARIO' (2012) 16 *MaxPlankUNYB* 282–327.

Mosler, H., 'The International Society as a Legal Community' (1973) 140(3) *RdC* 1–320, 11–12.

Murray, O., 'Piercing the Corporate Veil: The Responsibility of Member States of an IO' (2011) 8 *IOLR* 291–347.

Nakatani, K., 'Responsibility of Member States towards Third Parties for an International Wrongful Act of the Organization', in M. Ragazzi (ed.), *Responsibility of International Organizations: Essays in Memory of Sir Ian Brownlie* (Martinus Nijhoff 2013).

Ndiaye, T. and R. Wolfrum (eds.), *Law of the Sea, Environmental Law and Settlement of Disputes: Liber Amicorum Judge Thomas A. Mensah* (Martinus Nijhoff 2007).

Nijar, G., 'The Nagoya-Kuala Lumper Supplementary Protocol on Liability and Redress to the Cartagena Protocol on Biosafety: An Analysis and Implementation Challenges' (2013) 13 *INEA* 271–290.

Niner, A. et al., 'Deep-Sea Mining with No Net Loss of Biodiversity: An Impossible Aim' (2018) 5 *Front. Mar. Sci.* 53.

Nollkaemper, A., '"What You Risk Reveals What You Value", and Other Dilemmas Encountered in the Legal Assaults on Risks', in D. Freestone and E. Hey (eds.), *The Precautionary Principle and International Law: The Challenge of Implementation* (Kluwer 1996).

Nollkaemper, A. and D. Jacobs, 'Shared Responsibility in International Law: A Conceptual Framework' (2013) 34(2) *Mich. J. Int'l L.* 359–438.

Nolte, G., 'From Dionisio Anzilotti to Robert Ago: The Classical International Law and State Responsibility and the Traditional Primacy of a Bilateral Conception of Inter-State Relations' (2002) 13 *EJIL* 1083.

Nordquist, M., S. Nandan, S. Rosenne and M. Lodge (eds.), *United Nations Convention on the Law of the Sea 1982: A Commentary (Vol. VI)* (Martinus Nijhoff 2002).

O'Riordan, T. and J. Cameron (eds.), *Interpreting the Precautionary Principle* (Earthscan 1994).

Okowa, P., 'Procedural Obligations in International Environmental Agreements' (1996) 67 *BYIL* 275–336.

Ong, D. 'The 1982 UN Convention on the Law of the Sea and Marine Environmental Protection', in M. Fitzmaurice, D. M. Ong and P. Merkouris (eds.), *Research Handbook on International Environmental Law* (Edward Elgar 2010).

Orlando E., 'Public and Private in the International Law of Environmental Liability', in F. Lenzerini and A. Vrdoljak (eds.), *International Law for Common Goods* (Hart 2014).

Orrego-Vicuña, F., 'Responsibility and Liability for Environmental Damage under International Law: Issues and Trends' (1997) 10 *Geo. Int'l Envtl. L. Rev.* 279–308.

Oude Elferink, A., 'Environmental Impact Assessment in Areas beyond National Jurisdiction' (2012) 27(2) *IJMCL* 449–480.

Palchetti, P., 'Exploring Alternative Routes: The Obligation of Members to Enable the Organization to Make Reparation', in M. Ragazzi (ed.), *Responsibility of International Organizations: Essays in Memory of Sir Ian Brownlie* (Martinus Nijhoff 2013).

Pardo, A. and Carl Christol, 'The Common Interest: Tension between the Whole and the Parts', in St. J. Macdonald and D. Johnston (eds.), *The Structure and Process of International Law: Essays in Legal Philosophy Doctrine and Theory* (Martinus Nijhoff 1983).

Paulus, A., 'International Community', MPEPIL (last updated in March 2013).

Payne C. and P. Sand (eds.), *Gulf War Reparations and the UN Compensation Commission: Environmental Liability* (OUP 2011).

Peel, J., 'Precaution: A Matter of Principle, Approach or Process?' (2004) 5(2) *MJIL* 483.

Pellet, A., 'International Organizations Are Definitely Not States: Cursory Remarks on the ILC Articles on the Responsibility of International Organizations', in M. Ragazzi (ed.), *Responsibility of International Organizations: Essays in Memory of Sir Ian Brownlie* (Martinus Nijhoff 2013).

Peterson, S. et al., 'News from the Seabed: Geological Characteristics and Resource Potential of Deep-Sea Mineral Resources' (2016) 70 *Marine Policy* 175–187.

Pineschi, L., 'The Duty of Environmental Impact Assessment in the First ITLOS Chamber's Advisory Opinion: Towards the Supremacy of the General Rule to Protect and Preserve the Marine Environment as a Common Value?', in N. Boschiero et al. (eds.), *International Courts and the Development of International Law: Essays in Honour of Tullio Treves* (Asser 2013).

Pinto, M. C. W., 'Common Heritage of Mankind: From Metaphor to Myth, and the Consequences of Constructive Ambiguity', in J. Makarczyk and K. Skubiszewski (eds.), *Theory of International Law at the Threshold of the 21st Century: Essays in Honour of Krzysztof Skubiszewski* (Kluwer 1996).

'The Common Heritage of Mankind: Then and Now' (2012) 361 *RdC* 9–130.

Pinzauti, G., 'It Takes Two to Tango: States' Conferral of Powers on International Organizations and Its Implications for the Responsibility of the Organization and its Members', in D. Sarooshi (ed.), *Remedies and Responsibility for the Actions of International Organizations* (Martinus Nijhoff 2014).

Plakokokefalos, I., 'The Practice of Shared Responsibility in relation to Environmental Protection of the Deep Seabed', SHARES Research Paper 94 (2016).

Preller-Borquez, S., 'Integrating Sustainable Development into the Adoption of Emergency Orders for the Protection of the Common Heritage of Mankind and the Marine Environment' (2022) 37 *IJMCL* 73–88.

Proelss, A., 'The Role of the Authority in Ocean Governance', in H. Scheiber and J-h. Paik (eds.), *Regions, Institutions, and Law of the Sea* (Martinus Nijhoff 2013).

Pufendorf, S., *Two Books on the Elements of Universal Jurisprudence*, trans. W. A. Oldfather (Clarendon Press 1931).

Pyhala, M., A. Brusendorff and H. Paulomaki, 'The Precautionary Principle', in M. Fitzmaurice, D. M. Ong and P. Merkouris (eds.), *Research Handbook on International Environmental Law* (Edward Elgar 2010).

Ragazzi, M. (ed.), *International Responsibility Today: Essays in Memory of Oscar Schachter* (Martinus Nijhoff 2005).

Responsibility of International Organizations: Essays in Memory of Sir Ian Brownlie (Martinus Nijhoff 2013).

The Concept of International Obligations Erga Omnes (Clarendon 1997).

Ranganathan, S., 'Global Commons' (2016) 27 *EJIL* 693–717.

Remaoun, M., 'The International Seabed Authority and the Enterprise: How Africa is Reinvigorating the Principle of the Common Heritage of Mankind' (2021) 1(1) *JOGA*.

Røsæg, E., 'Compulsory Maritime Insurance' (2000) Marlus 258 SIMPLY.

Rosenne, S., 'Some Reflections *Erga Omnes*', in A. Anghie and G. Sturgess (eds.), *Legal Visions of the 21st Century: Essays in Honour of Judge Christopher Weeramantry* (Kluwer 1998).

Sand, P., 'Environmental Damage Claims from the 1991 Gulf War: State Responsibility and Community Interests', in U. Fastenrath et al. (eds.), *From Bilateralism to Community Interest: Essays in Honour of Bruno Simma* (OUP 2011).

'Environmental Dispute Settlement and the Experience of the UN Compensation Committee' (2011) 54 *JYIL* 151–189.

'The Evolution of International Environmental Law', in D. Bodansky, J. Brunnee and E. Hey (eds.), *The Oxford Handbook of International Environmental Law* (OUP 2008).

Sander, G., 'International Legal Obligations for Environmental Impact Assessment and Strategic Environmental Assessment in the Arctic Ocean' (2016) 31(1) *IJMCL* 88–119.

Sands, P., J. Peel, A. Fabra and R. MacKenzie (eds.), *Principles of International Environmental Law*, 3rd ed. (CUP 2012).

Sarooshi, D. (ed.), *Remedies and Responsibility for the Actions of International Organizations* (Martinus Nijhoff 2014).

International Organizations and their Exercise of Sovereign Powers (OUP 2005).

Savaresi, A., K. Kulovesi and H. van Asselt, 'Beyond COP26: Time for an Advisory Opinion on Climate Change?' *EJIL*: Talk! blog posted on 17 December 2021. Available at: www.ejiltalk.org/beyond-cop26-time-for-an-advisory-opinion-on-climate-change/.

Sax, J., 'The Public Trust Doctrine in Natural Resource Law: Effective Judicial Intervention' (1970) 68 *Mich. L. Rev.* 471–566.

Schermers, H., 'Liability of International Organizations' (1988) 1(1) *LJIL* 3–14.

Schermers, H. and N. Blokker, *International Institutional Law*, 5th ed. (Martinus Nijhoff 2011).

Schoenbaum, T., 'Environmental Damages in the Common Law: An Overview', in M. Bowman and A. Boyle (eds.), *Environmental Damage in International and Comparative Law* (OUP 2002).

Schrijver, N. and V. Prislan, 'From *Mare Liberum* to the Global Commons: Building on the Grotian Heritage' (2009) 30 *Grotiana* 168.

Schrijver, N., 'Managing the Global Commons: Common Good or Common Sink?' (2016) 37(7) *Third World Quarterly* 1252–1267.

'Permanent Sovereignty over Natural Resources', MPEPIL (2008).

Schrijver, N., *Development without Destruction. The United Nations and Global Resource Management* (Indiana University Press 2010).

The Evolution of Sustainable Development in International Law: Inception, Meaning and Status (Martinus Nijhoff 2008).

Sovereignty over Natural Resources: Balancing Rights and Duties (CUP 1997).

'The Status of the Precautionary Principle in International Law and its Application and Interpretation in International Litigation', in J. Pierre Cot (ed.), *Le procès international: liber amicorum Jean-Pierre Cot* (Bruylant 2009).

Schroder, M., 'Precautionary Approach/ Principle', MPEPIL (2009).

Schwartz, P., 'Principle 16: The Polluter-Pays principle', in J. Vinuales (ed.), *The Rio Declaration on Environment and Development: A Commentary* (OUP 2015).

'The Polluter-Pays Principle', in M. Fitzmaurice, D. M. Ong and P. Merkouris (eds.), *Research Handbook on International Environmental Law* (Edward Elgar 2010).

Scovazzi, T., 'Mining Protection of the Environment, Scientific Research and Bioprospecting: Some Considerations on the Role of the International Sea-Bed Authority' (2004) 19 *IJMCL* 383.

Seyersted, F., 'Objective International Personality of International Organization: Do their Capacities Really Depend upon the Convention Establishing Them?' (1964) 34(3) *Nordisk Tidsskrift Int'l Ret* 1.

Shackelford, S., 'The Tragedy of the Common Heritage of Mankind' (2009) 28 *Stan. Envtl. L. J.* 109–169.

Shelton, D., 'Stockholm Declaration (1972) and Rio Declaration (1992)', MPEPIL (2008).

'Common Concern of Humanity' (2009) 39(2) *Environmental Law and Policy* 83.

Shibata, A. (ed.), *International Liability Regime for Biodiversity Damage: The Nagoya-Kuala Lumpur Supplementary Protocol* (Routledge 2014).

'A New Dimension in International Environmental Liability Regimes: A Prelude to the Supplementary Protocol', in A. Shibata (ed.), *International Liability Regime for Biodiversity Damage: The Nagoya-Kuala Lumpur Supplementary Protocol* (Routledge 2014).

Shigeta, Y., 'Obligation to Protect the Environment in the ICJ's Practice: To What Extent *Erga Omnes*?' (2012) 55 *JYIL* 176–207.

Silva Soares, G. and E. V. Vargas, 'The Basel Liability Protocol on Liability and Compensation for Damage Resulting from Transboundary Movements of Hazardous Wastes and Their Disposal' (2002) 12(1) *YIntlEnvL* 69–104.

Simma, B., 'From Bilateralism to Community Interest in International Law' (1994-VI) 250 *RdC* 221–384.

'The Antarctic Treaty as a Treaty Providing for an "Objective Regime"' (1986) 19 *Cornell Int'L. J.* 189.

Singh, P., 'The Two-Year Deadline to Complete the International Seabed Authority's Mining Code: Key Outstanding Matters that Still Need to Be Resolved' (2021) 104804 *Marine Policy* 134.

SPC-EU Deep Sea Minerals Project, 'Manganese Nodules: A Physical, Biological, Environmental, and Technical Review' (2013) 23. Available at: http://dsm.gsd.spc.int/public/files/meetings/TrainingWorkshop4/UNEP_vol1B.pdf.

Spijkers, O., 'Intergenerational Equity and the Sustainable Development Goals' (2018) 10(11) *Sustainability* 3836.

Stoll, P-T., 'State Immunity', MPEPIL (last updated in April 2011).

Stumer, A., 'Liability of Member States for Acts of International Organizations: Reconsidering the Policy Objections' (2007) 48(2) *HILJ* 553–580.

Sun, L., 'Dispute Settlement Relating to Deep Seabed Mining: A Participant's Perspective' (2017) 18(1) *MJIL* 71–94.

Sverdrup, H. U., M. W. Johnson, and R. Fleming, *The Oceans: Their Physics, Chemistry, and General Biology* (Prentice Hall 1942).

Swords, D. and V. Ohio, 'United States Department of the Interior: A Contingent Step Forward for Environmentalists' (1991) 51(6) *La. L. Rev.* 1347–1376.

Tams, C., *Enforcing Obligation Erga Omnes in International Law* (CUP 2005).

Tanaka, Y., 'Obligations and Liability of Sponsoring States Concerning Activities in the Area: Reflections on the ITLOS Advisory Opinion of 1 February 2011' (2013) 60(2) *NILR* 205–230.

'Protection of Community Interests in International Law: The Case of the Law of the Sea' (2011) 15 *MaxPlanckUNYB* 329–375.

Tansley, A., 'The Use and Abuse of Vegetational Concepts and Terms' (1935) 16 (3) *Ecology* 284–307.

Telesetsky, A., 'Introductory Note to the Nagoya-Kuala Lumpur Supplementary Protocol on Liability and Redress' (2011) 50(1) *ILM* 105–113.

Tomuschat, C., 'Obligations Arising for States without or Against Their Will' (1993) 241(4) *RdC* 199–374.

Trouwborst, A., *Evolution and Status of the Precautionary Principle in International Law* (Kluwer 2002).

Precautionary Rights and Duties of States (Martinus Nijhoff 2006).

Tunnicliffe, V. et al., 'Strategic Environmental Goals and Objectives: Setting the Basis for Environmental Regulation of Deep Seabed Mining' (2020) 114 *Marine Policy* 103347.

Turner, P. et al., 'Deep-Sea Hydrothermal Vent Ecosystem Principles: Identification of Ecosystem Processes, Services and Communication of Value' (2019) 101 *Marine Policy* 118–124.

Van Doorn, E., 'Environmental Aspects of the Mining Code: Preserving Humankind's Common Heritage While Opening Pardo's Box?' (2016) 70 *Marine Policy* 192–197.

Van Dover, C.L. et al., 'Designating Networks of Chemosynthetic Ecosystem Reserves in the Deep Sea' (2012) 36 *Marine Policy* 378–381.

Van Dyke, J., 'The Evolution and International Acceptance of the Precautionary Principle', in D. Caron and H. Scheiber (eds.), *Bringing New Law to Ocean Waters* (Martinus Nijhoff 2004).

Villalpando, S., 'The Legal Dimension of the International Community: How Community Interests Are Protected in International Law' (2010) 21(2) *EJIL* 387–419.

Vinuales, J. (ed.), *The Rio Declaration on Environment and Development: A Commentary* (OUP 2015).

Von Bogdandy, A., M. Goldmann and I. Venzke, 'From Public International to International Public Law: Translating World Public Opinion into International Public Authority' (2017) 28(1) *EJIL* 115–145.

Wang, H., 'Ecosystem Management and Its Application to Large Marine Ecosystem: Science, Law, and Politics' (2004) 35 *ODIL* 41–74.

Warner, R., 'Oceans beyond Boundaries: Environmental Assessment Frameworks' (2012) 27(2) *IJMCL* 481–499.

Wedding, L. et al., 'Managing Mining of the Deep Seabed: Contracts Are Being Granted, but Protections Are Lagging' (2015) 349 *Science* 6244.

Wegener, A., *The Origin of Continents and Oceans*, trans. J. Biram (Dover 1966).

Weil, P., 'Towards Relative Normativity in International Law?' (1983) 77 *AJIL* 413–442.

Weiss, B., 'Invoking State Responsibility in the 21st Century' (2002) 96 *AJIL* 798–816.

Wellens, K., *Remedies against International Organizations* (CUP 2002).

Wetterstein, P. (ed.), *Harm to the Environment: The Right to Compensation and the Assessment of Damages* (OUP 1997).

White, L., 'The Historical Roots of Our Ecologic Crisis' (1967) 155(3767) *Science* 1203–1207.

Wilde, L., 'Scientific and Technic Advice: The Perspective of Iraq's Experts', in C. Payne and P. Sand (eds.), *Gulf War Reparations and the UN Compensation Commission: Environmental Liability* (OUP 2011).

Wilfred Jenks, C., *The Common Law of Mankind* (Stevens 1958).

Williams, B., 'Adaptive Management of Natural Resources: Framework and Issues' (2011) 92(5) *JEM Africa* 1364–1353.

Wolfrum, R., 'The Principle of Common Heritage of Mankind', MPEPIL (last updated November 2009).

'The Principle of the Common Heritage of Mankind' (1983) 43(2) *Max-Planck-Institut für ausländisches* 312–337. Available at: www.zaoerv.de/43_1983/43_1983_2_a_312_337.pdf.

Woodliffe, J., 'Environmental Damage and Environmental Impact Assessment', in M. Bowman and A. Boyle (eds.), *Environmental Damage in International and Comparative Law* (OUP 2002).

Wright, G. et al., 'Marine Spatial Planning in Areas beyond National Jurisdiction' (2021) 132 *Marine Policy* 103384.

Xu, X., *Responsibility to Ensure: Sponsoring States' Environmental Legislation for Deep Seabed Mining and China's Practice* (Brill 2021).

Yee, S., 'Member Responsibility and the ILC Articles on the Responsibility of International Organizations: Some Observations', in M. Ragazzi (ed.), *Responsibility of International Organizations: Essays in Memory of Sir Ian Brownlie* (Martinus Nijhoff 2013).

'The Responsibility of States Members of an International Organization for Its Conduct as a Result of Membership or Their Normal Conduct Associated with Membership', in M. Ragazzi (ed.), *International Responsibility Today: Essays in Memory of Oscar Schachter* (Martinus Nijhoff 2005).

Zemanek, K., 'State Responsibility and Liability', in H-P. N. Winfried Lang and K. Zemanek (eds.), *Environmental Protection and International Law* (Graham & Trotman 1991).

Zhu, L., *Compulsory Insurance and Compensation for Bunker Oil Pollution Damage* (Springer 2007).

ISA Documents

Secretary-General's Informal Consultations on Outstanding Issues Relating to the Deep Seabed Mining Provisions of the United Nations Convention on the Law of the Sea: Collected Documents (ISA, 2002).

Legislative History of the 'Enterprise' under the United Nations Convention on the Law of the Sea and the Agreement relating to the Implementation of Part XI of the Convention, 2002.

Regulations on Prospecting and Exploration for Polymetalic Nodules in the Area, 2000, ISBA/6/A/18, revised in 2013 at the 19th session, ISBA/19/C/17, approved by the Assembly, ISBA/19/A/9.

Regulations on Prospecting and Exploration for Polymetallic Sulphides in the Area, 2010, ISBA/16/A/12/Rev.1. Amendments to regulation 21, ISBA/20/A/10.

Regulations on Prospecting and Exploration for Cobalt-Rich Ferromanganese Crusts in the Area, 2012, ISBA/18/A/11. Amendments to regulation 21, ISBA/20/A/9.

Rules of Procedure of the Legal and Technical Commission, entered into effect on 13 July 2000.

Financial Regulations of the Authority, approved by the Assembly on 23 March 2000.

Recommendations for the Guidance of Contractors for the Assessment of the Possible Environmental Impacts arising from Exploration for Marine Minerals in the Area, July, 2013, ISBA/19/LTC/8 (earlier versions: 2001, ISBA/7/LTC/1/REV.1; 2010, ISBA/16/LTC/7).

Draft Regulations on Exploitation of Mineral Resources in the Area, ISBA/25/C/WP.1, 2019.

Revised Draft Regulations on Exploitation of Mineral Resources in the Area, ISBA/24/LTC/WP.1, 2018.

The Implementation of the Precautionary Approach by the International Seabed Authority, Discussion Paper No. 5 (March 2017).

Draft Regulations on Exploitation of Mineral Resources in the Area, 2017

Discussion Paper on the Development and Drafting of Regulations on Exploitation for Mineral Resources in the Area (Environmental Matters), 2017.

First Working Draft Regulations on Exploitation of Mineral Resources in the Area, 2016.

Draft standards and guidelines under phase 1

Annual Reports of the Secretary-General of the ISA under Article 166(4), UNCLOS (2000–2022).

Content and Development of Standards and Guidelines for Activities in the Area under the Authority's Regulatory Framework, Note by the Secretariat, ISBA/25/C/3, 2018.

Study on an Environmental Compensation Fund for Activities in the Area, ISA, Technical Study No. 27 (2021).

Towards an ISA Environmental Management Strategy for the Area, ISA Technical Study No. 17 (2017).

Environmental Assessment and Management for Exploitation of Minerals in the Area: Report of an International Workshop Convened by the Griffith University Law School in Collaboration with the ISA in Queensland, Australia, 23–26 May 2016, Technical Study No. 16 (2016).

Environmental Management of Deep-Sea Chemosynthetic Ecosystems: Justification of and Considerations for a Spatially-Based Approach, Technical Study No. 9 (2011).

Fauna of Cobalt-Rich Ferromanganese Crust Seamounts, Technical Study No. 8 (2011).

Biodiversity, Species Ranges and Gene Flow in the Abyssal Pacific Nodule Province: Predicting and Managing the Impacts of Deep Seabed Mining, Technical Study No. 3 (2008).

Addressing Serious Harm to the Marine Environment in the Regulations for the Exploitation of Mineral Resources in the Area, submitted by the delegation of the Netherlands, 2015, ISBA/21/C/13.

Strengthening Environmental Scientific Capacity of the ISA, a non-paper submission by Belgium to the ISA on June 22, 2018.

Egede, E., Mati Pal and Eden Charles, 'A Study related to Issues on the Operationalization of the Enterprise: Legal, Technical and Financial Implications for the International Seabed Authority and for States Parties to the United Nations Convention on the Law of the Sea', Technical Report 1/2019 of the International Seabed Authority.

Johnson, D. et al., 'Final report on the periodic review of the International Seabed Authority pursuant to article 154 of the United Nations Convention on the Law of the Sea', submission to the ISA, 30 December 2016.

ILC's Reports and Resolutions

Survey of State practice relevant to international liability for injurious consequences arising out of acts not prohibited by international law, prepared by the Secretariat, 1985, UN. Doc. A/CN.4/384.

Survey of liability regimes relevant to the topic of 'international liability for injurious consequences arising out of acts not prohibited by international law', 1995, UN. Doc. A/CN.4/471.

Survey of liability regimes relevant to the topic of 'international liability for injurious consequences arising out of acts not prohibited by international law', 2004, UN Doc. A/CN.4/543.

Reports submitted by the first Special Rapporteur Mr. Quentin-Baxter on the topic of international liability: The preliminary report, 1980, UN. Doc. A/CN.4/334; second report, 1981, UN. Doc. A/CN.4/346; third report, 1982, UN. Doc. A/CN.4/360 and Corr.1; fourth report, 1983, UN. Doc. A/CN.4/373 and Corr.1 and 2; fifth report, 1984, UN. Doc. A/CN.4/383 and Add.1;

Reports submitted by second Special Rapporteur Mr. Barboza on the topic of international liability: The preliminary report, 1985, UN. Doc. A/CN.4/394; second report, 1986, UN. Doc. A/CN.4/402 and Corr.1, 2 and 4; third report, 1987, UN. Doc. A/CN.4/405 and Corr.1 and 2; fourth report, 1988, UN. Doc. A/CN.4/413 and Corr.1; fifth report, 1989, UN. Doc. A/CN.4/423 and Corr. 1 and 2; sixth report, 1990, UN. Doc. A/CN.4/ 428 and Corr.1, 2 and 4; seventh report, 1991, UN. Doc. A/CN.4/ 437 and Corr.1; eighth report, 1992,

UN. Doc. A/CN.4/443 and Corr. 1 and 3; ninth report, 1993, UN. Doc. A/CN.4/450; tenth report, 1994, UN. Doc. A/CN.4/459; eleventh report, 1995, UN. Doc. A/CN.4/468; twelfth report, 1996, UN. Doc. A/CN.4/475 and Corr. 1 and Add. 1 and Add. 1/Corr. 1.

Reports submitted by the third Special Rapporteur Mr. Rao on the topic of international liability: The first report on the subtopic of prevention, 1998, UN. Doc. A/CN.4/487 and Add. 1; second report, 1999, UN. Doc. A/CN.4/501; third report, 2000, UN. Doc. A/CN.4/510; the first report on the subtopic of international liability, 2003, UN. Doc. A/CN.4/531; second report, 2004, UN. Doc. A/CN.4/540; third report, 2006, UN. Doc. A/CN.4/566.

The reports of the working group on the topic of international liability, 1996, UN. Doc. A/CN.4/L.533 and Add. 1; 1997, UN. Doc. A/CN.4/L. 536.

Draft articles on prevention of transboundary harm from hazardous activities, adopted by UNGA Res. 56/82 of 12 December 2001.

Draft principles on the allocation of loss in the case of transboundary harm arising out of hazardous activities, adopted by UNGA Res. 61/36 of 4 December 2006.

The second reports of the second Special Rapporteur Mr. Ago on the topic of State responsibility, 1970, UN. Doc. A/CN.4/233.

First reading of Articles on State Responsibility adopted by drafting committee in 1996, UN. Doc. A/CN.4/L.524 and Corr. 2.

Articles on state responsibility, adopted by UNGA Res.56/83 of 12 December 2001.

The first report by the Special Rapporteur Mr. Gaja on the topic of responsibility of international organizations, 2003, UN Doc. A/CN.4/532; second report, 2004, UN Doc. A/CN.4/541; third report, 2005, UN Doc. A/CN.4/553; fourth report, 2006, UN Doc. A/CN.4/564 and Add. 1–2; fifth report, 2007, UN Doc. A/CN.4/583; six report, 2008, UN Doc. A/CN.4/597; seventh report, 2009, UN Doc. A/CN.4/610; eighth report, 2011, UN Doc. A/cn.4/640.

Draft Articles on the Responsibility of International Organizations, with Commentaries, *Yearbook of the International Law Commission, 2011, Vol. II, Part Two*. Adopted by UNGA Resolution, UN Doc. A/RES/66/100.

IDI's Reports and Resolutions

Gaja, G., Obligations and Rights *Erga Omnes*: First Report, pp. 119–151 (Replies and Observations of the Commission to the First Report, pp. 152–187); and Second Report, pp. 188–202 (Replies and Observations of the Commission to the First Report, pp. 203–212), *Yearbook of the Institute of International Law*, Vol. 71-I, pp. 119–212, 2005.

Higgins, R., Report of The Legal Consequences for Member States of the Non-fulfilment by International Organizations of their Obligations toward Third Parties, *Yearbook of Institute of International Law*, Vol. 66-I, 1995.

IDI (the Fifth Commission) Resolution: *Obligations and Rights* Erga Omnes *in International Law* (rapporteur: Mr. Giorgio Gaja), adopted at Karkow Session on August 27, 2005. Available at: www.idi-iil.org/idiE/resolutionsE/2005_kra_01_en.pdf.

IDI Resolution (session of Lisbonne), The Legal Consequences for Member States of the Non-fulfilment by International Organizations of their Obligations toward Third Parties. Available at: www.idi-iil.org/idiE/resolutionsE/1995_lis_02_en.pdf.

IDI (the Eighth Commission) Resolution: Responsibility and Liability under International Law for Environmental Damage (Rapporteur: Mr Francisco Orrego Vicuña), adopted at the Session of Strasbourg on September 4, 1997. Available at: www.idi-iil.org/idiE/resolutionsE/1997_str_03_en.PDF.

ILA's Reports and Resolutions

Reports of the ILA Committee on Accountability of International Organizations: 1998, 2000, 2002, 2004.

ILA resolution No.1 (Berlin Conference), Accountability of International Organizations, 2004.

ILA New Delhi Declaration of Principles of International Law Relating to Sustainable Development, 2002.

London Statement of Principles applicable to the formation of general customary international law, adopted at the sixty-ninth Conference of the International Law Association, in London, on 29 July 2000.

Other Materials

The final report of The Managing Impacts of Deep Sea Resource Exploitation project ('MIDAS' 2016). Available at: www.eu-midas.net/sites/default/files/deliverables/D9.6_FINAL_lowres.pdf.

First Census of Marine Life 2010: Highlights of a Decade of Discovery. Available at: www.coml.org/highlights-2010.

Nautilus Minerals Niugini Limited, Environmental Impact Statement (Solwara 1 Project), Executive summary 2008 (prepared by Coffey Natural Systems, September 2008). Available at: www.nautilusminerals.com/irm/content/pdf/environment-reports/Environmental%20Impact%20Statement%20Executive%20Summary%20(English).pdf.

UNEP, The Meeting of the Group of Legal Experts to Examine the Concept of the Common Concern of Mankind in Relation to Global Environmental Issues (Co-Rapporteurs: A.A. Cançado Trindade and D. J. Attard), 1991. Available at: http://historico.juridicas.unam.mx/publica/librev/rev/iidh/cont/13/doc/doc29.pdf.

The reports of the SPC-EU deep seabed minerals project (2013). Available at: www.sopac.org/dsm/index.php/publications-and-reports.

Report of the Secretary-General pursuant to paragraph 19 of Security Council Resolution 687 (199), UN Doc. S/22559, 2 May 1991.

Governing Council Decision 7, Criteria for Additional Categories of Claims, UN Doc. S/AC.26/1991/7/Rev.1, 17 March 1992.

Comprehensive Environmental Response, Compensation and Liability Act (CERCLA) as amended (42 U.S.C. §§ 9601, et seq.).

Oil Pollution Act (OPA) (33 U.S.C. §§ 2701, et seq.).

U.S. DOI NRDA Regulations (CERCLA) 'Type A' NRDA Regulations, 43 C.F.R. 11.

U.S. DOI NRDA Regulations (CERCLA) 'Type B' NRDA Regulations, 43 C.F.R. 11.

U.S. DOC/NOAA NRDA Regulations (OPA) NRDA Regulations 15 C.F.R. 990.

Directive 2004/35/CE of the European Parliament and of the Council of 21 April 2004 on environmental liability with regard to the prevention and remedying of environmental damage.

Liability and Redress in the context of Paragraph 2 of Article 14 of the Convention on Biological Diversity – synthesis report on technical information relating to damage to biological diversity and approaches to valuation and restoration of damage to biological diversity, as well as information on national/domestic measures and experiences, UNEP/CBD/COP/9/20/Add.1, adopted on 20 March 2008.

Status of International Environmental-related Liability Instruments as of February 2008 in chronological order of adoption, UNEP/CBD/BS/GF-L&R/1/INF/1, 14–15.

IUCN World Conservation Congress 'Motion 069'. Available at: www.iucncongress2020.org/motion/069.

INDEX

2001 ASR, *see state responsibility*
Article 2, commentary to, 216
Article 31, 284
Article 36, 171
Article 42, 287
Article 48, 289
Article 55, principle of *lex specialis*, 280
2001 Draft Articles on Prevention
Article 2, commentary to, 165
Article 3, and commentary to, 121
Article 7, EIA, 135
Articles 8, 9, 12 and 13, 135
due diligence, 122
obligations of prevention, 10
significant environmental damage, 165
2006 Draft Principles, *see allocation of loss*
polluter-pays principle, 210
Principle 2, commentary to, 164
Principle 5, *see administrative approach*
2011 Advisory Opinion
Article 235(2) of UNCLOS, 227
defect of, 295
direct obligation, 125
due diligence obligations, 223
EIA, 133
full reparation principle, 284
obligation of conduct, 279
Principle 15 of the 1992 Rio Declaration, 124
Pulp Mills, 136
residual liability, 255, 283
responsibility to ensure, 114
sponsoring State, 15
trust fund, 246
2019 draft Exploitation Regulations
cost-based method, 196
delegation of power, 73
EIA process, 148
EIS templates, 146
environmental emergency, weight-shift in, 159
environmental performance standards, 86
ISO 14001, 152
monitoring programme, 151
Regulation 103, 265
Regulation 3, duty to cooperate, 105, 141
Regulation 56, Environmental Compensation Fund, 256
Regulation 80, 264
REMP, 96
results-based environmental regulation, 104

administrative approach, *see regulatory liability*
2010 Nagoya-Kuala Lumpur Supplementary Protocol, 257
paradigm evolution, 258
African Group
operationalization of the Enterprise, 76
strict environmental liability, 220
allocation of loss
civil liability, 13
compulsory insurance or financial security, 239
Environmental Compensation Fund, 247

allocation of loss (cont.)
  mechanisms, 213
  prompt and adequate compensation, 13
areas of particular environmental interests, xxi, 95
autonomy
  international organization, 299
  legal personality, 232
  the Enterprise, 78

best available scientific evidence, 154
best available techniques, 154
best environmental practices, 154

causal link, *see causation*
  between activity and enviornmental damage, 221
  as a condition, 273, 296
  presumption of, 222
  proof of
    risk involved, 223
    standard of, 223
  between wrongful acts and environmental damage, 221
causation, *see causal link*
CHM, *see community interest, common interest of mankind*
  1979 Moon Agreement, Article 11, 36
  distributive justice, 26
  DSM, 22
  elements of, 34
  implementation of, 111
  Malta's proposal, 22
  New International Economic Order, 29
  operationalization of, 57
common interest of mankind, *see community interest, CHM*
  Antarctica, 38
  outer space, 35
community interest, 23, *see CHM, common interest of mankind*
  duty to cooperate, 142
  marine environmental protection, 44
  obligations *erga omnes*, 43
contractor
  The Enterprise, 75, 231
  polluter-pays principle, 207, 255
  primary liability, 237
  private companies, 2
  publicly funded companies or institutions, 3
  State operator, 235
cost-based method, *see environmental damage, measure of*
  costs of monitoring and assessment activities, 180
  costs of post-spill environmental impact studies, 175
  costs of preventive measures, 172, 183
  costs of reasonable measures of reinstatement, 173
  costs of restoration measures, 184
  primary method, 178

decision-making procedure
  the Council, 62
deep-sea ecosystems, *see marine environment*
developing State
  effective participation of, 28
  the Enterprise, 79
  no preferential treatment, 29
  preferential treatment, 28
  reserved area, 29
  sponsorship, 29, 111
  training programmes, 28
DSM legal regime, 16
dual-track regulatory system, 112
due diligence
  Article 139 of UNCLOS, 119
  environmental risk, 125
  obligation of conduct, 119
  responsibility to ensure, 119
  standard of, 121, 125
    substantiation of, 158

EIA
  2001 Draft Articles on Prevention, 135
  Annex to the 1991 Protocol, 138
  Antarctica, 138
  Articles 204–206 of UNCLOS, 133
  common issues and concerns of, 135

Comprehensive Environment Evaluation, 138
contents of, 137
duty to cooperate, 140
environmental baseline, 144
environmental risk, 137
Espoo Convention, 134
in the global commons context, 138
ILC's Phase 1 Standards and Guidelines, 144
ILC's Recommendations on, 85
information, 133
Initial Environment Evaluation, 138
marine sciences and technologies, 146
practice, 145
procedures, 135, 140
Pulp Mills, 133
status of, 133
transboundary EIA, 134
emergency order, *see environmental emergency*
compliance of, 149
the Council, 92
serious environmental damage, 92
environmental baseline, 85
environmental damage
compensability, 172
damage through the environment, 20
damage to the environment, 20
damage to the marine environment *per se*, 19, 176, 228
victimless situation, 246
Emergency Order, 92
environmental baseline, 166
independent head of, 175
IOPC Funds, 167
pollution of the marine environment, 163
pure environmental damage, 177, 185, *see interim loss*
quantifiable elements, 171
remediation of, 191
threshold of, serious harm to the marine environment, 163
triggering element, 10, 161
UNCC 'F4' claims, 179
environmental emergency, *see emergency order*
the contractor, requirement of, 149
costs of, 196
Emergency Response and Contingency Plan, 150
ISA's response, 91
regulatory environmental liability, 261
environmental management
adaptive environmental management, 94
EMMP, 152
EMS, 151
ISO 14001, 152
LTC's guidelines, 86
regional environmental management, 95
REMP, xxiv, 95
environmental monitoring, 87
impact reference zones (IRZs), xxiv, 140, 153
preservation reference zones (PRZs), xxiv, 140, 153
environmental remediation
compensatory remediation, 192
complementary remediation, 192
primary remediation, 192
environmental risk
assessment of, 154
DSM, 137
EIA, 135
exploitation, 101
responsibility for risk, *see international liability*
environmental standards
LTC's Standards and Guidelines, 159
evolutionary approach
EPC and the Enterprise, 75
organs and subsidiary bodies, 59
the Secretariat, 70
expertise
independent expertise, 103
the LTC, 64
inadequacy, 68
the secretariat, 71
Exploration Regulations
annual report and review, 87
BEPs, 142

Exploration Regulations (cont.)
  certificate of sponsorship, 111
  cooperation, 137
  cost-based method, 196
  definition of marine environment, 162
  EIA, 133
  EIS, 144
  environmental emergency, 149
  issuance recommendations, by the LTC, 84
  joint liability or several liabilities, 206
  liability of the contractor, completion of the exploration, 205
  precautionary approach, 93
  programme to monitor, 151
  regulatory liability of the contractor, 261
  results of workshops, 100
  serious harm to the marine environment, 161
  standard clauses for exploration contract, 87, 196, 203, 206

fault
  civil liability, 214
  wrongfulness, in contrast, 220
full reparation principle, 283

GESAMP, 106
global commons, 24
good industrial practice, 154

insurance
  environmental liability insurance, 242
  insurability, 243, 246
  international maritime insurance market, 245
  limitation on liability, 243
  predictability of risk, 243
  risk spreading, 244
interim loss, 191
  non-use value, 197
  valuation of, 197
    contingent valuation methodology, xxii, 198
    methodologies, 198

international administration
  Articles 137 and 157 of UNCLOS, 34
  element of CHM in DSM, 25
  exercise of international public authority, 110
  international licensing system, 87
  the ISA, 26
  vis-à-vis the contractor, 113
international liability
  activity not prohibited by international law, 8
  civil liability, 10, 211
  civil liability approach, 227, 267
  civil liability treaties, 205, 206
  polluter-pays principle, 207, 263
  State liability *ex delicto*, 10, 276, 277
  State liability *sine delicto*, 8, 251
  triggering element, *see environmental damage*
international regulation, *see international administration*
invocation of liability
  of the contractor, parallel existence of two avenues, 228
  by the ISA, 261, 293
  of the ISA, member States, 307
  of the sponsoring state, 291, *see* 2001 ASR, Articles 42, 48
  by states, 291
  of state and non-state operator, 235
IPCC, 106

joint venture, 75

Legal and Technical Commission, *see LTC*
legal standing, *see locus standi*
lex specialis, 113
locus standi, 229, 287, 291, 308

marine environment
  definition of, 162
marine life, 54
marine mineral resources
  activities in the Area, 2, 82
  cobalt-rich ferromanganese crusts, 53
  HMS Challenger Expedition, 1

polymetallic nodules (manganese nodules), 1, 51
SMS deposits (polymetallic sulphides), 51
marine sciences, *see marine scientific knowledge*
development of, 104
HMS Challenger Expedition, 49
international cooperation, 108
scientific consensus, 106
significant role of, 49
unknowns, *see gaps in marine scientific knowledge*
marine scientific knowledge, *see marine sciences*
assessment
by the LTC, 105
new ways, 108
current status of, 49
gaps in, 55, 101, 199
marine scientific research, promotion and encouragement, 97
member State
membership, 298
no liability of, 300
responsibility of international organization, 298
moratorium
IUCN, 'Motion 069', 4

Natural Resources Damage Assessment, xxiii, 190, *see environmental damage*
restoration-based measure of damages, 191
no harm principle, 277, *see principle of prevention*

obligation of prevention, *see due diligence, principle of prevention*
obligation to cooperate (obligation of cooperation, duty to cooperate), 141
obligations *erga omnes*, 44, 290
operational arm, *see the Enterprise*
outcome-based environmental regulation, *see results-based environmental regulation*

P&I Clubs, 245
periodic review, 90
piercing the organizational veil, 301
polluter-pays principle
civil liability, 208
externality, 207
full implementation, 211
operator, 238
strict liability, 219
precautionary approach
basic legal elements of, 128
EIA as an implementation tool of, 133
environmental management tools, 94
international consensus about, 132
limitation of science, 127
nature of, 128
for policymaking, 127
precautionary measures, 130
Principle 15 of the 1992 Rio Declaration, 126
restrictive factors of, 124
science and value, 127
scientific uncertainty, 117
threshold of damage, 128
value judgment, 127
variability in interpretation, 127
precautionary principle, *see precautionary approach*
principle of prevention
Articles 192–194, UNCLOS, 118
as the cornerstone, 120
customary international law, general international law, 121
EIA as procedural corollary of, 133
no harm principle, 120
obligation of conduct, 121, *see due diligence*
preventive measures, 125
Principle 21/2, 120
Trail Smelter, 120
public trust doctrine, 259
administrative approach, 259

regulatory liability
discretion of the ISA, 265
environmental emergency, 264
monetary penalty, 264

regulatory liability (cont.)
  the regulator, 267
  reimbursement of the costs, 264
regulatory power, 57
  exercise of, 83
  scope of, 82
res communis, 24
responsibility of international organization
  legal personality, 231
responsibility to ensure, 88, 111, 119, *see due diligence*
restituto in integrum, *see full reparation principle*
restoration
  allocation of loss, 268
  compensatory restoration, 187
  cost of, 171
  ecological restoration, 224
  feasibility, 269, 286
  form of reparation, 283
  primary restoration, 187
  purpose of fund, 249
  terrestrial mining, 157
rules, regulations and procedures
  adoption of, 81
  the Assembly, 60
  Exploration Regulations, 16
  implementation of, 113
  the LTC, formulation, 83

Seabed Disputes Chamber (SDC)
  2011 Advisory Opinion, 17
  compulsory jurisdiction, 229, 232, 265, 292
  judicial review, 265
Secretariat, 70
  Secretary-General, 70
self-regulation, 155
solidarity, 250
sponsoring State
  as backup, dual-track regulatory system, 111
  State liability *ex delicto*, 276, 287
stakeholder survey, 103
state immunities, 235
State responsibility, *see 2001 ASR*
  internationally wrongful act, 214, 273
  invocation, 287
  locus standi, 287
  obligations *erga omnes*, 290
  State liability *ex delicto*, 10, 276, 277, 279
strict liability, 217
  environmental risk, 218
sustainable development
  emergency order, 92
  as the overarching principle, 115
  polluter-pays principle, 208
  principle of prevention, precautionary approach, 116

the Assembly
  decision-making competence, 79
  poor attendance, 60
the LTC
  attendance rate, 68
  recommendations, 84
  standards and guidelines, 84
two-year deadline
  Nauru, 4

UNCC, 167
UNCLOS
  Annex III, Article 4(4), 112, 119, 272
  Annex III, Articles 8 and 9, 28
  Annex III, Article 15, 28
  Annex III, Article 22, 200, 203, 221, 224, 261, 296
  Annex IV, Article 1(3), 234
  Annex IV, Article 2(1), 233
  Annex IV, Article 2(2), 232
  Annex IV, Article 2(3), 231
  Annex IV, Article 3, 78, 297
  Annex IV, Article 4, 233
  Annex IV, Article 11(4), 233
  Annex IV, Article 12(7), 234
  Annex IV, Article 13, 233
  Annex VI, Article 38, 16
  Article 1, paragraph 1(4), 163
  Article 136, 23, 291
  Article 137, 24
  Article 139(2), 275
  Article 140(1), 26
  Article 140(2), 27

Article 142(3), 19
Article 143(1), 26, 98
Article 143(2), 97
Article 144(2), 28
Article 145, 31, 81
Article 153, 27
Article 153(4), 112
Article 154, 70
Article 157, 32
Article 157(1), 57
Article 160(1), 59
Article 162(2), 63
Article 162, paragraph 2(a), 293
Article 162, paragraph 2(u), 294
Article 162, paragraph 2(w), 265
Article 163(2), 65
Article 163(3) and (4), 66
Article 165(1), 65
Article 165(2), 67
Article 165, paragraphy 2(e), 107
Article 166(3), 72
Article 168, 70
Article 169, 64
Article 170(2), 78, 231
Article 187(c), 226, 265
Article 187, paragraph b(i), 294
Article 188(1), 292
Article 189, 265, 308
Article 193, 118
Article 197, 141
Article 235(2), 227
Article 256, 98
Article 293(1), 16
Article 311(6), 309
Articles 176–183, 233
Articles 204–206, 133
Part XI of, 1
UNESCO-IOC, 105

For EU product safety concerns, contact us at Calle de José Abascal, 56–1°, 28003 Madrid, Spain or eugpsr@cambridge.org.

www.ingramcontent.com/pod-product-compliance
Lightning Source LLC
LaVergne TN
LVHW011702200926
848484LV00004B/1040
* 9 7 8 1 1 0 8 4 8 8 3 0 3 *